Fair Play

Fighting to Protect the Spirit of Sport

The Memoirs of a Sports Lawyer

Fair Play

Fighting to Protect the Spirit of Sport

The Memoirs of a Sports Lawyer

Jonathan Taylor KC

Bloomsbury Professional

LONDON • DUBLIN • EDINBURGH • NEW YORK • NEW DELHI • SYDNEY

BLOOMSBURY PROFESSIONAL
Bloomsbury Publishing Plc
50 Bedford Square, London, WC1B 3DP, UK
1385 Broadway, New York, 10018, USA
Bloomsbury Publishing Ireland Ltd
29 Earlsfort Terrace, Dublin 2, D02 AY28, Ireland

First published in Great Britain 2026

2

Printed 2026 and Reprinted 2026

British Library Cataloguing-in-Publication Data

A catalogue record for this book is available from the British Library.

ISBN: PB: 978 1 52653 523 8
Epdf: 978 1 52653 525 2
Epub: 978 1 52653 524 5

Typeset by Evolution Design and Digital Ltd (Kent)
Printed and bound by TJ Books, Padstow

For product safety related questions contact productsafety@bloomsbury.com

FSC www.fsc.org MIX Paper | Supporting responsible forestry FSC® C013056

Preface

Young sportsmen and women make enormous sacrifices to excel in their chosen sports, sports fans find the resulting competitive drama utterly compelling, and sports executives and investors love the enormous revenues generated by that demand. The cost side of that equation – the day-to-day work involved in regulating, administering, and policing sport – is far less glamorous. But having spent a quarter of a century providing legal advice to national and international sports governing bodies and event organisers, I am sure that if that work is not done effectively, there will be no meaningful product for anyone to enjoy.

Eminent ethicist Tom Murray describes the job of the sports regulator as follows:

> 'A sport and its stakeholders have the right to decide what values they want to celebrate and promote, and then to draw lines (eligibility rules, classification systems) that ensure their competitions emphasize such values and make them the determinant of success. What is unfair is decided, to a large extent, by the community of athletes and other stakeholders who understand and love the sport. […] The community must be satisfied that the new rules keep alive what it values, what natural talents enable athletes to excel, and what, in the end, is meaningful about participating and winning.'[1]

He is clear that what is meaningful about sport, what makes us value it so highly, is that it *'pursue[s] human excellence through the dedicated perfection of each person's natural talents'*.[2] He explains:

> 'Achieving excellence in sport requires a base of natural physical talents and the honing and perfection of those talents through a wide array of other human capacities such as the ability to study and learn from coaches, as well as human virtues such as perseverance, dedication, and a willingness to suffer in pursuit of a valued goal. … Becoming a great basketball player is made easier by being very tall; speed, strength, quick reaction time, large hands, and gracefulness are also natural advantages, susceptible in varying degrees to willful alteration. … But moral virtues are required to transform those talents into athletic success. Technique must be learned by repetition and practice; skeletal muscles, heart and lungs must be brought to their peak capacity by hour after hour of dedicated effort. Athletes in team sports must learn to cooperate, to lead, to motivate themselves and others. Different sports rely on different sets of natural talents and virtues. But all sports require some mix of both talents and virtues.'[3]

1 Murray T., *Making Sense of Fairness in Sports*, (2010) Hastings Center Report 40(2), pp.13-15.
2 WADA, *Fundamental Rationale for the World Anti-Doping Code*, 2021 World Anti-Doping Code, p.13; Murray T., *Ethics and Endurance-Enhancing Technologies in Sport*, in *Performance-Enhancing Technologies in Sport: Ethical, Conceptual and Scientific Issues* (Murray, Maschke, and Wasunna, eds., John Hopkins University Press 2009), pp.155-56.
3 Murray T., *Ethics and Endurance-Enhancing Technologies in Sport*, in *Performance-Enhancing Technologies in Sport: Ethical, Conceptual and Scientific Issues* (Murray, Maschke, and Wasunna, eds., John Hopkins University Press 2009), pp.155-56.

If that is right, if what we ultimately value about sport is that it presents us with '[c]ontests between people of different natural talents amplified by differences in self-discipline, perseverance and fortitude',[4] then the task of the sports governing body (SGB) is to design and implement rules that ensure the playing field in its sport is level and the outcome is determined solely by the athletes' natural talents, skill and effort, not by extrinsic factors that their natural talent, skill and effort cannot overcome, such as illicit performance-enhancing drugs, or equipment that is not available to everyone, or insuperable natural advantages such as age, sex, or weight.[5] So whenever a new element is introduced to the sport, if it strengthens 'the relationship between natural talents, their virtuous perfection, and athletic success', it should be encouraged, but if it allows a less talented or less dedicated athlete to triumph over athletes who are more talented and dedicated, then it should be excluded/prohibited.[6]

After describing in Chapter One (*Learning the Trade*) how I started my legal career in New York from 1990 to 1997, the solid foundations that experience gave me, and how I came back to England in 1997 and have practised sports law exclusively ever since, these memoirs recount how I have spent that time trying to help SGBs to devise and implement rules that advance this objective, and to defend those rules from legal challenge:

- Maintaining public confidence in the integrity of the sporting contest is obviously essential. If it turns out that the contest was not decided by the skill and effort of the participants, but instead by bribery and corruption, the public will be left with a very sour taste in the mouth that will see them quickly turn elsewhere for their entertainment. Therefore, athletes participating in elite sport are bound by strict anti-corruption rules that prohibit intentional underperformance to win a bet, or as the pay-off for a secret bribe, and SGBs need to be seen to police and enforce those rules rigorously and without compromise. In Chapter Two (*A Mortal Danger to Sport*), I illustrate these points by reference to a high-profile corruption case that I prosecuted on behalf of the International Cricket Council against the three Pakistani Test cricketers, Salman Butt, Mohammad Asif and Mohammad Amir.

- Allowing athletes to enhance their performances by doping would risk giving victory not to the athlete with the best talent and greatest effort, but rather to the

4 Murray T., *Ethics and Endurance-Enhancing Technologies in Sport*, in *Performance-Enhancing Technologies in Sport: Ethical, Conceptual and Scientific Issues* (Murray, Maschke, and Wasunna, eds., John Hopkins University Press 2009), p.151.

5 See Loland S., *Fairness in Sport*, in *Performance-Enhancing Technologies in Sport: Ethical, Conceptual and Scientific Issues* (Murray, Maschke, and Wasunna, eds., John Hopkins University Press 2009), pp.163-66: *'in most human practices, certain inequalities are considered relevant, acceptable and even admirable, whereas others are considered non-relevant and/or problematic and should be eliminated or compensated for. ... [I]f there are inequalities in person-dependent factors that will have an impact on performance that individuals cannot control or influence in any significant way, then these inequalities should be eliminated or compensated for'*. For example, in sport, competition categories are used to *'eliminate or compensate for essential inequalities between persons that cannot be controlled or influenced by individuals in any significant way and for which individuals cannot be deemed responsible'*, such as age, sex, body size. *'Inequalities in sex, body size, and age are biological and physical variables, and [therefore] qualify for elimination or compensation. Inequalities in genetic predispositions for strength or endurance, or in mental capacities such as willpower and determination, or in environmental factors, are not outside the sphere of individual effort and control and can be compensated for by hard training and effort'*.

6 Murray T., *Ethics and Endurance-Enhancing Technologies in Sport*, in *Performance-Enhancing Technologies in Sport: Ethical, Conceptual and Scientific Issues* (Murray, Maschke, and Wasunna, eds., John Hopkins University Press 2009), p.158.

athlete with access to the best drugs, which is not an attribute that the sporting public wishes to celebrate or reward.[7] Therefore, the World Anti-Doping Code, one of the most ubiquitous legal instruments ever written, in sport or otherwise, requires all athletes to submit to drug testing wherever and whenever requested, in order to demonstrate that they are not doping. In Chapter Three (*A Little Extra Chemical Kick*), I describe the enormous effort that goes into formulating and then enforcing the Code across the globe, including by reference to some of the doping cases that I have prosecuted against elite athletes before domestic tribunals and in particular before the Court of Arbitration for Sport (the 'CAS'), the so-called 'Supreme Court of Sport'. And in Chapter Four (*Russia's Doping Operation*) I explain the similar effort that goes into ensuring that all of the sports and countries that have signed up to the World Anti-Doping Code enforce it properly against their athletes and athlete support personnel, by reference to the work I did for the World Anti-Doping Agency (WADA), for World Athletics, for the International Paralympic Committee, and for the International Biathlon Union, in response to the state-sponsored doping that took place in Russia from 2011 to 2015.

- In sports that depend on power and strength, female athletes cannot compete against male athletes, not because of any lack of natural talent or effort, but because of the innate physiological differences between the sexes. As a result, the only way for female athletes, and society, to reap the many benefits that come from female participation in sport is to maintain separate male and female competition categories. But that means SGBs have to decide whether, and if so under what conditions, individuals who are biological males but have a female gender identity may participate in the female competition category. And that puts the SGBs squarely in the middle of what has become a very bitter culture war. World Athletics' president, Sebastian Coe, has not ducked the challenge presented. Instead he has explained that World Athletics and its members *'need to ensure its sport is as inclusive as possible, but there is also a responsibility to ensure fair and meaningful competition for all of our athletes to reward them for the huge commitment and sacrifice required to excel in the sport, and to inspire new generations to join the sport and aspire to the same excellence. … To do this we need to create competition categories within our sport that ensure that success is determined by talent, dedication and hard work, rather than by other factors that are not considered fair or meaningful, such as the enormous physical advantages that an adult has over a child, or a male athlete has over a female athlete'*.[8] In Chapter Five (*A Different Kind of Girl*), I describe how we initially stumbled but ultimately were able to demonstrate to the satisfaction of the CAS that rules designed to achieve that purpose are lawful.
- SGBs regulate the use of technology and equipment in their sports for many reasons, but in particular to ensure that *'[h]uman performance is the critical endeavour'*, not who has the best technicians.[9] In Chapter Six (*The Fastest Man On No Legs*), I explain how World Athletics applied its equipment rules to bar

7 Samuels M., *Suspicion hurts athletics*, The Times, 15 July 2025 (*'No wonder athletics is a hard sell if every feat comes with the suspicion of being taken for a ride'*).
8 *Coe reiterates reasons for new eligibility requirements for female classifications (DSD) in meeting with Athletics South Africa President,* IAAF press release dated 27 June 2018 (worldathletics.org/news/press-release/dsd-regulations-meeting-south-africa, accessed 14 October 2025).
9 IPC Policy on Sport Equipment (2 April 2011), section 3.1.4. See also UCI Cycling Regulations, Chapter III (Equipment), Section 2: *'Bicycles shall comply with the spirit and principle of cycling as a sport. The spirit presupposes that cyclists will compete in competitions on an equal footing. The principle asserts the primacy of man over machine'*.

US 400m double amputee Blake Leeper from its competitions on the ground that his prosthetic blades gave him an unfair advantage, and then successfully defended that position in proceedings before the CAS.

- I finish, in Chapter Seven (*Extra Time*), by describing a few other cases and matters I have worked on, in various different sports, that do not fit neatly into the other chapters but are still, I hope, worth including.

First, though, I want to acknowledge upfront with enormous gratitude and respect not only the excellent work that our clients have entrusted to us at Bird & Bird but also the superb guidance and support I have received throughout my career from many excellent mentors, clients and colleagues, most of whom are mentioned by name in what follows. Thanks also to those friends – including Stuart Miller, Stéphane Bermon, David Handelsman, Gunter Younger, Ross Wenzel, Iain Higgins, Jamie Herbert, Guy Taylor, and Jadine Scragg – whose comments and suggestions on chapter drafts improved them greatly. I am solely responsible for the content and for any deficiencies that remain. I also acknowledge the danger of memoirs descending into endless self-justification and unwarranted credit-taking, and have tried to avoid that as best I can. However, I note what Richard Feynman said in one of his memoirs: *'Recently I discovered a transcript of my speech, and what I said doesn't seem anywhere near as dramatic as the way I remember it. What I remember saying is much more wonderful than what I actually said!'*[10] There isn't a transcript of most of what I said or did, and so all that I have to go on is my memory of how wonderful and dramatic it was. My memory, like the rest of me, has definitely seen better days. Therefore, while I have striven for accuracy in all that follows, this is just how I remember it, and others – especially my adversaries in various cases – may well remember it very differently.

Finally, I note that these memoirs are not, and are not intended to constitute, legal advice, and therefore no reliance can or should be placed on any matters covered. In particular, the law firms that were instructed in relation to the matters I discuss are not in any way responsible for the content of these memoirs.

Jonathan Taylor KC

April 2026

10 Richard P. Feynman, *'What do you care what other people think?' Further Adventures of a Curious Character* (W.W. Norton & Company, 1st Edn, 1988), p.75.

Dedication

This book is dedicated to Kate, Sophie, and Emily.

As a cowboy once said, I wouldn't have nothing if I didn't have you.

Contents

Table of Abbreviations

ABA	American Basketball Association.
ABP	Athlete Biological Passport.
ACSU	Anti-Corruption & Security Unit.
ADAMS	Anti-Doping Administration & Management System.
ADO	Anti-Doping Organisation.
ADRV	Anti-doping rule violation.
AFI	Athletics Federation of India.
AIU	Athletics Integrity Unit.
ARAF	All-Russia Athletics Federation.
ASA	Athletics South Africa.
BCCI	Board of Control for Cricket in India.
BIU	Biathlon Integrity Unit.
BOA	British Olympic Association.
BCB	Bangladesh Cricket Board.
CAS	Court of Arbitration for Sport.
CAIS	Complete Androgen Insensitivity Syndrome.
CAH	Congenital Adrenal Hyperplasia.
CRC	Compliance Review Committee.
DCO	Doping Control Officer.
DHT	Dihydrotestosterone.
DSD	Difference in sex development.
FIA	Fédération Internationale de l'Automobile.
FIFA	Fédération Internationale de Football Association.
FINA	Fédération Internationale de Natation.
FIS	Fédération Internationale de Ski.
HMRC	Her Majesty's Revenue & Customs.
IAAF	International Association of Athletics Federation (now World Athletics).
IBA	International Boxing Association.
IBU	International Biathlon Union.
ICC	International Cricket Council.
IOC	International Olympic Committee.
IPC	International Paralympic Committee.

IP Report	Report of Richard McLaren dated 18 July 2016.
IRB	International Rugby Board (now World Rugby).
ISCCS	International Standard for Code Compliance by Signatories.
ITA	International Testing Agency.
ITF	International Tennis Federation.
IWF	International Weightlifting Federation.
KC	King's Counsel.
LIMS	Laboratory Information Management System.
MASH	Maximum Allowable Standing Height.
Met	The Metropolitan Police.
MTF	Male-to-female.
NADO	National Anti-Doping Organisation.
NBA	National Basketball Association.
NFL	National Football League.
NGB	National Governing Body.
NOC	National Olympic Committee.
NOTW	News of the World.
PAIS	Partial Androgen Insensitivity Syndrome.
PCOS	Polycystic Ovarian Syndrome.
QC	Queen's Counsel.
rEPO	Recombinant erythropoietin.
R&A	Royal & Ancient Golf Club of St Andrews.
RFU	Rugby Football Union.
ROC	Russian Olympic Committee.
RPC	Russian Paralympic Committee.
RSP	Running-specific prosthetics.
RTP	Registered Testing Pool.
RUSADA	Russian Anti-Doping Agency.
RusAF	Russian Athletics Federation.
RWF	Russian Weightlifting Federation.
SGB	sports governing body.
SRY	Sex-determining region of the Y chromosome.
UCI	Union Cycliste International.
UKAD	UK Anti-Doping.
UNESCO	United Nations Educational Scientific and Cultural Organisation.
UQ	University of Queensland.
USADA	United States Anti-Doping Agency.
USGA	United States Golf Association.
USOC	United States Olympic Committee.

USTA	United States Tennis Association.
UVa	University of Virginia.
WADA	World Anti-Doping Agency.
WADA I&I	WADA Intelligence & Investigations Department.
WADC	World Anti-Doping Code.
WTA	Women's Tennis Association.
5-ARD	5-alpha reductase deficiency.
17β	17β-hydroxysteroid dehydrogenase type 3 deficiency.

Chapter 1

Learning the Trade

School

I grew up in Wimbledon, in south-west London, and went to Wimbledon College, a state school run by the Jesuits. I played football and rugby avidly from the first opportunity, but my enthusiasm far exceeded my aptitude, and so there was never any prospect of a playing career. Instead, when we all took the Myers Briggs personality test at school, the teachers took one look at my results and said I was about as destined to be a lawyer as anyone could be.

Similarly determinative of my future was the fact that when our uncle Andrew took me and my brother Paul to see our first football match, on 2 November 1974, the team Andrew supported (Chelsea) was playing away, and so instead he took us to see Fulham beat Aston Villa 3:1 at Craven Cottage. At the time, Paul and I didn't realise what a lucky escape that had been, but we instantly fell in love with Fulham FC, and it was the start of a lifelong allegiance that has endured despite many trials and tribulations along the way. I agree with Simon Barnes' friend that supporting a football team is *'a bearable way of facing the fact that God doesn't love me'.*[1]

In April 1986, I went to the National Theatre to see *Hamlet*, which I was studying for A level English, and a week or so later I went to Craven Cottage on a cold Tuesday night to see Fulham play Carlisle in the old Second Division. *Hamlet* was a fantastic spectacle, but we all knew exactly what was going to happen in the final scene. At the Cottage, in contrast, the entertainment was extremely limited until the last minute, when a long punt over the top was met by the Fulham keeper, who smashed the ball against the chasing Carlisle striker and watched it rebound over his head into the empty net, consigning Fulham to a 1.0 defeat. That is what makes sport so unique and so compelling: you just never know what is going to happen. And most sports rules and regulations are ultimately aimed at preserving that uncertainty of outcome, while also trying to ensure that that outcome is decided solely by the relative skills of the competitors, ie their natural talents perfected by their hard work, not by other factors we do not value.

University

Fortunately, I was more successful in my Oxford entrance exam than Fulham were in League Division Two that season. They finished bottom and so went down to the Third Division, whereas I went up to University College, Oxford, joining Paul, who had gone up the year before. We spent three years happily playing football, rugby and cricket together for the college, albeit again with more enthusiasm than skill or success.

The English excel at time-honoured rituals that are sometimes so bizarre and unlikely that outside observers must wonder whether what they are seeing is real, or just some sort of Monty Python sketch. For example, a law degree at Oxford University, called a degree in '*Jurisprudence*', is delivered not in lecture form but rather in weekly tutorials where it is just you, or maybe you and one other student, and your tutor, often an eminent professor who asks for your critique of the august legal tome that he or she authored. I take this opportunity to apologise to Professor John Finnis for my butchering of his seminal work, *Natural Law and Natural Rights*. You have to pass an exam – called '*prelims*', or '*mods*' – after Hilary term of your first year, which comes after Michaelmas term and before Trinity term. But after that there is no continuous assessment, just study of eight subjects in turn, on which you will be tested only in final examinations ('*finals*') that take place over two weeks or so at the end of your third year. The class of degree you end up with depends entirely on how well you perform in those two weeks. And if that is not pressure enough, you have to sit those final exams dressed in '*sub fusc*', ie a dark suit with a white bow tie, worn under a black academic gown, the length of which depends on whether you are a '*commoner*' or have earned the academic distinction of becoming an '*exhibitioner*' or a '*scholar*', and a mortar board, which must only be worn outside, never indoors.

When I left Oxford in the summer of 1989, I was concerned that my '*Jurisprudence*' degree may not have prepared me properly for real world legal practice. What good was it to have learned about the Roman origins of the civil law system, practised on the continent, when England follows the common law system? How could I go into battle in an English court when I had no knowledge of such legal staples as the Sale of Goods Act 1979? I only realised later that the grounding I had been given in critical legal analysis and reasoning had equipped me to tackle any area of the law, no matter how arcane. At the time, however, I decided I was just not ready to start immediately down the path to qualification as a practising lawyer. Instead, relying on a late-night recommendation in the University College bar from my friend Kris Gledhill, who had blazed the same trail before me, I signed up for a master's degree at the University of Virginia Law School in Charlottesville, Virginia.

I enjoyed my year of US college life, including watching UVa's excellent basketball and (American) football teams. The football team attracted crowds of 70,000 to every home game, with most of the female fans wearing Laura Ashley dresses for some unexplained reason (their own version of '*sub fusc*', I suppose). In contrast, the University's rugby team, which I joined, attracted no spectators at all, but its players made up in endeavour for what they lacked in experience. We went on a very enjoyable tour to the Cayman Islands, where we played one game against the Cayman Islands Rugby Club and another against a team from the visiting HMS Penelope, on a verdant pitch that apparently owed its lushness to the turtle manure that was used to cultivate it. In the clubhouse after the games, someone put on a VHS tape of the latest Five Nations matches, and many of my teammates looked on in wonder, which was when I realised that none of them had actually seen any proper rugby matches before they started playing the game (a distinct disadvantage, in such an idiosyncratic sport). The rugby team was also my introduction to Scottish expat Ron Murray, who by then had retired from playing to become a referee, and who became a great friend, along with his wife Megan, until his untimely death in 2024.[2]

I also volunteered to help coach the women's '*junior varsity*' association football team, ie the UVa second team, but realised after only a couple of drills that they were all a lot better than me, and there really was nothing I could contribute to their development. At that stage, women's football in the US was far in advance of other countries, with the US team winning the inaugural FIFA Women's World Cup in China in 1991.

First job

Each year the major US law firms would visit the UVa Law School to interview potential recruits. And if they liked what they saw, they would fly you to their head office for further interviews. That sounded great to me, since I wanted to see Manhattan but couldn't afford to get there myself, so I signed up for interviews on campus with several New York firms. Bob Nash, a real estate partner from one of those firms, Schulte Roth & Zabel, was amused by my CV, with its references to exhibitions, scholarships, and other quintessential Oxford-isms. He said: *'I have no idea what any of this means. Is it any good?'* I said yes it was very good, and he shrugged and invited me to come up to New York for further interviews. I got through them as well, again probably more due to my novelty value than anything else, and was offered a place in Schulte Roth's litigation department.

Before I could start the job, I had to pass the New York State bar exam, but that turned out to be mainly multiple-choice questions, and so little more than a memory test. A friend and I drove down to a college in Richmond, Virginia, to sit the ethics component of the exam. He left the exam room early, and I eventually found him in a bathroom smoking a joint, which made me question whether he had fully embraced the spirit of the enterprise. In any event, in late August 1990 I drove up Route I-95 to New York from Virginia in a U-Haul van containing my meagre possessions. And in early September 1990 I started work in Schulte Roth's offices in midtown Manhattan, on the corner of Third Avenue and 54th Street.

The other new joiners in my cohort were all at least 24 or 25 years old, because in the US you have to have a four-year undergraduate degree before you can take the three-year law degree. On the other hand, unlike their English counterparts, graduates of US law schools are not required to spend time working as trainee solicitors or pupil barristers before they qualify professionally. Instead, once you graduate, as long as you pass a state bar exam, you are deemed to be qualified to practise law immediately. But I had only done a three-year undergraduate degree and then a one-year master's degree, and so when I started work at Schulte Roth in September 1990, I was still (for another two months) only 21 years old, and yet supposedly fully qualified and fit to practise law.

On my first day in the job, I was sent to see Bob Abrahams, one of the firm's most senior litigation partners, who was responsible for assigning an appropriate team of associates to work on each new case. When I went into his massive corner office, he was sitting reading my CV. I wondered if this would finally be the moment when my lack of qualifications for the job would be exposed, and I would be unceremoniously shown the door. But Bob's only question was whether I was a '*soccer*' fan, since he loved the beautiful game but was struggling at that point to find many others in the US who shared his passion. So football was an immediate common bond between us, and my friendship with Bob and his wife Carol endures to this day. We played together with other Schulte Roth lawyers and many other English expats in a 5-a-side league on Roosevelt Island in the East River, and on an 11-a-side team that played on various pitches of widely varying quality dotted around the Lower East Side of Manhattan.

Things have moved on a lot since then as far as the US attitude to football is concerned. Many Americans are now enthusiastic followers of the sport in general and English football in particular, with Premier League matches being shown live not just in pubs and bars, as happened when I was there in the 1990s, but also on US network television. In 2023, Lisa Lazarus, the CEO of the Horseracing Integrity and Safety Authority in the US, introduced me to its Kentuckian attorney, John Roach, and he turned out to be another avid Fulham fan, thanks to its long history of fielding American players, from Clint Dempsey and Brian McBride in the 2000s to Tim Ream and Antonee Robinson in recent years. Despite the transatlantic travel required, John is now a Fulham season ticket holder with a seat near me and Paul in our shiny new Riverside Stand.

I in turn enthusiastically followed baseball and basketball when I was in New York. When I got there in late 1990, I chose to follow the Yankees rather than the Mets, because the Yankees were much lower in the standings, and so apparently the underdog. I had not done any research, and so I did not realise the Yankees were in fact the Evil Empire, the Manchester United of baseball, but by the time I figured that out it was too late, my allegiance was fixed. I also loved going to Madison Square Garden to watch the Knicks' Patrick Ewing, Charles Oakley, John Starks and Antony Mason, who were a great team, even if they did seem to lose in the play-offs almost every year to Reggie Miller's bloody Indiana Pacers.

First day in a US court

In early 1991, Bob Abrahams and Geoff Amsel, another friend to this day, were representing a major bank in a dispute with a New York real estate developer (no, not that one) over the financing of a high-end residential development on Long Island, New York. Bob put me on the team, and I started by researching and drafting a legal submission for an application that was coming up for hearing. The day before the hearing, we got a surprise further submission from the other side, so Geoff and I worked long into the night preparing a response, which I then printed out to take to the hearing the next day, there being no such thing as electronic filing in those days. The next morning, I went with Bob and Geoff out to the state court in Mineola, Long Island, where the case had been filed. We met the bank's representatives in the cafeteria, and Bob sent me off to the courtroom to file our response before the hearing began.

When I got there, my first time ever in a US courtroom, there was no one around, and I had no idea where to go or what to do. Just then a grey-haired lady dressed in a sort of housecoat wandered in with a handful of files. I asked her if she knew where I could file some papers for that morning's hearing, and in a strong Long Island accent she said: *'Papers? What papers? The court has already read all of the papers for this hearing'*. I nervously replied that the court couldn't have read the papers I wanted to file, because we had only drafted them late the previous evening. She took them from me grudgingly, and told me to go and fetch my colleagues, because the hearing would start shortly.

I did that, and when we got back to the courtroom I settled down at the back with the bank's representatives to watch my first ever US oral argument. Then in came the judge, and I was startled to see that it was the same lady I had met before, who had now put on a long black robe over her housecoat. Bob stood up to begin his opening remarks, but the judge interrupted him and said: *'Hold on, where is that young man with the nice accent who was just up here? We don't want to start without him'*. Bob liked this a lot. *'Yes Your Honor, that young man is my colleague here, Mr Taylor from England, and you are right, he does have a nice accent'*, he replied, while I looked in vain for a hole in the ground to swallow me up. Bob recounted the tale with great glee at the next litigation department meeting, and recommended that his colleagues take me to all their hearings too, in case the judges in their cases were similarly partial to an English accent.

It will strike today's lawyers as absurd that we were not able to file our documents electronically with the court, a practice that is now ubiquitous. But this was a different age, technologically speaking. It was only when I started working at Schulte Roth in 1990 that I sent my first ever email; no one had the ability to send emails back at university in England. And it was only after a year or two at Schulte Roth that we were first able to access the Internet to conduct factual research. Until that point, we had to go and look at actual books, stored in a library. It was also a few years before we got phones that were not attached to the wall. And when I took a laptop back with me to England in 1993, when I took a break from Schulte Roth to teach for a year at University College, the students surrounded it in the library with great awe, as if it had been beamed down from outer space.

First advocacy

One major difference between legal practice in the US and England that had a big impact on my subsequent career is the way courtroom advocacy is handled. In England, most law graduates qualify as solicitors and work in law firms. They may specialise in litigation, and can appear in court in certain circumstances, but very few of them undertake any advocacy before a judge. Instead, when a case is scheduled for a court hearing, they instruct barristers (specialist advocates who are self-employed but work out of chambers they share with other barristers) to speak for the client in court. In the US, however, the profession is not split in this way. Instead, US litigators do all the work on the case, not just preparing the matter for hearing but also presenting the case at the hearing. They regard it as peculiar, and so did I when I eventually went back to England to practise, that a litigator would do all of the work preparing a case for hearing, but then hand over the advocacy – the best bit! – to another lawyer to do for them.

I was very happy with the US approach, because I definitely wanted to be an advocate. (If I had stayed in the UK instead of going to the US, I would most likely have gone to the Bar). In a large firm like Schulte Roth, however, the cases were so big, and the amounts at stake so substantial, that the only way for a young associate like me to get any advocacy experience was to work on a *'pro bono'* case, ie a public interest case taken on by the firm without charge to the client. One of Schulte Roth's *pro bono* clients, Human Rights Watch, gave me a case representing a Ugandan student who had claimed political asylum when he reached JFK Airport on the basis that he had a well-founded fear of persecution if he was forced to return to Uganda. He alleged that he had been arrested during a demonstration in

Kampala against the Ugandan president, Yoweri Museveni, and that he had been tortured by having his elbows tied together behind his back for hours at a time.

I interviewed the client, and gathered evidence to support his claim, including reports from Amnesty International about Museveni's violent crackdown on dissidents, as well as statements from the client's relatives and friends about his harrowing experiences. I then went to the hearing, nervous to be making my advocacy debut, particularly with a very anxious client in attendance for whom the stakes were very high. I started making my opening submissions, but just as I was getting into the detail, the judge held up his hand to stop me, lent over to turn off the recording device, and then said: *'You know, I used to be a US marine, and last night I saw that movie "Black Hawk Down", where they shot down that helicopter and killed all the soldiers. And as far as I am concerned, Idi Amin had the right idea. Bring back Amin, kill everybody'*. He then turned the recording device back on, and indicated that I should carry on with my submissions.

Too stunned to react on the spot, instead I just stumbled through my remaining arguments and got out of there as quickly as I could. But when I got back to the office, and had the chance to consult with much more experienced colleagues, I wrote to the judge, putting on the record what he had said while the tape-recorder was off. I said that his comments cast significant doubt on his ability to decide the case impartially, and asked that he therefore step down from the case. A few days later, I got an angry call from the judge, who said: *'I wasn't biased against your client before I got your letter, but I am now!'* I spoke to the people at Human Rights Watch, who contacted Willa Arpel, a journalist at New York Newsday, and she came and interviewed me. In the meantime, the judge granted my client's asylum application, presumably in an effort to avoid an appeal that would prompt scrutiny of what he had said. But Human Rights Watch was aware of several other cases in which he had made similarly outrageous remarks, and Willa went ahead and got the story published as a half-page editorial, titled *'Don't Tell It To This Judge'*. It was slightly sobering to see my name in black and white in the editorial, given how critical it was of the judge, and when a couple of weeks later a letter landed on my desk in a thick envelope embossed with the seal of the Chief Administrative Judge of the United States of America, I wondered for a moment if I was about to be deported as retribution for embarrassing the Immigration & Naturalization Service. But what the letter actually said was that the office of the Chief Administrative Judge had noted the New York Newsday editorial, that it had looked into the matter, and that I should please note that the judge in question had now retired.

More US advocacy

After that quite dramatic debut, I managed to get fairly regular advocacy opportunities, both in court and in different arbitration proceedings. One arbitration was held in the famous Peabody Hotel in Memphis, Tennessee, where ducks that live on the hotel roof travel down each morning in the lift to swim in the fountain in the lobby, and travel back up to the roof by the same route every evening. I was defending a broker-dealer against a claim that it had recommended unsuitable investments to an individual investor client. The investor had such a strong Mississippi accent that when I cross-examined him, I had no idea what he was saying in response to my questions, which made it very tricky to formulate sensible follow-up questions. The arbitration panel found this very amusing, and made no effort to help me out.

I also appeared in federal court in New York in a case arising out of a claim that Schulte Roth had brought for a large corporate client against its former senior executive. He responded by suing not only the corporation and several of its employees but also two Schulte litigation partners for malicious prosecution and various other torts, seeking damages of $365 million. I persuaded the district court to dismiss the complaint and also to fine my adversary for two false statements he had made during oral argument on the dismissal application.[3] He appealed that decision, which led to my one and only appearance before the Second Circuit Court of Appeals. It was an intimidating experience, particularly at the start of the hearing, when all three judges appear at once from behind a black curtain. But I survived, and so did the precedent that sanctions can be imposed on an advocate for false statements made during oral argument. The Second Circuit said: *'A lawyer fighting for his client's rights in a courtroom is expected to be as wily and resourceful as Daniel Webster was in his defense of Jabez Stone in the foreclosure action brought against him by the Devil, to whom Stone had sold his soul. Counsel must be able to think and argue on his or her feet in a courtroom, a forum where conditions change rapidly. Yet zealous oral advocacy must be conducted according to the rules and counsel may not "knowingly make a false statement of law or fact," Model Code of Professional Responsibility DR 7-102(A.5). To violate this professional standard may result in sanctions under Rule 11'*.[4]

In another case, our banking client had issued a letter of intent to make a substantial loan to a corporate customer, relying on the advice of a Schulte Roth real estate partner that the letter was not legally binding and so the bank could walk away if it wanted. When the bank did walk away, the customer sued for breach of contract. The real estate partner asked me, *'what happens now?'* I replied: *'We get to find out whether or not your advice was correct'*. That sums up the difference between litigators and transactional lawyers: litigators are almost always marked on their homework: their work product goes before a judge, who grants or refuses the relief they are seeking, based on the quality of their submissions; whereas transactional lawyers rarely are: their work goes into a closing binder, and often is only ever looked at again if the deal goes sour.*

The greatest sports deal of all time

In my nearly seven years at Schulte, I was only involved in one sports case, but it did relate to what has been described as *'the greatest sports deal of all time'*.[5] Today the National Basketball Association is one of the most valuable sports properties in the world, but in the 1970s its games were only broadcast on cable television, and generally on tape delay late in the evening rather than live. It also faced competition from a rival league, the American Basketball Association, which introduced innovations such as the tricolour ball and the three point line, and had the legendary player Julius Erving (*'Dr J.'*) as its main attraction. When merger discussions between the NBA and ABA stalled, the ABA teams adopted what has since become the standard strategy for upstart leagues in the US and Europe alike:

* I grudgingly acknowledge the counter-argument that every day that the bargain struck continues to deliver its promised benefits to the parties is a day in which the lawyers who papered the deal get at least a passing mark.

it threatened to file an antitrust suit against the NBA and its teams, alleging that they were conspiring to force the ABA out of business.

Eventually the NBA proposed to settle the case by accepting four ABA franchises into the NBA – the New Jersey Nets, the San Antonio Spurs, the Indiana Pacers, and the Denver Nuggets – but not the other three, the Virginia Squires, the Kentucky Colonels, and the Spirits of St Louis. The Squires folded, and the owners of the Colonels accepted a reported $3 million to walk away, but that left the Spirits owners, brothers Ozzie and David Silna, holding the keys to the kingdom, since their consent was required to drop the antitrust suit, and they were not shy about exploiting that leverage. The deadlock was eventually broken by the Silnas selling the Spirits franchise (which they had bought for $1 million) to the four new NBA teams in return for one seventh of each team's annual central NBA television revenues, in perpetuity. In other words, in return for giving up a failing franchise that was immediately liquidated by the acquiring teams, every year the Silnas would receive a total sum equal to four-sevenths of an NBA team's share of central television revenues for that year. And that would continue *forever.*

In the first year the deal kicked in, 1979, four-sevenths of one team's share only amounted to a couple of hundred thousand dollars, but with each new cycle thereafter the NBA central television revenues soared, so that by 2014 the Silnas were estimated to have received a cumulative $300 million, and with the NBA lining up a nine-year deal worth a reported $24 billion for the next cycle, starting in season 2016/17, their ongoing annual receipts were set to increase enormously again. On the other hand, this revenue-sharing obligation put the four NBA teams at a significant competitive disadvantage to their NBA rivals, and so they had to stop the bleeding. Eventually the Silnas allowed themselves to be bought out, reputedly for tax reasons, for *'a cool $500 million or so'*.[6]

New York state of mind

Throughout my time in New York, I was enormously impressed not only by how smart most of the lawyers were that I worked with or against, but also by the incredible amount of time and effort they put into ensuring that their work product, both written and oral, was flawless. If the other side did not match that effort, if their work product was poorly drafted, or showed anything less than complete mastery of the relevant facts and the applicable law, they had lost before they even got into the courtroom. I remember learning two lessons in particular, provided by two excellent Schulte Roth litigation partners who are sadly no longer with us:

- One time, I was struggling with how to phrase a particular point in a brief. Howie Godnick[7] said to me: *'What are you trying to say?'* I told him, and he said: *'Why don't you just say that then?'* In other words, I didn't have to dress up what I was trying to say in fancy legal terms, or rephrase it in pompous language.

Instead, plain (American) English was good enough.* That was very good advice that I have tried to follow ever since, and whenever a young lawyer sends me a draft letter for review that starts *'I enclose for your perusal ...'*, I pass on Howie's advice to them too.

- The other lesson came from Brooks Burdette,[8] who was crippled by polio, and treated litigation as a proxy for all the sports he loved but was unable to play himself. Late one night, we finally finished a 50-page brief that had to be filed with the court the next day, and I started to pack up, but Brooks insisted that first we sit and read the brief out loud to each other, because that would highlight unclear phrasing that you would not notice by simply reading it to yourself. He was absolutely right, we did improve the brief by doing this, and it was an excellent example of unflinching commitment to a faultless work product, but I nearly strangled Brooks for his languid Georgia drawl that night, as it extended the exercise by several hours.

When I came back to the UK in 1997, I insisted that we matched those standards, and only recruited lawyers who shared that commitment. I hope our clients and the judges and arbitrators we appear before would say we maintain those standards rigorously to this day. But if so, a lot of the credit goes to the lessons learned practising commercial litigation at Schulte Roth & Zabel in New York.

Becoming a sports lawyer back in the UK

In July 1994, I changed into my Fulham shirt in the office washroom and went down on the subway to City Hall to marry Kate, with her brother Ben (in his Wimbledon shirt) and her best friend Berni acting as witnesses. One of the highlights of the wedding celebrations was going to Giants Stadium to watch Bulgaria beat Germany 2:1 in the 1994 World Cup quarter finals. The winning goal, a stooping header by Letchkov, remains one of my favourite *'I was there'* sporting moments to this day.

The arrival of our first daughter, Sophie, in May 1997, prompted our return to England, because we wanted her to grow up near her grandparents and her many cousins (Kate's family also lived in Wimbledon, which is how we had met). I went to the big news-stand at Grand Central Station on a Wednesday, when the English papers from the previous day arrived, because in those days the best place to look for legal jobs was the Law section of the Tuesday edition of the Times. My eye was caught by an advertisement from Townleys, a small firm of solicitors that said it specialised in sports law and wanted to hire a litigator to build its sports disputes practice. I had never heard of sports law as a practice area, but I was worried that if I simply joined another commercial litigation department in a big English law firm, I would be forever comparing how they did things to how it was done in New York. I also wanted to be part of building something new, rather than just jumping on someone else's bandwagon, and obviously I loved sport and so liked the idea of

* 'American' English is most definitely not the same as 'English' English. In a case involving an allegation of document destruction, I said that documents had *'gone missing'*. My colleagues thought that was hilarious, and asked if it was the same as *'gone fishing'*. On the other hand, I was preparing once for a hearing, and the partner in charge asked me: *'is everything copacetic?'* I had to say I did not know, because I had no idea what *'copacetic'* meant.

working in the sports sector. So I took a deep breath and leapt into the unknown. I applied successfully for the Townleys job, took the Qualified Lawyers Transfer Test to become a qualified solicitor, and moved with Kate and Sophie to Wimbledon in September 1997. By happy coincidence, this was just when Kevin Keegan became Fulham manager and the club's fortunes were starting to turn for the better. By the time Sophie's sister Emily arrived in 2000, Fulham were only a season away from promotion to the Premier League.

I was also very lucky with my timing as far as the job move went. In late 1997, sports law was still a very immature practice area. Properties like the Premier League were growing in importance, but the full commercial value of sport was still only gradually emerging, and bluntly the degree of professionalism both within sport itself and among those who serviced the sector was variable. Townleys had a good number of sports sector clients, who had just started realising that they needed first class legal support to help them capture the growing commercial value of their sports and to manage the associated risks. And I was eager to exploit the opportunities that this presented.

Our clients were mainly governing bodies, event organisers, and other sports rights-holders, and we quickly became involved in a number of high profile disputes that raised fundamental issues about the nature of commercial sports rights and the competing claims to ownership and control of those rights. For example, when the Rugby Football Union announced in 1996 that the organising committee of the Five Nations Championship could no longer sell the broadcasting rights to Five Nations matches staged at Twickenham, because the RFU had sold the rights to those matches to Sky, the response of the Irish, Welsh and Scottish rugby unions was: '*That's nice. Who exactly are you going to play?*'

Gary Roberts, the eminent US sports law professor, subsequently told me about a very similar episode back in 1980, when Al Davis, the owner of the Oakland Raiders, decided to move the Raiders' home stadium to the Los Angeles Coliseum. Under the NFL rules at the time, Davis needed three quarters of the other NFL teams to agree the move, but had not secured their support. He sent a telegram to NFL Commissioner Pete Rozelle: *'Dear Pete. The Raiders are now the Los Angeles Raiders'*. Rozelle replied by return: *'Dear Al. Congratulations. Who are you planning to play?'* The Raiders had lost sight of a fundamental truth about competitive sport. Unlike other industries, sports teams *need* strong competition from rival teams in order to create a meaningful product that people will want to watch. And that basic and fundamental point has important legal ramifications.

To resolve the impasse with the RFU, Ireland's Tom Kiernan,[9] Wales's Vernon Pugh QC,[10] and Scotland's Allan Hosie, all fantastic rugby men, negotiated an Accord that required the RFU to pool the rights fee paid by Sky for its home Five Nations matches so that it could be shared among all five nations. We acted for the Five Nations Committee when it expelled the RFU from the Championship in 1999 for alleged breach of the Accord;[11] and when the RFU subsequently re-affirmed the Accord we acted for the Celtic unions in expert valuation proceedings to determine how much of the £87.5 million rights fee that Sky had paid the RFU was for its home Five Nations matches, and so had to be pooled, and how much was for its autumn internationals against Australia, New Zealand and South Africa, and so could be retained by the RFU. We also acted for the International Rugby Board (now World Rugby) in defence of proceedings filed by Cardiff RFC with the High Court and a parallel complaint filed by the English First Division Rugby clubs with the European Commission, attacking the IRB's rules requiring union approval for clubs to play cross-border matches and mandating that clubs release their players for international matches.[12] And (after Townleys was absorbed by another firm, Hammonds) we acted for The Football League when the owners of Wimbledon FC challenged the League's refusal to allow the club to move to Milton Keynes. That issue was eventually referred to a commission appointed by The Football Association, which – to my great regret – permitted the move.[13]

Over time my practice expanded beyond purely contentious matters to advising clients on the exercise of their regulatory and disciplinary powers, not only from an enforcement perspective but also from a constitutional perspective (complying with principles of good governance) and from a risk management perspective (minimising the risk of successful challenge on domestic and/or EU law grounds). That then progressed to advising the same clients on event organisation structures, such as drafting the Six Nations Constitution and the organisational documents for the Celtic League, and on the content of their event rules and regulations and competition participation agreements (eg for the European Rugby Cup, aka the Heineken Cup).

What is sports law?

In 2000, I was appointed Director of Studies in Sports Law at King's College, London. The course had been running for a few years, under the guidance of sports lawyer and agent Mel Stein,[14] but without the involvement of any of the eminent academics on the KCL Law Faculty. When at my interview for the job one of those academics questioned whether there was really any such thing as '*sports law*', I replied that the income statement of Townleys, a specialist '*sports law*' firm, suggested there was.[15] That was a crass answer, obviously, but there is a better one: even if the sports sector is subject to the same laws as everyone else, as opposed to a bespoke '*law of sport*', the application of any law is always sensitive to context, and so lawyers advising sports clients, and judges and arbitrators called upon to determine sports disputes, have to take due account of the '*specificities*' of the sports sector, ie the unique inherent characteristics that set it apart from other sectors.[16]

For example, competition law is highly suspicious of any sort of coordinated action between rival companies. But if sporting rivals did not agree on the rules and other terms of their engagement, they would not be able to compete, and therefore there would be no '*product*' for anyone to '*consume*'.[17] And to ensure that the teams are well-matched and so the outcome is uncertain, that coordination necessarily extends well beyond the rules of the game itself to encompass all sorts of financial and commercial restrictions and limitations that in any other industry would be blatantly unlawful. For example, the United States is obviously the bastion of free market principles, with a strong emphasis on individual economic freedom. But US professional sports teams accept the central sale of television rights to their matches and the sharing of the resulting revenues equally among all the teams. They also agree caps on spending on player wages, or the payment of a '*luxury tax*' on spending over an agreed limit. And they agree that the teams finishing bottom one season will get the best picks in the next player draft. Little wonder that one commentator has described North American sports as '*socialist*' in nature.[18] And these restrictions, like all other sporting rules, are lawful in the US and in Europe as long as they are proportionate, ie (1) they are the least restrictive way of achieving outcome uncertainty, and (2) any adverse side-effects do not outweigh the resulting benefits.

Advising an international SGB is a particular challenge, because its rules have to apply globally: *'an international federation deals with national federations and athletes from all over the world and it has to treat them on an equal basis. It therefore has to apply the same law to all of them. It is unacceptable that, based upon the same facts, a different result might be reached depending on the law applied'.*[19] The SGB may therefore specify that its rules are governed by the laws of a particular country – most often, the country where the governing body is headquartered, which is usually Switzerland. But a national court may still intervene if it considers that the rules contravene mandatory domestic laws. For example, in the mid-1990s the IAAF (as World Athletics was then called) specified that the penalty for a first doping offence was a four year ban, but a German court agreed with sprinter Katrin Krabbe that any ban greater than two years was disproportionate and therefore unenforceable under German law.[20] The only way for the IAAF to maintain a a global level playing field was to reduce its ban for a first doping offence to two years.

The Court of Arbitration for Sport (CAS)

This *'lowest common denominator'* approach obviously undermines efforts to protect the integrity of the sport. To tackle this and other issues, in 1994 the sports movement created the Court of Arbitration for Sport in Lausanne, Switzerland, the so-called *'Supreme Court of Sport'*,[21] with ultimate jurisdiction over all sports disputes, sitting in preference to any national courts, and providing definitive rulings that apply globally and so bind all participants in the sport, wherever they compete.[22] And CAS panels have employed various methods to ensure the international federation's rules are given uniform and consistent effect across the globe, irrespective of potentially conflicting national laws. For example, one CAS panel said that the federation's rules are the primary *'governing law'*, that national laws only supplement those rules where the rules are silent on an issue, and that even *'mandatory'* national laws do not trump those rules unless they reflect a fundamental legal principle of universal application.[23] And in *AEK Athens*, the leading CAS case on the issue, the panel explained: *'due to the transnational nature of sporting competitions, the effects of the conduct and deeds of international federations are felt in a sporting community throughout various countries. Therefore, the substantive and procedural rules to be respected by international federations cannot be reduced only to its own statutes and regulations and to the laws of the country where the federation is incorporated or of the country where its headquarters are. Sports law has developed and consolidated along the years, particularly through the arbitral settlement of disputes, a set of unwritten legal principles – a sort of lex mercatoria for sports or, so to speak, a "lex ludica" or "lex sportiva" – to which national and international sports federations must conform, regardless of the presence of such principles within their own statues and regulations, or within any applicable national law, provided that they do not conflict with any national "public policy" provision applicable to a given case. Certainly, general principles of law drawn from a comparative or common denominator reading of various domestic legal systems and, in particular, the prohibition of arbitrary or unreasonable rules and measures can be deemed to be part of such lex ludica'.*[24]

In January 2003 Butterworths published the first edition of *Sport: Law & Practice*, a 1200-page, multi-author guide to the practice of law in the sports sector. Adam Lewis QC of Blackstone Chambers and I were joint editors and wrote a significant part of that and each subsequent edition, alongside other leading sports law practitioners. In the fourth edition, published by Bloomsbury Professional in 2021, we identified from the CAS jurisprudence the following *'general principles of law'* that an international federation's rules must respect: the requirement of legal certainty (*nullem crimen, nulla poena sine lege certa*), the requirement of *'respect for fundamental rights'* (including the right to freedom of expression, the right to a fair hearing, and in particular the right to equal treatment), the need to act proportionately when restricting those rights to achieve legitimate objectives, the protection of acquired rights and legitimate expectations, the presumption against retroactivity (*tempus regit actum*), and the principle of good faith in the interpretation and application of the rules.[25] Anyone advising in the sports sector has to be fully conversant with all of these principles.

Another quirk of practice before the CAS is that most of the arbitrators on the CAS list[26] come from either civil law jurisdictions (in particular, Switzerland, Germany, France, and Italy) or common law jurisdictions such as the US, the UK, Australia, New Zealand, and India, and therefore when a three-person panel is appointed for a particular case, it usually includes a combination of civil law lawyers and common law lawyers. This is important because there are significant differences between the two systems:

- Substantively, the biggest difference is that in common law systems the judges' decisions become precedents that add to the corpus of law that judges in subsequent cases must either follow or distinguish (or overturn, if they sit in a superior court). Whereas in civil law countries the law is codified, and the role of judges is not to make new law but rather simply to interpret that code, so that (technically, at least) civil law judges are not supposed to give any weight to prior court decisions.[27] There is also the fact that as a general proposition *'international arbitration lacks a doctrine of precedent, at least as it is formulated in the common law system'*, with awards being considered simply the resolution of a dispute arising between the parties, and often being kept confidential and therefore not available for subsequent citation.[28] But in the context of sport, where you need a level playing field around the globe so that athletes everywhere are treated equally, decisions must be consistent from one case to the next. And therefore in practice CAS arbitrators from civil law jurisdictions tend to give exactly the same weight to prior CAS decisions as their common law counterparts.[29]

- Procedurally, the main difference is that civil law systems generally follow an *'inquisitorial'* approach in court cases, meaning that the judge directs and controls the proceedings, determining what facts are relevant to the outcome of the case and admitting evidence accordingly, including examining the witnesses him/herself, and the parties are largely limited to presenting arguments based on the evidential record the judge has developed; whereas in common law cases an *'adversarial'* approach is used, ie the parties gather the evidence, including by direct examination of their own witnesses and cross-examination of the other side's witnesses, and present the case as they see fit based on that evidence, while the judge's (much more passive) role is to make findings of fact and apply the law to those facts, based on the arguments presented by the respective parties. In short, *'[t]he inquisitorial process can be described as an official inquiry to ascertain the truth, whereas the adversarial system uses a competitive process between prosecution and defence to determine the facts'.*[30] The CAS Procedural Rules do not specify which approach is to be followed in CAS proceedings. Instead it is left to the CAS panel, which will be different in each case, to decide which system should be followed in the case before it.[31] However, the *de facto* approach – followed at least in the hundred-plus CAS cases in which I have been involved – is adversarial,[32] much to the surprise of one Italian lawyer I appeared against, who assumed the panel would question all of the witnesses itself, and was very surprised when he was abruptly told it was up to him to cross-examine our witnesses. Apparently the same issue arose at the Nuremburg trials of senior Nazis after the Second World War, where the stakes were as high as they could be: *'From the very beginning of the military tribunal, Allied representatives had struggled to make the requirements of their judicial systems compatible with one another. The Americans and British had presumed that the trials would proceed according to the adversarial procedures of common law, in which accusations of guilt would have to be cross-examined and argued in court. The Soviets and the French, on the other hand, operated according to the inquisitorial system of civil law, in which evidence is collected, prepared and evaluated by an examining magistrate and prosecutor before the start of proceedings'.*[33] But to me that is no excuse: whether the adversarial or inquisitorial system is to be used, the position should be spelled out clearly in the CAS Procedural Rules, so that no one is surprised or disadvantaged.

The CAS has often been criticised on the basis that it is a private body, not sufficiently accountable to public scrutiny, and not sufficiently independent of sport, although the latter charge at least has now been rejected by the European Court of Human Rights, in *Mutu/Pechstein.*[34] In my experience, however, while the CAS is far from perfect, it has many excellent arbitrators from many different jurisdictions, and they have shown themselves to be capable of resolving complex disputes in a manner that shows appreciation for the *'specificities'* of sport, and that seeks to strike an appropriate balance between the potentially conflicting rights of different stakeholders. The way that the CAS operates could undoubtedly be improved, but the simple fact is that if it did not exist, it would have to be created, because the global level playing field that each sport requires can only be achieved if there is one ultimate *'supreme court for sport'*. If the actions of a sports governing body could be challenged in the courts of any country where the sport is played, conflicting decisions would soon abound, the enforceability of rules and decisions would depend on the country you were in, and a global level playing field, delivering equal treatment of all athletes in a sport, wherever they compete, would be an idle dream.[35]

Taking silk

In 2017, having added 20 years of advocacy in sports cases to my seven years of advocacy in the US, I applied to be appointed one of *'Her Majesty's Counsel learned in the law'*, ie a Queen's Counsel ('*QC*'), or, since 2022, when King Charles III took the throne, a King's Counsel ('*KC*'). This does not mean, as it originally did, becoming a lawyer who represents the Crown. Technically, all it means is that you get to wear a special uniform in court (a short wig, silk gown, wing collar, and bands), you have the right to sit in the front row of the courtroom, and you have the right to address the court before any other advocates get to speak. But more importantly, it is a formal and recognised acknowledgement of the individual's expertise as an advocate, which is personally gratifying and helpful professionally.

My application to become a Queen's Counsel was unusual in two respects. First, I was a solicitor rather than a barrister. And second, almost all of my advocacy had taken place not in the English courts but rather in front of specialist sports tribunals, some in England but many overseas, especially at the CAS. SGBs have long written into their rules that any cases they bring against a participant for breach of the rules must go before a disciplinary panel, and that any appeals from the disciplinary panel's decisions, and any challenge to the SGB's decisions or actions, must be pursued not in the national courts (in England, the High Court) but before an external arbitral tribunal convened under the rules of a specialist service such as Sport Resolutions UK, or its international equivalent, the CAS. On the other hand, domestic sports tribunals and CAS panels are often chaired by a senior English barrister or former judge, and so I was able to obtain from them the references I needed to support my application. I was also able to cite my advocacy in various landmark cases at the CAS, several of which are described in these memoirs, as evidence of my credentials as an advocate.

The selection panel interviewed me in its first floor office in Hatton Garden, and kindly approved my application. I then had to get kitted out for the swearing-in ceremony, which took place before the Lord Chancellor in Westminster Hall in February 2017. That was when I discovered it is not just Oxford graduates who have to dress up in silly costumes for their passing out ceremonies. With the very generous help of Adam Sloane, then deputy senior clerk at Blackstone Chambers, one of the leading sports law sets, I went to Ede & Ravenscroft on Chancery Lane to rent the special outfit required for the ceremony, which consisted of a *'full-bottomed'* horsehair wig, a *'jabot'* (a lace frill) worn at the throat, a dress shirt with *'ruffles'* (lace cuffs), a waistcoat, black breeches extending to just below the knee, silk stockings, and shiny slip-on shoes with steel buckles, all covered by a long silk gown, which is why becoming a QC/KC is colloquially described as *'taking silk'*, and a QC/KC is referred to as a *'silk'*. I felt truly ridiculous in the outfit on the day, but my parents, as well as Kate, Sophie and Emily, seemed to enjoy the day despite, or perhaps because of, my discomfort.

Notes

1 Barnes S., *The Meaning of Sport* (Short Books, 2006), p.101.
2 Ronald Murray, 1947-2024, legacy.com obituary, accessed 14 October 2025.
3 *O'Brien v Alexander*, 898 F.Supp. 162, 176 (S.D.N.Y. 1995).
4 *O'Brien v Alexander*, 101 F.3d 1479 (2d Cir. 1996). The Daniel Webster reference in the judgment was to Benet, *The Devil And Daniel Webster And Other Writings* (Penguin Classics, 1999).
5 Burke M., *The NBA finally puts an end to the greatest sports deal of all time*, Forbes, 7 January 2014.
6 *The greatest sports deal*, Sports History Weekly, 7 March 2021; Burke M., *The NBA finally puts an end to the greatest sports deal of all time*, Forbes, 7 January 2014.
7 Howard Godnick obituary, dignitymemorial.com; Balsamini, *Peleton members do tribute rid for 'OG' member Howard Godnick*, New York Post, 11 December 2021.
8 Brooks Burdette's memorial service, 28 May 2009 (youtube.com/watch?v=KxqNlGYo8H8, accessed 14 October 2025).
9 Tom Kiernan obituary, The Times, 15 February 2002.
10 Vernon Pugh QC obituary, The Times, 25 March 2003.
11 Armstrong R., *Five Nations crisis as England are booted out*, The Guardian, 19 January 1999.
12 *Williams v Cardiff RFC v Pugh* [1999] Eu LR 195; *English First Division Rugby Complaint to the European Commission against the Rugby Football Union and the International Rugby Board*, Case No IV/36.994 (March 1998).

13 *Wimbledon FC v The Football League*, FA Arbitration Panel decision dated 29 January 2002; FA Commission decision date May 2002.

14 Obituary, The Times, 27 August 2022.

15 For a discussion of these conflicting views from a US standpoint, see Davis T., *What is Sports Law?*, 11 Marq. Sports L. Rev. 211 (2001).

16 See eg European Commission, *White Paper on Sport*, 11 July 2007, at p.13, referring to both *'the specificity of sporting activities and of sporting rules, such as separate competitions for men and women, limitations on the number of participants in competitions, or the need to ensure uncertainty concerning outcomes and to preserve a competitive balance between clubs taking part in the same competitions'*, and *'the specificity of the sport structure, including the autonomy and diversity of sport organisations, a pyramid structure of competitions from grassroots to elite level and organised solidarity mechanisms between the different levels and operators, the organisation of sport on a national basis, and the principle of a single federation per sport'*, and emphasising that *'[t]he case law of the European courts and decisions of the European Commission show that the specificity of sport has been recognised and taken into account'*.

17 As Gary Neville puts it, *'[n]o club is an island, independent of the rest'*: Neville G., *The People's Game: How to Save Football* (Hodder & Staughton, 2023), p.135.

18 Thompson D., *Why American sports are socialist*, The Atlantic, 20 June 2016.

19 *Foschi v FINA*, TAS 96/156, para 102.4.

20 *Krabbe v IAAF*, OLG Munich, judgment dated 28 March 1996, SpuRt 1996, p.133.

21 Goh CL and Anderson J., *The Credibility of the Court of Arbitration for Sport*, Harvard Journal of Sports & Entertainment Law (2022), Vol. 13, p.233; Casini L., *The Making of a Lex Sportiva by the Court of Arbitration for Sport*, German Law Journal, 2011;12(5):1317-1340, at 1321 (citing *A. et B. v IOC, FIS et TAS*, 4P.267/2002, 27 May 2003, BGE 129 III 445, 462) and at 1326.

22 For an account of the creation of the CAS from one of its main architects, see chapter 10 of *By The Way* (Chiselbury Publishing, 2024), the autobiography of Francois Carrard, a Swiss lawyer and former IOC Director General.

23 *Neue Grasshopper Fussball AG Zurich v Club Alianza Lima*, CAS 2008/A/1725, para 13.

24 *AEK Athens and SK Slavia Prague v UEFA*, CAS 98/200, para 156. See also generally Lindholm J., *The Court of Arbitration for Sport and Its Jurisprudence: An Empirical Inquiry into Lex Sportiva* (Asser Press, 2019).

25 *Sport: Law & Practice*, Lewis A. & Taylor J., eds. (Bloomsbury Professional, 4th Edn 2001), para B1.18 et seq. See also Foster K., *Is There A Global Sports Law?*, Entertainment Law, Vol.2, No.1, Spring 2003, pp.1-18.

26 CAS arbitrators (general list), tas-cas.org/en/arbitration/liste-des-arbitres-liste-generale.html (accessed 14 October 2025).

27 See eg Steffany S., *Comparison of Civil Law and Common Law in Australia and Surrounding Countries*, Jurnal Daulat Hukum (2022), vol. 5(3), pp.156-163. But see Kaufmann-Kohler G., *Arbitral Precedent: Dream, Necessity or Excuse?*, Arbitration International (2007) 23(3):357-378 at p.359 (*'In civil law countries, the precedential value of cases may be weaker than in common law countries, though it is nonetheless well established there. Indeed, civil law countries have such notions as* arrêt de principe *and* jurisprudence constante, *which are similar to* stare decisis *except that they do not require adherence to a legal principle that has been applied only once before'*). Cf The Hon. Mr Justice Ormiston, *The Common Law, The Civil Law, The Law of the Countries in South East Asia: A Comparative Study of Legal Systems*, The Arbitrator, May 1988, p.15, at p24 (*'The judges, of course, have the opportunity to fill in the interstices of the codes, especially one as broadly stated as the French Code Civile, but their decisions form only part of a pattern of decision making intended to throw general light on the operation of the code and not to alter or change its operation by means of binding precedent'*) and p.25 (*'If the common lawyer looks principally to what has been said in the courts, the civil lawyers looks to a written conceptualized law worked out in the Codes and expounded by the jurists and other academic writers. I concede that this is an oversimplification. Civil lawyers have for many years had to look at the decisions of their courts, and the common lawyer is increasingly dependent on the synthesis of reported decisions by academic and other textbook writers. Perhaps it is the precision of the written word in the French, German and Italian languages which has enabled the formulation of definitive legal rules, perhaps it is the greater respect given to the jurists and other institutional writers on the Continent, but in general terms the decisions of the courts play a lessor role in civilian systems, only to be looked at when it is possible to discern a pattern of accepted interpretation worked out from the written text'*).

28 Kaufmann-Kohler G., *Arbitral Precedent: Dream, Necessity or Excuse?*, Arbitration International (2007) 23(3):357-378 at p.357, and at p.365, quoting the following remark of Michael Mustill: *'a law is newly minted by the arbitrator on each occasion, with every contract the subject of its own individual proper law'*, although the focus there was on arbitration of purely

commercial disputes, and they were distinguished from sports disputes, where consistency and equal treatment from one case to the next are acknowledged to be more important (ibid, p.376).

29 See eg *UCI v Jogert*, CAS 1997/176, para 40 (*'Although in arbitration there is no stare decisis ... the Panel feels that CAS rulings form a valuable body of case law and can contribute to strengthen legal predictability in international sports law. Therefore, although not binding, previous CAS decisions can, and should, be taken into consideration by subsequent CAS panels, in order to help developing legitimate expectations among sports bodies and athletes'*); *Andersen v IOC*, CAS 2008/A/1545, para 55 (*'although a CAS panel in principle might end up deciding differently from a previous panel, it must accord to previous CAS awards a substantial precedential value and it is up to the party advocating a jurisprudential change to submit persuasive arguments and evidence to that effect'*). See also Casini L., *The Making of a* Lex Sportiva *by the Court of Arbitration for Sport*, German Law Journal, 2011;12(5):1317-1340, at 1331 (*'panels demonstrate a consistent deference to CAS jurisprudence; arbitrators often refer to prior CAS decisions'*); Kaufmann-Kohler G., *Arbitral Precedent: Dream, Necessity or Excuse?*, Arbitration International (2007) 23(3):357-378 at p.366 (citing cases that *'demonstrate the existence of a true* stare decisis *doctrine within the field of sports arbitration'*).

30 UN Office on Drugs and Crime, *Adversarial versus inquisitorial legal systems*, Organised Crime, Module 9, unodc.org.

31 Mavromati, D. and Reeb, M., *The Code of the Court of Arbitration for Sport: Commentary, Cases and Materials* (Kluwer Law, 2nd Edn, 2025), p.373.

32 Martens, D-R., *The Role of Arbitrator in CAS Proceedings*, CAS Bulletin, 2/2014, at p.35 (*'In international arbitration, there appears to be a trend towards conducting the proceedings "common-law style". The parties are given considerable freedom in shaping their case and the evidence. The arbitrators very often do not give any indication as to what arguments/evidence they consider to be crucial for the outcome of the case. As a result, parties very often inundate the panel with written submissions, documents and witness statements, which the arbitrators – due to their prior study of the case – already know will be irrelevant. Similarly, during the hearing, counsel go to great lengths in examining/cross-examining the witnesses on issues which have no impact whatsoever on the ultimate decision, thus ignoring the general advice to counsel never to tire or irritate the minds of those they seek to persuade. A lot of time and money is wasted in that way!'*).

33 Kinstler, L., *Come to This Court and Cry* (Bloomsbury 2022), p.47.

34 *Case of Mutu and Pechstein v Switzerland*, European Court of Human Rights, judgment dated 2 October 2018.

35 See *Case of Semenya v Switzerland*, European Court of Human Rights, judgment dated 10 July 2025, para 199 (*'As the Court noted in Mutu and Pechstein ..., it is certainly of interest for the settlement of disputes arising in a professional sports context, especially those with an international dimension, to refer them to a specialised body which is able to give a ruling swiftly and inexpensively. In that connection, it [is] observed that since high-level international sports events are held in various countries by organisations based in different States, and are open to sportspersons from all over the world, recourse to a single and specialised international arbitral tribunal facilitates a certain procedural uniformity and strengthens legal certainty; all the more so where the awards of that tribunal can be appealed against before the supreme court of a single country, in this case the Swiss Federal Supreme Court'*).

Chapter 2

A Mortal Danger to Sport

Match-fixing has apparently been around almost as long as sport itself: according to historians, in 388 BCE Thessalonian boxer Eupolos wanted an Olympic gold medal so badly that he bribed three of his rivals to let him beat them.[1] But the more usual scenario these days is for the contestant to lose a match deliberately, or to do something else deliberate during play, such as getting booked by the referee, so that others can make a killing by staking large sums on those outcomes in the (official or unofficial) betting markets. For example, in 1910 four Australian Rules footballers were banned from the sport, two of them for five years and two for life, for accepting bribes from bookmakers to underperform in club matches;[2] ten years later, eight members of the Chicago White Sox baseball team were banned for life for accepting $5,000 each from a gambling syndicate to throw matches in the 1919 World Series;[3] in 1951, the New York District Attorney arrested three stars of the national champion college basketball team for taking bribes to lose games deliberately;[4] in 1964, four English footballers were jailed for bribery, corruption and defrauding bookmakers after they agreed to lose a match and placed bets on that outcome;[5] and in 1994 accusations by The Sun newspaper that Liverpool goalkeeper Bruce Grobbelaar had accepted a bribe to underperform led to criminal corruption charges against Grobbelaar that ended in a mistrial, followed by a defamation claim by Grobbelaar against the newspaper's publishers that resulted in a House of Lords finding that Grobbelaar had '*acted in a way in which no decent or honest footballer would act and in a way which could, if not exposed and stamped on, undermine the integrity of a game which earns the loyalty and support of millions*'.[6]

It is hard to overstate the threat that such corruption presents to sport. To me, the image that *The Week* published on its front page in September 2010 – a shiny cricket ball riddled with worms and flies – summed it up perfectly. Sport is like a shiny apple – a juicy spectacle, ready to be enjoyed. But if you bite heartily into an apple, only to discover it is rotten inside, you will throw it away, disgusted, and will think long and hard before ever eating one again. And the same is true of sport: if ever you discover that the spectacle you were enjoying was a mirage, and the fix was in from the start, your confidence in the integrity of the sport will turn sour and it will be a long time, if at all, before you can put those suspicions behind you, and enjoy the sport again without any misgivings. As one commentator said: '*I look at cricket and all the things that have gone on about cricket match-fixing. If you see an unusual result, there is always the assumption that there is something wrong. I think […] if somebody puts in a magnificent performance, […] there are questions asked, as opposed to applauding the performance*'.[7] That is why SGBs have to come down so hard on match-fixing, putting in place rules and mechanisms that make such conduct more difficult, and its detection and swift and stringent punishment more likely, so that those who are tempted to stray decide the risks are too great. But if the SGB's efforts are inadequate, whether in the strength of the system put in place, or in the amount of resource committed to implementing that system, cheating is not deterred, and so the cancer spreads, and the long-term survival of its sport is put in peril.

Cricket

Cricket has long been prey to match-fixing, fuelled by the growth of illegal betting markets in India and elsewhere that has been chronicled by Ed Hawkins and others.[8] The high profile scandals involving South African captain Hanse Cronje, Indian captain Mohammad Azharuddin, and Pakistan captain Salim Malik, among others, ultimately prompted the International Cricket Council to commission a review by Sir Paul Condon, former Commissioner of the Metropolitan Police, and then, on his recommendation, to set up a dedicated anti-corruption unit chaired first by Condon himself and then by Sir Ronnie Flanagan, the former Chief Inspector of Constabulary for the United Kingdom, to police compliance by players, coaches, trainers, managers, team officials and others with a detailed anti-corruption code.[9] The ICC President at the time, Malcolm Gray, explained: *'we want followers of the game to have no doubt that the ICC is treating this issue with the utmost importance, and taking real steps to eradicate it. Our sole priority is to protect the long-term health of the sport, and no one should doubt our determination to achieve this aim'.*[10]

Starting on Sunday 29 August 2010, the efficacy of the ICC Anti-Corruption Code was put to a stern and very public test. I was on a family holiday in the Algarve at the time, splashing around in the swimming pool with my two young daughters, when I got a call from Iain Higgins, who had been a first-rate colleague of mine in private practice for several years before going to work for the International Cricket Council in Dubai. Iain told me to get hold of a copy of that day's News of the World as soon as possible and then call him back. This was in the days before automatic daily downloads of electronic copies of newspapers to your iPad. Instead, I had to ask the resort to get a copy of the paper faxed to them, which took ages and cost a fortune. When it finally inched its way out of the fax machine, the NOTW's front page headline was startling: *'CAUGHT! Match-fixer pockets £150k as he rigs the England Test at Lord's. We expose betting scandal that will rock cricket!'*

There followed a sensational story, spread out over 15 pages, alleging that Pakistan's captain Salman Butt had agreed to deliberately bat out a maiden order (ie to fail to score off six consecutive deliveries) during the Test match between Pakistan and England at The Oval on 21 August 2010, and that its strike bowlers Mohammad Amir and Mohammad Asif had bowled three deliberate no balls during the Lord's Test match on 28 August 2010, in return for £150,000 paid in cash to their agent, Mazhar Majeed, by *'Mohsin Khan'*, supposedly a corrupt Indian businessman but actually the infamous NOTW investigative journalist Mazher Mahmood, aka *'the Fake Sheikh'*, who had secretly recorded all of the key exchanges.[11]

According to the NOTW story, *'Khan'* and Majeed first met in person at the Park Lane Hilton on Monday 16 August 2010. *'Khan'* explained that he represented a group of businessmen who wanted to organise a cricket tournament in the Middle East and was hoping that the Pakistan players Majeed represented would be interested in participating. Majeed said he was sure they would, because they were not well paid, and needed to make money. The two men met again two days later, and when *'Khan'* hinted that the businessmen he represented were interested in match-fixing, Majeed said that he could provide them with information about fixes involving the Pakistan cricket team, as he was already providing that information to an Indian bookmaker: *'I deal with an Indian party, yeah. They pay me for the information. ... So say for example Mohammad Asif and Mohammad Amir are bowling, yeah. The market opens at ten overs and, let's say, 32 runs. Asif is going to indicate by bowling a dead ball at the start of the sixth over. ... That means he's going to do it. Then we know, then we start betting. ... my people know that the eighth, ninth and tenth over they are going to concede more than 18 runs. They're going to concede more than six runs an over, and the last ball of the tenth over is going to be a no-ball, okay'*. He explained they had also fixed the results of some of Pakistan's previous matches.[12] *'But we now are not going to do any results for the next two games because we want Salman Butt to be captain for long term. It's long-term thinking'*. *'Khan'* then said: *'Right, no, but a few no balls doesn't make any difference, does it?'* Majeed: *'Oh, no balls is easy. No balls, you know, there's not that much money anyway, we know that. You can't make that much money anyway. You can make a bet you know, if you wanted no balls you could probably get up to 10,000 each, yeah. That's simple'*.[13]

The Oval Test

At the close of play on the second day of the Oval Test, Thursday 19 August 2010, England had just started its second innings. That evening, Majeed introduced *'Khan'* to Pakistan captain Salman Butt and some of his team-mates at the Al-Shishawi restaurant on the Edgware Road. Then, in a conversation in a car outside the restaurant, Majeed said: *'Alright, just to show you that it's real, okay, I'm going to show you two no balls tomorrow'*. He said the price was £10,000 per no ball. *'Khan'* handed over £10,000 there and then, and promised to give Majeed the other £10,000 the next day. Majeed in turn promised to call *'Khan'* the next morning to tell him when exactly (which ball of which over) the Pakistani bowlers would be bowling the no balls. He also said that once this had been done, and *'Khan'* could see that Majeed was as good as his word, he would need to pay over another £150,000 as money on account, to be used to pay for tip-offs about fixes in subsequent matches.

The next morning, however, Majeed called *'Khan'* to explain that the two deliberate no balls he had promised could not be bowled that day, because Pakistan head coach Waqar Younis *'just sat down with the fast bowlers for half an hour about how many extras they gave last game ... we done five no balls yesterday, yeah, the day before, sorry. ... He's spent thirty minutes training with them about giving so many extras away, yeah, about putting their feet behind the line. ... They said after the talk this morning they don't want to do any no balls today. ... It's just because of this talk this morning, he doesn't usually do it ... . But bloody because he had this talk it's just going to look a bit suspicious'*.[14] Majeed promised *'Khan'* that the no balls would be bowled the following day instead.

Play ended that day with England nine wickets down in their second innings. Late that evening, Majeed called *'Khan'* again, and explained that with only one England wicket left, with Saeed Ajmal (who was not a party to the fixing arrangement) bowling at one end, and with the coach planning to put another spinner on at the other end, there was no guarantee that Amir or Asif would have a further opportunity to bowl the two promised no balls. So instead, Majeed said, Salman Butt would deliberately bat out a maiden in the first full over that he faced in

Pakistan's second innings. '*Khan*' protested that a maiden could happen anyway when a batsman had just got in. He therefore asked if Butt could also bat out the third over that he faced as a maiden. Majeed said: '*Yeah, could do that. ... I'll speak to him now. ... Why don't I do it on loudspeaker, then you can listen on the other line, yeah?*'[15] As a result, '*Khan*' overheard (and again secretly recorded) the following conversation between Majeed and Butt:[16]

Majeed:	'*You know the maiden yeah that we're doing for the first over yeah*'.
SB:	'*Yeah*'.
Majeed:	'*You know the third over you play yeah*'.
SB:	'*Yeah*'.
Majeed:	'*One more maiden*'.
SB:	'*Bro, just leave it, okay?*'
Majeed:	'*You don't want to do the next one, the third one?*'
SB:	[inaudible]
Majeed:	'*Right, I'll call you in the ...*'
SB:	'*We don't know what the situation will be at that time*'.
Majeed:	'*Okay, right, I'll call you in the morning and we'll speak then*'.

The next morning, '*Khan*' went to Majeed's house, and Majeed called Butt back and put the call on loudspeaker so that '*Khan*' could hear the conversation, which went as follows (English translations in square brackets):[17]

Majeed:	'*As-salamu alaykum*'.
SB:	'*Wa alaikum assalam. What?*'
Majeed:	'*Boss, just stick to what we said last night, okay. Just leave it as that. Okay.*'
SB:	'*Yes*'.
Majeed:	'*So, just, just the first full over you play, you just make sure you play a maiden, ok*'.
SB:	'*Theek hai*'. [okay]
Majeed:	'*Right and just do one thing though. Don't forget. After the second ball, just go and tap the middle of the pitch as a signal. Theek hai?*' [okay?]
SB:	'*Theek hai*'. [okay]
Majeed:	'*Okay, don't forget that, after the second ball, the signal. Boss good luck. I'll speak to you soon*'.
SB:	'*Okay*'.
Majeed:	'*Okay bye*'.

At the Oval later that morning, opener Yasir Hameed was out in the first over of Pakistan's innings, and so Salman Butt came in to replace him when the new ball was only five deliveries old. Butt did not give the pre-agreed signal after the second ball of the first full over he faced, and he did not bat out that over as a maiden. When '*Khan*' called Majeed afterwards for an explanation, Majeed said: '*He obviously felt the ball was doing too much off the pitch and he couldn't do a maiden so that's why he didn't do the signal. ... Yeah so he felt it might be risky trying to defend it with the new hard ball. Yeah, that it might pop up*'.[18] Majeed said the players were pushing him to get the £150,000 payment on account that '*Khan*' had promised. '*Khan*' said he would only pay it over if Majeed absolutely guaranteed that the two promised no balls would be bowled at the Lord's Test the following week. Majeed gave that guarantee without hesitation.

The Lord's Test

On Wednesday 25 August 2010, the day before the start of the Lord's Test, NOTW employees went to the Thomas Cook foreign exchange booth on Oxford Street to get £140,000 in £50 notes, made up of fifty-six bundles of £2,500 each. They marked the notes and recorded their serial numbers. They booked a suite at the Copthorne Tara Hotel, just off Kensington High Street, and Mahmood's technical expert Conrad Brown hid video and audio recording equipment around the suite, including a camera in a tissue box on the table facing a sofa. When Majeed got to the suite, '*Khan*' guided him to that sofa, and they had the following conversation, all captured by Brown's equipment:[19]

Majeed:	'*This is what it's going to be yeah. You're going to do this now to show me that you are serious ... then I'm going to prove to you, I'm serious. ... I'm going to give you three no balls, okay, to prove to you firstly that this is what's happening. ... There's no signal, nothing. These three are definitely happening*'.
Mahmood:	'*Okay*'.
Majeed:	'*They've all been organised, okay. So the first ball of the third over of the innings, yeah*'.
Mahmood:	'*Okay, first ball of the third over of the innings, right. So who's going to be opening?*'
Majeed:	'*Asif and Amir are going to be bowling*'.
Mahmood:	'*So do we know which one?*'
Majeed:	'*That is going to be Amir. Amir is going to bowl the first over, yeah*'.
Mahmood:	'*So the first ball ...*'.
Majeed:	'*Of the third over*'.
Mahmood:	'*Of the third over. Is there any signal?*'
Majeed:	'*No signal. It'll just happen*'.
Mahmood:	'*It's a no ball, okay*'.

Majeed:	*'Okay. Then the tenth, the last ball, sixth ball of the tenth over'.*
Mahmood:	*'Last ball of …'.*
Majeed:	*'… the tenth over'.*
Mahmood:	*'… the tenth over. Who's bowling it?'*
Majeed:	*'Asif will be bowling it'.*
Mahmood:	*'Okay'.*
Majeed:	*'And the next one, will be Amir … . … [W]henever the right hander comes in, he'll be going round the wicket. Okay?'*
Mahmood:	*'Okay'.*
Majeed:	*'… The first over he bowls around the wicket, the last ball of that over will also be a no ball. … After you see these three, yeah, you'll know that that's no coincidence, yes or no? … I've given you the three. … This is what's going to happen'.*
Mahmood:	*'Okay'.*
Majeed:	*'Okay. This is exactly what's going to happen, you're going to see these three things happen'.*
Mahmood:	*'Right'.*
Majeed:	*'Okay, then you're going to see that I'm, I'm talking 100 percent and I'm serious as well as you're serious'.*
Mahmood:	*'Okay. …'.*
Mahmood:	*'… So Asif will definitely be bowling the tenth over, yes?'*
Majeed:	*'For sure. The captain knows, he's the one that brings them on and brings them off. He will definitely do it'.*

Majeed then called Amir, and they had the following brief exchange, witnessed by '*Khan*' and recorded on tape:

Amir:	*'Hello, hello'.*
Majeed:	(in Urdu) *'Are you sleeping fucker?'*
Amir:	*'Yeah I was'.*
Majeed:	(in Urdu) *'Okay, sleep.'* (English) *'Just, we've spoken about everything before anyway. Okay, don't mind'.* (Urdu) *'You sleep, okay?'*
Amir:	*'Alright, okay'.*

'*Khan*' then gave Majeed a briefcase filled with £140,000 in bundles of £50 notes, so that with the original £10,000 already paid over, he had now given Majeed a total of £150,000. After counting it carefully, Majeed left with the briefcase and the cash. He told '*Khan*' to call him the next day, '*once it's happened*'.[20]

At Lord's the next morning, Salman Butt won the toss and put England into bat. While delivering the first ball of his second over of the day (the third over of England's first innings), Mohammad Amir overstepped the crease by a wide margin, and the umpire duly signalled a no ball. The CricInfo commentator said: '*Yikes, on replay that was an enormous no ball, good half a metre over the line*'. Mohammad Asif also overstepped while delivering the sixth ball of his fifth over (the tenth over of England's first innings), and the umpire again duly signalled a no ball.

Play ended early that day due to bad weather, and so Mohammad Amir did not have the opportunity to bowl the third no ball that Majeed had promised. At 10.15 pm, Majeed called '*Khan*' and told him that instead the third no ball would now be bowled the next morning, as the third ball of Amir's third full over (ie disregarding the three balls he still had to bowl from the over that he was halfway through when play was suspended that day). At 10.45 pm, Mahmood received a text from Majeed that read: '*Yaar [mate] after you finish your current over then 3 overs. Text back*'. Obviously Majeed had meant to send that text to Amir. Mahmood replied: '*Wrong person*'.[21]

The next day, Friday 27 August 2010, in his third delivery of his third full over, Mohammad Amir again overstepped the crease by a wide margin. The umpire immediately signalled a no ball and pointed out to Amir how far over the line he had stepped. Michael Holding, commentating for Sky Sports, said: '*How far over was that? Woh!*', and Ian Botham responded: '*It's like net bowling*'.[22]

The News of the World tells the Met Police about the fix

The NOTW was delighted with its scoop, but it did not want to lose the £150,000 in cash that Mahmood had paid to Majeed, and so it needed the police to apprehend Majeed and seize the money immediately after the Lord's fix happened. It therefore told the Metropolitan Police about the sting on the day of the three no balls, Friday 27 August 2010. The next day, the Met arrested Majeed on suspicion of conspiracy to defraud bookmakers, and that evening, after play had ended, they went to the Pakistan team hotel and searched the rooms of Butt, Asif, and Amir. In Butt's room they found £2,500 and in Amir's room they found £1,500 of marked NOTW £50 notes. The players claimed these were payments that Majeed had made to them for attending the opening of an ice-cream parlour in South London. No NOTW money was found in Asif's room. The Met also seized the mobile phones of all three players, but released the players without charge after they had undertaken to return to attend for questioning as and when required.

The story breaks and the ICC scrambles to react

Late that night, Saturday 28 August 2010, the News of the World broke the story online, in advance of the print edition the next day. The story immediately made headlines all around the world, and the ICC came under urgent and enormous pressure to react, prompting (among many other things) Iain Higgins' call to me in Portugal.

On 1 September 2010, ICC CEO Haroon Lorgat received a letter from Cressida Dick, who at that point was the Assistant Commissioner of the Metropolitan Police.

She confirmed that the Met was investigating Butt, Asif and Amir for conspiracy to defraud bookmakers, and said that the Met might need the ICC's help in arranging further interviews of the players. She acknowledged that the ICC might wish to take its own disciplinary action against the players, but asserted that the police investigation took precedence, and warned that the ICC should not do anything that might prejudice the criminal case, including interviewing the players.

This put the ICC in a difficult spot. Clearly it did not want to do anything that might prejudice the criminal case. But equally the Met had given no indication as to how long its investigation might take, and the ICC could not simply sit on its hands and allow the players to continue to play indefinitely. It had to act quickly and decisively, not only to maintain good order in the Test series itself – there were reports of exchanges of insults and scuffles between players from the two teams at Lord's before the start of play on the Sunday that the NOTW story came out – but also to reassure the watching public that the ICC was ready, willing and able to respond swiftly and rigorously to this apparent corruption of the sport. And that meant it had to charge the players as quickly as possible with breach of the ICC Anti-Corruption Code, which would then give it the power under the Code to suspend them from playing until the charges were resolved.

We therefore advised the Met that the ICC's responsibility to protect the sport meant that it would press forward with its disciplinary action unless the Met could show that doing so would materially prejudice its ability to pursue its criminal investigation. In response, we were told that the real concern of the Met and the Crown Prosecution Service was that any details of the ICC's disciplinary action against the players that got into the public domain might give the players an argument that the jury pool had been prejudiced and so they could not get a fair trial on any subsequent criminal charges against them. We therefore said we would go ahead and charge the players and provisionally suspend them, but if the players challenged their provisional suspensions: (a) any hearing on that challenge would take place in private; (b) the parties would be required not to disclose or make any public comment about any of the evidence produced during the process; (c) the decision would not be published beyond the parties; and (d) any public announcement by the ICC of the decision would make clear that the players were presumed to be innocent of the substantive charges unless and until the ICC proved otherwise at a full merits hearing. The Met and CPS were satisfied with this.

Charging and provisionally suspending the players under the ICC Anti-Corruption Code

We still had to satisfy ourselves, however, that we had sufficient authentic and admissible evidence to charge the players with breach of the ICC Anti-Corruption Code. Initially we only had the NOTW story and selected recordings of the Mahmood-Majeed dealings that the NOTW had posted online. Salman Butt had issued a strong denial (*'These are just allegations. Anybody can stand up and say things about you – it doesn't make them true'*) and so had Mohammad Amir, via his brother (*'He has told the family he will swear on the Koran he did not do these things. There is no way these allegations are true'*), while Pakistan's High Commissioner to London directly challenged the reliability of the NOTW recordings (*'We are not seeing on the video what the date or time is. Do you have answers to these questions? It could have been dated before the match or after the match, or at a different time'*).[23]

But the Met Police had already received copies of the complete recordings from the NOTW, and had confirmed to us that they believed the recordings to be authentic and (crucially) to have been made *before* the Test matches in question. Within a matter of days, the ICC also met with representatives of the NOTW, and was given its own complete copies and transcripts of the video and audio recordings, as well as a detailed explanation from Conrad Brown of how and when the recordings had been made. The NOTW also confirmed that, as long as the Met Police agreed, Mazher Mahmood would appear as a witness in any disciplinary proceedings brought by the ICC against the players, to authenticate the recordings and to testify as to his interactions with Majeed.

This was enough to establish a case for the players to answer, and so on 2 September 2010 we charged them with breaches of the Anti-Corruption Code, and suspended them from playing until the ICC Anti-Corruption Tribunal had ruled on the charges. We could not charge Majeed as well, because the ICC did not have jurisdiction over him. In summary, we alleged that:

- Majeed and the players had agreed that the players would fix aspects of Pakistan's matches, that Majeed would sell the information to gamblers, and they would split the proceeds between them.
- Majeed agreed with *'Mohsin Khan'* (Mahmood), whom he understood to be a representative of a Far East gambling syndicate, that Mohammad Amir and Mohammad Asif would each deliver a deliberate no ball at specific times during the Oval Test, in return for payment of £10,000 per no ball.
- When it became impossible to deliver those no balls at the Oval Test, Majeed promised *'Khan'* instead, with Salman Butt's agreement, that Butt would deliberately bat out a maiden over during Pakistan's first innings in the Oval Test.
- When that plan had to be called off, Majeed promised instead, again with the players' agreement, that Amir and Asif would deliver three deliberate no balls at specified times during the Lord's Test, in return for £150,000, which would also buy *'Khan'* information about future fixes.
- Amir and Asif duly bowled three deliberate no balls at the specified times in the Lord's Test.

Ed Hawkins, a sports journalist who has spent a lot of time investigating corruption in cricket, has suggested that no bookmaker would have accepted any significant bet on a specific delivery being bowled as a no ball, let alone a bet or bets paying out £150,000, because the risk of a fix is so great.[24] However, it was clear from the recordings that the cost of the no balls was £10,000 each, and the remainder of the £150,000 was a payment on account, to be drawn down when tip-offs were provided in the future about other fixes (not no balls, but match results and brackets – ie how many runs will be scored in a particular set of overs in a match), and so there was no need to recover the full £150,000 upfront. And in any event, in contrast to the subsequent criminal charges of conspiracy to cheat at gambling, which are discussed below, the disciplinary charges brought by the ICC did not depend on anyone actually betting on the fix. Instead, our case was that the players agreed to a corrupt plan to play to order. They may or may not have understood that others would make money on the betting markets from the fix, but either way their actions were still corrupt, and a clear breach of the ICC Anti-Corruption Code. They were still cheating the game, their teammates and the spectators, whether or not any bet was ever going to be placed on what they had corruptly promised to do.

When the ICC's charges and the players' provisional suspensions were announced, the press welcomed *'the swift action many in the game had demanded'*, and quoted with approval ICC CEO Haroon Lorgat's strong accompanying statement: *'We will not tolerate corruption in cricket – simple as that. We must be decisive with such matters and, if proven, these offences carry serious penalties up to a life ban. The ICC will do everything possible to keep such conduct out of the game and we will stop at nothing to protect the sport's integrity. While we believe the problem is not widespread, we must always be vigilant. It is important, however, that we do not pre-judge the guilt of these three players. That is for the independent tribunal alone to decide'.*[25]

The provisional suspension hearing

Salman Butt and Mohammad Amir immediately said they wanted to challenge their provisional suspensions, and it was announced that the Chair of the ICC Anti-Corruption Tribunal, Michael Beloff QC, a hugely respected English barrister with enormous sports law experience,[26] would hear that application on 30 and 31 October 2010 at the ICC's headquarters in Dubai. At that stage, both players were represented by Pakistani lawyers, Salman Butt by Mr Aftab Gul, and Mohammad Amir by Mr Shahid Karim.

At the hearing in Dubai, in order to persuade Mr Beloff to maintain the provisional suspensions of the players until a final decision was made on the charges against them, the ICC had to demonstrate a *'strong arguable case'* that each of them had breached the Anti-Corruption Code in the manner charged. To meet that burden, we presented the NOTW audio and video recordings, which we said showed: (1) that Salman Butt had agreed with Mazher Majeed on Friday 20 August 2010 and again early on Saturday 21 August 2010 that Butt would deliberately bat out a maiden over at The Oval on the Saturday; and (2) that on Wednesday 25 August 2010 and then again on Thursday 26 August 2010, Majeed had told '*Khan*' exactly when Amir and Asif would bowl three no balls during the following day's play at Lord's. We explained how those recordings had been provided to the ICC by the NOTW, and that the News International Legal Director, Tom Crone, had confirmed: (a) that he had received the recordings from Mazher Mahmood *before* the matches in question; and (b) that Mahmood would appear if necessary at the full hearing to authenticate the recordings and to testify as to his dealings with Majeed. We also presented a statement from David Kendix, Chairman of the Association of Cricket Statisticians and Historians, who explained that the odds of successfully predicting that three specific deliveries in a Test match would be no balls without having inside information to that effect were about 1.5 million to 1.

In response, Mr Gul and Mr Karim confirmed that their respective clients absolutely insisted that they had not been party to any fix, and contended that the fact that the CPS had not brought any criminal charges against their clients demonstrated their innocence. They argued that the provisional suspensions should be lifted unless the Tribunal was satisfied that the evidence presented by the ICC established the players' guilt beyond reasonable doubt, and asserted that that exacting standard had not been met, because Mahmood and the NOTW lacked credibility, the evidence they had provided was inadmissible because it had been obtained by a deceitful sting operation, and in any event the ICC had not established either that the NOTW recordings were authentic or, crucially, that they had taken place before the matches in question. In particular, Mr Gul confirmed that Mr Butt denied that it was him speaking to Majeed on the phone calls recorded on the NOTW tapes.[27]

At the end of the hearing, Mr Beloff ruled that the evidence presented by the ICC did establish a strong arguable case that the players had breached the ICC Anti-Corruption Code as alleged, and he therefore left their provisional suspensions in place pending the full merits hearing. He rejected the suggestion that evidence obtained by a sting operation must be disregarded, noting that such methods may be the only way to unearth evidence of corrupt behaviour. He said the only real question was whether the NOTW recordings were authentic and had been made before the matches in question. He said that at that stage the ICC's evidence that the News International Legal Director, Tom Crone, had confirmed that he received the recordings before the Lord's Test was enough to establish that there was a case to answer, given the absence at that stage of any evidence to the contrary. However, he emphasised that the case depended almost entirely on the authenticity of the recordings and (crucially) *when* they were made, and that therefore at the full hearing the ICC would need to be ready to prove those points to the requisite standard.

Gathering the evidence required for the hearing on the merits

Ensuring the players remained provisionally suspended from playing until the charges against them had been resolved was just the first step. To get the charges upheld at the full hearing, the ICC would have to produce authentic and admissible evidence – not just newspaper reports – that would prove the facts on which the charges were based to the standard of proof specified in the Anti-Corruption Code. That standard of proof was not the normal civil standard of balance of probabilities (more likely than not to be true). Instead, the Code specified that we would have to prove the most serious charges to the criminal standard of proof, ie beyond a reasonable doubt, and we would have to prove the other charges *'to the comfortable satisfaction'* of the Tribunal, a bespoke standard of proof borrowed from the World Anti-Doping Code (see p 49).

As Mr Beloff had said, the most crucial evidence was obviously the video and audio recordings of Salman Butt agreeing on the Saturday morning of the Oval Test to bat out the first over he would face that day as a maiden, and of Mazhar Majeed telling '*Mohsin Khan*' before the Lord's Test exactly when Amir and Asif would bowl the three no balls that they duly went on to bowl in that Test. We also knew the likely lines of attack on that evidence from the players. Mazher Mahmood's conviction for perjury in the 2014 trial of singer Tulisa Contostavlos was several years away,[28] but there had already been many public allegations about his and/or the NOTW's sharp practices and dubious investigative techniques in previous cases. In particular, we were of course aware that NOTW journalist Clive Goodman and his investigator Glenn Mulcaire had been jailed in 2007 for hacking into people's mobile phones to obtain compromising material, and that The Guardian had subsequently reported that such hacking was widespread at the NOTW. But

Mazher Mahmood emphatically denied that he had ever hacked anyone's phone[29] or that this investigation in particular had been triggered by unlawfully hacked information. Instead, he maintained that he had been tipped off by a source '*within the Pakistani cricket community*' about apparent fixing by Majeed and certain Pakistani players in relation to the ICC T20 World Cup in the West Indies in May 2010.[30] We were satisfied with this explanation, because the ICC's Anti-Corruption & Security Unit had received the same tip, and on that basis had opened a formal investigation into Majeed and had issued a formal demand to Salman Butt just a week before the Lord's Test, requiring him to provide details of the mobile phone numbers he had used while in the West Indies.

Previous Mahmood victims, including England football manager Sven-Goran Eriksson,[31] had also complained that Mahmood '*entrapped*' them, ie induced them to do something that they would never have done of their own accord. But that argument could not work in this case, because Majeed himself had said on tape that he and players on the Pakistan team had been fixing matches long before he ever met Mahmood. Mahmood had simply provided them with a further opportunity to profit from that fixing, which they had readily accepted without any need for him to apply any pressure.[32] Mr Beloff had already given short shrift to this argument in his provisional suspension decision, and Mr Butt and Mr Amir quietly dropped it before the merits hearing.

That left the crucial question of the authenticity of the recordings, and (in particular) *when* they had been made. We went back to the NOTW for the promised assistance on this point immediately after the provisional suspension hearing, and Mazher Mahmood said he would meet me in the bar of the Nobu Hotel on Portman Square. He was very concerned that no one should realise who he was or what we were discussing, and so we sat in a quiet corner of the bar. By chance, however, also in the bar that evening was Trevor East, a former senior Sky Sports executive who by that point had joined Pitch International, a client of mine. Trevor, a very gregarious man, spotted me and shouted over: '*Mr Taylor, I see you over there, what are you up to?*' I went over quickly to greet him and explain I was in a sensitive meeting and could not join him for a beer, much though I would like to, and he left us be after that. But Mazher Mahmood was not best pleased, given his concern that his alter ego as the Fake Sheikh should not be exposed. It also became clear that he was sceptical about whether the ICC was truly interested in pursuing the matter properly. But once he had calmed down and I had persuaded him that the ICC was indeed committed to the case, he agreed that he and Conrad Brown would provide detailed witness statements explaining his interactions with Majeed and how all of the recordings had been made. They would also include in their evidence an image of the very incriminating text message that Majeed had mistakenly sent to '*Khan*' instead of Amir on 26 August 2010, saying: '*Yaar [mate] after you finish your current over then 3 overs. Text back*'.

This was all very helpful, but in order to put the matter beyond any doubt, we also wanted to get records of the calls and texts made to and from the players' mobile phones in the relevant period, in order to establish that the phone conversations and other contacts between Majeed and the players that Mahmood/Khan had recorded had taken place *before* the Oval Test (in the case of the exchanges about the Oval fix) and *before* the Lord's Test (in the case of the exchanges about the Lord's fix). In the ordinary course, we would have simply used the powers given to the ICC under the Anti-Corruption Code to require the players to hand over their mobile phones so that we could look at the call logs and the texts received, but the Met Police had seized the players' mobile phones on the Saturday of the Lord's Test, and so we had to go to the Met for this information. They told us that they wanted to do all they lawfully could to assist the ICC, but they could not hand over any phone data without a court order. The ICC Anti-Corruption Tribunal had no power to order third parties to hand over evidence, and so we applied to the High Court pursuant to Civil Procedure Rule 34.3(1),[33] seeking a witness summons requiring the Commissioner of the Metropolitan Police to provide the ICC with details of the phone contacts between Majeed and the players in the key periods. That application is one of only two times that I have appeared as an advocate in the English courts, because (as already explained: see p 15) almost all sports disputes are resolved by way of arbitration proceedings before bodies such as Sport Resolutions UK and the Court of Arbitration for Sport in Lausanne. The Master signed the witness summons, and the Met duly provided a witness statement confirming that the phone data in its possession showed that all three players had called Majeed before start of play at The Oval on Friday 20 August 2010 (just after they had been warned by the coach to ensure they did not bowl any extras) and that Majeed had called Salman Butt at 11.41 pm that night, and the call had lasted for 57 seconds. That was exactly the time that Majeed spoke to Butt on the call recorded by Mahmood, when Majeed asked Butt to bat out a second maiden over and Butt told him no, and their conversation on the tape lasted 57 seconds as well. The records also established that Salman Butt telephoned Majeed at 8.14 am on Saturday 21 August 2010, and the call lasted for 41 seconds. Again that was exactly the time that Butt called Majeed on the second call recorded by Majeed, when Majeed told Butt '*just stick to what we said last night … . So, just the first full over you play, you just make sure you play a maiden, okay?*' and Butt replied '*Okay*', and their conversation lasted 41 seconds on the tape as well. This demonstrated that Mr Butt's evidence that it was not him on the other end of the phone in those two conversations was untrue.

The hearing in Doha on the merits

On 12 November 2010, Mr Beloff directed that Albie Sachs (former judge on South Africa's Constitutional Court) and Sharad Rao (former Attorney-General of Kenya) would sit alongside him on the Anti-Corruption Tribunal to determine the charges on the merits. He also directed that the merits hearing would be held at the Qatar Financial Centre in Doha, Qatar, from 6-11 January 2011, and that each side had to file its evidence and written submissions prior to that date. That tight timetable was set at the request of the lawyers for Mr Butt and Mr Amir, because they wanted their clients to be cleared in time to play in the ICC Cricket World Cup tournament scheduled for February and March 2011. Given the evidence we had, I was surprised that they were so confident of their case, but that was a matter for them, not me.

Mr Butt subsequently got new counsel, namely English barristers Ali Bajwa and Yasin Patel, who changed tack and applied for a stay of the disciplinary proceedings pending a charging decision from the CPS and pending resolution of any criminal charges that were brought. We opposed this application vigorously, arguing that the ICC Anti-Corruption Code had to be enforced speedily and effectively in order to maintain public confidence in the integrity of the sport, and that Mr Butt had not shown that he would face a real risk of injustice in the criminal proceedings if the disciplinary proceedings happened first. By this stage, Mohammad Asif was represented by Addleshaw Goddard, instructing Alexander Cameron QC, the brother of the then-Prime Minister, David Cameron. They agreed with the ICC that the disciplinary hearing should go ahead without waiting for the outcome of the Met's investigation and any subsequent criminal charges. Mr Beloff duly rejected Mr Butt's request for a stay, and Jamie, Iain and I quickly gathered the following evidence for the merits hearing in Doha, with the crucial help of ACSU head Ravi Sawani and his team of investigators, and with the steadfast and unequivocal backing of the ICC Board, ICC CEO Haroon Lorgat, ICC General Counsel David Becker, Giles Clarke (the chair of the ICC's Pakistan Taskforce), and ACSU chair Sir Ronnie Flanagan:

- The witness statement of Mazher Mahmood, Investigations Editor of the News of the World, describing how he had posed as '*Mohsin Khan*' and secretly recorded audio and video footage of his dealings with Majeed, including: (a) when Majeed telephoned Salman Butt and confirmed the Oval fix agreement with him; (b) when Majeed told '*Khan*', the night before the first day of the Lord's Test, exactly when Amir and Asif would bowl no balls at the Lord's Test; and (c) when Majeed told '*Khan*', the night before the second day of the Lord's Test, exactly when Amir would bowl the third no ball the next day. Transcripts of all of the highly incriminating conversations recorded on that footage were attached as exhibits to Mahmood's statement, along with photographs of the text messages that Mahmood had received from Majeed.

- The witness statement of Conrad Brown, who had organised and so was also able to authenticate the audio and video recordings of Mahmood's dealings with Majeed, and to corroborate the dates and times of those dealings.

- The witness statement of Tom Crone, Legal Director for News International, the publishers of the News of the World, who confirmed (by exhibiting copies of emails that he had received by Mahmood during the investigation) that Majeed had told Mahmood exactly when Amir and Asif would bowl the three no balls at the Lord's Test *before* those no balls were bowled.

- The witness statement of David Kendix, official scorer at the Lord's Test and Chairman of the Association of Cricket Statisticians and Historians, explaining that the odds of successfully predicting that three specific deliveries in a Test match would be no balls without having inside information to that effect were about 1.5 million to 1.

- The Met Police witness statement confirming the dates and times of the key telephone contacts between Majeed and the players, taken from the call logs on the mobile phones seized from the players.

- The witness statement of Martin Vertigen of the ACSU, attaching phone records that had been obtained mainly by using the powers given to the ACSU under the Anti-Corruption Code to require the players to provide formal consent to their service providers to give the ACSU records of calls and texts made to and from their phones in the relevant periods, including in particular calls and texts to/from Mazher Majeed. This evidence revealed that the phone contacts between Majeed and the players reflected *exactly* his interactions with '*Khan*' on the NOTW tapes. In particular, they showed that Majeed had spoken with and/or texted each of Butt, Amir, and Asif several times shortly before and shortly after the meeting at the Copthorne Tara Hotel on 25 August 2010 where '*Khan*'

> gave Majeed £140,000 in cash. They also showed that there was a flurry of further texts and calls between the same men after the close of play at Lord's the next day, when the time to bowl the third no ball had had to be re-arranged. And they showed that the same evening, just after Majeed had mistakenly sent '*Khan*' a text intended for Amir that said '*Yaar [mate] after you finish your current over then 3 overs. Text back*', and '*Khan*' texted back '*Wrong person*', Majeed immediately texted Amir, who duly texted Majeed straight back.

None of the players disputed the evidence of Conrad Brown, Tom Crone, the Met Police, or Martin Vertigen, and therefore that evidence was accepted into the record without them having to appear at the hearing. However, the players did dispute the evidence of Mazher Mahmood, and so he turned up in person in Doha, with elaborate precautions being taken to keep his face concealed from the members of the press who gathered outside the hearing venue each day. On cross-examination by counsel for the players, Mr Mahmood suffered glancing blows based on general criticisms of his and/or the NOTW's investigative techniques, but the core of his evidence of his interactions with Mr Majeed was unshaken, because it was all captured on tape. And in light of all of the evidence we had provided about the provenance of those recordings, and the phone records that backed them up and confirmed when they were made, Mr Butt and Mr Amir were forced to abandon their previous arguments that the recordings were not authentic/were not made prior to the matches in question. In particular, Mr Butt was now forced to admit what he had denied at the provisional hearing, namely that it *was* him on the other end of the phone to Majeed in the NOTW recordings, agreeing to deliberately bat out a maiden over at the Oval Test, which was of course enormously damaging to the credibility of his denials of any knowledge of any fix. And all three players now had to explain how Mazhar Majeed had been able to tell '*Khan*' in advance exactly when Amir would bowl two no balls and Asif would bowl one no ball in the Lord's Test. Needless to say, they did not have any plausible innocent explanation. Salman Butt accepted that Majeed must have had inside information, but said it did not come from him. Mohammad Asif also accepted that Majeed must have had inside information, said the source must have been Butt, and alleged that Butt had manipulated him into bowling his no ball by telling him immediately prior to that delivery to run in faster. Mohammad Amir also denied any knowledge of a fix. He insisted that his first no ball was due to slippery conditions and his second was due to him wanting to bowl a bouncer to drive the batsman back into his crease, but he was unable to explain how Majeed had been able to tell '*Mohsin Khan*' in advance exactly when those two no balls would be bowled. As the Tribunal noted in its eventual decision: '*When taxed to supply an explanation for what seemed to be inexplicable unless Mr Amir had agreed directly or through an intermediary to bowl those no balls at those times, Mr Karim like Hamlet accepted that "that is the question". But with great charm he left the Tribunal to resolve it; from him, as from his client, answer came there none*'.[34] Ultimately, all three players simply argued they had not been party to any agreement to fix any part of either Test match, and submitted that the evidence submitted by the ICC did not prove beyond any reasonable doubt that they had.

The hearing lasted for six days. At one point, agitated about some disputed point that I cannot now remember, I went to see opposing counsel, who were together in a meeting room with their clients. I started vigorously complaining, and Alex Cameron interrupted and asked me to step outside with him, where he said quietly: '*Jon, no need to be so aggressive, we are all just trying to represent our clients properly, just as you are trying to represent the ICC properly*'. I realised he was right, took a deep breath, and apologised to him and his colleagues. His suggestion that I should maintain professional detachment from the case I was presenting was very good advice, albeit there will be plenty of adversaries who will say I have often failed to heed it in the years that followed. Sadly Alex died from pancreatic cancer in 2023.[35] I also have a lot of respect for Ali Bajwa (now KC) and Yasin Patel, who together represented Salman Butt very ably at the full hearing before the Tribunal. As counter-intuitive as it may seem, I have always found it a lot easier to litigate a case when the other side is experienced and knows what it is doing, and when you know you can trust them not to misstate facts or play games. It means you can get to the key issues much more quickly, without having to waste time unnecessarily on peripheral issues and distractions, which saves a lot of time and money, and makes for a much more efficient and effective decision-making process.

At the end of the hearing, the Tribunal said it would hand down its decision in a few weeks. That evening, the ICC legal team (me, Iain Higgins, and Jamie Herbert) ate in one of the restaurants at the W Hotel in Doha, near to where the hearings had been held, with opposing counsel Alex Cameron QC, Ali Bajwa, and Yasin Patel. While we were on our way there, we bumped into Tribunal chair Michael Beloff, and invited him to join us. Halfway through the meal, a NOTW journalist came up to the table unannounced, shoved a camera and microphone in Michael's face, and asked him aggressively: '*Why are you being so cosy with counsel for the players?*' I pointed out that we (counsel to the ICC) were also there, so that nothing inappropriate was happening, and told him to leave us alone. After the meal, we went for a drink in the hotel bar. Alex Cameron was admiring the dizzying array of spirits and liquors on display behind the bar, and lamenting that his brief fee would not stretch to cover the cost of any of them, when the NOTW journalist suddenly appeared, apologised for the disturbance over dinner, and offered to buy us both drinks. Immediately, without missing a beat, Alex Cameron turned, gestured towards the top shelf and said, '*Well in that case I'll have a …*' and rattled off the name and vintage of a very expensive-sounding brandy that I had never heard off and that caused the NOTW journalist's face to blanch when he got the bill. This demonstrated Alex's sophistication, and was and remains the only time in my life that I have regretted the potential limitations of a state school education.

The decision on the merits, and the sanctions hearing

On 4 February 2011, while Jamie and I were on the plane flying back to Doha to receive the Tribunal's decision and (if necessary) to address the Tribunal on the issue of sanctions, the CPS announced that it had charged Mazhar Majeed and the three players with conspiracy to accept corrupt payments, contrary to section 1 of the Prevention of Corruption Act 1906, and with conspiracy to cheat at gambling, contrary to section 42 of the Gambling Act 2005. This timing by the CPS was not coincidental: the criminal charges triggered application of the Contempt of Court Act 1981, meaning that the media would have to be very careful, in its reporting of the Tribunal's decision, not to say anything that risked prejudicing the trial of the criminal charges.

When we got to Doha, we were all given the lengthy written decision of the Tribunal, which explained in careful detail why it was upholding most of the charges the ICC had pressed against the players. The Tribunal noted that the players had sought to cast doubt on the integrity of the NOTW and Mr Mahmood, but for the Tribunal the proof was in the pudding:[36]

> From a journalistic point of view, establishing that the captain of the Pakistani team was involved in the alleged fix would strongly boost the value of his investigatory coup. Moreover, the finesse with which he [Mazher Mahmood] played his part in the "sting" indicates that he is a master of dissimulation. Nevertheless, all the core elements of his testimony were borne out by uncontroverted video and tape-recorded evidence. This was the rock on which counsel for Mr Amir's general critique of the not altogether unblemished record of the NOTW and of MK in other matters founded. The recordings spoke vividly for themselves – he had no need to gild the lily.

The Tribunal also noted that the players had not challenged the phone data evidence from the Met Police and the ACSU that established the time and duration of calls and text messages between Majeed and the three players. It said: '*With these materials to hand, we are in a position to construct a dependable and at times vivid narrative of the events which preceded and led up to the bowling of the three no balls*'.[37] And as explained above that narrative was utterly damning of Majeed and the players.

The Tribunal upheld the charge that Mr Butt had failed to disclose Mazhar Majeed's request that he bat out a maiden at the Oval Test,[38] but rejected the separate charge that he had actually agreed to do so, because '*the evidence on that charge did not satisfy us beyond reasonable doubt that he seriously intended to follow through with the proposed fix*'.[39] As to the Lord's Test, the Tribunal concluded:[40]

> 187. … the evidence against all three players concerning the Lord's fix agreement to bowl three no balls at pre-determined moments in the game is overwhelming. The fundamental point is that Mr Majeed, who acted or purported to act as their agent, is captured on video and audio tape predicting exactly when in the game the three no balls would be delivered, and by whom. …
>
> 188. There is further unchallenged evidence of intense telephone and text communication between Mr Majeed and each of the three players, frequently at or near midnight or even in the early hours of the morning, in the middle of a hard-fought test match.
>
> 189. In addition, the explanations offered by the players were in each case, quite implausible, and none of them had been advanced at the time the story first broke in the media, or by the time of or at the provisional hearing that took place in October 2010.
>
> 190. For these and other reasons dealt with in detail in this Determination, we have no doubt at all that all three players were parties to the fix at Lords regarding the bowling by Mr Amir of two no balls and by Mr Asif of one no ball, at predicted moments in the game.

Having digested the Tribunal's decision at great speed, we had to return later that day to address it on the question of sanctions. The Anti-Corruption Code provided that the sanction for the most serious offences was a ban of between five years (minimum) and life. We submitted that the key consideration for the Tribunal, in deciding where to land in that range, was the need to maintain public confidence in the reputation and integrity of the sport and in the ability of the ICC to defend that integrity from corrupt acts on the part of players and player support personnel. In our view, that factor weighed heavily in favour of sanctions at the highest end of the scale. In response, Mr Bajwa for Mr Butt cited the infamous case of Puerta v ITF (see p 60) as authority for the proposition that the Tribunal could go lower than the minimum ban prescribed in the Code where that ban was disproportionate on the facts of the case before it. The Tribunal did not agree with him, but ruled that in any event the facts of this case would not have warranted any reduction below the five year minimum.[41] On the other hand, the Tribunal considered there were factors mitigating against a life ban: the fix was initiated by Majeed rather than the players; it had been confined to three no balls at Lord's and had had no impact on the outcome of either Test match; none of the players appeared to have received any reward for the fix (the Tribunal decided we had not proved beyond reasonable doubt that the NOTW money found in the hotel rooms of Butt and Amir was payment for the fix[42]); and the players had all lost their reputations and their livelihoods, and now faced criminal penalties as well. Taking all of these circumstances into account, the Tribunal banned Mr Butt for ten years, with the last five suspended on condition that he participated in programmes of public education and rehabilitation; it banned Mr Asif for seven years, with the last two suspended on the same condition; and it banned Mr Amir (whose impressionable age of 18 appeared to garner much sympathy with the Panel) for the minimum five years. Of the public education and rehabilitation elements, the Tribunal said: '*We sense that a restorative process of that kind would be well received by the general cricket loving public, and the ICC. If that would encourage young people in particular about the need to resist temptations to take irregular short cuts in life, something really good can emerge from the process. Repentant sinners have in other areas, including the sporting, made the best teachers*'.[43]

The News of the World was furious, and so were many other commentators, because in their view the players' egregious conduct had warranted life bans all round, and these lesser bans called into question whether cricket was really serious about fighting corruption.[44] My immediate reaction was to agree with them. But Iain Higgins pointed out why the Tribunal may have focused not just on punishment but also on redemption. One of its three members, Albie Sachs, a former ANC activist, had lost his right arm and been blinded in one eye by a car bomb planted by the South African security forces while he was in exile in Mozambique. However, when the struggle against apartheid ended, he had returned to South Africa, declared that '*punishment is not the only form of justice*', championed the work of the Truth & Reconciliation Commission, and advocated for '*soft vengeance*' in the form of creation of a free, democratic South Africa living under the protection of a constitution, a bill of rights, and the rule of law.[45] I was forced to acknowledge that Mr Sachs was probably better qualified than me to determine what would best serve the interests of justice in this case.

The ICC Anti-Corruption Code provided that the players could appeal the Tribunal's decision to the Court of Arbitration for Sport. All three players did so within the 21-day deadline, but they subsequently agreed that those appeals should be stayed until the criminal proceedings against them were concluded. Presumably they hoped that those criminal proceedings would turn up exculpatory evidence that they could deploy at the CAS.

The criminal proceedings

Far from producing exculpatory evidence for the players, however, the criminal proceedings later that year only produced further incriminating evidence that we had not been aware of in Doha. In particular, that evidence showed that on 17 August 2010, ie the day before the Oval Test, Mohammad Amir had texted his bank details to a number in Pakistan, belonging to an '*Ali*', and had sent the following messages: '*How much and what needs to be done*', '*This is going to be too much*', and '*so in first 3, bowl however you want, and in the last 2, do 8 runs?*', all apparently without the involvement of Majeed.[46] Mr Amir also subsequently admitted that on the Saturday of the Lord's Test, after the police had come to search his hotel room, he had texted the same Ali and told him to delete from his phone all evidence of their contacts.[47] There is an obvious tension between this and Mr Amir's subsequent claim to Michael Atherton that he had been a naif whose youthful gullibility had been exploited by Majeed and Butt.[48]

Majeed and Amir both pleaded guilty to the criminal charges. Butt and Asif pleaded not guilty but were convicted on all counts by a jury at Southwark Crown Court in autumn 2011. Mr Justice Cooke sentenced Mazher Majeed to two years and eight months in prison, on the basis that he and Salman Butt were the '*architects*' of the fixing, and because of the evidence that Majeed's corrupt activities in cricket started well before the Oval and Lord's Tests in August 2010. He imposed a more lenient prison term on each of the players than he said he would otherwise have done because in each case he considered that the ban from cricket was already '*considerable punishment for a man in your position*'. However, '*these crimes of which you have been convicted require that a sentence be imposed which marks them for what they are and acts as a deterrent for any future cricketers who may be tempted*'. He sentenced Salman Butt to two years and six months in prison because of his leadership status in the Pakistan team, because '*you were the orchestrator of this activity, as you had to be, as captain, in arranging for these bowlers to be bowling the overs which were identified in advance to Majeed and which he identified to the NOTW journalist*', and because of his '*key role in directing the corrupt activities*', in particular his recruitment of Mohammad Amir. He gave Mohammad Asif 12 months in prison, and Mohammad Amir six months in a young offender institution.[49]

The Court of Appeal rejected the subsequent appeals of Butt and Amir, saying:[50]

> ... the corruption was carefully prepared. It was not set up on the spur of the moment. Nor was it the result of a sudden temptation to which either appellant succumbed in effect on the spur of the moment. The criminality was that these three cricketers betrayed their team, betrayed the country which they had the honour to represent, betrayed the sport that had given them their distinction, and betrayed the very many followers of the game throughout the world. In exchange for the privilege and advantages of playing Test cricket it was required of them that at all times they should perform honestly and play to the best of their respective abilities – no more, but certainly no less. If for money or any other extraneous reward it cannot be guaranteed that every Test player will play on the day as best he may, the reality is that the enjoyment of many millions of people around the world who watch cricket, whether on television or at Test Matches, will eventually be destroyed. ... [I]n the long term the game would be utterly impoverished

> if the court failed to make it clear that conduct like this is not simply a matter of breaking the rules of the game and therefore subject to internal regulation and discipline by the ICC, but that it is also criminal conduct of a very serious kind which must be marked with a criminal sanction.

These prison sentences sent further huge shockwaves throughout the sport. To the best of my knowledge, this was the first time that cricketers had ever been sent to prison for match-fixing, and they had to serve their sentences in a foreign country to boot. Even with time off for good behaviour, Mohammed Amir served about three months before being released in February 2012, Mohammad Asif served about six months before being released in May 2012, and Salman Butt served about seven months before being released in June 2012.[51] I know the ACSU believes this outcome has had a huge deterrent effect on other cricketers.

The CAS appeals

Mr Amir subsequently withdrew his appeal to the CAS against his five-year ban from cricket, and in March 2012, after his release from custody, he gave a lengthy interview to Michael Atherton in which he finally admitted his guilt.[52] He also gave a full confession to the ICC, and appeared in an educational video talking about his experience, which I understand has been extremely impactful when shown to other players as part of the ACSU's educational efforts.

Mr Butt also abandoned his appeal to the CAS against the Tribunal's finding that he had breached the ICC Anti-Corruption Code, but maintained his appeal against the length of the ban he had been given (ten years, five suspended), arguing that it was irrational and disproportionate and should be replaced with a ban of less than five years. In April 2013, the CAS Panel, chaired by Graeme Mew, with Romano Subiotto QC and Robert Reid QC as wing members, rejected that appeal. They said that a minimum five-year ban for spot-fixing could not be said to be irrational, given that the CAS has upheld life bans for similar or lesser offences in other sports. Mr Butt argued that the ban he had received was disproportionate because his misconduct was spot-fixing only, not match-fixing, it only involved three no balls and had no impact on the course or result of the match, it would not have happened but for the NOTW undercover operation, Pakistani players were uniquely vulnerable to spot fixing because they were not well-paid (they were not paid much to play for Pakistan, and the Indian ban of Pakistani players after the terrorist attacks in Mumbai in October 2008 meant they could not play in the lucrative Indian Premier League competition), and he had already suffered from a period of imprisonment and from no longer being able to earn a living at cricket. The CAS Panel gave these points short shrift. It noted that Mr Butt had been the captain of the Pakistan team and so was supposed to be a role model, but instead had been the orchestrator of the fix. It also noted that the ICC Anti-Corruption Tribunal had already taken into account most of the mitigating factors now cited by Mr Butt, and that Mr Justice Cooke had reduced his prison term in light of the ban the Tribunal had imposed, meaning that the CAS did not need to reduce that ban based on the prison term imposed. It also said: '*while the Panel has sympathy for Mr Butt's suffering, Mr Butt made no express apology for his actions or for the detriment caused to the game. In those circumstances, a plea for leniency has less resonance*'. It said it considered the ten-year ban (five suspended) imposed by the Tribunal to be '*lenient*' in all the circumstances.[53]

The same day, the same panel also issued an award rejecting Mr Asif's appeal against his seven-year ban (two suspended). It noted: '*given the history of corruption in cricket and the considerable adverse publicity caused by this episode, the Panel considers that strong enforcement action is necessary to send a signal of deterrence. The Panel also notes that the sanction could be described as lenient when considered in context*'.[54]

After the bans ended in September 2015, Mohammad Amir returned to international cricket. He played in the 2016 ICC World Twenty20, in the 2017 ICC Champions Trophy (which he helped Pakistan to win by taking three wickets in the final against India), in the 2019 ICC Cricket World Cup, where he was Pakistan's leading wicket-taker, and in the 2024 ICC World Twenty20, before retiring from international cricket in December 2024. In contrast, while Salman Butt and Mohammad Asif both played domestic cricket in Pakistan, neither of them ever played international cricket again. In December 2023, the Pakistan Cricket Board announced that it had appointed Salman Butt as a consultant to its selection panel, but it quickly reversed that decision in the face of public outcry;[55] and in April 2025 the franchises in the Pakistan Super League competition objected to his inclusion on the PSL 10 commentary panel on the grounds that it would undermine the tournament's reputation.[56]

Meanwhile Mazher Majeed pleaded guilty in 2014 to HMRC charges of tax fraud relating to his property business, for which he received a further two-year prison sentence on top of the two years and eight months he had received for his orchestration of the cricket match-fixing. According to media reports, after his eventual release from prison he became a boxing agent/promoter.[57]

The Dhaka Premier League in Bangladesh

I also want to mention briefly one of the other match-fixing cases I was involved in for the ICC. The ICC Anti-Corruption Code adopted the '*substantial assistance*' provision found in the World Anti-Doping Code (see p 50), giving a player an opportunity to get part of his ban for match fixing suspended by providing information that helps the ICC to enforce the Code against his co-conspirators or others. In 2013, following various leads that had come to the ACSU, Iain Higgins and ACSU investigator Colin Tenant used that mechanism to get detailed information from former Bangladesh captain Mohammad Ashraful about the fixing of matches in the Dhaka Premier League (the Bangladesh domestic T20 competition) in 2013. I was instructed to prosecute the alleged conspirators under the Bangladesh Cricket Anti-Corruption Code, on behalf of the Bangladesh Cricket Board, before a domestic tribunal sitting in Dhaka, the capital of Bangladesh.

When I got to Dhaka a day or two before the start of the hearing, together with the ICC's in-house lawyer, Sally Clark, our BCB minder told us that because of rumours that organised crime figures had been behind the fixing, we would have armed guards accompanying us when we were driven from the hotel to the hearing room and back each day. Sure enough, the next morning, parked outside the front entrance of the hotel alongside our minivan, there was an open-topped truck with 12 soldiers sitting facing each other in two rows of six, fully uniformed and each armed with a rifle. The sight was made all the more surreal by the fact that the soldiers all sported beards that were dyed bright orange, in the longstanding Bangladeshi tradition. They drove in front of our minibus to and from the hearing centre every day for the next three weeks.

The night before the last day of the hearing, when the closing arguments would be delivered, the newspapers reported that there would be a national strike the next day, and noted that the strikers had threatened to throw petrol bombs at any vehicles that ventured onto the roads in defiance of the strike. I politely enquired of our BCB minder how we would be getting to the hearing the next morning, given this peril. He said I did not need to worry, they were going to take two additional steps to protect us. First, the soldiers in the accompanying truck would have bullets in their rifles the next day. Apparently we would have been utterly defenceless to any attack prior to that date, as the soldiers' rifles had been unloaded to that point. And second, we would be driven to the hearing in an ambulance, because the rioters would not throw petrol bombs at an ambulance. I enquired whether it was appropriate for us to be using an ambulance when the people who were having petrol bombs thrown at them might need it more, but he told me not to worry. I understood why when I came down to the front entrance of the hotel the next morning, and found our boxes being loaded into the same white minibus that we had travelled to the court in every day for the past three weeks, only now someone had painted the windows of the minibus white, had painted '*AMBULANCE*' in reverse across the windscreen, and had put a fake siren on the roof. I am happy to report that, thanks to these sterling efforts, our journey to and from the hearing centre that day passed off without incident.

Notes

1 Shavin N., *The Ancient History of Cheating in the Olympics*, The Smithsonian Magazine, 3 August 2016.
2 Fagan S., *How Gambling Ruined Sport*, sfaganweb.wordpress.com/2012/12/02/how-gambling-ruined-sport (accessed 30 October 2025).
3 Asinof E., *Eight Men Out: The Black Sox and the 1919 World Series* (Owl Books, 1963).
4 *Sport: The Big Money*, Time Magazine, 26 February 1951.
5 For several years, professional footballer Jimmy Gauld had systematically interfered with Football League matches, enticing players into fixing matches and betting on the outcome. His criminality came to light in December 1962, after he approached Sheffield Wednesday player David Layne, a former colleague at Mansfield Town, to identify a new target game. Layne suggested that Wednesday were likely to lose their imminent match against Ipswich Town, and proposed to his fellow players Peter Swan and Tony Kay that they ensure that outcome. The three all bet against their own side in the match. In 1964, Gauld sold his story to the Sunday People for £7,000, incriminating not only the three Wednesday players, but also himself. All four received prison sentences. See Inglis S., *Soccer in the Dock* (Collins, 1985).
6 *Grobbelaar v News Group Newspapers Ltd* [2002] UKHL 40, at para 24, per Lord Bingham. See Thomas D., *Foul Play* (Corgi Books, 2004).
7 Andrew Bingham MP, House of Commons Digital, Culture, Media and Sport Committee, *Combatting doping in sport*, 5 March 2018 (publications.parliament.uk/pa/cm201719/cmselect/cmcumeds/366/366.pdf, accessed 31 August 2025). See also ICC Anti-Corruption Code, 2010, Article 1 (*'All cricket matches are to be contested on a level playing field with the outcome to be determined solely by the respective merits of the contesting teams. .... Public*

confidence in the authenticity and integrity of the cricket match is vital. If that confidence is undermined, then the very essence of cricket, the characteristics that deliver its unique appeal, are shaken to the core'); Higgins I. et al, Match-Fixing and Related Corruption, in *Sport: Law & Practice* (Bloomsbury, 4th Edn, 2021), at para B4.1 (*'If the authenticity of the sporting spectacle is exposed just once as a façade, confidence in every sporting achievement is eroded. The story of the young baseball fan pleading with the 1919 World Series fixer, "Shoeless" Joe Jackson – "Say it ain't so, Joe" – may well be apocryphal, but it captures succinctly the faith-shattering betrayal of trust that such corruption represents. That is why match-fixing is seen as a "mortal danger" to sport, "a cancer that eats at the health and the very existence of the game". And that is also why … the English courts and the Court of Arbitration for Sport alike have consistently upheld robust regulatory efforts to stamp out that "cancer", and why sports have gone to great lengths to investigate the problems that they face, and to address them both at the level of prior prevention and at the level of detection and sanction, in a manner designed to restore confidence in the integrity of competitions'*); *ECB v Kaneria & Westfield*, ECB Disciplinary Panel decision dated 22 June 2012, p.1 (*'Self-evidently corruption, specifically spot fixing, in cricket or any other sport for that matter, is a cancer that eats at the health and very existence of the game. For the general public, supporting the game and their teams within it, there is no merit or motivation to expend time, money or effort to watch a match whose integrity may be in doubt. The consequence of the public's disengagement from cricket would be catastrophic. Furthermore, the game of cricket simply cannot afford to have its reputation tarnished in the eyes of commercial partners. These partners could not and would not link their brand to a sport whose integrity has been so undermined. For players who have devoted their entire careers to the pursuit of hard fought and properly competitive sport, to have those genuine achievements called into question by the corrupt actions of a tiny minority, may tend to devalue their worth. Accordingly we have no doubt that this is a cancer which must be rooted out of the game'*); England cricketer Paul Collingwood, *After this sickening summer, I can't wait to play a team who are trying 100%*, Mail Online, 10 October 2010 (*'[O]nce those allegations were made, it just devalued everything we had achieved in the series. … Poor Jonathan Trott and Stuart Broad, both of whom had made brilliant hundreds to get us out of the mire at 102-7, were devastated by the allegations. I have no doubt that Pakistan were trying their hardest to break their partnership and that Trott and Broad's achievement was 100 per cent valid, but inevitably people start to see shadows everywhere. … If we cannot provide something the public can believe is 100 per cent straight, then forget it, the game is gone. No player will want to play it and no spectator will want to watch it. That's why I advocate penalties and the strongest deterrents. To me, anyone found guilty of match-fixing or spot-fixing should be banned for life'*; sentencing remarks of Mr Justice Cooke, *R v Majeed, Butt, Asif and Amir*, 3 November 2011, para 1 (espncricinfo.com/story/spot-fixing-controversy-sentencing-remarks-of-justice-cooke-539088, accessed 14 October 2025) (*'It is the insidious effect of your actions on professional cricket and the followers of it which make the offences so serious. … Now, whenever people look back on a surprising event in a game or a surprising result or whenever in the future there are surprising events or results, followers of the game who have paid good money to watch it live or to watch it on TV … will be led to wonder whether there has been a fix and whether what they have been watching is a genuine contest between bat and ball. What ought to be honest sporting competition may not be such at all'*).

8 Hawkins E., *Bookie Gambler Fixer Spy: A Journey to the Heart of Cricket's Underworld* (Bloomsbury 2012).

9 *Report in short: The Condon inquiry*, The Guardian, 24 May 2001.

10 *ICC to act on Anti-Corruption Unit Report recommendation*, icc.cricket.com, May 2001.

11 See generally Mahmood M., *Confessions of a Fake Sheikh* (Harper Collins 2008); British Scandal podcast, *The Fake Sheikh: From Robes to Riches*, 2024 (open.spotify.com/episode/5MndUphc3U7txCdXRRs5rz, accessed 14 October 2025).

12 NOTW, *'CAUGHT! Match-fixer pockets £150k as he rigs the England Test at Lord's. We expose betting scandal that will rock cricket!'*, 29 August 2020; *ICC v Butt, Asif and Amir*, decision of Anti-Corruption Tribunal dated 5 February 2011 (redacted version published by ICC), para 49.

13 NOTW, *'CAUGHT! Match-fixer pockets £150k as he rigs the England Test at Lord's. We expose betting scandal that will rock cricket!'*, 29 August 2020.

14 NOTW, *'CAUGHT! Match-fixer pockets £150k as he rigs the England Test at Lord's. We expose betting scandal that will rock cricket!'*, 29 August 2020; *ICC v Butt, Asif and Amir*, decision of Anti-Corruption Tribunal dated 5 February 2011 (redacted version published by ICC), para 59.

15 *ICC v Butt, Asif and Amir*, decision of Anti-Corruption Tribunal dated 5 February 2011 (redacted version published by ICC), para 63.

16 *ICC v Butt, Asif and Amir*, decision of Anti-Corruption Tribunal dated 5 February 2011 (redacted version published by ICC), para 65.

17 *ICC v Butt, Asif and Amir*, decision of Anti-Corruption Tribunal dated 5 February 2011 (redacted version published by ICC), para 69.
18 NOTW, *'CAUGHT! Match-fixer pockets £150k as he rigs the England Test at Lord's. We expose betting scandal that will rock cricket!'*, 29 August 2020; *ICC v Butt, Asif and Amir*, decision of Anti-Corruption Tribunal dated 5 February 2011 (redacted version published by ICC), para 75.
19 NOTW, '*CAUGHT! Match-fixer pockets £150k as he rigs the England Test at Lord's. We expose betting scandal that will rock cricket!*', 29 August 2020; *ICC v Butt, Asif and Amir*, decision of Anti-Corruption Tribunal dated 5 February 2011 (redacted version published by ICC), paras 80-85.
20 *ICC v Butt, Asif and Amir*, decision of Anti-Corruption Tribunal dated 5 February 2011 (redacted version published by ICC), paras 85-87.
21 *ICC v Butt, Asif and Amir*, decision of Anti-Corruption Tribunal dated 5 February 2011 (redacted version published by ICC), paras 101-102.
22 *ICC v Butt, Asif and Amir*, decision of Anti-Corruption Tribunal dated 5 February 2011 (redacted version published by ICC), para 108.
23 Greenslade N., *The Thin White Line* (Pitch Publishing 2020), p.117, p.120, p.196.
24 Hawkins E., *Bookie Gambler Fixer Spy: A Journey to the Heart of Cricket's Underworld* (Bloomsbury 2012), p.150 et seq.
25 Gibson O. and Hopps D., *Three Pakistan players suspended by ICC and charged under anti-corruption code*, The Guardian, 2 September 2010.
26 See Beloff M., *MJBQC: A Life Within and Without the Law* (Bloomsbury 2022), Chapter 10 (*'My Sporting Life'*). Michael has been described as *'the Godfather of Sports Law'*, albeit only by me, in *Lawyer of the week: Jonathan Taylor, QC for IAAF in Caster Semenya case*, The Times, 9 May 2019.
27 See also *NOTW sting not reliable – Salman Butt*, espncricinfo.com, 28 October 2010 (*'"I do not want to comment on The News of the World because everybody knows what kind of paper it is," Butt told Associated Press. "Everybody knows about its reputation across the world." Butt said that Majeed "must have made lots of claims … clearly exaggerating things to show his authority. I think he might have said a lot of things in that video because it was edited. So nobody knows what has gone wrong in that video"'*).
28 *R v Mazher Mahmood & Alan Smith*, sentencing remarks of HHJ Gordon, 21 October 2016 (judiciary.uk/wp-content/uploads/2016/10/mahmood-sentencing-remarks-20161021.pdf, accessed 14 October 2025); Greenslade N., *The Thin White Line* (Pitch Publishing 2020), chapter 8.
29 Mr Mahmood reiterated that denial in his first witness statement to the Leveson Inquiry, dated 14 October 2011 (discoverleveson.com/evidence/Witness_Statement_of_Mazher_Mahmood/6153/media, accessed 14 October 2025), at para 38 (*'I have never engaged in or procured anyone to engage in computer hacking in order to source stories or for any other reason. Neither am I aware of anyone else at the newspaper doing so – save insofar as that term includes phone hacking, about which I have no knowledge other than that which is in the public domain'*) and at the criminal trial of Butt and Asif that took place the following month. See also Greenslade N., *The Thin White Line* (Pitch Publishing 2020), p.179 (Mahmood: *'I had no knowledge of that in my 20 years at the paper'*).
30 Greenslade N., *The Thin White Line* (Pitch Publishing 2020), pp.18-19, p.180, and pp.237-38 (printouts originally came from owner of repair shop to whom Majeed had given his phone to fix, and were distributed from that source to *'others within the Pakistani cricket community'*, one of whom sent them to Mahmood and also to the ICC). See also sentencing remarks of Mr Justice Cooke, *R v Majeed, Butt, Asif and Amir*, 3 November 2011, para 1 (espncricinfo.com/story/spot-fixing-controversy-sentencing-remarks-of-justice-cooke-539088, accessed 14 October 2025) para 20 (to Salman Butt: *'you bear the major responsibility for the corrupt activities, along with Majeed. The evidence of the text exchange between you and Majeed in the West Indies in May 2010 shows your involvement in such activities outside the scope of the period covered by the indictment'*).
31 *Reporter's string of scoops*, BBC News, 15 January 2006.
32 See sentencing remarks of Mr Justice Cooke, *R v Majeed, Butt, Asif and Amir*, 3 November 2011, para 1 (espncricinfo.com/story/spot-fixing-controversy-sentencing-remarks-of-justice-cooke-539088, accessed 14 October 2025), para 3 (*'I bear in mind that this was a sting by the News Of The World (NOTW), but that does not render your culpability any the less, once it is recognised that you were involved in discussing such activities outside the scope of the sting, as it is clear that you Majeed, Butt and Amir were'*) and para 11.4 (to Majeed: *'It is clear from the telephone schedules that you were in touch with contacts in India and Dubai and were passing on information relating to the Oval and Lord's test matches in relation to gambling activity there. I find that this was all part of your corrupt activity because you were intent on passing the same*

information about fixed events to different people so they could place bets based on them in different markets- Dubai, India, and as you thought, the Far East where the journalist said his punters were involved').

33 Which stated: '*The court may issue a witness summons in aid of an inferior court or of a tribunal.*' And see CPR 34.4(3) ('*In this rule, "inferior court or tribunal" means any court or tribunal that does not have power to issue a witness summons in relation to proceedings before it'*.

34 *ICC v Butt, Asif and Amir*, decision of Anti-Corruption Tribunal dated 5 February 2011 (redacted version published by ICC), para 170.

35 Alec Cameron KC obituary, The Times, 23 March 2023.

36 *ICC v Butt, Asif and Amir*, decision of Anti-Corruption Tribunal dated 5 February 2011 (redacted version published by ICC), para 11.

37 *ICC v Butt, Asif and Amir*, decision of Anti-Corruption Tribunal dated 5 February 2011 (redacted version published by ICC), para 45.

38 *ICC v Butt, Asif and Amir*, decision of Anti-Corruption Tribunal dated 5 February 2011 (redacted version published by ICC), paras 185-86.

39 We had dropped the charges against the two bowlers relating to the Oval Test, because we had less evidence that they had been asked and had agreed to bowl the no balls at the Oval, whereas we had strong evidence that they had been asked and had agreed to bowl them at Lord's the following week.

40 *ICC v Butt, Asif and Amir*, decision of Anti-Corruption Tribunal dated 5 February 2011 (redacted version published by ICC), paras 187-190.

41 *ICC v Butt, Asif and Amir*, decision of Anti-Corruption Tribunal dated 5 February 2011 (redacted version published by ICC), para 208.

42 *ICC v Butt, Asif and Amir*, decision of Anti-Corruption Tribunal dated 5 February 2011 (redacted version published by ICC), para 223. The subsequent criminal proceedings eventually yielded further incriminating evidence on this point. See the sentencing remarks of Mr Justice Cooke to Mazher Majeed, *R v Majeed, Butt, Asif and Amir*, 3 November 2011 (espncricinfo.com/story/spot-fixing-controversy-sentencing-remarks-of-justice-cooke-539088, accessed 14 October 2025), para 8 ('*The fact that of the £150,000 that you actually received, only £2500 in marked notes was found in Butt's possession and £1500 in Amir's possession, together with the evidence of payment of £13,000 into Butt's bank account and some £23,000 into your company's accounts, suggests that you took the lion's share of the cash paid by the journalist'*).

43 *ICC v Butt, Asif and Amir*, decision of Anti-Corruption Tribunal dated 5 February 2011 (redacted version published by ICC), para 231.

44 Radford B., *Caught Out: Shocking Revelations of Corruption in International Cricket* (John Blake Publishing Ltd, 2011), p.68-69.

45 Sachs A., *The Soft Vengeance of a Freedom Fighter* (Grafton Books, 1990).

46 *R v Amir & Butt* [2011] EWCA Crim 2914, para 10; sentencing remarks of Mr Justice Cooke, *R v Majeed, Butt, Asif and Amir*, 3 November 2011, para 1 (espncricinfo.com/story/spot-fixing-controversy-sentencing-remarks-of-justice-cooke-539088, accessed 14 October 2025), at para 42 ('*there is evidence, in the shape of texts and telephone calls with a Pakistani number of your involvement in discussions about fixing brackets at The Oval during the period of the indictment, though there is no evidence that such fixing actually occurred. That discussion did not relate to Majeed'*).

47 Atherton M., *Full transcript of Mohammed Amir interview*, espncricinfo.com, 20 March 2012; Greenslade N., *The Thin White Line* (Pitch Publishing 2020), p.186.

48 Atherton M., *Full transcript of Mohammed Amir interview*, espncricinfo.com, 20 March 2012.

49 Sentencing remarks of Mr Justice Cooke, *R v Majeed, Butt, Asif and Amir*, 3 November 2011, para 1 (espncricinfo.com/story/spot-fixing-controversy-sentencing-remarks-of-justice-cooke-539088, accessed 14 October 2025).

50 *R v Amir & Butt* [2011] EWCA Crim 2914, paras 32, 35.

51 *Amir released from jail*, skysports.com, 1 February 2012; *Pakistan's Asif released from prison*, icc-cricket.com, 4 May 2012; *Lawyers: Salman Butt released*, ITV News, 21 June 2012.

52 Atherton M., *Full transcript of Mohammed Amir interview*, espncricinfo.com, 20 March 2012.

53 *Butt v ICC*, CAS 2011/A/2364, para 75.

54 *Asif v ICC*, CAS 2011/A/2362, para 72.

55 Atherton M., *Banish fixer Salman Butt for good – captains should know better*, The Times, 6 December 2023 ('*On what grounds did the PCB think it was a good idea to bring him back? … Butt abused his position of responsibility … at a time … when captains and players should have been far more aware, far less naïve. As a result, he should have forfeited his right to a return to any position of authority within the governing body'*).

56 *PSL franchises object to Salman Butt's inclusion in commentary panel*, cricexec.com, 10 April 2025.

57 Kershaw T. and Lawton M., *How agent jailed over cricket fixing scandal became major figure in boxing*, The Times, 13 January 2024; Kershaw T., *Cricket spot-fixer who became boxing big fish is declared bankrupt*, 12 April 2025; Kershaw T. and Lawton M., *Cricket fixer 'won't be involved in any fights shown on BBC'*, The Times, 9 August 2025.

Chapter 3

A Little Extra Chemical Kick

In 2008 Jacques Rogge, the president of the International Olympic Committee, said: *'It is naïve to believe that no-one will take drugs. Cheating is embedded in human nature'.*[1] Canadian sprinter Tony Sharpe agreed: *'The glory is too sweet, the dollars are too much'.*[2] And Grigory Rodchenkov, the former head of the Moscow anti-doping laboratory, has pointed out: *'If sport was "clean" that would ... favour[] naturally gifted athletes over their less advantaged rivals. Without doping, there is no way to overcome the ability gap'.*[3]

The organisers of the '*Enhanced Games*', aka the '*Steroid Olympics*',[4] see no problem with athletes taking drugs to enhance their performance. They maintain that *'athletic excellence is the pursuit of expanded human ability through the dedication to perfection of talent, technology, and scientific advancement'*, and therefore performance-enhancing drugs *'should be embraced and celebrated in elite competition'.*[5] But the premise of this book is that a governing body of a sport must strive to ensure that the contest is determined solely by natural talent and hard work. Allowing athletes to overcome their rivals' superior talents and work ethic by taking performance-enhancing drugs would effectively give victory not to the best athlete but to the athlete with the best pharmacologist, and why would anyone want to celebrate that?[6]

Dick Pound, first President of the World Anti-Doping Agency, has been clear: *'[D]oping in sport ... is cheating. It may be dangerous cheating, depending on the substance or method used. It is destructive of the essential ethical values in sport. It needs to be prevented and, if it cannot be prevented, then it must be detected and swift measures taken to ensure that the athletes and officials involved in such practices are removed from the sport. This does not require nuance. It requires firm and consistent action'.*[7] However, the main reason governments have intervened in this fight is not to defend sporting integrity, but rather because of the serious health risks that doping presents to elite athletes and to the youngsters who see them as role models. Taking anabolic steroids in supra-therapeutic quantities increases the risk of stroke, heart attack, cancer, manic behaviour, and dangerous mood swings;[8] while blood doping increases the risk of stroke, heart attack, and cerebral or pulmonary embolism.[9] One academic review identified 19 athlete/workout deaths between 1990 and 2012 linked to the abuse of anabolic steroids,[10] while a *Guardian* journalist suggested that the deaths of 20 young Belgian and Dutch cyclists between 1987 and 1990 and of eight cyclists under 35 between 2003 and 2004 were likely due to blood doping.[11] However, more than half of approximately 300 elite athletes surveyed in the 1980s said that they would take a drug that guaranteed them victory in every competition they entered in the next five years, even if it was also guaranteed to kill them after that;[12] and data analysed in 2015 *'yield[ed] an estimation of 14-39% of current adult elite athletes who intentionally used doping'.*[13] The reliability of these surveys may be debatable, but clearly we are not just talking about a tiny minority of actual or potential dopers. And drug-taking even by a small minority forces their competitors to join them or else be left in their wake,[14] creating a doping arms race that ratchets up the health risks until eventually parents will simply not let their children take up sport at all.

The sports movement and public authorities around the world have therefore joined together to create the World Anti-Doping Agency and to issue the World Anti-Doping Code, which prohibits doping by athletes and facilitation of doping by their support teams, and polices that prohibition by requiring athletes to submit to drug testing on demand, and requiring the anti-doping authorities to vigorously investigate any evidence of doping. In this chapter, I discuss the enormous effort that goes into implementing and enforcing the Code across the globe.

Pre-WADA

There is evidence that athletes used drugs to boost their performances as far back as Ancient Greece.[15] According to anti-doping pioneer Arne Llungqvist, however, drug use in sport really accelerated in the late 1950s and early 1960s, when athletes in the Eastern bloc were given access to amphetamines and testosterone, and athletes in the West started taking the same *'to measure up with their competitors from the East. ... Pharmacies became some kind of indispensable smorgasbord for athletes. A good diet, enough sleep, training and technique just wasn't enough to compete any longer. That little extra chemical kick had become indispensable'.*[16] But most sports bodies only began to take notice in the late 1960s, after the high-profile death from amphetamine abuse of English cyclist Tony Simpson during the 1967 Tour de France. The IOC introduced testing for stimulants and narcotics at the 1968 Olympic Games in Mexico City, with the sole stated aim of protecting athletes' health. It started testing for steroids at the 1976 Olympics in Montreal, although detection was difficult until gas chromatography and mass spectrometry analysis techniques were introduced in 1983, prompting the withdrawal of numerous athletes from that year's Pan-American Games. It is now possible to detect tiny quantities of drugs in a urine sample, sometimes even long after their ingestion. In addition, other techniques have been developed that enable the detection in a blood sample of doping substances such as recombinant erythropoietin and human growth hormone, as well as of evidence of the use of blood doping methods such as blood transfusions.[17]

Ben Johnson's positive test for stanozolol, a powerful anabolic steroid, after his 100m victory at the 1988 Seoul Olympics, was a seminal moment.[18] *'This drew attention, as never before, to the problem of drug use in sport. It did not, by any means stop such use, but it served notice that the problem was far greater than sports officials had yet acknowledged'.*[19] The subsequent Dubin Inquiry in Canada concluded that *'banned performance-enhancing substances and in particular anabolic steroids are being used by athletes in almost every sport, most extensively in weightlifting and track and field'.*[20] And after the fall of the Berlin Wall in 1989, evidence emerged of systematic misuse of drugs by East German athletes, eventually leading to criminal prosecutions of the doctors and coaches for causing grievous bodily harm to athletes who had been minors at the time.[21] In the wake of these various revelations, the pressure on sports regulators to take effective action continued to build.

In 1994, the IOC signed an agreement with the Summer and Winter Olympic Federations and National Olympic Committees to unify their anti-doping rules and procedures, and in September 1994 a Medical Code was presented that included the first IOC List of Prohibited Substances and Prohibited Methods. But compliance with that code (subsequently re-named the Olympic Movement Anti-Doping Code) was not mandatory, and so significant differences persisted from sport to sport in terms of what was banned, what was permitted, and what sanctions were imposed. Those disparities, and the disunity they reflected, significantly undermined the fight against doping.[22]

The creation of the World Anti-Doping Agency (WADA)

In July 1998, French criminal investigators uncovered evidence of systematic drug use by Festina and other teams competing in that year's Tour de France, leading to seven teams withdrawing or being expelled from the event. This scandal, and in particular the opprobrium heaped on the Union Cycliste International, the world governing body of cycling (the '*UCI*'), for its perceived failure to police the sport effectively, prompted the IOC to organise a World Anti-Doping Conference in Lausanne in February 1999 to discuss the establishment of an independent anti-doping agency with authority over all sports. Dick Pound, IOC member and first WADA President, recalls what he did at the conference to persuade the IOC and the public authorities to commit to this new joint venture:[23]

> When the time came for me to explain the structure of the proposed international anti-doping agency, the government appetite for criticizing the IOC had not yet been sated. About forty governments were present, and they all declared the model to be unthinkable. They would not even consider participating unless they had at least 50 percent control. ... I said [to IOC President Juan Samaranch]: *'We already know that the Olympic movement is incapable of controlling the use of drugs in sport on its own. We do not have the legal or the financial means to do so and, frankly, there is little enthusiasm for the struggle itself among many of the International Federations. If we bring the governments to the table as full partners, we will have all the necessary means at our disposal, and we can lay off half the costs of the initiative on them'.* This revived him somewhat and he sent me off to meet with the government representatives. The meeting was short. I said, *'I understand that you have irreconcilable disagreements with the model I put forth.' 'Yes,'* they said. *'You insist that you have 50 per cent control?'* I questioned. *'We do'*, they answered. *'You've got it,'* I replied. *'What?'* they exclaimed. *'We agree,'* I said. They could hardly believe their ears.

As a result, all of the delegates to the 1999 World Anti-Doping Conference from the Olympic Movement, the United Nations, governments, national anti-doping agencies, athletes and the medical profession, publicly agreed that the only effective strategy to fight doping in sport was a uniform approach by all sports, coordinated on a global scale as a partnership between the sports movement and the public authorities.[24] WADA was formally established on 10 November 1999, with a mission to coordinate and monitor the fight against doping in sport on a worldwide basis.[25] It has a 42-member Foundation Board, half from the Olympic Movement and half from public authorities, as well as a 16-strong Executive Committee, including the

WADA President and Vice-President, five sports movement representatives and five public authority representatives (one from each continent), and (since 2021) the chair of the WADA Athletes Committee and three independent members. It gets half of its funding from the Olympic Movement and half from the public authorities.[26] WADA is therefore a true (and unique) public-private partnership between the governments of the world and the sports movement, a *'recognition of the fact that governments and the sporting movement must act together to fight doping and that neither sector will be successful without the collaboration and cooperation of the other'.*[27]

The World Anti-Doping Code

WADA immediately turned its attention to creating a new global anti-doping code, using the IOC's Olympic Movement Anti-Doping Code as the starting point. The principal draftsman was Rich Young, a US lawyer with extensive experience as a sports litigator and as a CAS arbitrator, and a man of enormous charm and self-effacement, qualities I have seen him use many times to disarm opponents and build consensus in support of the Code.[28] Following publication of the first version of the Code in 2003, Rich's partner in arms for the revised versions published in 2009, 2015, and 2021 has been Ulrich Haas, a similarly accomplished German law professor and CAS arbitrator whose civil law perspective complements Rich's common law approach. On occasion, Rich and Ulrich have let me propose one or two provisions for inclusion in the Code, but no doubt my most important contribution to the cause came during a trip to Beijing, when my speedy intervention saved them both from serious injury when overenthusiastic market traders attempted to attract their custom by hitting them over the head repeatedly with fake Nike trainers. Who knows where the fight against doping in sport would be now if I had not been so courageous?

The Code that Rich and Ulrich and their colleagues on the Code drafting team have produced includes the following core provisions:

- At Article 2, a uniform definition of doping offences, referred to (because Rich is American) as *'anti-doping rule violations'* (or *'ADRVs'*):
  - First there are the offences of presence in an athlete's sample of a prohibited substance or of evidence of use of a prohibited method, as well as the separate offences of use/attempted use of a prohibited substance or method. It is a cornerstone principle of the World Anti-Doping Code that an athlete bears *'strict liability'* for any prohibited substance found in their body, meaning that *'the violation occurs whether or not the Athlete intentionally or unintentionally used a Prohibited Substance or was negligent or otherwise at fault'*. The reason is obvious: the international federation or NADO or other enforcement body (referred to collectively in the Code as *'Anti-Doping Organizations'*) generally has no idea, and no way of finding out, how and when the athlete ingested the prohibited substance, so if the ADO had to prove the athlete's degree of fault, *'it is likely that even intentional abuse would in many cases escape sanction for lack of proof of guilty intent. And it is certain that a requirement of intent would invite costly litigation that may well cripple federations [...] in their fight against doping'.*[29] And if a performance is tainted by the presence of a banned substance in the athlete's system, their

results must be disqualified even if they bear no fault for it, because they have received an unfair advantage either way.

- Then there are offences designed to prevent conduct that undermines the sample collection process. So it is an ADRV to evade or to fail or refuse to submit to sample collection; to fail to provide accurate information about your whereabouts so that you can be found for sample collection; and to tamper or attempt to tamper with sample collection or other parts of the doping control process. These all require proof of fault.
- The next group of offences are possession of, trafficking or attempted trafficking in, and administration or attempted administration of prohibited substances or methods, as well as complicity or attempted complicity in another's ADRV, which all require proof of intent.
- Finally, there are the offences of associating with an athlete or coach while they are serving a doping ban, and discouraging or retaliating against someone for blowing the whistle on another person's doping activities, the latter of which was introduced in the 2015 Code in response to threats made to Russian whistleblowers Yuliya Stepanova (see p 77) and Grigory Rodchenkov (see p 73).

- At Article 3, there are provisions establishing burdens and standards of proof. In particular, the burden is put on the ADO to prove the ADRV charged *'to the comfortable satisfaction of the hearing panel, bearing in mind the seriousness of the allegation which is made. This standard of proof in all cases is greater than a mere balance of probability but less than proof beyond a reasonable doubt'*. This is a bespoke standard of proof peculiar to sports cases, coming from a CAS case dating back to the 1996 Atlanta Olympics,[30] and based on the civil law concept of *'inner conviction'*, ie, whether the arbitrator is personally satisfied that the allegation is true.[31]
- At Article 4, provision for an agreed list of prohibited substances and methods, to be updated at least annually, which distinguishes between short-acting substances that are only banned in competition (eg stimulants and narcotics), and substances with a longer effect (eg anabolic agents, growth hormones) that are banned at all times.
- At Article 5, an explanation of the overlapping roles and responsibilities of different ADOs for the testing and investigation of athletes and athlete support personnel who come under their jurisdiction.
- At Article 6, a requirement that all doping samples are sent to laboratories accredited by WADA, so that they are all tested in accordance with standardised analytical procedures and requirements.
- At Articles 7 and 8 respectively, a requirement for the ADO to follow due process when charging an athlete or athlete support person with an ADRV, including particular requirements for the imposition of a provisional suspension prior to a merits hearing, and a general requirement to afford the athlete or athlete support person in question a fair hearing on the charge before an independent and impartial tribunal.
- At Article 9, where an athlete commits an ADRV in connection with a competition (eg they refuse to provide a sample after a race, or they provide a sample that tests positive for a prohibited substance), there is automatic disqualification of their result in that competition, including forfeiture of any medal or other prize.

And Article 10 provides for potential disqualification of the results they achieve in other competitions at the same event (eg another race, over a different distance) (Article 10.1) or at subsequent events (Article 10.10).

- Article 10 establishes a carefully calibrated framework for determining the length of the ban to be imposed on the athlete or athlete support person who is found to have committed an ADRV, combining fixed starting points (to ensure consistency and equal treatment) with carefully constrained opportunities to move up or down from those starting points in exceptional circumstances (to ensure proportionality). In particular:

  - If a substance that is a recognised doping agent (eg an anabolic steroid or a growth hormone) is found in an athlete's sample, the ADRV is presumed to be intentional and a four-year ban applies unless the athlete can prove they did not use it intentionally, in which case the ban is reduced to two years. For these purposes, proving lack of intent means proving that they did not *'engage in conduct which they knew constituted an anti-doping rule violation or knew that there was a significant risk that the conduct might constitute or result in an anti-doping rule violation and manifestly disregarded that risk'*, ie it encompasses recklessness (or, in civil law terms, *dolus eventualis*).

  - On the other hand, if the substance is a *'Specified Substance'* – ie, a substance that is *'more likely to have been consumed or used by an Athlete for a purpose other than the enhancement of sport performance'* – then the presumption is reversed, meaning that a two-year ban applies unless the ADO can prove the athlete's use was intentional (using the same test), in which case it goes up to four years.

  - A two-year ban for a substance that is not a *'Specified Substance'* will be reduced by up to half if the athlete can show they bear *'No Significant Fault or Negligence'* for the presence of the drug in their system, and it will be eliminated completely if they show they bear *'No Fault or Negligence'*. If the substance is a *'Specified Substance'*, or was in a contaminated product, or a minor or recreational athlete is involved, the two-year ban may be reduced by up to 100% based on No Significant Fault or Negligence. In each case, fault is assessed by determining how far the athlete departed from their duty to use *'utmost caution'* to avoid ingesting any prohibited substance or using any prohibited method.

  - For the other ADRVs, the ban varies from one to two years (for a whereabouts violation), two to four years (for refusal or failure to submit to sample collection, or for tampering with doping control), two years to life (for complicity and for acts of retaliation), or four years to life (for trafficking or administering prohibited substances to others).

  - In a provision inspired by US criminal sentencing rules,[32] whatever ban is fixed may be part-suspended if the athlete provides *'substantial assistance'*, ie useful information about ADRVs or other non-compliance committed byothers.

- To ensure consistent application and enforcement of this global scheme:

  - International federations are given the right to appeal against national-level decisions that they consider not Code-compliant; NADOs are given the right to appeal against international decisions; and WADA is given the right to appeal against both. In each case, the (sole or ultimate) appeal is to the Court of Arbitration for Sport (Article 13).

- ○ Subject to those appeal rights, every Code signatory is required to recognise and give effect to other signatories' decisions, including in particular provisional suspensions and periods of ineligibility (Article 15). For example, when Martina Hingis was banned for two years under the Tennis Anti-Doping Programme,[33] she was not able to participate in equestrian sports either during that ban.[34]

Detailed regulations supporting and implementing these Code provisions can be found in a series of International Standards, including:

- the International Standard for Testing and Investigations, the main purpose of which is to help Signatories *'to plan for intelligent and effective Testing, both In-Competition and Out-of-Competition, and to maintain the integrity and identity of the Samples collected from the point the Athlete is notified of the Test, to the point the Samples are delivered to the Laboratory for analysis'*, together with standards for the gathering of intelligence and the conduct of investigations, which are becoming more and more important in uncovering doping (see Chapter 4);
- the International Standard for Laboratories, which sets out the analytical standards that laboratories must meet when testing samples in order to secure and thereafter to maintain WADA accreditation;
- the International Standard for Therapeutic Use Exemptions, which identifies the criteria to be used and the process to be followed to determine whether there is medical justification for an athlete to use particular prohibited substances or methods;
- the International Standard for Results Management, which sets out the core responsibilities of ADOs in relation to results management, from initial review and notification of alleged ADRVs, through provisional suspension, to issue of a decision on the merits, and appeal; and
- the International Standard for Code Compliance by Signatories, setting out a system for ensuring that all Code Signatories adopt and implement effectively anti-doping rules that comply with the Code (see pp 57 and 99).

Still further detail is provided in a series of Technical Documents and guidelines sitting under the International Standards.

The role of fault in doping cases

Because the World Anti-Doping Code makes an athlete strictly liable for any prohibited substance found in their sample, whether they took it intentionally, recklessly, negligently, or even unknowingly, most of the contested Article 2.1 cases (presence of prohibited substance in athlete's sample) are about whether the detailed requirements for collection and analysis of samples were followed. But if the integrity of the sample and the reliability of the positive result are established, all that is left to argue about is what consequences should be imposed.

If the sample was collected in competition, the athlete's results in that competition are automatically disqualified, whether or not they were at fault, because either way their performance was tainted. But the Code recognises that any further punishment (in particular, any ban from future competition) must be commensurate with the athlete's fault. To respect that principle while still ensuring a robust and consistent sanctioning framework, as just explained the Code creates a series of presumptions. For example, if the substance found in the athlete's system is a steroid or other serious doping agent, the presumption is that they took it intentionally, to enhance performance, and therefore the presumptive ban is four years, and the burden is put on the athlete to rebut that presumption by proving that they did not ingest the drug intentionally or recklessly (to take the ban down to two years) or with any significant fault or negligence (to take the ban down to one year) or with any fault or negligence at all (to eliminate the ban entirely).

Imagine, then, that the lab reports that it has found a very low concentration of a prohibited substance in an athlete's urine sample, consistent with what you would see at the tail-end of an extended doping programme. But the athlete strenuously denies cheating, and instead insists that the substance must have got into their body without their knowledge, as a contaminant of something they ate or drank. And that might feasibly be true. For example, in some countries cattle are injected with steroids to bulk them up prior to slaughter, and a urine sample collected shortly after an athlete has eaten meat from the carcass could test positive for very low levels of those steroids. Meanwhile lots of sports supplement products contain steroids or simulants that are prohibited by WADA, many of which are not mentioned on the product's list of ingredients. And hearing panels have accepted that even medications and drinking water may be contaminated with diuretics.[35]

Now imagine that you are the arbitrator who has been appointed to hear this case and to decide what consequences should be imposed. How are you going to decide if the athlete is telling the truth?

The athlete's vigorous denials of cheating cannot be enough, in themselves, to resolve the point, no matter how heartfelt they may seem, because, as leading CAS arbitrator Michael Beloff KC once famously said, *'the currency of such denial is devalued by the fact that it is the common currency of the guilty as well as of the innocent'*.[36] In other words, *'the guilty are just as likely as the innocent to express surprise, disbelief, and a profound sense of injustice'*.[37] For example:

- Multiple Olympic champion Marion Jones insisted in her 2004 autobiography, using capital letters to drive home her point: *'I HAVE ALWAYS BEEN UNEQUIVOCAL IN MY OPINION: I AM AGAINST PERFORMANCE-ENHANCING DRUGS. I HAVE NEVER TAKEN THEM AND I NEVER WILL TAKE THEM'*.[38] Three years later, she was forced to admit that was a lie.[39]

- Multiple Tour de France winner Lance Armstrong said in 1999: *'I have been on my deathbed, and I'm not stupid. I can emphatically say I am not on drugs'*.[40] He even sued his main accuser, Sunday Times journalist David Walsh, for defamation, before being exposed by some excellent work from USADA[41] and eventually admitting his extensive doping to Oprah Winfrey.[42]

- Another cyclist who took a tortuous path to righteousness was Armstrong's team-mate Floyd Landis: *'In the wake of his dramatic Tour de France victory in 2006 and his following disqualification for doping, the cyclist Floyd Landis convinced thousands of his US supporters that he was the victim of national prejudice, conspiracy, and injustice. Having launched appeals on social media, he collected nearly half a million dollars to fund legal challenges. In the course of five full days*

> *of hearings before CAS, Landis referred to his deeply religious background which would supposedly make him too ashamed to lie. He was assisted by experts and lawyers who did not hesitate to conduct aggressive cross-examination of the modest technicians from the lab which had detected his doping, and to accuse them of far worse than incompetence. His defense failed in June 2008, whereupon he launched an action in a US federal court seeking the annulment of the award, denounced what he asserted to be the illegitimacy of CAS, and continued vehemently to protest his innocence until suddenly recanting in April 2010, admitting to years of doping and ultimately avoiding criminal prosecution for having defrauded his donors only by undertaking to make restitution of the money raised'.*[43]

So how do you distinguish truthful denials from false ones? Polygraph tests are not reliable lie detectors (Armstrong and Jones both passed them);[44] and nor are judges, because, as Malcolm Gladwell has shown, you cannot reliably assess the accused's veracity simply by observing their demeanour under questioning.[45] In fact, it is impossible to determine whether an athlete is at fault for the presence of a prohibited substance in their sample unless you know how it got there. And that is why the Code says that, as a general rule, an athlete's denial of fault cannot even be considered unless they first show how the prohibited substance got into their system.[46] CAS panels have made it clear that it is not enough for an athlete simply to deny any knowing wrongdoing and say that *'therefore'* the explanation *'must be'* something for which the athlete bears no blame, such as contaminated food or a spiked drink. Again Michael Beloff has put it succinctly: *'Seeking to eliminate by such an approach all alternative hypotheses as to how the substance entered his body and thus to proffer the conclusion that what remains must be the truth reflects the reasoning attributed to the legendary fictional detective Sherlock Holmes by Sir Arthur Conan Doyle in "The Sign of Four",*[47] *but is reasoning impermissible for a judicial officer or body'.*[48]

Most often the explanation offered for the athlete's positive test is that the prohibited substance found in their sample was an ingredient or a contaminant of something they ate (eg the flesh or internal organs of livestock that had been injected with growth promoters prior to slaughter[49]) or something they drank (eg coca leaves in a herbal tea drunk in Peru[50]) or of a medication or supplement they took. The more exotic claims include that the prohibited substance came from eating the flesh and/or organs of uncastrated wild boar (the explanation given by boxer Tyson Fury, which I made sure that I tested on cross-examination while standing just outside his enormous reach);[51] or that it was in the saliva of a person that the athlete kissed (the explanation given by tennis player Richard Gasquet, which led to me cross-examining him about the difference between a *'bisou'* [a peck on the cheek] and a *'galoche'* [a French kiss]);[52] or that it was in bodily fluids of another that were passed to the athlete during sexual intercourse;[53] or that it was in a cream the athlete had used to promote moustache growth;[54] or in a pill that promised to strengthen and sustain his erection.[55] Or the argument might be that the foreign cells found in the athlete's blood were not illicitly infused, but rather were due to the fusion of his foetus in the womb with the foetus of an unborn twin.[56] To maintain the integrity of the system, there is *'a stringent requirement to offer persuasive evidence that the explanation [the athlete] offers for [a positive test] is more likely than not to be correct, by providing specific, objective and persuasive evidence of his submissions'.*[57] That may on occasion mean that innocent athletes who are unable to identify the cause of their positive test are banned,[58] *'but the possible unfairness to such athletes is outweighed by unfairness to all athletes if proffered, but maybe untruthful, explanations of spiking are too readily accepted'.*[59]

Getting the World Anti-Doping Code adopted and implemented globally

After the first World Anti-Doping Code came into effect in 2004, the immediate focus was on ensuring that all Code Signatories adopted Code-compliant rules. That led to two important cases going to CAS.

First, in 2004 FIFA objected to the Code provision mandating a two-year ban for a first offence with only limited possibility to reduce or eliminate the ban in exceptional circumstances. It argued this was contrary to the Swiss law *'principle of culpability'*, which requires an individual assessment of the sanction based on the objective and subjective circumstances of each case. WADA maintained that the Code provisions on sanctions were compatible with Swiss law. FIFA and WADA jointly requested an advisory opinion from a CAS panel, which advised as follows:

- As the international federation recognised by the IOC for the sport of association football, FIFA is bound by the Olympic Charter, including the obligation set out in Rule 26 of the Olympic Charter to adopt and implement the World Anti-Doping Code in its sport.
- The FIFA Anti-Doping Rules contain all of the Code ADRVs, including making an athlete strictly liable for the presence of a prohibited substance in their sample without having to prove intentional, reckless or even knowing use. They also use the same list of prohibited substances and methods.
- The Code mandates a two-year ban for a first offence of presence of a prohibited substance in the athlete's sample, with the possibility to eliminate the sanction entirely if the athlete can show they bear no fault or negligence for that offence, or to reduce it by up to half if they can show they bear no significant fault or negligence. In contrast, the FIFA Anti-Doping Rules leave it to the hearing panel to decide on the period of ineligibility within the range six to 24 months *'according to the degree of the offender's guilt and the objective and subjective circumstances of the case'*, taking into account *'generally recognised principles of law'*, ie the doctrine of proportionality. In other words, two years is the default penalty under the World Anti-Doping Code, and the maximum penalty under the FIFA rules.
- '[M]andatory Swiss law does not require FIFA to draft its Anti-Doping Rules as it did'. Swiss law states that a sanction must be commensurate to the fault of the offender and must go no further than is necessary to achieve the objectives underlying the rules. That principle *'requires the sanctioning body not only to evaluate the individual misconduct and the impact of the sanction on the athlete, but also to take the overall goal and the need for a uniform and harmonized concept in the fight against doping into account'*. The sanctioning scheme in the World Anti-Doping Code meets those requirements and is not disproportionate or excessive, because it is based on the athlete's fault – how far they departed from the duty of utmost caution to avoid prohibited substances entering their system – and if the athlete departs significantly from that standard, a fixed two year ban is necessary to punish that failure and to incentivise others to take their duty of utmost caution seriously.

- Most importantly, the aim of harmonisation and the principle of equal treatment mean there should be no difference in the sanctioning scheme from one sport to the next. Arguments that football is different do not hold water: '*Although it is true that especially the economic consequences of two years*' ineligibility for a professional football player may be different from those which would affect an amateur athlete, … it would be grossly unfair if an athlete would receive "less severe treatment" which allowed him to return to the lucrative professional sport earlier, just because he had previously earned a high salary'.[60]

FIFA was therefore required to amend its rules to comply with all of the mandatory provisions of the World Anti-Doping Code, including the full sanctions regime.

The second case related to Code Article 23.2.2, which specifies the Code provisions that must be incorporated verbatim into a Signatory's anti-doping rules, and states that no provisions may be added that change the effect of those mandatory provisions. In 2008 the IOC adopted a rule that any athlete who is banned for more than six months for a doping violation is also ineligible for the next edition of the Olympic Games, even if the ban has expired before those Games start. The British Olympic Association already had a similar rule, which stated that any athlete who commits a doping offence is not eligible to be selected by the BOA for any subsequent Olympic team, even after the doping ban has expired, unless he or she can show that '*his or her offence was minor or committed without fault or negligence or that there were mitigating circumstances for it*'. The bye-law said an offence would be considered minor if the Code specifies a ban of six months or less for it.

These rules were an excellent example of '*Freakonomics*', ie, a regulatory intervention that ends up having the opposite effect to what was intended, such as a rule that seeks to stop parents picking up their kids late from day care by imposing a late pick-up charge, but is seen by the parents as giving permission to pick their kids up late in return for the stated fee, so that late pick-ups only increase.[61] A panel hearing a case brought by an ADO under Code-compliant rules might consider that the athlete's ADRV warrants a ban of (say) 12 months, but the IOC or BOA rule means that a 12-month ban would also trigger exclusion of the athlete from the next Olympics (the IOC rule) or from all subsequent Olympics (the BOA rule). If the panel considers that would be a disproportionate punishment, it is driven instead to impose only a six-month ban in order to avoid these additional consequences. As a result, while the IOC and BOA rules were intended to be tough on doping, their effect was to *reduce* the bans imposed, and so to reduce the deterrent effect of those bans.[62]

The US Olympic Committee challenged the IOC rule at CAS on the basis that it improperly added to the mandatory sanctions regime set out in the World Anti-Doping Code, in breach of Code Article 23.2.2, which has been incorporated into the Olympic Charter. The IOC argued in response that its rule was not a disciplinary sanction but an eligibility rule, determining who was suitable to represent a country in the Olympics. The CAS panel agreed with the USOC that the rule was a sanction not an eligibility rule, on the basis that eligibility rules do not bar an athlete from competing due to their prior undesirable behaviour, but rather serve to facilitate the organisation of the competition and to ensure the athlete meets the performance standards. It therefore also agreed that the IOC rule was contrary to Code Article 23.2.2, and so was void and unenforceable.[63]

When the USOC award was handed down, WADA wrote to the BOA and three other NOCs that had similar rules. It acknowledged that it had previously accepted their position that those rules were merely a selection policy, not a sanction, but noted that the USOC award had made it clear that they were in fact a sanction, and therefore invited them to repeal those rules. All did so bar the BOA. When WADA duly declared the BOA non-compliant with the Code, in December 2011 the BOA appealed that decision to the CAS. WADA's Director-General, David Howman, asked me to represent WADA in that appeal, my first time acting for it, while David Pannick QC and Adam Lewis represented the BOA. Following the IOC line, they argued that the BOA bye-law was not a sanction but simply the implementation of a selection policy aimed at ensuring that only '*the most appropriate athletes*' were selected to represent Team GB at the Olympics. We pointed out in response: that the BOA bye-law is triggered by an anti-doping rule violation under the Code; that the consequence applied under the bye-law is determined by the sanctions that are applied under the Code for that violation; and that the BOA's purported characterisation of the bye-law consequence as a selection bar rather than an ineligibility rule is '*a distinction without a difference*'. In other words, if it walks like a duck and quacks like a duck, then it probably is a duck. The CAS panel agreed with our assessment, and said: '*The purpose of Article 23.2.2 WADA Code is indeed the very purpose of the WADA Code: the harmonization throughout the world of a doping code for use in the fight against doping. This worldwide harmony is crucial to the success of the fight against doping. The WADA Code is intended to be an all-encompassing code that directs affected organizations and athletes. The WADA Code ensures that, in principle, any athlete in any sport will not be exposed to a lesser or greater sanction than any other athlete; rather, they will be sanctioned equally. By requiring consistency in treatment of athletes who are charged with doping infractions or convicted of it – regardless of the athlete's nationality or sport – fairness and proper enforcement are achieved. Any disharmony between different parties undermines the success of the fight against doping. For these good reasons, NOCs and other Signatories agreed to limit their autonomy to act within their own spheres with respect to activities covered by the WADA Code*'.[64]

Many years later, when Adam Lewis (who by then had taken silk) suggested over a pint that he had never lost a case to me, I pointed to the BOA award. Adam said that did not count, because he was led in that case by David Pannick QC, who therefore had to take the loss. If so, then my record against Adam may not be great, but I have an unbeaten record (1:0) against Lord David Pannick KC, one of the English Bar's leading advocates. Of course, the victory was pretty straightforward once the CAS panel in USOC had overturned the very similar IOC rule, but I say it still counts.

In any event, assisted by these CAS decisions, global adoption of the World Anti-Doping Code has now been achieved. After the United Nations Charter and the Vienna Convention for the Protection of the Ozone Layer, which are two quite important legal documents, the World Anti-Doping Code is the most ubiquitous legal instrument in the world. All but one of the 193 member states of the United Nations have committed, via the UNESCO International Convention against Doping in Sport, to adopt appropriate laws, regulations or other measures to help the sports movement fight doping in sport based on the Code in their respective countries. The only UN member state that has not adopted the World Anti-Doping Code is Afghanistan under the Taliban, and the only recognised sports that have not implemented it are the US professional leagues (American football, baseball, basketball, and ice hockey) and some of the bodies that sanction professional boxing/fighting. That is a remarkable achievement.

However, getting Signatories to adopt Code-compliant rules was just the first stage. To ensure harmonisation and equal treatment of all athletes, they also have to *implement* those rules in a comprehensive and effective way. To motivate them to do this, and to ensure that implementation could be properly monitored and policed, in 2018 WADA adopted a new International Standard for Code Compliance by Signatories (see p 99), which requires Signatories to report on exactly what they are doing to implement a Code-compliant anti-doping programme, to submit to WADA audits of those programmes, and to respond to WADA's information requests and corrective action reports. The ISCCS has transformed the compliance process from mere box-ticking (have you adopted Code-compliant rules?) to a robust compliance exercise (show us your test distribution plan, show us the risk assessment on which it is based, show us your athlete education efforts, etc). By the end of 2019, more than ten thousand corrective actions had been completed by Signatories,[65] and many more have been completed since then. Each one of those corrective actions represents one more step towards a global level playing field.

Getting the World Anti-Doping Code adopted and implemented in the UK

Consistent with its traditional non-interventionist approach to sport,[66] the UK Government historically took a relatively hands-off approach to the regulation of drug use in sport. It endorsed the Olympic Movement Anti-Doping Code, and was an early signatory to the Council of Europe's 1989 Anti-Doping Convention. However, it never passed any specific legislation to incorporate those instruments into domestic law, or to require sports bodies to adopt anti-doping programmes reflecting their provisions. Instead, it largely left the regulation, policing and enforcement of anti-doping rules in sport in the United Kingdom to the national governing bodies of the respective sports.

After the advent of the World Anti-Doping Code in 2003, however, the UK signed the UNESCO Anti-Doping Convention, committing to adopt appropriate laws, regulations or other measures in the UK to help fight doping in sport based on the Code. At the government's direction, the Drug-Free Sport Directorate of UK Sport, which was the UK NADO at that time, made adoption and enforcement of Code-compliant anti-doping rules a condition of NGB eligibility for public funding; it issued model anti-doping rules that NGBs could adopt to fulfil the first part of that commitment; it established an independent National Anti-Doping Panel to hear cases arising under those rules; and it started to exercise the right of appeal given to it under those rules to ensure that anti-doping decisions issued by that Panel or by tribunals appointed by those NGBs were consistent with the Code. And in 2007 the UK Sport board announced that it was recommending that the government require NGBs, as a further condition of eligibility for public funding, to transfer exclusive results management authority – ie the authority to investigate matters and determine whether there is a case to answer under the doping rules – to a new independent NADO, UK Anti-Doping.

Following extensive consultation with the sports movement, in December 2009 the UK Government published the National Anti-Doping Policy.[67] I drafted that policy, which requires UK NGBs to adopt either the UK Anti-Doping Rules issued by UK Anti-Doping or other Code-compliant anti-doping rules mandated by their international federations, to delegate results management and case prosecution responsibility to UK Anti-Doping, and to appoint the National Anti-Doping Panel to hear and determine all charges that the anti-doping rules have been breached, unless UK Anti-Doping agrees that the NGB's own results management systems and tribunals are Code-compliant. UKAD supports and monitors ongoing NGB compliance with these requirements by means of a formal assurance framework.[68]

In my opinion, and in the opinion of the Department of Culture, Media & Sport following a review in 2018,[69] the creation of UK Anti-Doping and the National Anti-Doping Panel, and the powers given to them by the National Anti-Doping Policy have significantly enhanced the fight against doping in sport in the United Kingdom. As just one example, giving one central and independent body a clear public mandate and authority to investigate violations and manage results across all sports has facilitated information-sharing by the police, Customs, and other public agencies. For example, UK Anti-Doping obtained a four-year ban of an athlete when the police shared a transcript of an interview in which he stated that steroids found in his home were not for selling to others but rather for his personal use in training for competition, and another four-year ban of a boxer for repeated online purchases of prohibited substances, based on evidence supplied by US law enforcement.[70]

Ensuring equal treatment by making CAS the ultimate arbiter

To ensure that all athletes are treated equally and the playing field remains level, the World Anti-Doping Code requires NADOs and international federations to report all case resolutions to each other and to WADA, and gives those bodies the right to appeal the decisions to the Court of Arbitration for Sport if they do not apply the Code properly. A good example of this system working effectively is the case of Blake Leeper, a US Paralympic athlete whose remarkable story I tell in Chapter Six. A urine sample collected by USADA from Mr Leeper at an athletics event in the US in June 2015 tested positive for cocaine, and USADA therefore charged him with an ADRV. In response, he denied knowingly ingesting cocaine. The domestic hearing panel ordered him to provide a hair sample for testing, to try to determine whether he had ingested cocaine over a period, but USADA reported that he showed up at the laboratory '*with all the hair shaved off his body such that a sample could not be taken*'.[71] Nevertheless, based on the very low level of the cocaine metabolites found in Mr Leeper's sample, the domestic hearing panel accepted his claim that he had used cocaine out of competition in a context unrelated to sports performance, therefore found that he had not intentionally doped, and so reduced the four year ban that would otherwise have applied under the World Anti-Doping Code down to two years. However, the panel rejected Mr Leeper's submission that he had inadvertently ingested cocaine by mistakenly using the toothbrush of someone else who had used cocaine. It therefore rejected his plea that he bore no (or no significant) fault or negligence for his positive test, and so declined to eliminate the ban or to reduce it from two years to one.[72]

Neither USADA nor Mr Leeper appealed that decision. In January 2016, however, they entered into a '*settlement agreement*' in which USADA accepted a different explanation for Mr Leeper's positive test – that he had taken the cocaine while intoxicated and so while his judgement was impaired – and therefore agreed to reduce his ban from two years down to one year, expiring on 20 June 2016, which happened to be just before the deadline for selection for the US team for the 2016 Paralympic Games in Rio.[73]

The International Paralympic Committee refused to recognise that agreement. Instead it said it would continue to recognise the two-year ban imposed by the domestic hearing panel, meaning that Mr Leeper would not be eligible to compete in Rio. I advised the IPC on the issue, and at one point I received a call from USADA's attorney, Bill Bock, asking why the IPC would not simply accept USADA's judgement that a one-year ban was appropriate in all the circumstances of the case. I responded that the IPC has to review all national-level cases to ensure athletes from different countries receive equal treatment, and to guard against hometown decisions. Mr Leeper subsequently appealed to the CAS, arguing that the IPC's refusal to recognise his agreement with USADA was in bad faith. The CAS rejected that appeal, agreeing with the IPC that Mr Leeper's degree of fault did not justify a reduction of the two-year ban down to one year, and instead *'[t]he period of ineligibility imposed on the Athlete in the Settlement Agreement was clearly dictated first and foremost by the (understandable, however not justifiable) desire to allow the Athlete to compete at the Paralympics'*.[74] In this way, consistent treatment of all Paralympic athletes was maintained.

A test of nerve

But of course, an appeal to CAS only works to ensure harmonisation and equal treatment across the globe and across all sports if all CAS panels are prepared to apply the Code rigorously in every case. That is not always straightforward because, as one CAS panel has noted: *'It is the nature of [Code-compliant] rules that they are inflexible in principle yet applied to a great variety of circumstances on a one-size-fits-all basis'*.[75] That is particularly true of the Code's sanctioning regime:

> [T]he one-size-fits-all characteristics of the rule on reduction of ineligibility may tempt arbitrators to make allowances for specific circumstances – such as the great difference from sport to sport of the likelihood of being able to compete at an elite international level of competition, and thus the different impact of the same period of ineligibility on athletes whose international competitiveness may be of greatly contrasting duration given the physical demands of their sport. But the time and place for making such allowances is when such rules are drafted (and amended), not in making individual decisions.[76]

Therefore, while CAS panels have noted that anti-doping rules must comply with general legal principles such as the requirement of proportionality, they have accepted that they may not depart from a Code-mandated sanction just because that sanction feels *'uncomfortable'* in the circumstances of a particular case, but only if it *'were to constitute an attack on a personal right which was serious and totally disproportionate to the behaviour penalised [...]'*.[77]

Ultimately this becomes a test of nerve for the CAS arbitrators. Are they ready to apply the Code-mandated rules in order to ensure harmonisation and equal treatment, even if they think that on the facts of the particular case the result is very harsh? Put more starkly, do they have the stomach to sacrifice the few in order to protect the many?[78]

This tension between harmonisation and proportionality came to a head in the case of *Puerta v ITF*. A urine sample collected from Mariano Puerta after his defeat in the 2005 French Open men's singles final tested positive for a very small and in no way performance-enhancing concentration of etilefrine, a banned stimulant. He said that in the players' lounge just before the final, his wife had used his water glass to take some medication that included etilefrine, and there must have been some dregs of the medicine left in the drops of water in the glass when she handed it back to him. That explanation was accepted by the tribunal, and on that basis it also accepted that he bore No Significant Fault or Negligence for his ADRV. In the ordinary course, this would have led to a reduction of the presumptive two-year ban to a ban of between 12 and 24 months. However, this was Mr Puerta's second ADRV, and therefore the 2003 Code mandated a life ban, and only permitted mitigation on grounds of No Significant Fault or Negligence down to an eight-year minimum. In circumstances where both of his ADRVs arguably had compelling mitigating features, however, the CAS panel felt compelled to impose only a two-year ban. It insisted that this was *not* a departure from the Code, but rather a filling of an inadvertent gap in the Code's otherwise comprehensive sanctioning regime, namely the failure to cater for a situation where two ADRVs were committed that both had significant mitigating features.[79] It explained:

> 11.7.17 It is undoubtedly, and commendably, the aim of WADA and of the signatories to the WADC to ensure that the WADC established a coherent and reasonable policy for sanctioning athletes who were found to have broken anti-doping regulations, and thereby cheated both their fellow athletes and the sporting public at large. The Panel has no doubt that the WADC has achieved that aim admirably, and is an invaluable tool in the fight against doping. Indeed, in all but the very rare case, the WADC imposes a regime that, in the Panel's view, provides a just and proportionate sanction, and one in which, by giving the athlete the opportunity to prove either "No Fault or Negligence" or "No Significant Fault or Negligence", the particular circumstances of an individual case can be properly taken into account.
>
> 11.7.18 But the problem with any "one size fits all" solution is that there are inevitably going to be instances in which the one size does not fit all. The Panel makes no apology for repeating its view that the WADC works admirably in all but the very rare case. It is, however, in the very rare case that the imposition of the WADC sanction will produce a result that is neither just nor proportionate. It is argued by some that this is an inevitable result of the need to wage a remorseless war against doping in sport, and that in any war there will be the occasional innocent victim. There may be innocent victims in wars where bullets fly, but the Panel is not persuaded that the analogy is appropriate nor that it is necessary for there to be undeserving victims in the war against doping. It is a hard war, and to fight it requires eternal vigilance, but no matter how hard the war, it is incumbent on those who wage it to avoid, so far as is possible, exacting unjust and disproportionate retribution.

[...]

11.7.23 Any sanction must be just and proportionate. If it is not, the sanction may be challenged. The Panel has concluded, therefore, that in those very rare cases in which Arts 10.5.1 and 10.5.2 of the WADC do not provide a just and proportionate sanction, ie when there is a gap or lacuna in the WADC, that gap or lacuna must be filled by the Panel. That gap or lacuna, which the Panel very much hopes will be filled when the WADC is revised in the light of experience in 2007, is to be filled by the Panel applying the overarching principle of justice and proportionality on which all systems of law, and the WADC itself, is based.

11.7.24 It would be a disaster for the WADC, and for the fight against doping in sport, if the WADC were to be struck down in any jurisdiction as not producing a just and proportionate sanction.

11.7.25 The Panel does not consider that to fill the gap or lacuna that it believes to exist in the WADC requires it, or any tribunal, to exercise a general discretion. [...] Indeed, the existence of such a general discretion would be inimical to the WADC, which seeks to achieve consistency and certainty. The Panel does not believe that such a discretion exists, and would not welcome its existence.

Despite these clear words, it has since become standard for athletes' counsel to invoke *Puerta* in any case where the rules mandate a fixed ban, whether for doping or for some other misconduct (see p 36). While most panels have responded by holding the line, as the *Puerta* panel exhorted them to do,[80] a few have not, and in my view the fight against doping has been the worse for it.

Ironically, in 2020 the Argentinian media reported that Mr Puerta had admitted making up the explanation that the etilefrine had got into his system through his inadvertent ingestion of his wife's medication. According to those reports, he said the etilefrine must have been in ginseng and caffeine pills that his fitness coach's friend (who he had never met) had prepared for him.[81] If that explanation had been offered at the time, then (given all the red flags) his plea of No Significant Fault or Negligence would very likely have been rejected, and the outcome would have been very different.

Making testing effective

Drug testing is not just about catching cheats; it is also about vindicating the achievements of innocent athletes. Imagine making all the extreme sacrifices required to win gold, only for the public to assume that achievement must have been fuelled by drugs.[82] If the testing that is done is intelligent and effective, then it allows innocent athletes to point to their clean testing records as evidence that their results are credible. But what if the testing is unintelligent and ineffective, if the holes in the net are so big that cheating athletes can also slip through? Not only does that give a false veneer of credibility to a cheat's claims of innocence, such as Lance Armstrong's infamous comment, when he retired from cycling in 2011: *'Twenty-plus-year career, 500 drug controls worldwide, in and out of competition. Never a failed test. I rest my case'.*[83] In addition, if and when that cheat is eventually caught by other means (USADA famously exposed Lance Armstrong by persuading his team-mates to testify against him in exchange for reduced bans of their own[84]), that tells the world that drug testing is not effective to sort the innocent from the guilty. And so the innocent athletes suffer twice, first by being cheated of victory, and then by being cheated of public belief in the credibility of their own achievements.

So how can we know whether a sport's testing programme is intelligent and effective? One thing for sure is that it is not just a numbers game. It would be easy to design a testing programme that had thousands and thousands of drug tests but was guaranteed not to catch anyone, eg by collecting the samples at the wrong time, or not running all of the relevant analyses on those samples at the laboratory. That is why WADA requires ADOs to conduct detailed risk assessments of the sports they have jurisdiction over, and then to design intelligent test distribution plans that make use of all available tools and techniques to ensure the testing addresses those risks effectively.[85]

One of the first questions for WADA when it comes to monitoring compliance with this requirement is whether the ADO is doing enough out-of-competition testing. Drug testing during competitions is obviously important, to give the participating athletes and the watching public confidence that no one has taken (for example) a fast-acting stimulant to fight off fatigue and improve their focus and alertness on the field of play. But in-competition testing is like a fixed speed camera: everyone knows it is there, and therefore *'[o]nly a fool, or a Ben Johnson who took a calculated risk that his last late steroid programme would clear before he competed in Seoul, gets caught'*.[86] And an athlete may take nothing just before the match itself, but could well still be benefiting from the long-term effects of drugs taken weeks or months before the match – eg steroids that built muscle, or rEPO that increased the amount of oxygen in the blood – that have long since passed through the body and so are no longer detectable in the urine or blood by the time the match comes around. The only way to address this risk is to collect urine and blood samples outside of competition. And the only way to do that without giving the athlete advance notice of the testing – which would allow them to avoid the test, or to frustrate it, eg by temporarily halting their drug intake, or by drinking enough water to dilute the urine so that the concentration of the drug in their urine sample is too low to trigger a positive result – is to require the athlete to give you details of where they are going to be whenever they are out of competition, so that they can be found at any time, without any advance notice. Genuine no notice out-of-competition testing is like a mobile speed camera, much more effective at catching cheats, and therefore much more effective at deterring cheating. And it also helps clean athletes to persuade the public that their own achievements are genuine (*'I can't take drugs, I could be tested literally at any time'*).

Under the 2003 World Anti-Doping Code, WADA left the ADOs to determine for themselves how to find athletes for testing when they were not in competition. Many did not try very hard at all. Others did, but struggled to find an approach that achieved the objective (enabling the athlete to be found at any time) without being disproportionate (holding an athlete accountable for a missed test any time they departed from their previously-declared routine). Some required the athlete to provide '24/7' whereabouts information, but if the Doping Control Officer could not find the athlete where they had said they would be, the DCO would either: (1) call the athlete and give them more time to report for testing; or else (2) come back the following day in the hope they would be there. Others required details of the athlete's whereabouts for only one hour per day, which was more reasonable but limited the ADO's ability to find the athlete for testing outside that hour.

Therefore in 2007 WADA's Director of Standards & Harmonization, Rune Andersen, brought together a group of experts – Kate Mittelstadt and Jenn Schrier from USADA, Thomas Capdevielle from the IAAF, and Andy Parkinson and Nicole Sapstead from UK Sport's Anti-Doping Directorate – to share their experiences and ideas for an optimal set of whereabouts rules. I supported their discussions and drafted the resulting rules. The group came up with the following system, which we thought brought together the best of the different approaches in place at that time, and added new features to strengthen the system overall:

- Each international federation has to put the highest priority athletes in its sport into an international registered testing pool. Each NADO has to put the highest priority athletes in the highest priority sports in its country into a national registered testing pool.
- Each athlete in a registered testing pool (national or international) must log onto WADA's centralised database, the Anti-Doping Administration and Management System ('*ADAMS*'), before the start of each quarter, and must enter for each day in the following quarter: (1) the times of any regular activities (eg work, training, school); and (2) where they will be staying each night. They also have to specify (3) precisely where they will be for one hour each day between 6 am and 11 pm. Any failure to provide any of this information is recorded as a filing failure.
- Any ADO with testing authority over the athlete (the international federation, the NADO, an event organiser, etc) can access the information in ADAMS about the athlete's whereabouts in order to locate them for testing when they are out of competition.
- Where an athlete's plans change, they must log into ADAMS and update their previous filing. If necessary, they can log into the system up to one minute before their chosen one-hour slot to say that their plans have changed, in which case they must give a new location and/or a new time slot later that day. But whether they update their original time slot or location, or leave it as originally specified, they have to be at the location they have specified during the hour specified. If an ADO tries to test them during the hour they have specified, at the place they said they would be, but they are not there, and do not have a very good excuse, a missed test is recorded.
- A single filing failure or missed test is not a rule violation. But any combination of three filing failures and/or missed tests in any 18-month period (subsequently reduced to 12 months) is an ADRV, and carries a ban of between one and two years.

Rune and I presented this proposed scheme to WADA's stakeholders, many of whom had never collected proper whereabouts information from their athletes and therefore had never had any proper out-of-competition testing in their programmes prior to this point. We dealt one by one with the various concerns they raised:

- Many worried that this would be an untenable administrative burden for athletes in the registered testing pool. We explained how athletes would be able to make their quarterly ADAMS filings and their day-to-day updates on any desktop or laptop computer or even on their mobile phones if they wanted.

- Some player associations complained this was a gross invasion of the privacy of the athletes. We pointed out that it is a much greater invasion of their privacy to require them to let a DCO follow them into a toilet and watch them pee into a cup, but that is nevertheless accepted because everyone knows there is no other way to ensure the test is done properly. Everyone also accepts that in-competition testing alone is not enough to police the ban on doping; instead, no notice out-of-competition testing is also essential. We asked whether the player associations could tell us a less intrusive way of enabling such testing than requiring athletes to file information in ADAMS about their whereabouts when out of competition. They could not.
- One person was concerned that the system could interfere with an athlete's love life. What if they met someone in a bar and decided to go back to that person's place rather than return to the place they had entered in their whereabouts filing as their overnight address? We pointed out that the rules gave athletes the flexibility to choose not only the location but also the time (between 6am and 11pm) for their time slot, and so anyone with an unpredictable love-life could avoid a missed test simply by not designating their home late at night or early in the morning for their time slot.
- Another concern was that we would end up banning athletes for purely administrative errors. We said it would be up to the international federations and NADOs to train the athletes they put in their registered testing pools on how to meet the filing requirements, and they were also free to provide administrative support to the athletes to help them meet these requirements. In addition, a ban is only imposed if the athlete commits three whereabouts failures. In other words, two whereabouts failures do not trigger any consequences, and the system includes various warnings and reminders to avoid a third failure. Furthermore, after a short period – originally 18 months, subsequently reduced to 12 months – a whereabouts failure '*expires*' and the athlete is back down to one strike, or none, so that it will only be the truly negligent who will get a third strike in that period and so face a ban.
- Others worried that determined cheats could circumvent the system too easily. For example, they could deliberately wait until just before their designated one-hour time slot and then at the last minute change their filing in ADAMS to designate a different location more than an hour away, so that any DCO who turned up at the original location would not have time to get to the second location. That was true, but we pointed out that the athlete would have to pull this trick every day while they were doping, and that such repeated last-minute updating would be an enormous red flag, identifying the athlete as someone the ADO should investigate and target test; and it might also amount to evading sample collection, or tampering with the doping control process, both separate ADRVs that attract significant bans of their own.
- The team sports pleaded for special treatment, arguing that in team sports athletes train, travel and compete together rather than individually, and so it is much easier to find them for testing when they are not playing in a match. We said that was fine, athletes on teams could delegate their whereabouts filings to a team official, who could file details of their training and competition schedules, and they could designate their one-hour time slot during those collective activities if they wanted. But they would also have to provide details of where they would be sleeping each night, and of any regular activities conducted on an individual basis when they were not with the team. And if they delegated

the filing of their whereabouts information to a team official, they would remain personally liable for any incomplete or inaccurate filings by the team official, as well as for a missed test if they were not where the team official had said they would be during the one-hour time slot.

Rune and I presented the proposed rules at the World Anti-Doping Conference held in Madrid in November 2007, but various stakeholders, led by the German NADO, raised objections. Eventually the WADA Executive Committee decided that our proposal should be referred for further consultation. Rune was furious. He came over, pinned me with his steely blue eyes, summoning up the spirits of his ferocious Viking ancestors, and said: *'We will go to Bonn, and we will crucify them'.* Never mind the German NADO, he terrified *me*. At the subsequent meeting at the German NADO's headquarters in Bonn, we had several rounds of tense exchanges. The Germans insisted that a one-hour *'missed test'* time slot gave athletes too much scope to avoid testing outside of that hour. In response, we explained that requiring the athlete to be liable for a missed test for the entire 24 hours of every day was impracticable and disproportionate. In addition, the one-hour time slot anchors the athlete to a certain location for a particular day. Combined with the information that the athlete must provide as to where they will be residing, training, competing and conducting other *'regular'* activities during that day, it should be possible to locate the athlete for testing not only inside but also outside the time slot. The discussion dragged on without any progress being made, but just when I thought the meeting was going to collapse in acrimony, someone's mobile phone went off loudly with Abba's *'Dancing Queen'* as the ringtone. The debate abruptly stopped, and a red-faced Rune grabbed his phone to take the call from his wife. That moment of levity punctured the tension in the room, we all took a break, during which I had a quiet word with the NADO's lawyer, Anja Martin, and after the break we managed to make progress.

The new whereabouts rules were duly approved by the WADA Executive Committee in May 2008, came into force in 2009 as part of the International Standard of Testing,[87] and have been in effect ever since. With various tweaks as we learned from daily practice, the ADAMS system has held up pretty well, and so have the rules, enabling ADOs to locate athletes for testing at any time without having to give them advance notice of the test. Understandably, no one is happy about the administrative burden, but most athletes seem to have recognised the benefits. In 2009, Roger Federer said: *'It's a tough system, no doubt. It's a significant change to what we were used to before, so I think it takes some getting used to it… I feel like this is how you're going to catch them, right? You're not going to catch them ringing them up and saying, "Look, I would like to test you maybe in two days." The guy's cheating and they're smart, right? It's an hour a day. I know it's a pain, but I would like it to be a clean sport, and that's why I'm OK with it'.* His fellow tennis player Bob Bryan said: *'It's a little strict. They've been showing up a lot at our house, especially last year before the Olympics, but we want fairness in our sport. We don't want it looked upon like baseball. We want integrity in our sport'.* And Olympic swimmer Rebecca Adlington said: *'I get tested all the time. Before the trials last week I got tested three times in the space of two weeks. At the Olympics you are tested every time you race and have to have blood tests. I did blood profiling before the Olympics as well so that if anybody ever said "She's on drugs" I can prove I'm not'.*[88]

The whereabouts rules have also stood up to legal scrutiny. A number of French athletes and player unions filed an action arguing that the rules infringed their right under Article 8 of the European Convention of Human Rights to respect for their private and family lives, because they meant that even when the athletes were not training or playing they were still *'on duty'*, they could not go hiking or camping anywhere too remote, and even their homes were not free of intrusion by doping control officers. In short, the claimants complained, *'their situation was comparable to that of sex offenders who were on a register or individuals wearing an electronic tag who had to declare their whereabouts. Top-level athletes were presumed to be potentially engaged in doping'*. Putting aside the obvious hyperbole, this is a good example of a claimant simply complaining about the restrictive nature of a rule without considering what the restrictions are aimed at achieving, or whether there is any better way of achieving it. In April 2018 the European Court of Human Rights agreed with the claimants that the whereabouts rules encroached significantly on their right to a private and family life. In fact, the court acknowledged that the requirements were *'onerous'*, going well beyond what is required of most working people. However, it also found that, because many drugs are eliminated quickly from the body but have a long-lasting effect, a doping control programme can only be effective if it tests athletes not just in competition but also out of competition, which is only possible if you know where the athletes are when they are not competing. Therefore, the court found, the whereabouts rules are a necessary means of ensuring the effectiveness of doping controls, and they are also proportionate, because they contain various checks and balances and procedural safeguards, and the claimants had not been able to identify a less intrusive set of requirements that would offer sufficient protection from cheating.[89]

Postscript

It is not surprising that a system of rules that applies in virtually every sport in virtually every country in the world sometimes throws up difficult challenges, difficult cases, and difficult results. Nor, given the stakes, is it surprising that cases arising under these rules can be very hard-fought and expensive. And the rules are necessarily tough and relatively inflexible, to ensure that there is consistency and rigour in every sport and in every country where the Code applies, which can lead, in some extreme cases, to the harsh punishment of a few innocent athletes along with the guilty. But for all of that, I doubt that many people who care about the integrity of sport would wish for a return to the days before the World Anti-Doping Code came into effect.

Notes

1 *Drug-free sport is Utopia – Rogge*, BBC, 24 November 2008.

2 Quoted in Simson V. & Jennings A., *The Lords of the Rings: Power, Money & Drugs in the Modern Olympics* (Simon & Schuster, 1992), p.187. See also Dwain Chambers, *TEDx Talks*, 3 January 2024 (youtube.com/watch?v=tJrho1yhB-o, accessed 11 October 2024); *Dwain Chambers: I told my mum I'd change nothing about my life*, The Times, 12 January 2024 (*'I knew I was breaking the rules. But to be number one was more important. The fame, the glory, the money, the success – it came thick and fast. [...] I knew it was wrong from the start. I didn't know what pharmacology was, but I knew it was more than running round a track. In my eyes, I was underperforming. If you're down, you're susceptible. That's when they get you. I had to be in the top three in the world or my contract would get cut in half. I was living a flash lifestyle that I was not able to maintain'*).

3 Rodchenkov G., *The Rodchenkov Affair: How I Brought Down Putin's Secret Doping Empire* (Penguin 2021), p.87. See also Gladwell M., *Man and Superman*, The New Yorker, 9 September 2013 (using drugs to enhance performance *'is a vision of sports in which the object of competition is to use science, intelligence, and sheer will to conquer natural difference. Hamilton and Armstrong may simply be athletes who regard this kind of achievement as worthier than the gold medals of a man with the dumb luck to be born with a random genetic mutation'*).
4 *'Steroid Olympics': athletes to compete at 'Enhanced Games'*, Channel 4 News, 5 June 2025 (youtube.com/shorts/p-2j03lk1xs, accessed 7 October 2025).
5 Enhanced.com (accessed 7 October 2025) and '*The First Declaration on Human Enhancement*'.
6 See generally Sandbakk, Ø., & Loland, S., *Records at What Cost? A Critique of the Enhanced Games*, Int J Sports Physiol Perform, 2025 Dec 10:1-4.
7 Pound R., *Inside the Olympics* (Wiley, 2004), p.84.
8 Harrison G. et al, *Adverse Health Consequences of Performance-Enhancing Drugs: An Endocrine Society Scientific Statement*, Endocrine Reviews, Volume 35, Issue 3, 1 June 2014, pages 341–375; National Health Service, *Anabolic Steroid Misuse* (nhs.uk/conditions/anabolic-steroid-misuse/, accessed 6 October 2025). The state-sponsored athlete doping programme undertaken in East Germany in the 1970s and 1980s led to liver damage, cardiovascular complications, early mortality, and (for the female athletes) irreversible masculinization, reproductive issues, and psychological trauma. See Franke W. and Berendonk B., *Hormonal doping and androgenization of athletes: a secret program of the German Democratic Republic government*, (1997) Clinical Chemistry, 43:1262–1279.
9 Mayo Clinic, *Performance-enhancing drugs: Know the risks* (mayoclinic.org/healthy-lifestyle/fitness/in-depth/performance-enhancing-drugs/art-20046134, accessed 6 October 2025).
10 Frati P. et al, *Anabolic Androgenic Steroid (AAS) related deaths: autoptic, histopathological and toxicological findings*, Curr Neuropharmacol. 2015 Jan;13(1):146-59, cited in Favretto D. et al, *Post-mortem investigation into a death involving doping agents: The case of a body builder*, Drug Test Anal. 2022 Oct;14(10):1795-1799, Epub 2022 Aug 14.
11 Siddique H., *Blood doping: what is it and has anyone died as a result of it?*, The Guardian, 2 August 2015.
12 Goldman R. and Klatz R., *Death in the Locker Room, Drugs & Sports* (Elite Sports Medicine Publications, 1992), pp.23-24. Note however that subsequent research commissioned by WADA suggests that the number of athletes who would answer the same way today has dropped significantly, even if a small proportion of athletes would still prioritise winning over health and/or legality: Connor J et al, *Would they dope? Revisiting the Goldman dilemma*, J Br J Sports Med 2013;47:697-700; Woolf J et al, *The Goldman Dilemma is dead: what elite athletes really think about doping, winning, and death*, (2016): International Journal of Sport Policy and Politics, 9(3), 453-467; and Woolf J. et al, *How athletes conceptualise doping, winning and consequences: insights from using the cognitive interviewing technique with the Goldman dilemma*, (2017): Qualitative Research in Sport, Exercise and Health, 9:3, 303-320.
13 de Hon O, Kuipers H, van Bottenburg M., *Prevalence of doping use in elite sports: a review of numbers and methods*, Sports Med. 2015 Jan;45(1):57-69.
14 *National Federation of Sportspersons' Associations and Unions & Others v France*, European Court of Human Rights, 48151/11 and 77769/13, judgment dated 18 January 2018, para 166 (*'The use of doping agents in order to gain an advantage over other athletes unfairly eliminates competitors of the same level who do not have recourse to them, is a dangerous incitement to amateur athletes, and in particular young people, to follow suit in order to enhance their performance, and deprives spectators of the fair competition which they are entitled to expect'*); Alex Zulle, Festina cycling team: *'Everybody knew that the whole peloton was taking drugs and I had a choice. Either I buckle and go with the trend or I pack it in and go back to my old job as painter'*, quoted in Camporesi S. and Knuckles J., *The solution to doping is to extend the blame beyond athletes*, Aeon, 22 July 2016; Lance Armstrong: *'If I was racing in 2015, no, I wouldn't do it again because I don't think you have to. If you take me back to 1995, when doping was completely pervasive, I would probably do it again'* (Strachan, *Lance Armstrong: If I Had To Do It All Over, I'd Probably Cheat Again*, huffingtonpost.com, 26 January 2015).
15 Galen, writing in the third century BC, noted the practice of Olympic competitors consuming, apparently for performance-enhancement purposes, *'the rear hooves of an Abyssinian ass, ground up, boiled in oil and flavoured with rose hips and petals'*: Olympedia, Doping (olympedia.org/definitions/131, accessed 5 October 2025).
16 Ljungqvist A., *Doping's Nemesis* (SportsBooks Limited, 2008), p.48.
17 See generally Mottram D., *'An evolution of doping and anti-doping in sport'*, in Mottram D. and Chester N., *Drugs in Sport*, 7th Edn (Routledge, 2018), Simson V. & Jennings A., *The Lords of the Rings: Power, Money & Drugs in the Modern Olympics* (Simon & Schuster, 1992), Chapter 15 (Before Your Very Eyes), and see p. 75 for a brief explanation of the Athlete Biological Passport indirect detection method.

18 Moore R., *The Dirtiest Race in History* (Bloomsbury, 2012).
19 Pound R., *Inside the Olympics* (Wiley, 2004), p 53.
20 Mr Justice Charles Dubin, *Report of the Commission of Inquiry into the Use of Drugs and Banned Practices Intended to Increase Athletic Performance* (Ottawa 1990), p 517; and see the discussion of the impact of Dubin Report in Simson V. & Jennings A., *The Lords of the Rings: Power, Money & Drugs in the Modern Olympics* (Simon & Schuster, 1992), Chapter 15 (Before Your Very Eyes).
21 Franke W. and Berendonk B., *Hormonal doping and androgenization of athletes: a secret program of the German Democratic Republic government*, (1997) Clinical Chemistry, 43:1262–1279; Ungerleider S., *Faust's Gold: Inside the East German Doping Machine* (St Martins Press, 2001); Ljungqvist A., *Doping's Nemesis* (SportsBooks Limited, 2008), Chapter 8 (The Anti-Doping Police and the East German Underworld).
22 Vrijman E., *'A Commentary on Current Issues and Problems'*, in *Drugs and Doping in Sport* (Cavendish, 2001), p.147. See Ljungqvist A., *Doping's Nemesis* (SportsBooks Limited, 2008), pp.116-17 (*'Country after country, sport after sport, and federation after federation had introduced their own regulations. Different sports' anti-doping rules sometimes conflicted. Different sports or different countries might dish out different punishments or reach different judgements for different offences. The co-ordinated regulations across all sports found in Sweden were absent on an international level. Sometimes, conflicts arose between the national and international regulations'*).
23 Pound R., *Inside the Olympics* (Wiley, 2004), pp.70-74. See also Pound R., *The World Anti-Doping Agency*, [2002] International Sports Law Review 53; Hanstad D.V., Smith A., Waddington I., *The Establishment of the World Anti-Doping Agency: A Study of the Management of Organizational Change and Unplanned Outcomes*, International Review for the Sociology of Sport 2008; 43; 227.
24 *Declaration on Doping in Sport*, World Anti-Doping Conference (Lausanne, 1999). See Pound R., *Inside the Olympics* (Wiley, 2004), pp 69–74; Houlihan B., '*The World Anti-Doping Agency: Prospects for Success*', in *Drugs and Doping in Sport* (Cavendish, 2001), p 125.
25 According to its constitution, WADA's objects are *'(1) to promote and coordinate at international level the fight against doping in sport in all its forms including through in and out-of-competition; to this end, the Foundation will cooperate with intergovernmental organizations, governments, public authorities and other public and private bodies fighting against doping in sport, inter alia the International Olympic Committee (IOC), International Sports Federations (IF), National Olympic Committees (NOC) and the athletes; it will seek and obtain from all of the above the moral and political commitment to follow its recommendations; (2) to reinforce at international level ethical principles for the practice of doping-free sport and to help protect the health of athletes; (3) to establish, adapt, modify and update for all the public and private bodies concerned [...] the list of substances and methods prohibited in the practice of sport; [...] (4) to encourage, support, coordinate and, when necessary, undertake, in full cooperation with the public and private bodies concerned, [...] the organization of unannounced out-of-competition testing; (5) to develop, harmonize and unify scientific, sampling and technical standards and procedures with regard to analyses and equipment, including the homologation of laboratories, and to create a reference laboratory; (6) to promote harmonized rules, disciplinary procedures, sanctions and other means of combating doping in sport, and contribute to the unification thereof, taking into account the rights of athletes; (7) to devise and develop anti-doping education and prevention programmes at international level, in view of promoting the practice of doping-free sport in accordance with ethical principles; [and] (8) to promote and coordinate research in the fight against doping in sport'*.
26 See wada-ama.org/en/who-we-are/governance (accessed 8 October 2025).
27 UNESCO Director-General's Final Report on the Preparation of the International Convention Against Doping in Sport, ED/2005/CONV-DOP Rep1 (Paris, February 2005), para 7.
28 Dick Pound clearly has the same view, recounting how Rich would always be *'explaining things with endless patience and good cheer, in such a non-threatening manner that no one could take offense'*: Pound R., *Inside the Olympics* (Wiley, 2004), p.53.
29 Comment to Article 2.1 of the 2003 World Anti-Doping Code, quoting *USA Shooting & Quigley v Union Internationale de Tir*, CAS 94/129, para 36.
30 *Korneev & Gouliev v IOC*, CAS OG 1996, Arbitration No. 003-4, p.17.
31 See Hwang M. and Chern C., *Standards of Proof and Requirements for Evidence in Special Situations*, Global Arbitration Review, 12 October 2023 (*'Common law legal systems apply the "balance of probabilities" test, which calls for a claim to be upheld if the tribunal is convinced by the evidence that the claim is more likely than not true. Conversely, civil law legal systems apply the 'inner conviction' test, which asks whether the arbitrator regards the evidence to have reached a level at which they are personally satisfied with the veracity of an allegation'*); *Adamu v FIFA*, CAS 2011/A/2426, para 88 (*'The Panel is of the view that, in practical terms, this standard of proof of personal conviction coincides with the "comfortable satisfaction" standard*

widely applied by CAS panels in disciplinary proceedings. According to this standard of proof, the sanctioning authority must establish the disciplinary violation to the comfortable satisfaction of the judging body bearing in mind the seriousness of the allegation. It is a standard that is higher than the civil standard of "balance of probability" but lower than the criminal standard of "proof beyond a reasonable doubt". The Panel will thus give such a meaning to the applicable standard of proof of personal conviction').

32 See 18 United States Code section 3553(e) (*'Upon motion of the Government, the court shall have the authority to impose a sentence below a level established by statute as a minimum sentence so as to reflect a defendant's substantial assistance in the investigation or prosecution of another person who has committed an offense'*); US Sentencing Commission, *The Use of Federal Rule of Criminal Procedure 35(b)* (January 2016).

33 *Hingis handed two-year suspension*, BBC Sport, 4 January 2008.

34 *Hingis will not come back after two-year drug ban*, Essential Tennis, 26 October 2009.

35 *WADA v UK Anti-Doping & Banks*, CAS 2024/A/10647, paras 135-36 (pharmaceutical products); *UCI v Burke & CCA*, CAS 2013/A/3370, paras 173-78 (mains water).

36 *Meca-Medina and Mejcen v FINA*, CAS 99/A/234 and CAS 99/A/235, para 10.17.

37 *WADA v Swimming Australia, Sport Integrity Australia & Shayna Jack*, CAS 2020/A/7579, para 101.

38 Jones M., *Life in the Fast Lane* (Grand Central Publishing, 2004), p.173 (emphasis in original).

39 Zinser M. and Schmidt L., *Jones Admits to Doping and Enters Guilty Plea*, New York Times, 6 October 2007.

40 McMillan S., *Lance Armstrong's doping denials – in quotes*, The Guardian, 18 January 2013.

41 *USADA v Armstrong*, reasoned decision dated 10 October 2012 (usada.org/wp-content/uploads/ReasonedDecision.pdf, accessed 10 October 2025).

42 Schrotenboer B., *Lance Armstrong to Oprah: Story was 'one big lie'*, USA Today, 17 January 2013.

43 *WADA v Swimming Australia, Sport Integrity Australia & Shayna Jack*, CAS 2020/A/7579, para 105.

44 For example, the Supreme Court of Western Australia has noted that *'it has not been shown that the polygraph technique is a reliable method for determining truth or untruth and nor is there the degree of acceptance within the relevant scientific community which would indicate that it is being seen as so'*: *Mallard v The Queen* [2003] WASCA 296, at para 369. The English courts agree that *'there is no place in a court or tribunal for such evidence'*: *Allen v FCA* [2014] UKUT 0348 (TCC), para 15; *Fennell v Jerome Property Maintenance Ltd*, QBD, Tucker J, The Times (26 November 1986) (*'As a matter of principle, evidence produced by the administration of a mechanically or chemically or hypnotically induced test on a witness so as to show the veracity or otherwise of that witness [is] not admissible in English law'*). Similarly, the Canadian Supreme Court has held that, *'based upon a consideration of rules of evidence long established, the polygraph has no place in the judicial process where it is employed as a tool to determine or to test the credibility of witnesses' because it does not assist the trier of fact (the judge or jury) and the human fallibility that is inevitably present in that process would 'be fortified with the mystique of science')*: *R v Béland*, [1987] 2 SCR 398, pp.416-419. The United States Supreme Court came to the same conclusion in *United States v Scheffer* (1998) 523 US 303, paras 1266-1267.

45 Gladwell M., Talking to Strangers (Penguin, 2020), pp.36-43, 153-54, 164-67. See also *WADA v Swimming Australia, Sport Integrity Australia & Shayna Jack*, CAS 2020/A/7579, para 102 (*'Yet presentational skills of appellants – what one may call the "likeability" factor – undeniably play a role. In this case, the Appealed Decision includes a statement by the Sole Arbitrator, whose sincerity is not in doubt, that in his 40 years of experience as an advocate the Athlete was "one of the most impressive" witnesses he had ever seen: "completely straightforward, genuine and honest [...] emotional at times [...] but not inappropriately or theatrically so". In recent cases where the period of ineligibility was reduced notwithstanding the absence of proof of the source of the prohibited substance, such as Lawson and Jamnicky, three-member tribunals comprised of highly experienced arbitrators were also clearly influenced by the personal charisma of the appellants'*), *para 103* (*'It is perfectly possible not only that wholly deserving appellants may be personally unattractive, but that indeed this very charmlessness reflects innocent sincerity. Appellants may be honestly outraged at a system which allows them to be fingered as cheaters, upset at being treated as miscreants by unsympathetic officials, incredulous at impersonal rules which they find hard to understand and impossible to accept, and bewildered by their first humiliating exposure to formal adjudication by individuals whom they have no inclination to trust – and even less so if their supporters, including their home public as well as national officials whose own reputation may be at stake, encourage them in this disbelief. When they address their judges, they may have the choice between expressing themselves in a foreign language in which they may sound harsh, hesitant, and defensive, or through interpreters lacking the ability to covey personal qualities which would be apparent in the appellants' own communities'*), and *para 104* (*'Thus the outcome may be affected by presentational skills and the cultural affinities*

of the accused and the judge. The former may not have a high level of educational level and cognitive ability, or come from a background of privilege, all of which may safely be assumed to have a positive correlation with the ability to appear convincing. In some sports athletes may reach an international level at a young age. They may be a tongue-tied and nervous for reasons that have nothing to do with guilt. They may lack the support of a confidence-boosting entourage. Such factors should not be decisive').

46 See generally Taylor J., *Case Comment: Lawson v IAAF*, CAS 2019/A/6313, 2020 Vol.20, Issue 3, International Sports Law Review, p.47.

47 In Arthur Conan Doyle's *The Sign of Four*, Sherlock Holmes famously states: *'When you have eliminated all which is impossible, then whatever remains, however improbable, must be the truth'.*

48 *IWBF v UK Anti-Doping & Gibbs*, CAS 2010/A/2230, para 11.5.

49 Eg *UCI v Contador & RFEC*, CAS 2011/A/2384.

50 *Hipperdinger v ATP*, CAS 2004/A/690, para 45.

51 In December 2017, UKAD settled the proceedings with Mr Fury on the basis that the anti-doping rule violations based on the reported presence of elevated levels of nandrolone metabolites were upheld, Mr Fury received a two-year period of ineligibility, back-dated to 13 December 2015 to take account of delays in the process and his provisional suspension, and his results from his fights in February 2015 were disqualified: UKAD press release, *UKAD and Mr Tyson Fury and Mr Hughie Fury issue joint statement*, 12 December 2017.

52 *ITF v Gasquet*, CAS 2009/A/1926; *WADA v Gasquet*, CAS 2009/A/1930. A similar claim was made by the athlete in *WADA v FIE & T.*, CAS 2024/A/10748.

53 Associated Press, *USADA clears Virginia Fuchs of doping violation caused by sex*, espn.co.uk, 12 June 2020; Orme D., *Triathlete avoids doping ban after failed test caused by 'sexual contamination'*, mirror.co.uk, 27 October 2025. See also Dennehy C., *A positive doping test after sex?*, Irish Examiner, 6 March 2024, listing cases.

54 *South Korea striker takes 15-game drug ban after blaming moustache cream*, The Guardian, 15 June 2015.

55 *USADA v Merritt*, AAA No. 77 190 00293 10, award dated 15 October 2010, para 7.8.

56 *Hamilton v USADA & UCI*, CAS 2005/A/884, para 59. Cyclist Tyler Hamilton confessed in his subsequent book that he had been receiving regular blood transfusions, supposedly of his own previously-extracted blood, but potentially mixed (by mistake) with another rider's blood: Hamilton T. & Coyle D., *The Secret Race. Inside the Hidden World of the Tour de France: Doping, Cover-ups, and Winning At All Costs* (Bantam Books, 2012), p.229.

57 *IRB v Keyter*, CAS 2006/A/1067, paras 13-14.

58 *WADA v UK Anti-Doping & Banks*, CAS 2024/A/10647, para 157 (*'It does not follow from the above, and the Panel most certainly has not concluded, that the Athlete cheated; rather, the Panel once again acknowledges that the Athlete presented as a person of integrity as an athlete trying to avoid the taking of prohibited substances and she has devoted substantial resources to find the source of the presence of chlortalidone in her Sample. The Panel is nevertheless required to apply the rules, in particular the ADR, which were enacted to safeguard one of the most important principles in sport of ensuring a level playing field and fairness to all athletes, without which the existence of all sports may be jeopardised. The Panel therefore concludes that the Athlete was unfortunately not able to discharge her burden of proving how the prohibited substance entered her body'*). For Ms Banks' detailed account of the case that gives a real insight into the experience of an athlete accused of breaking the anti-doping rules, see her blog at lizzybankscouk.wordpress.com.

59 *IWBF v UK Anti-Doping & Gibbs*, CAS 2010/A/2230, para 11.12 (requiring proof of source *'is prima facie proportionate. To permit an athlete to establish how a substance came to be present in his body by little more than a denial that he took it would undermine the objectives of the Code and Rules. Spiking and contamination – two prevalent explanations volunteered by athletes for such presence – do and can occur; but it is too easy to assert either; more must sensibly be required by way of proof, given the nature of the athlete's basic personal duty to ensure that no prohibited substances enter his body. The Sole Arbitrator has sympathy with athletes who are – as, he accepts they can be – victims of spiking without evidence to prove its occurrence; but the possible unfairness to such athletes is outweighed by unfairness to all athletes if proffered, but maybe untruthful, explanations of spiking are too readily accepted'*).

60 *FIFA and WADA advisory opinion*, CAS 2005/C/976 & 986. The last three excerpts quoted in the text are from (respectively) paragraphs 173, 157, and 153 of that opinion.

61 See Levitt S. & Dubner S., *Freakonomics: A Rogue Economist Explores the Hidden Side of Everything* (Penguin, 2007), pp.15-16. See also generally Levitt S. & Dubner S., *Super Freakonomics: Global cooling, patriotic prostitutes, & why suicide bombers should buy life insurance* (Allen Lane, 2009).

62 For example, the CAS panel in *US Olympic Committee v IOC* noted an American doping case where the panel *'appears to have fixed the suspension at exactly 6 months in order to*

avoid the application of the IOC Regulation': *US Olympic Committee v IOC*, CAS 2011/O/2422, fn 3. The case in question was *USADA v Brunemann*, AAA No. 77 190 E 00447 08 JENF, decision dated 26 January 2009, in which the national-level panel noted (at footnote 27): *'Because Respondent's sanction does not exceed six months, there is no need for the Panel to address Respondent's arguments that a period of ineligibility would preclude Respondent from participating in the 2012 Olympics (and would effectively constitute a life-ban) because of application of the new Rule 45 of the Olympic Charter, which would result in a disproportionate sanction in violation of the doctrine of proportionality. Had the Panel determined that a sanction of more than six months was warranted, the Panel would have had to seriously consider Respondent's proportionality argument'*.

63 *US Olympic Committee v International Olympic Committee*, CAS 2011/O/2422.

64 *British Olympic Association v WADA*, CAS 2011/A/2658, including at paras 35 and 22.

65 WADA press release, *End of term message to stakeholders from WADA President, Sir Craig Reedie*, wada-ama.org, 30 December 2019.

66 See Prime Minister Tony Blair, Foreword, *A Sporting Future for All – The Government's Plan for Sport* (DCMS PP374, March 2001) (*'The Government does not and should not run sport'*).

67 UK National Anti-Doping Policy, version 1.0, 14 December 2009.

68 UKAD, *Assurance Framework: Ongoing support and compliance process*, version 1.0, 2023.

69 DCMS, *Tailored Review of UK Anti-Doping*, January 2018.

70 *UK Anti-Doping v Burns*, NADP Tribunal decision dated 10 December 2012, paras 46–47; *UK Anti-Doping v Olubamiwo*, NADP Consent Order dated 13 June 2012.

71 *USADA v Leeper*, AAA Panel decision dated 6 November 2015, para 4.18.

72 *USADA v Leeper*, AAA Panel decision dated 6 November 2015, paras 7.18 and 7.19.

73 USADA press release, *US Paralympic Track & Field Athlete, Leeper, accepts sanction for anti-doping rule violation*, usada.org, 1 February 2016.

74 *Leeper v International Paralympic Committee*, CAS 2016/A/4502, para 125.

75 *WADA v Swimming Australia, Sport Integrity Australia & Shayna Jack*, CAS 2020/A/7579, para 181.

76 *WADA v Swimming Australia, Sport Integrity Australia & Shayna Jack*, CAS 2020/A/7579, para 106.

77 *Squizzato v FINA*, CAS 2005/A/830, para 10.23.

78 *USA Shooting & Quigley v Union Internationale de Tir*, CAS 94/129, para 15 (upholding strict liability rule because *'it appears to be a laudable policy objective not to repair an accidental unfairness to an individual by creating an intentional unfairness to the whole body of other competitors'*); *IWBF v UK Anti-Doping & Gibbs*, CAS 2010/A/2230, para 11.10 (*'It was well recognised that the continued battle to eliminate doping from competitive sport waged by lawyers and laboratories on one side against (some) scientists and sportsmen on the other is necessary if sport is to preserve its integrity and its attraction. It is also recognized that there may in consequence of that battle be innocent victims. … [A] rule which at first sight may appear to be unfair to one athlete may on mature consideration be justified as fair to athletes as a whole'*) and para 11.12 (*'The Sole Arbitrator has sympathy with athletes who are – as, it accepts they can be – victims of spiking without evidence to prove its occurrence; but the possible unfairness to such athletes is outweighed by unfairness to all athletes if proffered, but maybe untruthful, explanations of spiking are too readily accepted'*); *WADA v UK Anti-Doping & Banks*, CAS 2024/A/10647, para 157 (*'the Panel most certainly has not concluded that the Athlete cheated; rather, the Panel once again acknowledges that the Athlete presented as a person of integrity as an Athlete trying to avoid the taking of prohibited substances and she has devoted substantial resources to find the source of the presence of chlortalidone in her Sample. The Panel is nevertheless required to apply the rules, in particular the ADR, which were enacted to safeguard one of the most important principles in sport of ensuring a level playing field and fairness to all athletes, without which the existence of all sports may be jeopardised'*).

79 *Puerta v ITF*, CAS 2006/A/1025, para 74.

80 See eg *ITF v Sharapova*, Independent Tribunal decision dated 6 June 2016, para 102 (*'The rules cannot be circumvented by invoking the principle of proportionality. It would be contrary to the principles underlying the code, in particular respect for the rules which must apply equally to all, to allow an unprincipled exception to or waiver from the rules on the grounds of proportionality of sanction as it affects the particular circumstances of this player'*); and on appeal, Sharapova v ITF, CAS 2016/A/4643, para 99 (*'The Panel is also of the view that there is no basis for reducing her sanction further by applying principles of proportionality. The Panel's basis for this position is that the WADC, from which the ITF ADP is derived and on which it is based, has been found repeatedly to be proportional in its approach to sanctions, that the question of fault is built in to analysis of length of sanction under the ITF ADP, and that no case has been cited that could justify a further reduction of the Player's sanction here'*).

81 Associated Press, *Mariano Puerta admits lying to CAS about doping*, espn.co.uk, 3 August 2020.

82 Wood K., '*Casual viewers link performances like these with doping. That's the sport's legacy. But the presumption of innocence applies*': *Tadej Pogacar defended against suspicion*, cyclinguptodate.com, 11 October 2025.
83 Lance Armstrong, Facebook post, 20 May 2011.
84 *USADA v Armstrong*, reasoned decision dated 10 October 2012 (usada.org/wp-content/uploads/ReasonedDecision.pdf, accessed 10 October 2025).
85 See WADA International Standard for Testing & Investigations, section 4; WADA Guidelines for Implementing an Effective Testing Program V.2, 1 January 2023; WADA Technical Document for Sport Specific Analysis, v.11, 1 January 2026; Lauritzen F. and Holden G., *Intelligence-based doping control planning improves testing effectiveness: Perspectives from a national anti-doping organisation*, Drug Test Anal. 2023 May;15(5):506-515; Thevis M, Kuuranne T, Geyer H., *Annual banned-substance review-Analytical approaches in human sports drug testing, 2021/2022*, Drug Test Anal. 2023 Jan;15(1):5-26.
86 Simson V. & Jennings A., *The Lords of the Rings: Power, Money & Drugs in the Modern Olympics* (Simon & Schuster, 1992), p.185.
87 WADA International Standard for Testing, January 2009.
88 *Athlete Testimonies on Whereabouts System* (wada-ama.org/sites/default/files/resources/files/WADA_Athlete_Testimonies_Whereabouts_EN.pdf, accessed 10 October 2025).
89 *National Federation of Sportspersons' Associations and Unions & Others v France*, European Court of Human Rights, 48151/11 and 77769/13, judgment dated 18 January 2018, paras 125, 169, and 191 ('*The Court does not underestimate the impact of the whereabouts requirements on the applicants' private lives. Nevertheless, the generalinterest considerations that make them necessary are particularly important and, in the Court's view, justify the restrictions on the applicants' rights under Article 8 of the Convention. Reducing or removing the requirements of which the applicants complain would be liable to increase the dangers of doping to their health and that of the entire sporting community, and would run counter to the European and international consensus on the need for unannounced testing. The Court therefore finds that the respondent State struck a fair balance between the different interests at stake and that there has been no violation of Article 8 of the Convention*').

Chapter 4

Russia's Doping Operation

The World Anti-Doping Agency is very clear that *'[i]t is crucially important for the global system that Anti-Doping Organizations are held to the same high standards that we expect from athletes'*.[1] As its first President, Dick Pound, has said: *'WADA's challenges are extensive, since its activities must transcend distance, culture, attitudes, customs, beliefs and politics. Code compliance can only be successful when all parties commit to honouring values-based compliance and maintain a strong anti-doping culture that seeks to serve athletes, irrespective of their nationality or federation. When violations of the Code [by Signatories] are alleged, WADA must act not only to ensure enforcement of regulations, but also to protect all clean athletes …'*.[2]

Russia's remarkable state-sponsored corruption of the anti-doping system was exposed in late 2014 by two very brave Russian whistle-blowers. The story hit the front pages in New York and around the world, and remained there for several years as more and more details of the conspiracy slowly emerged. This chapter recounts how the sports movement scrambled to respond, and how the different responses revealed serious weaknesses in the protection offered by the global anti-doping framework, weaknesses that it took several years to address.

'The Fraud of the Rings'[3]

Dr Grigory Rodchenkov, the former head of the Moscow anti-doping laboratory, now tells it plainly: *'I helped run the most successful sport doping enterprise in world history. As director of Russia's ironically named Moscow Anti-Doping Centre, my job was to make sure that the hundreds of Russian athletes participating in international events were never caught with banned substances in their body fluids during training camps and competitions. … But I certainly did not work alone – in fact, I administered Russia's doping operation under the close scrutiny of the secret police: the FSB, the former KGB. The Ministry of Sport monitored my every move. And all this took place under the watchful eye of the sport-obsessed judo fan himself, President Vladimir Putin. … [T]his was a fraud of unspeakable proportion. It undermines all accomplishments and the whole system of doping control in sports'*.[4]

President Putin is not the first autocrat to have craved success in international sport to whip up nationalist fervour and demonstrate his country's superiority over its rivals. Nor is Russia the first country to resort to systematic doping of its athletes to achieve that success.[5] But Russia under President Putin is the first (at least, as far as we know) to have attempted wholesale corruption of every level of the anti-doping system in an effort to ensure its misdeeds were not detected. In summary, and as subsequently described in the various reports referenced below:

- Russia won only three gold medals at the 2010 Winter Olympics in Vancouver, and only 15 medals altogether, putting it 12th in the gold medal table and sixth in the overall medal table. This was simply unacceptable to President Putin, and he was very clear that it must not happen again.
- His Ministry of Sport and its agency, the Centre for Sports Preparation of National Teams of Russia, therefore quickly devised a scheme to dope elite Russian athletes to victory in international competition without detection and disgrace. They targeted in particular the 2013 IAAF World Championships, which Russia would host in Moscow in August 2013, and the 2014 Winter Olympics, which Russia would host in Sochi in February 2014.
- Dr Grigory Rodchenkov, the head of Moscow's WADA-accredited anti-doping laboratory, devised a cocktail of three anabolic steroids (trenbolone, oxandrolone, and metenolone) mixed with whisky or vermouth, called the '*Duchess*' cocktail, after a popular brand of lemonade sold in Russia. These powerful steroids enabled athletes to recover quickly from exertion and so to compete at the top level over successive days. But they were absorbed quickly into the system and long-term metabolites were not formed, so that they could only be detected in the urine for a few days after consumption. The CSP and other state-trained scientists distributed the Duchess cocktail of drugs to elite athletes in track & field and in various winter sports.
- Russia had signed up (via the UNESCO International Convention Against Doping in Sport) to the World Anti-Doping Code, and had set up the Russian Anti-Doping Agency, whose job was to collect athletes' urine and blood samples and deliver them to the Moscow laboratory to be tested for the presence of prohibited substances, with the results reported into WADA's ADAMS database, and with RUSADA then responsible for pursuing the sanctions mandated by the World Anti-Doping Code against any athlete whose sample had tested positive for prohibited substances.
- When athletes who were part of the doping programme were tested by RUSADA, they would take a note of the number engraved on the main and reserve bottles (A and B samples) into which they poured their urine, and pass that number on to the CSP. If the Moscow laboratory's screening procedures flagged a potential prohibited substance in an athlete's A sample, Dr Rodchenkov would secretly report the sample bottle number to the Ministry of Sport, which would find out from RUSADA whether that sample had come from an athlete who was part of the doping programme. If so, Deputy Sports Minister Yuri Nagornykh would issue a '*save*' order, and Dr Rodchenkov would then tell his staff not to run the normal confirmation procedures. Instead they would halt the analysis of the sample and enter the test result as negative in the Laboratory Information Management System and in WADA's ADAMS database. This has become known as the '*Disappearing Positives*' methodology.
- This did not provide complete protection, however, and therefore further measures were also required:
    - First, the WADA rules require accredited laboratories to store all reserve (B) samples for at least three months, and WADA has the right to have those B samples sent to another laboratory for testing at any time. Such testing would have revealed both that the athlete providing the sample had doped and that the Moscow laboratory had not tested their A sample properly the first time around. Therefore agents of the FSB (the federal security service of

the Russian Federation) developed special tools to open the sealed B sample bottles, pour out the tainted urine, and replace it with clean urine from the athletes in question, before re-sealing the B samples and returning them to storage in the laboratory (the '*Sample Swapping*' methodology).

- Second, international federations could send foreign Doping Control Officers to collect samples from Russian athletes at any time, whether the athletes were in Russia or abroad, and those samples could be sent to WADA-accredited laboratories outside of Russia for testing. Therefore, the Russian authorities ensured that Russian athletes got notice when the foreign DCOs were in Russia, so that they could hide until they were clean. And the CSP collected samples from the athletes before they left the country, and had them tested by the Moscow laboratory to ensure the steroids the athletes had taken were no longer detectable ('*wash-out testing*').

- Third, the WADA rules also allow for the collection and analysis of blood samples to test for evidence of blood doping, which was also common among elite Russian athletes. And while it is difficult to detect the presence of blood-doping substances in blood directly, in 2009 WADA introduced a new indirect detection method, the Athlete Biological Passport, which tests blood samples taken from an athlete over time not for the blood-doping agent itself, but instead for variations in natural markers such as haemoglobin concentration and reticulocyte count, which will vary in predictable ways if the athlete is doping.[6] RUSADA and the Moscow laboratory could delay reporting the results of their own ABP testing into ADAMS, to avoid exposing doped Russian athletes before major competitions. However, several international federations (including athletics and biathlon) also started collecting ABP samples from Russian athletes, and those samples were not always sent to the Moscow laboratory, which meant the Russians could not interfere with that testing to avoid the reporting of suspicious results. Instead, therefore, they bribed the leaders of the athletics and biathlon federations to avoid or at least delay the processing of those ABP results and the consequent bringing of disciplinary charges against the athletes in question.

- These various measures enabled Russian athletes to dope themselves with steroids and rEPO/blood transfusions without fear of exposure. And the results were impressive. At the 2012 London Olympics, Russian athletes came third in the medal table, winning 24 golds, 26 silvers, and 32 bronze medals, without any of their samples collected during the Games testing positive for any prohibited substances. And at the IAAF World Championships held in Moscow in 2013, where the Moscow laboratory was able to bury positive A sample results and the FSB was able to swap out the corresponding B samples for clean urine, Russia finished top of the medal table with seven golds, one ahead of the USA, without any doping scandals involving Russian athletes being reported.

- Russian success at the 2014 Sochi Winter Olympics was deemed so important that the athletes in the scheme were told to continue doping right up to and even at the Games themselves, which necessitated further measures to cover up that doping:

  - The '*Disappearing Positives*' scheme would not work in the satellite anti-doping laboratory in Sochi, because IOC and WADA representatives would be present in the laboratory throughout the Games, observing the sample analysis process closely. So the FSB agents repeated the sample swapping scheme they had first tried out successfully at the 2013 IAAF World Championships. Each night during the Sochi Games, Dr Rodchenkov's minions would pass urine samples collected from doped Russian athletes through a specially-drilled mousehole in the sample storage room to FSB agents waiting in a secret adjacent room. The FSB agents would then use their special tools to open the sample bottles (A and B), pour out the tainted urine, and replace it with clean urine that had been collected from those athletes prior to the Games, before re-sealing and passing the samples back through the mousehole to Dr Rodchenkov's team, who could then put them through the normal analytical procedures, in full view of WADA and the IOC, safe in the knowledge that the A samples would test negative, no one would suspect anything untoward had happened, and if any further testing took place at a later date, the B samples would test negative as well.

- ○ The IOC's doping control programme for the Sochi Games also required the collection of ABP blood samples from athletes for overnight testing at the Sochi laboratory and immediate reporting into ADAMS, so that any abnormal deviation in the values of the haemoglobin concentration and/or reticulocyte percentage in those samples compared to the values reported in previous samples could be identified and the athlete could be immediately suspended from competing in the Games. However, when an ABP sample was collected from a Russian athlete who was still blood-doping during the Games, Dr Rodchenkov's men deliberately delayed analysis of that sample beyond the 36-hour deadline set in WADA's ABP rules, so that when the results were eventually reported into ADAMS, they were automatically invalidated.

- This scheme also worked very well. All of the urine samples collected at the Games from doped Russian athletes were swapped out for clean urine, out of sight of the WADA observers, and no samples provided by Russian athletes tested positive at the Games. In addition, any abnormal ABP values were invalidated due to late reporting, and so no ABP violations were triggered. And when the Games ended on 23 February 2014, Russia was at the top of the final medal table, with 13 golds, 11 silvers, and nine bronze medals.

Johannesburg, November 2013

I first came into contact with the scheme, albeit unknowingly, more than a year before it was first exposed. In November 2013, at the World Anti-Doping Conference in Johannesburg, I sat on a disciplinary committee with former WADA president Dick Pound and USADA scientist Larry Bowers that had to decide whether the Moscow anti-doping laboratory should have its accreditation suspended for failing to analyse samples in accordance with the requirements of WADA's International Standard for Laboratories. This was the first time I encountered Dr Grigory Rodchenkov, the director of that laboratory, a colourful character whose story has since been captured in his own book, *The Rodchenkov Affair*,[7] and in an Oscar-winning documentary, *Icarus*.[8] In the book, Dr Rodchenkov says he has *'an enthusiastic and excitable personality that isn't ideally suited to adversarial legal questioning'*,[9] and based on that hearing in Johannesburg I would agree with him. At the time, however, the conspiracy he was part of had not yet been uncovered, and therefore the evidence before us was confined to certain technical performance issues. As a result, we decided to impose only a provisional suspension on the

Moscow laboratory,[10] which meant it was still permitted to operate the satellite laboratory at the 2014 Olympic Games in Sochi.[11] If we had known in Johannesburg the full picture of what the Russians had been doing, the outcome would obviously have been very different.

ARD documentary, December 2014

Vitaly Stepanov worked as a DCO for RUSADA, collecting urine samples from Russian athletes and sending them to the Moscow anti-doping laboratory for analysis. During his work he met and eventually married Yuliya Rusanova, an elite Russian middle-distance runner, who took his name and became Yuliya Stepanova. Their remarkable story is told in David Walsh's book, *The Russian Affair*.[12] Yuliya told Vitaly that she and her team-mates were given steroids by Dr Sergei Portugalov of the CSP, who also headed the medical commission of the All-Russia Athletics Federation (*'ARAF'*). She made secret recordings of her exchanges with athletes and coaches involved in the scheme. Vitaly passed the evidence to WADA's Jack Robertson, but until the 2015 World Anti-Doping Code came into effect, WADA lacked investigative powers of its own,[13] and so Robertson passed that evidence on to Hajo Seppelt, a German investigative journalist. Hajo's exposé, *'The Doping Secret: How Russia Creates its Champions'*, was broadcast on German television channel ARD in December 2014.[14] The documentary asserted that Russian officials had supervised the systematic doping of elite Russian athletes, and had hidden that cheating by enlisting Dr Rodchenkov to ensure the Moscow laboratory did not report their samples as positive. It accused Valentin Balakhnichev, ARAF President and also IAAF Treasurer, of extorting bribes from elite Russian athletes (including marathon runner Liliya Shobukhova) to cover up their doping, and suggested other high-ranking IAAF officials were complicit in that scheme.

Following the broadcast of the documentary, Mr Balakhnichev stepped down as IAAF Treasurer, Dr Gabriel Dollé resigned as director of the IAAF Medical & Anti-Doping Department, and Papa Massata Diack, son of IAAF President Lamine Diack, resigned from his position as a *'marketing consultant'* to the IAAF. WADA commissioned its former President, Dick Pound, together with Richard McLaren, a Canadian law professor and CAS arbitrator, and Gunter Younger, Head of the Cybercrime Department at the Bavarian Landeskriminalamt, to investigate the ARD allegations and determine whether RUSADA or the IAAF or any other Code signatories had breached the Code, whether the Moscow laboratory had breached the International Standard for Laboratories, whether any athletes, coaches, doctors or other support personnel had breached applicable anti-doping rules, and whether any officials were complicit in such breaches.[15] But there was no further reaction at the IAAF until Lamine Diack's fourth and final term as President came to an end in August 2015, and Seb Coe was elected to replace him.

Fake news – the IAAF 'blood-doping' scandal, August 2015

There are many examples, some of them covered in this book, of investigative journalists doing excellent work to expose corruption in elite sport. One of the best is David Walsh of The Sunday Times, who exposed the cheating of Lance

Armstrong and others at the Tour de France, undaunted by the sustained legal and political attacks on his character by Armstrong and the sport's international federation, the UCI.[16] Sport needs journalism like this to help it root out corruption, and it is hardly surprising when those journalists are cynical about the good faith of the international federations they are investigating. But when a supposed exposé is misinformed, and the allegations of corruption have no merit, the international federation has a duty to defend itself as well as any wrongly impugned athletes, because if the public loses confidence in the ability and the commitment of the international federation to protect the integrity of the sport, all is lost.

On 1 August 2015, ARD broadcast another sensational documentary, *'Doping – Top Secret: The Shadowy World of Athletics'*,[17] proclaiming that an IAAF database of blood test results, leaked to ARD by an unnamed *'whistle-blower'*, indicated that the IAAF had known about widespread doping by elite athletes in the years 2001 to 2012 but had done nothing about it. The next day The Sunday Times covered the same story, reporting that two experts they had consulted, Robin Parisotto and Michael Ashenden, had concluded that the blood test results of more than 800 athletes in the database were *'highly suggestive of doping or at the very least abnormal'*. Those 800+ athletes included a third of the medal winners in endurance events at the Olympics and IAAF World Championships in the period 2001 to 2012, of which seven were Brits, one of them *'a top UK athlete'*. Robin Parisotto said: *'Never have I seen such an alarmingly abnormal set of blood values. ... So many athletes appear to have doped with impunity, and it is damning that the IAAF appears to have sat idly by and let this happen'*; while Michael Ashenden said it was *'a shameful betrayal of* [the IAAF's] *primary duty to police their sport and to protect clean athletes'*.[18]

In response, Seb Coe, who at the time was running for election as IAAF President, did not pull any punches:

> It is a declaration of war on my sport. I take pretty grave exception to that. This, for me, is a fairly seminal moment. There is nothing in our history of competence and integrity in drug testing that warrants this kind of attack. We should not be cowering. We should come out fighting.
>
> Nobody should underestimate the anger at the way our sport has been portrayed. The fightback has to start here. We cannot be portrayed as a sport that is in any way dragging our heels.
>
> The use of that database, however it got into their possession, displayed either breath-taking ignorance or a level of malevolence around a set of readings you simply cannot extrapolate beyond. The idea that my sport sat there either covering up wrongdoing or just being incompetent could not be wider of the mark.
>
> The use of this stuff, the sensationalising, this is absolutely an attempt to destroy the reputation of the athletes and our sport. Nobody is remotely suggesting that news organisations don't have the right to question and challenge and kick the tyres but this selective use of this so-called information is just wrong.

> We will not bend a knee to any other sport in the way we've led the way on this [blood testing].[19]

However, ARD and The Sunday Times did not back down, and so WADA asked the Pound Commission to consider these allegations in addition to ARD's original December 2014 allegations. On 14 August 2015, Dick Pound issued a statement urging commentators to be careful not to jump to any unwarranted conclusions:

> Several media releases have been issued and statements made that have tended to confuse the situation, rather than to make clear exactly what can be relied upon as evidence of doping and what cannot. By way of summary, and based on the experts' initial analyses, until the Athlete Biological Passport (ABP) was introduced in 2009, none of the test results contained in the database could be used as the basis for a definitive finding that doping had occurred. At best, they could only be used as indicators of the need for targeted future testing of athletes having abnormal or unusual values.
>
> The IC [Independent Commission] considers this to be an essential point of focus, which bears repeating in the circumstances: no test data derived from the IAAF database prior to the adoption of the ABP in 2009 can be considered to be proof of doping. It would be reckless, if not libellous, to make such an allegation. The reported values may be suspicious and lead to targeted testing of the athletes involved, but nothing more could be done with the information.[20]

The UK House of Commons' Digital, Culture, Media and Sport Committee was apparently not satisfied with this, and nor was it content to leave the Pound Commission do its job. Instead, the Committee saw fit to start its own enquiry into the prevalence of doping in international athletics. It held its first session on 8 September 2015, hearing evidence by video-link from Michael Ashenden, who doubled down on his original criticisms of the IAAF's blood-testing efforts. The Committee members were apparently unable or unwilling to challenge anything that Mr Ashenden was saying, notwithstanding the Pound Commission's express warning. Instead, they simply sent up a few gentle lobs for him to smash over the net:

> Q3/19/20 Ashenden: ... Essentially, the blood database was the same format as what we would use as experts to interpret the blood if it was coming through the [Athlete Biological] Passport, for example. ... [T]hroughout those 12 years the IAAF knew there was a problem with Russia. They knew there was something going on and, from what I can see, there was no meaningful action. Certainly there was no action that I am aware of at a federation level to make some kind of intervention. The IAAF deliberately set up a blood-testing protocol that was designed to establish longitudinal blood profiles. That is what it was for. There is no question that it was fit for purpose and so, yes, there has been this data that they could have acted on. I am aware of their comments where they do not believe that they could have but, frankly, that does not correspond with the evidence.
>
> ...

Q26 Damian Collins: Do you feel that the scale of the problem—the research over that 12-year period indicated about the scale of blood doping within athletics—is so big that the IAAF just did not want to confront it, did not want to confront the reality of what that data suggested?

Ashenden: Of course, I cannot tell you what the IAAF is thinking but my impression ... is that they seem to be overwhelmed. They had an opportunity to stem the tide back in 2005 when it really became glaringly obvious. They did not take any action then; it just got worse and worse and worse. Then, with the introduction of the [Athlete Biological] Passport in 2009, there have been—no question—a lot more athletes removed once that passport was in place. But essentially, they were then fighting an uphill battle because there were so many events that had been contaminated, so many medals that had been won by dope cheats, that to confront that would have been an absolute PR disaster. I think that explains the aggressiveness of their response to this story and, essentially, they have had their pants pulled down. I understand that they are angry and they would not have liked this, but in my view if you have had 12 years to take care of a problem and you haven't, something needs to change and some sort of attention needs to be focused on it. In my opinion, bringing this to the awareness of the public and the media is perhaps the best chance that we have to really get something to change.

...

Q53 Jesse Norman (chair): To be clear, you have been very specific and in your evidence, which we are going to publish, you have been clear that the IAAF's position, which is that the pre-2009 blood values have no legal standing, is incorrect and indeed the IAAF itself has relied on those values in enforcement or legal proceedings?

Ashenden: That is correct. I can elaborate for you a little if you would like, but what you are saying is correct.

...

Q62 Norman: Yes, and the final quote [from Seb Coe], "The idea that my sport just sat there could not be wider of the mark. There is nothing in our history of competence and integrity in drug testing that warrants this kind of attack". Both of those things sound tenuous to say the least, given your evidence today. It sounds as though the IAAF did sit back after 2001. It sounds as though it has been grievously short of energy, at least for long periods over the last 15 years, as regards enforcement and requirements on individual federations to do their job. It sounds as though they have been dilatory in not following the lead set by other agencies in other aspects of world sport in combating blood doping and, therefore, far from there being nothing in their history that warrants this kind of attack, a large chunk of their history warrants this kind of scrutiny, if not an attack. Is that true?

Ashenden: In my opinion, yes.[21]

In the same evidence session, Mr Norman asked David Kenworthy, the chair of UK Anti-Doping: *'When you hear that the London Marathon, potentially the winners or medallists at the London Marathon, potentially British athletes are under suspicion for very high levels of blood doping … when you think of the effect that has on young people and the community nature of that event, what are your emotions about that, how do you feel about that?'.* Given that Paula Radcliffe was the only British athlete who had won the London Marathon in the 20th century, and one of only two British athletes who had finished in the top three in that period, she was forced to defend herself:

> I categorically deny that I have resorted to cheating in any form whatsoever at any time in my career, and am devastated that my name has even been linked to these wide-ranging accusations. I have campaigned long and hard throughout my career for a clean sport. I have publicly condemned cheats and those who aid them. These accusations threaten to undermine all I have stood and competed for, as well as my hard-earned reputation. By linking me to allegations of cheating, damage done to my name and reputation can never be fully repaired, no matter how untrue I know them to be.
>
> Whilst I have the greatest of respect for anyone responsibly trying to uncover cheating in sport, and of course for Parliament itself, it is profoundly disappointing that the cloak of Parliamentary privilege has been used to effectively implicate me, tarnishing my reputation, with full knowledge that I have no recourse against anyone for repeating what has been said at the committee hearing.[22]

Seb Coe was outraged at these false smears and wanted us to put in an uncompromising response, both on behalf of the IAAF and on behalf of Paula Radcliffe. Thomas Capdevielle of the IAAF Medical & Anti-Doping Commission, Huw Roberts (the IAAF's in-house lawyer) and I put one together that again did not pull any punches:

> The IAAF has consistently been a pioneer in the war against blood doping in sport, using every tool available to it to catch blood dopers in athletics and with considerable success. The Athlete Biological Passport (ABP) began in 2009. The IAAF in consultation with WADA was the first sports organisation to adopt the ABP across the whole sport. Prior to 2009, the IAAF screened nearly 8000 blood samples for potential markers of blood doping, and followed up with thousands of urine tests to detect the presence of rEPO. That strategy, which continues to this day, has led to 145 athletes being caught with rEPO in their systems (including Rashid Ramzi, one of the athletes highlighted by The Sunday Times), and another eight athletes (including the four Russian athletes highlighted by The Sunday Times) being caught and banned for manipulating the tests in an attempt to evade detection.
>
> The IAAF has created ABP profiles for more than 5500 athletes, based on more than 13,000 ABP samples collected from those athletes. As a result, 56 more athletes have been caught and sanctioned for blood doping with 13 further cases pending, and 12 more currently in the pipeline. This is significantly more ABP cases than every other anti-doping organisation in the world put together.

ARD/The Sunday Times and their consultants cannot deny any of this. Instead, they argue that the abnormal values found in the blood screening tests conducted by the IAAF from 2001-2009 (i.e., pre-ABP) were not just indicators of potential doping that could be used to target expensive urine tests for rEPO, but instead constituted "compelling evidence" of blood doping, so stating the IAAF should have charged the athletes based on that evidence alone, without the need for any further testing.

The IAAF fundamentally disagrees with that assertion, and it is not alone. WADA and Dick Pound, the chair of its Independent Commission, have also stated clearly and unequivocally that *"no test data derived from the IAAF database prior to the adoption of the ABP in 2009 can be considered to be proof of doping. It would be reckless, if not libellous, to make such an allegation. The reported values may be suspicious and lead to targeted testing of the athletes involved, but nothing more could be done with the information"*.

In the response published today, the IAAF sets out in detail why that is correct, and why the contrary stance of ARD/The Sunday Times and their retained consultants lacks any scientific or legal basis.

The results of testing of an athlete's blood samples are only reliable, and may only be fairly compared with the results from other samples in that athlete's profile, if all of the samples are collected in strict compliance with stringent and standardised sample collection, transport and analysis procedures. If not, any apparent differences in results from one sample to the next have no scientific validity. Those standardised procedures were only introduced in 2009, with WADA's adoption of the ABP programme. The samples collected by the IAAF before that date were not collected pursuant to those procedures. Therefore, while they could be used to help focus expensive urine testing for rEPO on potentially suspicious athletes, they certainly could not be used as evidence of doping in and of themselves.

Furthermore, even if the pre-2009 values had been reliable and fairly comparable with each other, deviations in those values could be caused not by blood doping but rather by innocent factors (such as altitude, exercise, medical conditions, etc.). Therefore, an abnormal value is not evidence of doping, which is a classic 'prosecutor's fallacy'.[23] Instead, information has to be gathered so experts can assess and seek explanations for the abnormal readings an athlete's profile. Only if they conclude that the abnormal reading is highly likely to be due to blood doping, and that no other potential explanation is plausible, can blood doping charges be brought. But these potentially confounding factors were only fully identified when the ABP programme was adopted by WADA in 2009. Prior to that time the necessary information was not collected by anyone to enable these other factors to be assessed. As a result, no charge could ever be brought based on the pre-2009 data, for fear of mistaking an abnormal reading for blood doping when it could have been entirely innocent.

Paula Radcliffe's case illustrates the point perfectly. She has been publicly accused of blood doping based on the gross misinterpretation of raw and incomplete data. When all of the necessary information is considered, however (as the WADA ABP protocols require), there are clearly plausible

> explanations for the values in her profile that are entirely innocent. For example, in two of the cases highlighted by The Sunday Times, the samples were collected immediately after competition (when dehydration causes a decrease in plasma concentration, and so an increase in reported haemoglobin concentration, even though there has been no increase in red blood cells). Any competent scientist would therefore immediately conclude that they should be disregarded. Furthermore, the IAAF followed up by testing Ms Radcliffe's urine samples for rEPO, and her blood samples for evidence of blood transfusions, and all of those tests came back negative.
>
> ---
>
> The IAAF is far from complacent. It understands that there is always more that can and should be done to fight the scourge of doping in sport. It also acknowledges the important role played by journalists not only in unearthing evidence of doping but also in scrutinising the efforts made by antidoping organisations to fight doping in their sports and countries. Such scrutiny, when it is well informed, fact-based, and fair, plays an important part in holding the anti-doping movement to account and so maintaining the public's confidence that the IAAF and its fellow stakeholders in that movement are ready, willing and able to do everything necessary to fight doping in sport.
>
> When journalism is not well-informed, fact-based, or fair, however, i.e., when it is simply wrong both as a matter of science and as a matter of law, and therefore gives rise to wholly groundless accusations of inaction/incompetence on the part of the IAAF, as well as damaging false assertions and inferences about individual athletes, then the IAAF has not only the right but also an obligation to set the record straight.[24]

We hoped that Michael Ashenden and Robin Parisotto would take the time to consider the detailed rebuttal arguments that accompanied that statement, so that they could determine whether they needed to revisit their original positions. Instead, however, they declared overnight that the response was *'25 pages of hair-splitting, ... no doubt intended to muddy the waters ...'*. They maintained their allegations against the IAAF in full, and said: *'Let's wait and see who is sitting on the right side of history'*.[25]

Fortunately, we did not have to wait too long to find out the answer to that.

On 2 December 2015, Seb Coe and Thomas Capdevielle appeared before Jesse Norman's committee. I was in the audience, sitting in front of Hajo Seppelt, the journalist behind the ARD documentaries, who was a noisy and hostile (to the IAAF) spectator. Seb and Thomas quickly set them straight:

> Q189/191 Seb Coe: ... I will die in a ditch for the right of media groups to challenge me, to impugn my motives, to question my judgments, to take to task the sport that I am currently the head of, but the issue that I took exception to was the very selective use of data that could not possibly be used in and of itself to prove positive tests. The very nature of the collection of the data there—and there are two very clear histories here—is what was being collected before the biological passport was in place in 2009 and the

> protocols that were not in place before 2009, dating back to some of the discussions and allegations around 2001. ... The issue that I want to make clear here was the selective use of data ... to imperil the reputation of clean athletes, and to extrapolate from one or two readings a pathology of positive and sanction, you cannot do. You can't do it legally, it is not good medically and it is not within the WADA Code. ...
>
> ...
>
> Q197 Damian Collins: Country is clearly a factor but the problems are widespread. It is not like it is just concentrated in one country, but the issue is the number. Is this a failure of governance in the IAAF if you can have a system where potentially from 5,000 athletes 700 may have produced sample results which are not being followed up on? Who is checking on that? Who knows? I am not expecting individual athletes to be named but just the numbers saying, *"We have concerns, say, over 700. We have only charged 200. We don't know how many others are being pursued"*. If that is the case, isn't that a failure of governance of the system?
>
> Thomas Capdevielle: Sir, with due respect, the question of whether the IAAF did a proper follow-up is very clear for us. We duly followed up according to the protocols in place at the time. We did a follow-up of every block of data that was regarded as atypical according to the protocols in place at the time. We stick to this and I think we explained it in great detail in our rebuttal. We also showed it to the Independent Commission. ... [T]he only purpose of doing blood screening at the time was an indicator to trigger for testing of urine. We followed up with urine testing and with EPO detection. We did more than 8,000 tests at the time. ... [W]e could not catch all the athletes who may have been identified as atypical because of the limitation of the then applicable EPO method. That is the reason why we put all our efforts into putting in place the Athlete Biological Passport with a handful of other organisations, including the UCI, including a few national anti-doping agencies, to be able to view this blood data not as an indicator but as direct evidence of doping. That is what we did and, to date, we have prosecuted more cases than any other organisations [taken] altogether. It is 71 cases as we speak.[26]

Mr Ashenden and Mr Parisotto refused to give us a copy of the analysis they had done of the results in the leaked database (why?), but they did give it to WADA's experts, who considered that analysis, and the IAAF's rebuttal document, and declared the rebuttal to be scientifically sound. WADA confirmed that the IAAF had started collecting blood samples before there was any obligation to do so, and that until the ABP was introduced in 2009, there was no reliable basis to use blood values as evidence of blood doping, because of the lack of standardisation in the way blood samples were collected, transported, analysed and interpreted, and also because there weren't any appropriate procedures to demonstrate proper chain of custody, results validity, identity and integrity.[27]

On 21 December 2015, Huw Roberts and I flew to Montreal with Pierre-Yves Garnier to thrash out the issues with the members of the Pound Commission and with

Michael Ashenden. The Pound Commission's conclusions, published the following month,[28] were unequivocal:

> The IC [i.e., the Pound Commission] does not accept the conclusions in the reports of Drs Ashenden and Parisotto provided to the ARD and Sunday Times, in which it is stated that sanctions could have been obtained on the basis of the values reported in the IAAF database provided to them for analysis. The IAAF rebuttal was accepted as scientifically sound by the WADA expert group assisting the IC, and the IC concurs with that judgment.
>
> The IAAF was among the most active ADOs in the field of testing under the original EPO protocols and, subsequently, the ABP protocols. It has consistently followed accepted methodologies and has played an active role in the advancement of the applicable science. ... Follow up activities in the face of suspicious values have generally been thorough and reasonable in the circumstances.
>
> The IC does not endorse suggestions that the IAAF has not been sufficiently active in relation to EPO testing from the outset of a reliable test for rEPO. While nothing is perfect, the IAAF has been extremely active in this aspect of the fight against doping in sport.[29]
>
> [A]ll information required for a proper evaluation of a blood passport, as collected from 2009 for each ABP test ... was not included in the database. Although it may be hard to blame Drs Ashenden and Parisotto, since they did not have such information in hand, to draw definite conclusions on the basis of incomplete data is a serious issue and they should have taken more precautions in that regard.
>
> Ashenden himself was fully aware that no successful prosecution of a suspected doping infraction could likely have occurred on the basis of pre-2009 data, although such data might, in certain circumstances, be used to supplement ABP data. He provided no references to any scientific publications in which it may have been suggested that successful prosecutions could have occurred on the basis of such data nor to any case brought on the basis of such data alone. ... [T]he IC finds that it would not have been legally possible to bring a successful sanctioning process against any athletes based on the values in the IAAF database.
>
> The IC was provided with no explanation for the differences in approach and cautions expressed by the same scientists in previously written scholarly publications on the subject matter and the opinions expressed in the work commissioned by The Sunday Times. The differences are quite significant.

In response, Mr Ashenden and Mr Parisotto both issued short statements accepting the Pound Commission's conclusions.[30] They did not see fit to apologise for making baseless allegations against the IAAF based on profoundly flawed scientific analysis. But they did say they were willing to let Seb Coe lead the IAAF moving forward, which I am sure he really appreciated.

In the newspapers the next day, Paula Radcliffe reiterated her complaints about the false smears of her reputation by The Sunday Times and its so-called experts, and Seb described the Select Committee proceedings as *'McCarthy-esque'*, and suggested that the way Paula had been (falsely) implicated by Jesse Norman, the Committee chairman, was *'really shabby'*.[31] I agreed with Paula and Seb then, and I agree now.[32] All this episode did was divert time and money away from the efforts of Seb and his team to deal with the real issues that were facing the IAAF at that time, which were: (1) how to restore public confidence in the IAAF's ability to protect the integrity of its sport, following ARD's revelations that certain former IAAF officials had helped to cover up the Russian doping scheme; and (2) how to address the doping culture that had clearly pervaded Russian athletics.

Seb advanced the first objective by persuading the IAAF Council in October 2015 to agree to the creation of a new Athletics Integrity Unit, funded by the IAAF but with Thomas Capdevielle, Huw Roberts and other committed anti-doping specialists working under the oversight of an independent board chaired by David Howman, the former WADA Director-General. The AIU was designed by Huw and by Maria Clarke, another international sports integrity expert. It started operating in April 2017, and quickly became a model of its kind, copied by several other sports.[33]

Achieving the second objective, however, was a much longer haul.

The Pound Commission's first report

On 9 November 2015, the Pound Commission issued its first report into the ARD allegations. It concluded that the Russian Ministry of Sport had instilled *'a deeply rooted culture of cheating'* in Russian athletics, that there had been *'consistent and systematic use of performance enhancing drugs by many Russian athletes'*, organised by Russian coaches and doctors employed by ARAF (including in particular Dr Portugalov), and covered up by RUSADA (through intentionally inadequate testing efforts) and by Dr Rodchenkov and others at the Moscow anti-doping laboratory (by burying positive tests, by substituting clean urine for urine that would have tested positive, and by destroying more than 1400 tainted samples prior to a WADA onsite visit). The Commission also noted that there had been *'corruption and bribery practices'* within the previous IAAF leadership, including delays in following up abnormal ABP results that allowed a number of Russian athletes to compete at the 2012 London Olympics when they should not have done so. The Commission said it had passed the key evidence about that corruption and bribery to the relevant criminal authorities for appropriate follow-up.[34] It withheld final judgment on the IAAF pending feedback from the criminal authorities, but noted that *'the allegations of corrupt behaviour affect a fraction of the many hardworking and committed men and women of the IAAF'*, and that *'[k]ey individuals within the IAAF provided exemplary cooperation with the IC investigation team'*. It also pointedly noted that *'there is no reason to believe that Athletics is the only sport in Russia to have been affected by the identified systemic failures'*. It recommended that WADA declare RUSADA non-compliant with the Code, so that it could not carry out drug-testing of Russian athletes until its failings identified in the report had been addressed; that WADA also revoke the accreditation of the Moscow laboratory and insist Dr Rodchenkov be sacked; that the IAAF suspend ARAF for non-compliance with its anti-doping obligations; and that the IOC not allow any Russian track & field athletes to compete in the Olympic Games until ARAF had addressed the issues identified in the report.[35]

The IAAF and WADA reacted swiftly. On 13 November 2015, the IAAF Council suspended ARAF's membership of the IAAF with immediate effect. It stated that RusAF would only be reinstated when it had completed a long list of corrective actions, and until then Russian athletes would not be permitted to participate in international competitions, including the Olympic Games.[36] (IAAF Competition Rule 22.1(a) stated that any athletes whose national federation is suspended by the IAAF are ineligible to compete in international events). Former WADA director Rune Andersen (with whom I had worked on the whereabouts rules when he was at WADA: see p 63) was appointed to chair a special taskforce to police the reinstatement requirements, alongside IAAF Council members Abby Hoffman, Anna Riccardi, Geoff Gardner, and Rožle Prezelj, and I was appointed as counsel to the Taskforce. Meanwhile on 18 November 2015 WADA's Foundation Board declared RUSADA non-compliant with the Code, so that it could no longer collect samples or conduct investigations or results management, and revoked the Moscow laboratory's accreditation to test athletes' samples.[37]

Two months later, on 14 January 2016, the Pound Commission issued its second report, which concluded that:

- In addition to doping their athletes with steroids, the Russians were also giving their athletes rEPO and blood transfusions. However, they did not understand the power of the ABP to detect blood doping until 2012, by which time many ABP cases were in progress against Russian athletes, and so the Russian authorities had to find a way to get those cases derailed or at least delayed.
- Due to a lack of proper governance checks and balances at the IAAF, Lamine Diack (its President from 1999 to August 2015), his son Papa Massata Diack (engaged as an IAAF marketing consultant), and their legal advisor Habib Cissé were able to interfere with the efforts of the IAAF Medical & Anti-Doping Department to address the Russian doping cases. In particular, Habib Cissé took over management of the ABP profiles of Russian athletes that indicated likely doping. He gave a list of those athletes to ARAF President Valentin Balakhnichev, who told one of the athletes on the list, marathon runner Liliya Shobukhova, that she had a problem. Aleksey Melnikov, the Russian national team's coach for long distance running and race walkers, told Ms Shobukhova she had to pay the dollar equivalent of 450,000 euros in order to avoid being banned from the 2012 Olympics. In June 2012, the IAAF Medical and Anti-Doping Department issued a formal demand to Ms Shobukhova to explain her suspicious ABP results, but Cissé took charge of the demand, and it was never delivered to her.
- Ultimately Mr Cissé delayed the IAAF's pursuit of the ABP cases so that all of the athletes on the list remained available for selection for the Russian team for the 2012 London Olympics.
- When, in late 2012, Huw Roberts became aware of the Russian athletes on the list, he confronted President Diack, who confirmed that it had been agreed not to proceed with the cases. Huw immediately resigned but Diack promised him the cases would be taken forward in full compliance with IAAF Rules, and subsequently ensured that none of the athletes on the list competed at the 2013 IAAF World Championships in Moscow. After those championships, however, Huw was prevented from taking the cases forward, and so he resigned again in January 2014, and, after the matter was reported to the independent

IAAF Ethics Board, he left the IAAF in April 2014, coming to join me at Bird & Bird instead.

- In March 2014, Ms Shobukhova was told she would have to accept a sanction, and was repaid 300,000 euros from a Singapore bank account controlled by an associate of Papa Massata Diack.[38]

- The Commission stated: *'The IC commends the work, in particular, of Messrs Capdevielle, Garnier and Roberts, who did their best often in difficult circumstances, to ensure that anti-doping measures were properly and diligently implemented'.* But it also said: *'The IAAF Council could not have been unaware of the extent of doping in Athletics and the non-enforcement of applicable anti-doping rules. There was an evident lack of political appetite within the IAAF to confront Russia with the full extent of its known and suspected doping activities'.*[39] This was yet more evidence, if any were needed, that Seb's subsequent creation of the Athletics Integrity Unit to police and enforce the sport's integrity rules had not come a moment too soon.

The confirmation of the Russian doping scheme poses a dilemma for the sports movement: should there be a blanket ban of Russian athletes, or individual assessment?

In October 2015, Dr Rodchenkov suspected that he was about to be arrested by the Russian authorities and made a scapegoat for the corruption exposed by ARD and the Pound Commission. He therefore fled from Moscow to the US, where he collaborated with film-maker Bryan Fogel to get his side of the story told. In May 2016, the New York Times reported that Dr Rodchenkov had confirmed the details of the Russian state-sponsored doping scheme, and that he had saved on his laptop evidence from the Moscow laboratory's computer files of the thousands of positive samples collected from Russian athletes that he and his team of analysts had buried and misreported. He also went into detail about the sample swapping at the Sochi satellite laboratory during the 2014 Olympics: '"*We were fully equipped, knowledgeable, experienced and perfectly prepared for Sochi like never before,*" he said. "*It was working like a Swiss watch*"'.[40] WADA quickly appointed Richard McLaren to investigate Dr Rodchenkov's account and to identify any athletes who might have benefited from the scheme, with a requirement to report back by 15 July 2016, ie three weeks before the start of the 2016 Rio Olympic Games, so that the IOC, the IPC, and the relevant international federations could decide which of the athletes on the entry lists that had been submitted by the Russian Olympic Committee and the Russian Paralympic Committee respectively should be blocked from competing in Rio.[41]

This limited mandate highlighted a fundamental weakness in the anti-doping rules in place at that time. The 2015 World Anti-Doping Code gave the WADA Foundation Board the power to decide that a Code Signatory was non-compliant with its obligations under the Code, but WADA itself could impose only very limited consequences for that non-compliance (basically, only loss of membership of WADA committees). It was up to the IOC, the IPC, the international federations, and other major event organisers to decide whether to impose any more significant consequences.

The IOC announced that it would host an *'Olympic Summit'* in Lausanne on 16 June 2016 to *'coordinate and harmonise the approach among the International*

Federations, which take the first decision on the eligibility of athletes with respect to qualification for and participation in the Olympic Games. The discussion will have to address the difficult decision between collective responsibility and individual justice'.[42] At the summit meeting itself, it was decided that the international federations would have to assess each athlete that the ROC proposed to enter for their respective competitions, to determine based on that athlete's anti-doping record whether he or she should be permitted to compete.[43]

Richard McLaren issued his report on 18 July 2016. It said that the laboratory data and other evidence that Dr Rodchenkov had saved on his laptop confirmed that the Russian Ministry of Sport had directed, controlled and overseen a *'state-dictated failsafe system'* in which the CSP doped elite athletes and the Moscow anti-doping laboratory *'disappeared'* their positive samples, reporting them as negative to WADA, ie the Disappearing Positives scheme described by the Pound Commission; while at the 2014 Winter Olympics in Sochi, doped athletes' samples were passed to FSB agents through a mousehole in the laboratory wall, and they prised open the bottles, replaced the incriminating urine with clean urine that had been collected from the athletes before the Games began, replaced the bottle caps, and returned the clean samples back through the mousehole to the laboratory for analysis, ie the Sample Swapping scheme also described by the Pound Commission. Professor McLaren said the evidence showed that the conspiracy had operated from late 2011 to August 2015, and covered mainly athletics and weightlifting but also more than 28 other sports. He noted that because of the very tight reporting deadline, he had not yet had time to identify which individual athletes may have benefited from the conspiracy.[44]

WADA reacted immediately: *'In the face of such evidence of state sponsored subversion of anti-doping processes, WADA ... calls on the Sports Movement to impose the strongest possible measures to protect clean sport for Rio 2016 and beyond'.* It asked the IOC and IPC to consider excluding the entire ROC and RPC teams from the 2016 Olympics and Paralympics, and to admit instead only individual Russian athletes who could meet *'very strict criteria'*, with any such athletes to participate on a neutral basis, not as representatives of Russia. It also asked the international federations of the sports implicated in the McLaren report to *'consider their responsibilities'* under the World Anti-Doping Code to take action against their Russian national federation members.[45]

The IAAF leads the way

The IAAF had already made its call. On 17 June 2016, the IAAF Council had met at the Grand Hotel in Vienna to consider whether to lift the suspension of the Russian national athletics federation, ARAF (by now, re-named the Russian Athletics Federation, or RusAF), and permit its athletes to participate in the track & field competitions at the Rio Olympics. Rune Andersen's Russia Taskforce recommended that the Council maintain RusAF's suspension, because several of the key reinstatement requirements set by the IAAF Council (see p 87) had not yet been met. In particular, the Taskforce reported: *'a. the deep-seated culture of tolerance (or worse) for doping that led to RusAF being suspended in the first place appeared not to have changed materially;*[46] *b. a strong and effective anti-doping infrastructure capable of detecting and deterring doping had still not been created; and c. there were detailed allegations, which are already partly substantiated, that the Russian authorities, far from supporting the anti-doping effort, have in fact orchestrated systematic doping and the covering up of adverse analytical findings'*. The Taskforce said: *'If RusAF was reinstated so that Russian athletes can compete in International Competition, even though the prevailing doping culture has not yet been corrected, and the necessary anti-doping infrastructure has not yet been put in place, then not only would the IAAF lose the ability to force through real and lasting change in Russia. In addition, its claim to be ready to take the tough decisions that are necessary to protect the integrity of the sport would lose any credibility. Undoubtedly, non-reinstatement of RusAF would mean that some clean Russian athletes will miss out on Rio. But while that is unfortunate, it is nothing compared to the injustice that so many athletes have suffered in the past in being cheated out of medals, prize money and glory by their Russian competitors, and that so many more could suffer in the future if this opportunity to solve the problem is wasted. In short, this is the price that has to be paid for the failure of the Russian authorities to fix the problem before now, and the Russian authorities alone are to blame for that'*.[47]

The IAAF Council accepted the Taskforce's recommendation in full, meaning that RusAF remained suspended and therefore unable to enter its athletes in international events, including the Rio Games. But the Council also adopted a new IAAF Competition Rule 22.1A, which Huw Roberts and I had drafted, which provided a route for athletes affiliated to a national federation that had been suspended for anti-doping failings to compete in international competitions in an individual capacity, ie as *'neutral athletes'*, if they could show the IAAF's Doping Review Board that they had been outside the country and subject to other, effective anti-doping systems *'for a sufficiently long period to provide substantial objective assurance of integrity'*. In addition, the new rule gave the same benefit to any athlete who had made *'a truly exceptional contribution to the protection and promotion of clean athletes, fair play, and the integrity and authenticity of the* sport', and so provided a route for Yuliya Stepanova to apply for permission to compete in Rio based on her bravery in exposing the Russian doping scheme. There was a heady atmosphere in the Grand Hotel bar that night after the IAAF Council meeting had finished, with a real feeling that the IAAF's strong stand for clean sport had made a difference. David Walsh seemed to agree. In that weekend's Sunday Times, he remarked that *'Friday in Vienna was one of the better days in the fight against doping'*.[48]

The IAAF Doping Review Board subsequently considered applications from 68 Russian athletes for permission to compete in Rio pursuant to IAAF Competition Rule 22.1A, but ultimately denied them all, based on the Pound Commission's determination that during the relevant period – from 1 January 2014 to summer 2016 – the drug-testing regime in Russia, where they had all been based, had been completely corrupted.[49]

In the last week of June 2016, I got a call from Mike Morgan, who advised that his firm, Morgan Sports Law, had been instructed by the ROC to challenge the IAAF's exclusion of the Russian track & field athletes from the Rio Games. We agreed to submit the dispute to the CAS on an expedited timetable, so that the CAS Panel could issue an award on or before 21 July 2016, which was two days before the deadline for entries for the Games. Morgan Sports Law filed a complaint with the CAS on 3 July 2016, arguing that IAAF Competition Rules 22.1(a) and 22.1A were unlawful and so unenforceable, and therefore could not be used to block any Russian athlete from competing in Rio. They therefore maintained that the athletes entered by the ROC should be accepted if they met the IAAF's normal qualification standards, even if they did not meet the additional (unjustified) eligibility requirements set out in Rules 22.1(a) and 22.1A. And they argued that in any event, the IAAF did not have the right to say the Russian athletes had to compete at the Olympics in a neutral capacity, rather than as representatives of Russia. And (just in case those arguments failed) they also appealed against the Doping Review Board's denial of the 68 athletes' individual applications for permission to compete in Rio.

The argument advanced was that IAAF Competition Rules 22.1(a) and 22.1A were unlawful because they effectively sanctioned athletes based on RusAF's alleged anti-doping failures and based on *'suspected anti-doping breaches'* by the athletes themselves, which (they claimed) amounted to nothing more than an (unwarranted) presumption that the athletes were tainted by the alleged failures in the Russian anti-doping system. They said this *'guilt by association'* operated as a sanction on top of those mandated by the World Anti-Doping Code, and therefore was invalid and unenforceable, ie the same argument as had been deployed in *USOC v IOC* and in *BOA v WADA* (see p 56). They also argued that the IAAF could not take any action based on RusAF's failures because certain IAAF officials had been complicit in those failures. And they argued that the IAAF rules violated the principles of equal treatment (because they effectively treated athletes differently depending on whether they lived inside or outside Russia), of legal certainty (because they imposed an indefinite sanction), and of proportionality (because they punished athletes based on wrongs committed by others, and effectively presumed guilt based on nationality), as well as the requirement of fair and non-discriminatory treatment.

A week later, on 10 July 2016, after a lot of work from Huw and from Bird & Bird's Lauren Pagé and Edwina Haddon, we filed the IAAF's response. We pointed out that it was made clear at the Olympic Summit that the international federation of a sport has the sole right to set its sport's eligibility rules for the Olympic Games, and we insisted that the IAAF rules at issue here were clearly an eligibility rule, not a sanction. We said that the Russian athletes were not being excluded from international competitions as a sanction for their own doping misconduct. Instead, their exclusion was simply a consequence of the fact that their national federation had been suspended from membership for failing to subject them to an anti-doping system that met the mandatory requirements of the World Anti-Doping Code and the IAAF Anti-Doping Rules, a suspension that had not been challenged by RusAF or the claimants. We said the ROC's arguments conflated the general eligibility rule set out in IAAF Competition Rule 22.1(a) – that a federation's athletes may only participate in international competitions if the federation complies with its membership obligations – with the exception to that rule set out in IAAF Rule 22.1A, which does not make anyone ineligible, but instead provides a route to competition for athletes affiliated to a suspended federation. We said the other arguments failed on the facts, but also because they were arguments that apply to sanctions, and only RusAF had been sanctioned, not the individual athletes.

The hearing took place on 19 July 2016 in Geneva. The CAS Panel was made up of Luigi Fumagalli (chair), Jeff Benz, and Robert Reid QC. Olympic champion pole-vaulter Elena Isinbaeva was the only athlete to give evidence. Mike Morgan and Howard Jacobs argued the case for the ROC and the affected Russian athletes, and I argued the case for the IAAF. The CAS Panel issued its decision two days later, on 21 July 2016. It ruled that IAAF Competition Rules 22.1(a) and 22.1A were valid and enforceable, and so the ROC was not entitled to nominate athletes who were ineligible under those rules to compete at the Rio Olympics. It also issued a separate award rejecting the 68 athletes' appeals against the Doping Review Board's decisions. The CAS Panel's reasoned award, which was issued in October 2016, explained that it agreed with the IAAF that the suspension of a national federation for anti-doping failures and the consequent exclusion of its athletes from competition are both consistent with the World Anti-Doping Code. In particular, the exclusion of athletes affiliated to the suspended national federation *'is not ... a doping sanction for the athletes concerned. It is a rule which affects the eligibility of athletes to enter into International Competitions and is a consequence of the organizational structure of international sport: national federations are members of international federations, and have the duty to respect the obligations deriving from such membership; athletes participate in organized sport, as controlled by an international federation, only on the basis of their registration with a national federation, which is a member of the international federation in question. ... The athletes are ineligible because RusAF has been sanctioned, and has accepted that sanction, not because of what the athletes have done'*. The CAS Panel rejected the athletes' estoppel and unequal treatment arguments on the facts (because no IAAF officials had been involved in the creation and implementation of the Russian doping scheme, and because the rules applied equally to any national federation, not just to RusAF), and rejected the other arguments on legal grounds, including that because Rule 22.1A does not impose a sanction, it does not have to pass any proportionality test, and in any event it is *'a proportionate means of encouraging NFs to comply with the IAAF's rules'*, in particular because if athletes of a suspended national federation are not excluded from competition, the suspension will have no meaningful impact on the national federation's behaviour. The Panel also noted that *'Rule 22.1A is an inclusionary rule, and only created an opportunity, not a bar, for the Claimant Athletes. It would not assist the Claimants for the rule not to be applied, since they would not, in any case, regain eligibility. It would only have the effect of harming any other Russian athlete who satisfied Rule 22.1A(b)'*.[50]

This was an important decision. It established that blanket exclusions of a country's athletes based on the failure of that country to implement an effective anti-doping structure are not unlawful. The athletes were not liable for the failures of their national federation, but they derived their eligibility to compete internationally from their national federation, and therefore if that federation was suspended from membership for failing to implement an effective domestic anti-doping system, its athletes would automatically lose their eligibility for international competition. This ruling gave the sports movement a strong weapon to punish the Russian state for corrupting the country's national anti-doping system, and to deter any recurrence.

The reaction of the other Summer Olympic sports

On 19 July 2016, the IOC announced that Professor McLaren's report (the *'IP Report'*) had revealed *'a shocking and unprecedented attack on the integrity of sports and on the Olympic Games. Therefore, the IOC will not hesitate to take the toughest sanctions available against any individual or organisation implicated'*. It said it had established a special commission (the Schmid Commission) to consider what action should be taken against the officials from the Russian Ministry of Sport and other officials mentioned in the report. However, *'[s]ince, for the IOC as an international non-governmental organisation, the Russian Ministry of Sports and its subordinated organisations such as the Center of Sports Preparations of National Teams of Russia (CSP) and the Russian Federal Research Center of Physical Culture and Sport (VNIIFK) are beyond its reach, it will forward the results of its inquiries to UNESCO and WADA to take further measures and sanctions in application of the UNESCO "Convention against Doping in Sport" and the World Anti-Doping Code'.* It also announced the creation of a second commission (the Oswald Commission) to conduct an inquiry into the Russian team that had competed at the 2014 Sochi Games, to include the re-analysis of samples that had been collected from them in Sochi. It added: *'The EB reiterates and supports the measure already announced by the Olympic Summit on 21 June 2016 to reverse the "presumption of innocence" of athletes from Russia with regard to doping. This means that the eligibility of each Russian athlete will have to be decided by his or her International Federation (IF) based on an individual analysis of his or her international anti-doping record'.* It noted that because Professor McLaren had not had time to compile the data required to establish anti-doping rule violations by individual athletes, the international federations would *'now have to evaluate the IP Report and then take the appropriate measures, according to their respective rules'.*[51]

As a result, while the ROC could enter a team for the 2016 Olympic Games, it could only include a particular athlete on that team if the athlete's international federation was satisfied with his or her anti-doping record. Given that the opening ceremony for the Rio Games was less than two weeks away, the international federations involved in those Games were now under intense pressure to decide which of the Russian athletes that the ROC had entered for their competitions should be permitted to compete. They responded in different ways.

On 29 July 2016, the International Weightlifting Federation decided to exclude all athletes and officials of the Russian Weightlifting Federation from the Rio Games, on the basis that four of the eight weightlifters that the RWF had nominated to compete in Rio were mentioned in the McLaren report as previous beneficiaries of the Disappearing Positives methodology, and two others had prior anti-doping rule violations. In addition, the McLaren report asserted that 61 Russian weightlifters in total were part of the state-sponsored doping programme, and upon re-analysis the samples of all nine Russian weightlifters who had competed at the London Games and/or the Beijing Games had tested positive for Turinabol. The IWF said the RWF and its athletes had therefore brought the sport into disrepute, which triggered a power for the IWF to *'take such action as it deems fit to protect the reputation and integrity of the sport'*, and it was exercising that power to exclude the entire Russian weightlifting delegation from the Rio Games. On 1 August 2016 the RWF applied to the CAS for a ruling that the IWF's *'blanket ban'* of Russian weightlifters was invalid and unenforceable. In Rio two days later, a CAS panel rejected that application on the ground that the findings in the McLaren report were a sufficient basis for the IWF to exercise the power conferred on it by its rules.[52]

Each of the other Summer Olympic international federations conducted an individual assessment of each Russian athlete that the ROC had put forward for their respective competitions in Rio. The federations' decisions were reviewed by a three-person panel, which decided that 44 of the athletes entered by the ROC in the sports in question (mainly swimmers and rowers) should be excluded from the Games on the ground that they had not shown they were untainted by the conspiracy, and/or because they had not been subject to sufficient reliable anti-doping testing in the lead-up to Rio.[53]

In total, then, of the 389 athletes originally nominated by the ROC to compete in Rio across all sports, the IAAF excluded 67, the IWF excluded eight, and the other Summer Olympic sports excluded a further 44, leaving 270 Russian athletes who were permitted to compete, not as neutral athletes but as representatives of Russia.[54]

The reaction of the IPC

On 22 July 2016, four days after receiving the McLaren report, the IPC followed the IAAF's approach by opening suspension proceedings against the Russian Paralympic Committee. Based on the account of state-sponsored doping of Russian Paralympic athletes set out by Richard McLaren, the IPC Executive alleged that the RPC had breached its obligation to strive to ensure that its athletes and athlete support personnel complied with the World Anti-Doping Code and the IPC Anti-Doping Rules. On 7 August 2016, the IPC Governing Board upheld that allegation, therefore suspended the RPC's membership of the IPC, and consequently excluded the entire Russian team from the 2016 Paralympic Games. I attended the press conference in Rio where the decision was announced. IPC President Philip Craven spoke powerfully, saying that the Russian Government had *'catastrophically failed its athletes'*, and that *'[t]he medals over morals attitude disgusts me'*.[55] It was very refreshing to hear another sports leader speak so bluntly and so unequivocally, and it appeared to make quite an impression on the journalists in attendance.[56]

The RPC immediately appealed to the CAS, seeking annulment of the IPC Governing Board's decision, or alternatively an order permitting Russian Paralympic athletes who were not implicated in the McLaren report and who had been subject to non-Russian drug testing in 2016 to compete in Rio. Liz Riley (the IPC's general counsel, who had previously been at Bird & Bird), Lauren Pagé and I had only four days to file an answer, and I was busy chairing the WADA Independent Observer Team in Rio at the time. Fortunately, Jim Bunting and Carlos Sayao, the first-rate Canadian lawyers who had been against us the year before in the *Chand* case (see p 142), were also in Rio, assisting the Canadian Olympic Committee, and they very kindly agreed to help the IPC. With their support, and after several very late nights, we filed our answer to the RPC appeal by the deadline, along with a sworn affidavit from Richard McLaren explaining that his team of investigators had determined that the Moscow laboratory had sought '*save*' or '*quarantine*' instructions from the Russian Ministry of Sport for up to 44 samples from Paralympic athletes spanning 26 sports, and had subsequently '*saved*' seven Russian Paralympic athletes. He also said there was evidence that 21 samples collected from seven different Russian Paralympic athletes at the Sochi Games had been swapped out for clean urine.

At the hearing in Rio on 22 August 2016, Jim Bunting and I split the advocacy duties. The chair of the CAS Panel, Annabelle Bennett, was amused to see us side by side in this way, since she had also presided over the *Chand* case where we had been in vigorous opposition. Counsel for the RPC relied heavily on the fact that the McLaren report did not say that the RPC was involved in the state-sponsored doping scheme described in the report. That was true. In fact, there was little if any evidence that the RPC and its board members were directly involved in the conspiracy, and the CAS Panel declined to make any such finding. The RPC also argued that it had necessarily relied on RUSADA and the Moscow anti-doping laboratory to police its anti-doping rules, that it had no oversight or control over those entities, and it could not be held responsible for their misconduct. We strongly resisted that argument on the basis that the RPC had a positive and non-delegable duty to ensure that its athletes were subject to a compliant anti-doping system, and the CAS Panel emphatically agreed,[57] saying:

> 59. However, the obligation vigorously to pursue all potential anti-doping rule violations within its [the RPC's] jurisdiction and to investigate cases of doping ([WADA Code] Article 20.4.10), are not passive. The IPC Constitution and IPC Anti-Doping Code make compliance with those obligations a condition of each NPC's membership of the IPC. These are positive obligations to ensure compliance. Indeed, the RPC's constitution recognises the obligation to ensure the spirit of fair play, to promote the creation of drug-free sport together with WADA, to maintain compliance with the IPC Handbook and to implement the WADA Code so as to ensure compliance with the domestic anti-doping policy and rules.
>
> 60. These obligations are those of the RPC and remain so within its jurisdiction, whether or not there is delegation to other bodies such as RUSADA, the accredited WADA laboratory or WADA itself as the world-wide international organisation responsible for fighting doping. Still, on a national level and within the structure of the IPC as stipulated in the Constitution, the RPC is the responsible entity having the obligation to the IPC as well as to the IPC's members to ensure that no violations of the anti-doping system occur within Russia. The existence of the system as described in the IP Report and in the McLaren affidavit means that the RPC breached its obligations and conditions of membership of the IPC.

The RPC also argued that it was disproportionate to suspend the RPC and to exclude its athletes from the Rio Paralympic Games, because the RPC was not implicated in the McLaren report, it did not control the persons involved in the Russian doping scheme, it had done everything required of it under the WADA Code and the IPC Anti-Doping Code, and it had ensured since 2016 that all testing of its athletes was conducted by foreign organisations. And it argued that *'a blanket prohibition is not justified, as it has not been established that all para-athletes nominated by the RPC have ever been implicated in doping'*. The CAS Panel also rejected these submissions, for reasons similar to those deployed by the IAAF and upheld in *ROC v IAAF*:

> 81. The IPC was faced with probative evidence of widespread systemic doping under the RPC's "watch". It has described the findings of the IP Report as disclosing the "the biggest doping scandal in sports history". Following the publication of the IP Report, WADA issued a statement which included a recommendation that the IOC and IPC consider, under their respective Charters, to decline entries, for Rio 2016, of all athletes submitted by the Russian Olympic Committee and the RPC. The IOC followed this recommendation, in principle, but delegated the decision to the international federations, together with guidelines to be applied. The IPC chose to act in a different way, insofar as it did not delegate the decision, whether or not to enter Russian para-athletes, to its members but decided to handle the matter uniformly for all of its members. The fact that the IPC chose to proceed in this way in light of the IP Report does not establish, per se, the disproportionality of the Decision.

82. The IPC points to its hierarchical and federal structure according to which its members govern and implement the respective sport exclusively in a specific geographic region. In order to promote and govern the sport on a world-wide level, the IPC is, thus, dependent on its (national) members to implement its policies on a national level. Consequently, the IPC relies on the RPC to ensure compliance in Russia with its zero tolerance anti-doping policy. The IPC points out that this is not particular to Paralympic sport. Rather, this federal system with complementary international and national obligations is the core back-bone of the fight against doping, as is evidenced by the respective articles in the WADA Code [...]. The IPC says that the assertion by the RPC that it did not know what was happening and that it had no control over those involved in the system described by Professor McLaren does not relieve the RPC of its obligations but makes matters worse. [...]

83. The decision of the IPC to suspend the RPC was within its power, has a proper legislative basis and was not irrational, or perverse, or outside the margin of discretion open to it. The Decision was not evidently or grossly disproportionate. It was a unanimous decision of the IPC's Governing Board, which included six Paralympians and representatives from around the world. The IPC explained that it made the decision as it viewed suspension as the only way to ensure that the system, and systematised doping, in Russia no longer continued. Suspension cannot be said to be evidently or grossly disproportionate in view of the overwhelming evidence of the IP Report and the information that followed that directly affected Paralympians in Russia, including in the Sochi Paralympic Games.

...

86. [...] The RPC had a non-delegable responsibility with respect to implementing an anti-doping policy in conformity with the WADA Code in Russia. As an athlete cannot escape the consequences of an anti-doping rule violation by delegating his or her responsibility in relation to the personal duty to ensure that no prohibited substance enters his or her system (Art. 2.1.1 WADA Code), the RPC cannot delegate the consequences where other bodies within Russia acting as its agent implement a systemic system of doping and cover-up. Delegation is permissible and practical and may, indeed, be necessary but, as is recognised in many legal situations, it is not a means of avoiding all responsibility.

...

88. The IPC took the view, which was not unreasonable in the circumstances of the scale and the nature of the doping and cover-up, that the purpose of a suspension of membership was threefold. On the one hand, the measure was designed to provoke behavioural change (for the future) within the sphere of responsibility of the RPC. On the other hand, the suspension took into account that the failures in the past had resulted in a distorted playing field on an international level, because the IPC anti-doping policy was not being adequately enacted and enforced vis-à-vis para-athletes affiliated to RPC. Finally, the IPC submitted that in view of the fact that Paralympic sports had been specifically mentioned in the IP Report, a strong message had to be issued to restore public

confidence, since the Paralympic movement depends – much more than other sports – on the identification with moral values.

89. The Panel notes that all three goals pursued by the IPC are legitimate and that the measure taken is suited to achieve the goals pursued. The suspension of the RPC was a means of restoring a level playing field and was, in addition, a powerful tool to provoke behavioural change within the RPC's sphere of influence. The Russian stakeholders responsible for the systemic doping used the RPC to enter (doped) athletes into the competitions. By suspending the RPC this ability was and will be undermined. The measure taken was also a powerful message to restore public confidence. There was no submission to the Panel of an alternative measure that would, comparably and effectively, restore a level playing field for the present and the immediate future, affect future behavioural change and restore public trust.

The day after the hearing, I left Rio, and finished drafting the report of the WADA Independent Observer Team on the plane on the way back to London.[58] I was exhausted, but also satisfied that the CAS rulings in *ROC v IAAF* and in *RPC v IPC* had established important principles that could be used to underpin the compliance efforts of WADA and the sports movement moving forward.

Post-Rio challenges

Once the dust had settled from Rio, WADA had two pressing issues to address:

- First, the system for enforcing Code compliance by NADOs, international federations and other Code signatories had to be radically reformed. Reasonable people might disagree about the right response to the state-sponsored doping scheme: a ban of the entire Russian team, as per the IAAF, IWF, and IPC, or individual assessment of each athlete's case, as per the other Summer Olympic sports. But what hurt the anti-doping movement was the varying responses from sport to sport, rather than one central decision that everyone stood behind and enforced, in the same way as Code Article 15.1 obliges all Code Signatories to recognise and enforce every individual athlete's doping ban within their respective spheres of authority. Dick Pound had put his finger on this problem in the first Pound Commission report: *'WADA also has the duty to monitor Code compliance by Code Signatories [but …] [t]he compliance responsibility does not enable WADA to issue sanctions against a party that is Code non-compliant. WADA is limited, in the event that it identifies non-compliance, to advising the responsible authority, such as the International Olympic Committee (IOC), the applicable international federation (IF) and UNESCO of such non-compliance. It then becomes the responsibility of the notified parties to take the appropriate action'.*[59] And on 24 July 2016, in the midst of the chaos leading up to the Rio Games, the IOC Executive Board had noted *'its serious concerns about the obvious deficiencies in the fight against doping. The IOC thus emphasises again its call to WADA to fully review their anti-doping system. The IOC will make its contribution to this review by proposing measures for clearer responsibilities, more transparency, better supervision procedures and more independence'.*[60] With that impetus behind it, in November 2016 the WADA Foundation Board mandated the development of a new international standard that would give WADA the power to police Code compliance by Signatories and to impose meaningful consequences for non-compliance that all Signatories would be required to recognise and enforce.

- Second, effective action had to be taken to ban and disqualify the results of the individual Russian athletes who had been doped as part of the state-sponsored scheme from 2011 to 2015. To achieve that, however, WADA had to obtain the Moscow laboratory's analytical data relating to the positive tests that had been '*disappeared*', as well as any remaining samples of those athletes that were still stored at the Moscow laboratory, so that they could be re-tested and/or examined for evidence of sample-swapping. On 9 December 2016, Richard McLaren published his second report, which announced that the evidence he had reviewed indicated that more than 1,000 Russian athletes *'appear to have been involved in or benefited from systematic and centralised cover up and manipulation of the doping control process'*. He said that the screening results of more than 500 samples, including some provided by *'well-known and elite athletes'*, had generated presumptive positive results that had subsequently been *'disappeared'* in the Moscow laboratory's records. He provided '*Evidence Disclosure Packages*' to the international federations of the athletes involved, but he noted that he had not personally assessed whether the evidence was sufficient to establish individual anti-doping rule violations in each case. He also noted that the Moscow anti-doping laboratory had been asked to hand over all of the original data from its testing of those athletes' samples, so that the Disappearing Positives could be tracked down, as well as any of those samples that it still had in storage, so that they could be re-tested by a trusted laboratory. But he had been told the data and the samples had been sealed off and withheld by order of the Russian Investigative Committee, a criminal investigation agency that reports directly to President Putin.[61] Clearly that was not acceptable. Access to the data and samples was needed to ensure the international federations had all the evidence required to ban and to disqualify the tainted results of the athletes who had doped as part of the state-sponsored scheme. Unless the data and samples were provided, not only would cheating athletes avoid justice. In addition, Russian athletes who had not cheated would not be able to clear their names and so would always have a cloud of suspicion over them.

At the WADA Foundation Board meeting in Glasgow in November 2016, I was appointed chair of WADA's Compliance Review Committee, which would be closely involved in the efforts to address these two issues. My colleagues on the CRC were Beckie Scott (a Canadian former cross-country skier and Olympic gold medallist, and the chair of the WADA Athlete Committee), World Archery Secretary-General Tom Dielen (sports movement representative), who I knew from a previous exchange (see p 228), Bente Skovgaard-Kristensen (representative of the public authorities), and Henry Gourdji and Barbara Leishman (independent compliance experts from the air transport industry and the pharmaceutical industry respectively). They all proved to be very fine colleagues in the challenging times that lay ahead.

The International Standard for Code Compliance by Signatories

We quickly put together a new International Standard for Code Compliance by Signatories that represented a paradigm shift in the monitoring and enforcement of Code compliance by international federations, NADOs, and major event organisations. Whereas previously WADA had simply determined whether or not a Signatory had adopted Code-compliant rules, the draft ISCCS gave WADA various tools to monitor whether the Signatory was actually implementing those rules in a comprehensive and effective way. And instead of leaving others to determine the consequences to be imposed on a Signatory for non-compliance, the ISCCS set out a formal procedure that mirrors as closely as possible the procedures followed in cases of Code non-compliance by individuals: WADA sends a formal notice to the Signatory, alleging non-compliance and proposing consequences from the range of consequences specified in ISCCS Article 11, and the Signatory either admits the non-compliance and accepts the proposed consequences or else disputes them, in which case the matter is referred to the CAS for determination, with WADA having the burden to prove that the Signatory is non-compliant and that the consequences and reinstatement conditions that WADA has proposed are necessary and proportionate. Importantly, any other Signatory who would be affected by the consequences and reinstatement conditions imposed would have a right to intervene in the proceedings to protect its interests, but whatever consequences were ultimately accepted by the non-compliant Signatory or imposed by the CAS would have to be recognised and given effect to by all other Signatories. In other words, instead of multiple, disparate responses to Signatory Code non-compliance, there would now be one single process, with all affected Signatories having the right to participate and protect their interests, but once a final decision was made, if necessary by the CAS, every Signatory would be bound by it and would have to give effect to it within its own sphere of authority.

In addition, ISCCS Article 9.5 introduced a fast-track procedure to get cases of non-compliance with *'Critical'* requirements processed quickly, where *'urgent intervention is required in order to maintain confidence in the integrity of a sport or sports and/or of a particular Event or Events'*. And to prevent Signatories trying to avoid responsibility by blaming others for their failure to comply, we included the following provision at ISCCS Article 9.4.3:

> ... In no circumstances, however, shall it be an acceptable excuse, or a mitigating factor (1) that the Signatory's failure to comply with its obligations under the Code and/or the International Standards has been caused by interference by, and/or a failure to provide support or other act or omission by, any governmental or public authorities. Each Signatory has voluntarily accepted the obligation to comply with its obligations under the Code and the International Standards, which includes an obligation to devote sufficient resources, and, where applicable, an obligation to secure the support of governmental and other public authorities required to achieve and maintain Code compliance; or (2) that the Signatory assigned the task of complying with some or all of its obligations under the Code and/or the International Standards to a third party ... .
>
> *[Comment to Article 9.4.3.2: As CAS ruled in RPC v IPC, CAS 2016/A/445, (a) a body with an obligation to enforce the Code within its sphere of authority remains*

> *fully liable for any violations even if they are due to the actions of other bodies that it relies on but that it does not control; and (b) just as an athlete cannot escape the consequences of an anti-doping rule violation by delegating his or her responsibility to comply with his or her anti-doping obligations to others, so too a Signatory has an absolute and non-delegable obligation to comply with requirements of the Code and the International Standards. The Signatory has the right to decide how to meet that obligation, including the right to assign certain tasks to appropriate third parties, should it see fit, but it remains fully responsible for complying with the Code and the International Standards, and is fully liable for any non-compliance caused by any failures of such third party.]*

I presented the draft ISCCS to the WADA Executive Committee and Foundation Board in May 2017, and proposed an expedited stakeholder consultation process, so that the finalised ISCCS could be presented again for formal approval in November 2017. That proposal was accepted, the draft ISCCS attracted widespread support among stakeholders, and it was duly approved in November 2017 and came into effect in April 2018.

Getting the analytical data and urine samples out of the Moscow laboratory

As a reminder, RUSADA had been declared non-compliant in November 2015 (see p 87). In summer 2017, ie before the new ISCCS came into effect, WADA issued a list of conditions that RUSADA had to meet in order to be deemed Code-compliant again, which became known as the '*Roadmap to Code Compliance*'. In its accompanying press release, WADA noted that the Roadmap had been *'developed and agreed with'* RUSADA, the Russian Ministry of Sport, and the ROC.[62] Most of the Roadmap requirements were aimed at improving the governance and operational effectiveness of RUSADA, eg hiring a new director-general and supervisory board members; establishing and implementing an effective test distribution plan; hiring new DCOs and chaperones and getting them trained by UK Anti-Doping; and ensuring the DCOs were given access to athletes living in *'closed cities'*, ie cities subject to strict security access measures to protect the military/other assets located in or near those cities. Those requirements were soon satisfied, under the supervision of two international experts, Peter Nicholson and Ieva Lukosiute-Stanikuniene. By September 2017, the only two Roadmap requirements that remained outstanding were: (1) that the responsible authorities for anti-doping in Russia, including RUSADA, the ROC, and the Russian Ministry of Sport, *'publicly accept the reported outcomes of the McLaren* Investigation', ie accept that a state-sponsored doping scheme existed in Russia from 2011 to 2015; and (2) that WADA be given access to the electronic data for all sample analyses conducted from 2011-2015 in the Moscow laboratory, as well as to any of those samples that remained in storage at the Moscow laboratory.

On the first point, it seemed obvious to me that if the Russian authorities did not acknowledge what had happened from 2011 to 2015, no one could have any confidence that it would not happen again. However, Russian delegate Vitaliy Smirnov insisted at the WADA Foundation Board meeting in Glasgow in November 2016 that *'Russia had never had a state-sponsored system of doping'*.[63] On the second point, the Russian Ministry of Sport and the ROC maintained that access could not be provided to the samples and data in the Moscow laboratory because the Russian Investigative Committee had started an investigation into the allegations in the McLaren report, and the samples and data were evidence in that investigation. The CRC did not accept this excuse, because (as the CAS panel had stated in *RPC v IPC*) just as an athlete cannot avoid strict liability for compliance with his obligations by blaming his failures on his coach or trainer, so too a NADO cannot avoid liability by blaming third parties such as governmental authorities for its failure to comply with its obligations.[64]

In October 2017 WADA received from a whistle-blower a database of analytical data copied from the Moscow laboratory's Laboratory Information Management System that confirmed the Disappearing Positives scheme had been in effect in the laboratory between January 2012 and August 2015. As explained below, this database would ultimately prove to be very useful, but it was not a substitute for the original data and the samples held by the laboratory, which were still needed in order to take effective action against the athletes who had been doped as part of the scheme. Unless WADA was given direct access to the servers on which that data was stored, subsequent efforts to discipline the implicated athletes would be undermined by arguments about the authenticity of that data.

In November 2017, I attended the WADA Executive Committee and Foundation Board meetings in Seoul in my capacity as CRC chair. ROC President Alexander Zhukov also attended. He insisted that RUSADA was *'a completely reformed organisation with a new leadership, independent of the government, and properly funded'*, and that it was fully compliant with its responsibilities under the Code. He also said: *'The McLaren report had become a key reason for the total reorganisation of the Russian anti-doping system. Russia accepted the fact that the national anti-doping system had failed. It had also been recognised by the country's top leadership that the failure had been the result of organised activities aimed at manipulating doping samples of Russian athletes by a group of individuals for their own personal benefit. That group had consisted of a number of individuals within RUSADA, the Moscow anti-doping laboratory and other anti-doping institutions. The level of involvement and the guilt of certain individuals would be determined by the Investigative Committee of Russia at the end of its investigation. At the same time, Russia absolutely denied the existence of a state-sponsored doping system'*, and therefore it could not unconditionally recognise the conclusions of the McLaren report. Mr Zhukov insisted that the requirement to publicly accept the McLaren report was *'an artificial obstacle of a political nature, not related to sport'*. Meanwhile his colleague, Minister Pavel Kolobkov, addressed the second outstanding requirement, saying that *'in accordance with the requirements of the criminal procedure legislation, the samples stored in the laboratory and the electronic database had been sealed. According to the provisions of the criminal procedure code of the Russian Federation, material and evidence had to be kept with the criminal case. ... Once the investigation was completed, the samples and electronic data would be transferred to the relevant organisations'*.[65]

In response to those comments, WADA Athlete Committee member Adam Pengilly asked pointedly how athletes around the world could have any faith in the new anti-doping system that Mr Zhukov said had been put in place in Russia *'unless there was a real acknowledgement of the extent of everything that had taken place?'* He got no answer from the Russian delegates. I in turn suggested that it was clearly not enough for Mr Zhukov to say that *'a group of individuals within RUSADA, the*

Moscow anti-doping laboratory and other anti-doping institutions' had orchestrated the scheme *'for their own personal benefit'*. Instead, the Roadmap requirement was to publicly accept Richard McLaren's conclusion that the conspiracy had been directed by Ministry of Sport officials and implemented in Sochi by members of the FSB, and until that was done the CRC could not say that this requirement had been met. As for Mr Zhukov's argument that these were *'political requirements'* that did not relate to RUSADA's operational capabilities, and therefore should not be a barrier to RUSADA's reinstatement, I noted that: (1) the Russian authorities had accepted these two requirements as pre-conditions to RUSADA reinstatement when they agreed to the Roadmap to Code Compliance; and (2) while RUSADA's operational reforms were encouraging, RUSADA worked within a particular environment and was dependent upon that environment for the success of its operations, and *'in a circumstance in which there were findings by a WADA independent investigation that the previous RUSADA's operations had been utterly corrupted by Ministry of Sport officials directing RUSADA, laboratory officials and the FSB, however good the reform at RUSADA, how could [WADA] be confident that they would not be corrupted again if the findings made and set out in detail with the evidence to support them had not been addressed, refuted if they could be, but otherwise addressed, so that athletes could have comfort that, in the future, that would not be repeated?'* After due deliberation, WADA's Executive Committee agreed that RUSADA should not be reinstated until these two remaining requirements were met.[66]

Hopes were raised of resolution of the first point when the Schmid Commission issued its report on 2 December 2017, finding that there had been *'a widespread culture of doping in Russia, affecting numerous sports for a long period of time'*, and declaring that the evidence confirmed *'the involvement of a number of individuals within the Ministry of Sport and its subordinated entities, such as CSP, VNIFK, RUSADA, Moscow and Sochi Laboratories'*, even if it also declared that *'no indication, independent or impartial evidence appeared to corroborate any involvement or knowledge at a higher level of the State'*. The Schmid Commission recommended that the IOC Executive Board *'take the appropriate measures that should be strong enough to effectively sanction the existence of a systemic manipulation of the anti-doping rules and system in Russia, as well as the legal responsibility of the various entitles involved (ie including [prohibition of the use by Russian athletes of their national] uniform, flag and anthem), while protecting the rights of the individual Russian clean athletes …'*.[67] Three days later, the IOC Executive Board suspended the ROC and its President, which meant that the ROC could not enter a Russian team in the 2018 Winter Olympic Games in Pyeongchang, but a mechanism was established to permit Russian athletes who satisfied a committee that they were not tainted by the doping scheme to compete in the Games as *'Olympic Athletes from Russia'*, under the Olympic flag and with an Olympic anthem.[68] Of a list of 500 athletes produced by the ROC, ultimately only 168 Russian athletes were cleared by the committee on this basis and so were permitted to compete in Pyeongchang.[69] A CAS panel sitting in Pyeongchang denied applications by 47 of the 332 excluded athletes to be allowed to compete. It rejected their argument that they had been impermissibly sanctioned despite not having been found guilty of doping, finding instead that the suspension of the ROC meant that no Russian athletes could be entered for the Games, and therefore (citing the *ROC v IAAF* award) the special entry process established by the IOC was not a sanction but an eligibility decision, providing a route for individual athletes who had not been tainted by Russian state-sponsored doping to compete notwithstanding the ROC's suspension, and that process had been operated in a manner that was neither discriminatory, nor arbitrary, nor unfair.[70]

On 16 May 2018, the day of the next WADA Executive Committee meeting, WADA received a letter signed by Mr Kolobkov and the ROC and RPC presidents, acknowledging that certain (unnamed) individuals had corrupted Russia's anti-doping system, but denying that the Russian state or any of their respective organisations authorised or even knew about their actions. I was in Montreal for that meeting, as well as the meeting the next day of WADA's Foundation Board. Sports movement representatives on the Executive Committee argued that since everyone agreed RUSADA was now operating effectively, it should be provisionally reinstated on the basis that the reinstatement could always be reversed at a later date if the outstanding requirements were not met. Craig Reedie steered the Executive Committee to decide instead to ask the CRC to consider whether the new letter met the first requirement (acknowledgement of the McLaren findings), and also to consider the argument that the second requirement (access to the samples and testing data) was a *'political condition'* that was therefore not *'appropriate'* and should be dropped. At the Foundation Board meeting the next day, Clayton Cosgrove, the representative of the New Zealand government, spoke forcefully against that argument, saying that *'WADA had taken a strong position on Russia, sending a clear signal that doping would not be tolerated, and he and all of the public authorities commended WADA for that. Any move that changed, undermined or weakened that position or the International Standard for Code Compliance by Signatories fundamentally undermined the credibility and integrity of that institution'*.[71]

The CRC met again on 14 June 2018 in Montreal. We decided that the first outstanding requirement for the reinstatement of RUSADA was not met by Minister Kolobkov's May 2018 letter, but it would be met if the Russian authorities specifically acknowledged the findings of the Schmid Commission, which included a finding that *'a number of individuals within the Ministry of Sport and its subordinated entities'* were involved in the conspiracy. We also took the view that the second requirement should not be dropped, but that it could be considered satisfied if the Russian authorities made an unconditional commitment that WADA would be given, by a specified date in 2018: (1) access to the servers in the Moscow laboratory, so that it could take an authentic copy of the LIMS data and of the raw analytical data linked to the initial and confirmation testing procedures run on the samples referenced in the LIMS data; and (2) access to any samples that the data indicated may have been misreported as negative, so that they could be re-tested. In other words, we changed the requirements to provide the data and samples from a prerequisite for reinstatement to post-reinstatement conditions. WADA President Craig Reedie communicated this to Minister Kolobkov on 22 June 2018.[72]

The CRC discussed the matter at length before deciding to change its recommendation in this way, and we all agreed that it was the right decision. While we knew that many stakeholders would not like the idea that RUSADA should be reinstated before the data and samples had been handed over, there was a very good reason to make that change:

- Misconduct can only be punished in accordance with the laws in place when the misconduct happens, not laws adopted subsequently.[73] Therefore the new regime set out in the ISCCS could not be used to punish non-compliance that had taken place and had been identified and declared before the ISCCS came into force on 1 April 2018 (such as the Russian state-sponsored doping scheme).

Instead, it could only be used to punish non-compliance that took place after 1 April 2018.

- Therefore, if WADA continued to insist that RUSADA could not be reinstated until the data and samples had been provided:
  - If the samples and the data were handed over without any gaps and without any tampering, then RUSADA could be reinstated, and the IOC, IPC and international federations could use the data and samples to establish ADRVs by, and therefore obtain bans and disqualification of results of, the Russian athletes who had been part of the doping conspiracy.
  - But if the samples and data were not provided in full, or were tampered with prior to delivery (Gunter Younger, who was by now the head of WADA's Intelligence & Investigations Department, assured us that his investigators would be able to detect that tampering), and so RUSADA was not reinstated, the pre-ISCCS regime for sanctioning Signatory non-compliance would apply, which risked a re-run of the disparate responses to Russian non-compliance that had preceded the Rio Games.
- On the other hand, if RUSADA was reinstated first, and provision of the samples and of a complete and authentic copy of the data were made '*Critical*' post-reinstatement conditions, then if the data and samples were not provided, WADA could take action against RUSADA under the ISCCS, seeking the significant consequences set out in that Standard for non-compliance with Critical requirements. And whatever consequences the CAS decided to impose, all other Signatories would have to recognise and give effect to them.

The reinstatement of RUSADA

At its meeting on 21 August 2018, the CRC decided that a response received from Minister Kolobkov on 13 August 2018[74] did not satisfy either the requirement to acknowledge the findings of the Schmid Commission or the requirement to commit that WADA would get access to the samples and data by a specified date in 2018. We therefore issued a recommendation to the WADA Executive Committee that RUSADA should not be reinstated to the list of Code-compliant signatories.

On 13 September 2018, WADA received a letter from Minister Kolobkov that purported to address both requirements:[75]

- First, it said that *'[t]he Russian Federation fully accepted the decision of the IOC Executive Board of December 5, 2017 that was made based on the findings of the Schmid report'.*
- Second, it provided the following commitment: *'After the reinstatement of RUSADA and the consent of the Russian Investigative Committee, we will provide as soon as possible to an independent expert, agreeable to WADA and the Investigative Committee, the access to the analytical equipment to retrieve (under the supervision of the Russian Investigative Committee and under conditions that preserve the integrity of the evidence) an authentic copy of the LIMS data and of the raw*

analytical data mentioned in your letter. If based on the LIMS data and the raw data, potential Adverse Analytical Findings are identified in respect of samples stored in the laboratories sealed by the Investigative Committee, we will work in a spirit of cooperation with WADA and the Investigative Committee and in compliance with the Russian Criminal Procedural Code to enable the independent re-testing of these samples in accordance with the International Standard for Laboratories'.

The CRC met the same day by conference call. We decided that Minister Kolobkov's new letter was enough to meet the first outstanding requirement, because the Schmid report had endorsed and relied upon the core findings of the McLaren report, including the finding that Ministry of Sport officials and FSB agents were involved in the manipulation of the anti-doping system in Russia. We noted that the letter did not meet the second requirement, because the commitment made to provide the data and samples was conditional on the agreement of the Russian Investigative Committee, and because no firm deadline was given by which the data and samples would be provided. Seeing an urgent need to break the deadlock, we decided to recommend that the WADA Executive Committee go ahead and reinstate RUSADA on two conditions, namely that RUSADA and the Russian Ministry of Sport must *'procure'*: (1) that WADA receives an authentic copy of the LIMS data and a copy of the raw analytical data linked to the initial and confirmation testing procedures carried out by the Moscow laboratory on the samples referenced in the LIMS data by no later than a fixed date to be determined by the Executive Committee; and (2) that any re-analysis of samples required by WADA following review of that data is completed within six months of that fixed date. We said the two conditions should be classified as *'Critical'* requirements, which would increase the consequences to be applied under the ISCCS in the event the conditions were not satisfied.

Later that day, however, someone leaked the CRC's August 2018 recommendation – that RUSADA should not be reinstated because the data and samples had not been provided – to the BBC's Dan Roan, who published it on Twitter.[76] WADA therefore wanted to announce that the CRC had subsequently decided to recommend that RUSADA be reinstated immediately, with the provision of the data and samples made Critical post-reinstatement requirements. When I advised the CRC of this, Beckie Scott called me and said that, having seen UK and US athletes in the media calling on WADA to stick to the Roadmap conditions, she was concerned we would be greatly criticised for changing our position and allowing RUSADA to be reinstated before the data and samples had been handed over. She therefore wanted the CRC to discuss the issue further before proceeding with its revised recommendation. The next morning, Beckie advised the CRC by email that, having had time to reflect, and having seen many athletes calling on WADA to stick to the original recommendation, she no longer supported the revised recommendation to the WADA Executive Committee. I spoke to each of the other CRC members in turn. They agreed with me that Beckie should be allowed to change her vote retrospectively, but also confirmed that they continued to support the revised recommendation, meaning it was now carried by a majority of four to one, rather than unanimously, and I duly wrote to WADA Director-General Olivier Niggli on that basis.[77] In response, Beckie resigned from the CRC, asserting that *'politics have trumped principle'*.[78] When the CRC's revised recommendation was made public the next day, we faced a torrent of criticism, just as Beckie had predicted, with Jim Walden (Dr Rodchenkov's lawyer) calling it *'the greatest treachery against clean athletes in Olympic history'* (which I found slightly ironic, given his client's leading role in the doping conspiracy itself), USADA's Travis Tygart saying it was *'bewildering and inexplicable ... a devastating blow to the world's clean athletes. ... Frankly it stinks to high heaven'*,[79] and the UK Anti-Doping Athlete Commission describing it as *'a catastrophe for clean sport'*.[80] Ed Moses, the chairman of USADA, wrote in an op-ed in The New York Times that the proposal to reinstate RUSADA *'has sparked shock among sports fans and clean athletes worldwide, who, like me, and with no transparency from the global anti-doping body, are scratching their heads at this abrupt, curiously timed development'*.[81]

It was in this febrile atmosphere that I flew out a few days later to attend the WADA Executive Committee meeting in the Seychelles. And the atmosphere was no less febrile there, with accusations and counter-accusations flying from all sides, alongside rumours that the Russians were trying to bug the Executive Committee meeting. The minutes of that meeting have since been published on the WADA website.[82] When the CRC recommendation was tabled for discussion, the representatives of the public authorities pushed for its consideration to be delayed until the next Executive Committee meeting, in Baku in November 2018, but that proposal was defeated by six votes to five. Then each of Linda Helleland (WADA's Vice-President), Clayton Cosgrove and Beckie Scott spoke forcefully in favour of not reinstating RUSADA until it had produced the data and samples. Beckie noted that multiple athlete committees from different sports supported that position, and emphasised that WADA's first duty was to those clean athletes. When it was my turn to speak, I noted that everyone agreed that the lab data and samples had to be handed over, and the only disagreement was how to achieve that handover as quickly as possible. I explained that in my view WADA would be in a stronger position to get the data and samples if RUSADA was reinstated immediately and the requirement to hand over the data and samples was designated a *'Critical'* post-reinstatement requirement, because RUSADA would then come under the new compliance regime set out in the ISCCS, and so would be subject to significant consequences if it failed to provide the data and samples. I suggested RUSADA be given until 31 December 2018 to produce the data, and six more months to provide the samples, accompanied by a clear message that if either deadline was not met, WADA's response would be uncompromising. That recommendation was accepted by 9 votes to 2, with Linda Helleland and Clayton Cosgrove dissenting (Beckie did not have a vote, and nor did I). The WADA press release noted: *'These conditions are critical requirements under the ISCCS, which came into force on 1 April 2018. If they are not met, then the ExCo will consider proposals from the CRC to address such non-compliance based on the relevant provisions of the ISCCS'*.[83]

Despite my explanation at the WADA Executive Committee meeting, the storm of criticism from certain stakeholders re-doubled when the decision was announced. Former WADA Director-General David Howman said that WADA had favoured *'money over principle'*,[84] even though WADA would not benefit financially from RUSADA's reinstatement. And on 31 October 2018, representatives of various NADOs announced their attendance at an *'anti-doping summit'* at the White House organised by USADA CEO Travis Tygart, where *'Government representatives lined up to criticise ... the controversial decision to lift the ban on Russia last month'*.[85]

Did the strategy work?

The WADA Foundation Board met again in Baku on 15 November 2018. Asked to explain the next steps, I said that the Executive Committee's decision in September had made it clear what the Russian authorities had to do, and when they had to do it, and had specified that the requirements to produce the data and samples were *'Critical'* requirements under the ISCCS, meaning that a failure to meet them would entitle WADA to pursue the most significant potential consequences set out in the ISCC, on a *'fast-track'* basis. I was asked if RUSADA could avoid responsibility by saying the data and samples were part of a crime scene and therefore the Russian Investigative Committee would not release them. I said this was *'an issue that had been litigated in a case related to the IPC and the RPC around the Rio Paralympic Games. In that case, the CAS had said that an Anti-Doping Organization had an obligation to ensure that it got the support of all necessary authorities in its country to live up to the obligations imposed upon it. Therefore, RUSADA would be legally accountable if there was a failure to provide the data and the samples. A case based on that non-compliance would stand up at the CAS. There were numerous legal arguments that [...] would be made. They had been anticipated and factored into the recommendation made to the Executive Committee and the decision taken by the Executive Committee. No lawyer would give any guarantees, but the issues had been thought about and, if there was a legal fight, [I] would expect WADA to prevail'.*[86]

On 17 December 2018, the WADA Intelligence & Investigations team travelled to Moscow to retrieve the laboratory data, but was denied unconditional access and so left empty-handed, meaning the 31 December deadline was missed. This prompted another storm of protest from USADA and others, including biathlete Sebastien Samuelsson, who posted an open letter online on 3 January 2019 noting that the deadline had been missed without any consequences being imposed, and accusing the CRC of *'siding with the cheats instead of the honest athletes'*, and *'doing everything within its power to help the nation that committed doping fraud'.*[87] But we stayed calm and trusted in the process set out in the ISCCS that all stakeholders had agreed on just one year previously. On 1 January 2019, WADA advised the Russians that the failure to provide access to the laboratory data by 31 December amounted to non-compliance with a Critical requirement that would be dealt with on a fast-track basis. The Russians quickly responded by promising to provide that access. The WADA I&I team went back to Moscow on 10 January 2019, was given direct access not only to the LIMS database but also (at its insistence) to the laboratory instruments and servers, and made forensic copies of around 24 terabytes of data (equivalent to more than 24 million documents) relating to the analysis of samples at the laboratory between 1 January 2012 and 31 August 2015. And in April 2019 a total of 2,262 samples that had been in storage in the Moscow laboratory were shipped to the Lausanne anti-doping laboratory for re-testing. Therefore, both post-reinstatement conditions were met, assuming that the laboratory data provided to WADA was authentic and had not been tampered with.

WADA I&I retained a team of forensic experts from the Institute of Forensic Science of the University of Lausanne to verify the copy of the LIMS database that it had taken from the Moscow laboratory's servers in January 2019 by comparing it to the 2015 copy of that database that WADA had received from a whistle-blower in October 2017. After various exchanges with their Russian counterparts, the Lausanne experts reported that:

- The 2019 copy of the LIMS database matched the 2015 copy in many respects. In particular, the 2019 copy confirmed that many presumptive adverse analytical findings had not been reported by the Moscow laboratory but instead had been *'disappeared'* into a secret part of the LIMS database.

- A significant number of those presumptive adverse analytical findings had not been tampered with, and those findings (and the related raw data from the laboratory instruments) were being shared with the relevant international federations, so that they could pursue ADRVs against the athletes in question.

- However, other presumptive adverse analytical findings stored in the secret part of the LIMS database, including 145 of the 300 cases that WADA had identified as high priority, had been deleted, and the related raw data from the laboratory instruments had been deleted or altered, in December 2018 and January 2019, just before the WADA team came to Moscow to copy the database. These deletions and alterations had been concealed by back-dating computer systems and data files to make it appear that the Moscow data had been in its current state since 2015. The commands issued to execute the manipulations, deletions and back-dating were also deleted, in an attempt to cover up the cover-up.

- In addition, someone had deleted 25 forum messages from the 2019 copy of the LIMS database that showed laboratory staff member Evgeny Kudryavtsev manipulating the laboratory data and samples in 2013 and 2014, including swapping out tainted samples in advance of an anticipated site visit by WADA in December 2014. And they had inserted in their place fabricated messages purporting to show Dr Rodchenkov and two other laboratory staff members falsifying data in order to extort money from athletes. The fabrications were so clumsy and contrived – for example: *'I propose we enlighten Kudryatsev about our scheme involving the sample. We need to tell him straight and clearly that we are creating the appearance of dirty samples, and the athletes and their trainers are bringing us bonuses'* – that they would have been laughable if the attempted deception had not been so serious.[88]

WADA I&I and its experts had come through, just as Gunter had promised me they would. In November 2019 the CRC recommended that WADA send RUSADA a formal notice under the ISCCS alleging that it had failed to comply with the *'Critical'* requirement to provide an accurate and complete copy of the LIMS database and the related raw data, asserting that the deliberate tampering with the data and attempt to frame Dr Rodchenkov were aggravating factors, and therefore proposing as a consequence that Russian government representatives, ROC officials, and Russian athletes should be excluded from any major event staged in the next four years, including the 2020 Summer Olympics in Tokyo and the 2022 Winter Olympics in Beijing, as well as all other major events and all world championships held in that four-year cycle, that the Russian flag should not be displayed and the Russian anthem should not be played at those events, and that only Russian athletes who could prove they were not tainted by Russia's anti-doping failures – ie they were not involved in the institutionalised doping programme, their data were not part of the manipulation, and they were now subject to credible testing – should be permitted to compete in those events, but only as neutral athletes, not in Russia's colours. In addition, Russia should not be permitted to host or to bid to host any Olympic events or world championships in the next four years.[89]

At a specially convened meeting on 9 December 2019, the WADA Executive Committee accepted the CRC's recommendation, and the notice commencing formal non-compliance proceedings was sent to RUSADA the same day.[90] David Walsh applauded this step, saying that it sent a clear message that Russia was *'the pariah of world sport'*, and that the consequences proposed by the CRC struck the right balance between strong punishment for the Russian state and leniency for those Russian athletes who could show they were not tainted by the conspiracy.[91] UK Anti-Doping and others also expressed their support for the decision.[92] But some stakeholders, including some members of the WADA Athletes Committee, believed this was not a severe enough proposed punishment for what the Russian authorities had done; instead a blanket ban on all Russian athletes should be imposed.[93] I therefore explained the thinking behind the CRC's recommendation in an interview with Sean Cottrell of LawInSport:[94]

> There is a starting point in the appendix to the Standard that says in a Critical case, here is your starting point, you move up or down. We just went through them one by one and said, what do we do here? Do we go this far? Does that achieve the objectives? Does it go too far? Is it disproportionate? We applied the usual legal analysis. We said, *'what consequences are required to punish, to send a message to deter people from doing this again?'* We set this out plainly and transparently in the decision, which is available on the WADA website. …
>
> Now people may say, *'if the athletes are there, then it's a sham. There's nothing to it, Russia's really there'*. Believe me, the response that we've got is very clear. For Russia, a state that uses sport as a symbol of national power and pride, not to have your President, your government officials there, not to have the Olympic Committee officials there, not to have the flag, not to have the colours of the country there is a very significant blow to their pride. I think, and I don't shy away from that, this is what we want. We want them to feel shamed. We want them to know that they forfeited their right to be there … .
>
> Our judgment was that you balance what we think is the impact of that against the unfairness of innocent athletes being excluded. We thought it was right to draw the line where we did. Again, I don't mind people saying *'you're wrong, that's too weak'*. I think we can see reasonable people disagree, because even the WADA Athlete Committee is split down the middle. I've seen various athletes' committees come out and say it's too weak and others say, no, we agree with it. So, I have no problem with the argument. I do have a problem with people saying *'you disagree with me so you lack integrity'*.
>
> … I do think that it will have an impact and it sends a message: *'You, Russia, have forfeited your place at the top table'*. I do think people need to take a look at the whole of the proposed consequences and judge it over overall, not just focusing on the point that some athletes will be able to compete in Tokyo.

RUSADA responded to WADA's formal notice the following week, disputing both the alleged non-compliance and the proposed consequences. WADA therefore filed a request for arbitration of the dispute with the CAS. WADA and RUSADA both filed extensive legal submissions and expert evidence in support of their respective cases. The onset of the Covid epidemic and the consequent postponement of the

Tokyo Olympic Games from 2020 to 2021 lessened the urgency somewhat, and so the hearing did not take place until November 2020. At the hearing, the Russian witnesses insisted that the Moscow laboratory data had not been tampered with before it was handed over to WADA I&I, which prompted some merciless cross-examination from WADA's lead counsel, Ross Wenzel, and there were also extensive submissions by all parties on a host of legal arguments and counter-arguments.

The CAS Panel (chaired by Mark Williams SC, sitting with Luigi Fumagalli and Dr Hamid Gharavi) issued its 186-page award on 17 December 2020.[95] In summary:

- It ruled that WADA had been right to categorise the requirement to provide the Moscow laboratory data as a *'Critical'* requirement in the fight against doping, *'as it concerns the provision of authentic doping sample data in the context of a state-sanctioned doping program'*.[96]
- It rejected the argument that RUSADA could not be held strictly liable for alleged failures by other Russian government agencies, ruling: *'[T]here can be no serious challenge to the proposition put by WADA that if a NADO could avoid a compliance action by blaming the interference of public authorities or other third parties, the system would be toothless. It would mean that countries with unscrupulous governments or sports authorities with the power and the will to undermine proper anti-doping regulation would be able to do so without consequences, so that, in effect, the overriding aim of harmonised anti-doping regulation would only be possible in those countries where authorities were willing to play by the rules. ... The nature and extent of Russian doping violations revealed during recent years, and accepted by RUSADA, demonstrate how third parties can interfere with and corrupt the anti-doping program and processes. For WADA and the world sporting movement to be able to prevent these abuses and protect clean sport, it is necessary to effect change by acting through its Signatories, if necessary on the basis of strict liability. The compliance consequences for Signatories are necessary to fight against doping and to ensure the level playing field regardless of fault'*.[97] This was a crucial ruling, which built on the *ROC v IAAF* and *RPC v IPC* decisions described above. Any other ruling would have undermined the entire system.
- The panel accepted the evidence of WADA's forensic experts that the Russian Investigative Committee had subjected the Moscow laboratory data to *'deliberate, sophisticated and brazen alterations, amendments and deletions ... intentionally carried out in order to remove or obfuscate evidence of improper activities carried out by the Moscow Laboratory as identified in the McLaren Reports or to interfere with WADA's analysis of the Moscow Data ... . [A]lterations were made to Forum Messages in the Moscow Data in order to deceptively inculpate certain employees of the Moscow Laboratory (Dr Rodchenkov and Dr Sobolensky) in a contrived extortion scheme while exonerating others (Mr Kudryavtsev) from wrongdoing. ... This conduct, which went well beyond mere deletion of incriminating doping samples or data, was breathtaking in its audacity'*.[98]
- The panel was clear that *'[t]he steps taken to manipulate the Moscow Data and deceive WADA could hardly be more serious'*:

> 708. As WADA submitted, far from recognising the opportunity to come clean and draw a line under a scandal that has plagued, and drained resources from, international sport for years, the Russian authorities unfortunately saw it as an opportunity to fraudulently promote their fabricated defence strategy and mitigate or avoid the consequences of the

doping scheme. [...] When the cover-up of the doping scheme began to unravel, the solution adopted by the Russian authorities was not to come clean but rather to double down by seeking to cover up the cover-up.

709. [...] The Panel agrees with the view expressed in the CRC Recommendation that the non-compliance in this case "could hardly be more serious". By manipulating and deleting the Moscow Data, the Russian authorities interfered with, and undermined, the anti-doping system in the most cynical and sophisticated manner. Rather than concede the fact of the manipulations in view of the damning forensic evidence, Russian experts assisting the Ministry of Sport offered explanations that were wholly inadequate, unconvincing and far-fetched and also sought to rely on the fabricated and manipulated Forum Messages and New Data.

...

- The panel then turned to consider what consequences should be imposed. Its analysis was strong and uncompromising:

710. These manipulations show that the Russian authorities remain as willing as ever to interfere with, and corrupt, the anti-doping system. Having done so in the past (in a manner previously considered unthinkable), it is necessary to take robust action to attempt to deter any repetition.

711. The Panel accepts that it is necessary to impose serious consequences not only in the interest of the fight against doping in general, but also specifically in the long-term interest of RUSADA, the protection of Russian athletes, and clean Russian sport. To attempt to ensure that RUSADA can fulfil its role of fighting against doping in Russia, it is necessary to effect a fundamental change in attitude at the level of public authorities in Russia, who have demonstrated frequently that they are able and willing to interfere with the anti-doping infrastructure and processes and also in respect of those athletes who have been willing to engage in doping. It is necessary to impose meaningful consequences to attempt to ensure the confidence of clean athletes, stakeholders and the wider public in the ability of WADA to defend the integrity of sport against doping. Otherwise, the clear message will be that governments and public authorities can corrupt and manipulate anti-doping programs and that WADA is unable to do anything about it. The Panel accepts that WADA is motivated not by ill will against Russia or Russians, but rather by the desire for an effective and independent Russian anti-doping program, to protect a new generation of Russian athletes and for clean Russian sport.

- However the panel then noted:

717. In considering relief, the Panel recognises the need to consider the respective structures of the various organisations that will be required to implement the measures ordered, and to make sure that such measures will neither unduly interfere with those structures nor impact essential and beneficial work that is done by or on behalf of those organisations. It also recognises the need to avoid, where possible, ancillary disputes which may cause delay and increase the time and costs incurred preparing for major events, including the Olympic Games and Paralympic Games, particularly in the light of disruption occasioned by the COVID-19 pandemic. Further,

the Panel acknowledges that imposing severe consequences upon an entirely new generation of Russian athletes may go further than necessary to achieve the objectives of the WADC.

718. ... The relief to be granted must, as submitted by IOC, strike a balance between the toughest consequences in light of the seriousness of the non-compliance, following any applicable rules of natural justice and respective human rights, and be sufficiently specific to be implemented without unnecessary risk of ancillary disputes.

- The panel then declared that the consequences proposed by WADA would be imposed for a set period, ie Russia would be barred from hosting any world championships, its officials would be barred from sitting on the boards or committees of any international federation, and it would be barred from entering any team in the Olympics or Paralympics or any world championships as representatives of Russia, or under the Russian flag and anthem. Instead Russian athletes would have to compete as neutral athletes, albeit in uniforms that bear the Russian colours. However, the panel said that *'principles of proportionality'* meant that period should be two years, rather than the four proposed by WADA, so that it would run till the end of 2022, not 2024.[99]

As a result, at the 2020 Summer Olympics in Tokyo, which was delayed until August 2021 due to Covid, and at the 2022 Winter Olympics in Beijing, Russian athletes competed under the team name *'ROC'* rather than *'Russia'*, their team uniforms did not feature the Russian flag, and when they won medals the Russian flag was not flown and the Russian national anthem was not played at the medal ceremonies or anywhere else at any Games venue. The same restrictions applied in the world championships of Signatory sports taking place between December 2019 and the end of 2022.

The CAS Panel's decision to apply the consequences for only two years, rather than the four years requested by WADA, was undoubtedly disappointing.[100] It prompted renewed criticisms of WADA and the CRC from both sides of the argument. ROC President Stanslav Pozdnyakov said: *'In this case, common sense prevailed over some elements of hatred of our country, one single British lawyer'*.[101] I reject that allegation: I don't hate Russia; the CRC was reacting to irrefutable evidence of cheating by the Russian authorities, and its reaction would have been the same if any other country had cheated on such a grand scale. On the other hand, Travis Tygart's response – *'it's clear that WADA ... has told athletes that it did not hear them and that they don't matter. Russia has claimed victory today and, for them and their ability to corrupt global sport, deceive the world, and cheat the global anti-doping system, they are right'*[102] – was also wrong. WADA had committed huge resources to the case in an effort to vindicate the rights of clean athletes, but the ISCCS – which USADA had supported – made it clear that the final decision on consequences must be made not by WADA but by an independent CAS panel, based on its own analysis of what is proportionate in all the circumstances of the case. And while Mr Pozdnyakov may have been *'claiming victory'*, tell that to the Russian athletes who had to compete as neutrals at these elite events rather than under the Russian flag and who were denied the chance to celebrate their achievements with the Russian national anthem.

Ultimately the question is whether the memory of this humiliation will be enough to deter the Russian authorities, and their counterparts in other countries, from ever again conspiring to corrupt the anti-doping system in the way it was corrupted from 2011 to 2015. Or, if not, whether it might embolden future generations of Russian athletes to refuse to acquiesce in such schemes. None of us can know this; we will all just have to wait and see. What is clear, however, is that the data and samples that were retrieved by WADA I&I from the Moscow anti-doping laboratory in 2019 have enabled WADA and its stakeholders to bring many of the Russian athletes who doped as part of the 2011-2015 scheme to justice, with their results disqualified and their places and medals being withdrawn and re-allocated to the rightful winners. On 13 August 2025, WADA reported that the data and samples had generated a total of 322 cases to that date, of which 280 had resulted in findings of anti-doping rule violations, 29 were still pending, and 13 were still under investigation by the relevant WADA stakeholders.[103] By November 2025, 298 cases had resulted in sanctions, and nine cases were still pending.[104] In other words, in 298 cases so far (and counting), justice has been served in a way that would not have been possible if the data and samples had not been retrieved. In particular, Russian athletes have been stripped of seven gold medals, nine silvers and four bronzes originally awarded at the 2012 London Summer Olympics, as well as of five of seven golds and two of four silvers originally awarded at the 2013 IAAF World Championships, and three of 13 golds and one of eleven silvers originally awarded at the 2014 Sochi Winter Olympics.[105] In addition, 87 athletes that the ROC put forward for the Pyeongchang Olympics were excluded from that Games because they were implicated by the LIMS data recovered from the Moscow lab (see p 107). That is by no means everything we might have wished for, but it is consequential nevertheless.

The reinstatement of RusAF

Going back to athletics, since its appointment in June 2016 the IAAF Taskforce had worked hard to assess the efforts of RusAF to reform Russian athletics. This included meeting with Vitaly Stepanov, Hajo Seppelt, and Gunter Younger to understand the extent of ARAF and RUSADA corruption, as well as 19 meetings (including ten in Moscow) with representatives of RusAF and various other Russian authorities to assess their reform efforts.[106] The most memorable of these were a meeting in early 2016 with Russian Sports Minister, Vitaly Mutko, who insisted in an extraordinarily tedious hour-long monologue that his Ministry strongly supported the fight against doping in sport and had never been involved in the doping of Russian athletes; and an extremely tense meeting with Colonel Zherdev of the Russian Investigative Committee, who did not take kindly to being pressed on whether his committee would be investigating the alleged involvement of Ministry officials and FSB agents in the cover-up of that doping. RusAF implemented a number of reforms quickly, including replacing Valentin Balakhnichev with a new president, Dmitri Shlyakhtin, and rolling out anti-doping education programmes for its athletes and coaches. But the failure to change the underlying doping culture in Russian athletics, demonstrated by the continuing hostility shown to whistleblowers like Yuliya Stepanova, who was branded a *'Judas'*,[107] and the emergence of more and more evidence that the Russian Sports Ministry had indeed been involved in the doping conspiracy, prompted the Taskforce's June 2016 recommendation (discussed at p 89 above) that RusAF's membership should remain suspended, and that only untainted Russian athletes should be permitted to compete (as '*neutral athletes*') in the Rio Olympics.

By July 2018, RusAF had made the required improvements to its governance and operations, but three reinstatement conditions remained outstanding:

(1) the Russian authorities had not yet acknowledged and addressed (or refuted) the McLaren and Schmid findings that Russian Sports Ministry officials were implicated in the doping conspiracy;

(2) RUSADA had not yet been reinstated as a fully reformed and independent NADO, capable of conducting reliable testing of Russian athletes; and

(3) the AIU had not yet been given access to the analytical data and samples that it needed to resolve the suspicious test results of Russian track & field athletes from the period 2012-15 that were stored in the hidden section of the Moscow laboratory's LIMS database.

By June 2019, those three conditions had also been met (see pp 105–107), but the Athletics Integrity Unit advised the World Athletics Council that Mr Shlyakhtin and two other senior RusAF officials had been complicit in the provision of fabricated medical records by high jumper Danil Lysenko in an attempt to avoid a whereabouts violation; while (as noted above: see pp 107–108) in September 2019 WADA I&I's forensic experts concluded that the Russian authorities had deliberately tampered with the LIMS data before providing it to the AIU, in an attempt to cover up doping by Russian track & field athletes. In November 2019 the World Athletics Council suspended the reinstatement process, and in March 2020, after RusAF sacked Mr Shlyakhtin and his colleagues and admitted the AIU charges, the Council fined RusAF $10 million for the Lysenko tampering, warned that any repeat would likely prompt a proposal to expel RusAF from membership, and asked the Taskforce to devise a new strategic plan and operational roadmap for the lifting of RusAF's suspension, to be supervised on the ground in Russia by international experts, including Peter Nicholson, fresh from his role helping WADA oversee RUSADA's reinstatement.[108]

In 2022, RusAF acknowledged the historic cheating by Russian athletes implicated by the LIMS data, rolled out a comprehensive anti-doping education programme for new generations of Russian athletes, and facilitated comprehensive testing of those athletes by RUSADA.[109] After a successful independent audit of RusAF's operations in late 2022, the World Athletics Council agreed in March 2023 to lift the suspension of RusAF's membership, subject to its continuing compliance with various special conditions designed to ensure that there could be no backsliding. This meant there was no longer any anti-doping bar to RusAF entering teams in international competitions.[110] By that point, however, the World Athletics Council had banned Russia due to its invasion of Ukraine in March 2022, and so the Russian athletes continued to be excluded from international competition in any event.

Cleaning house at the international federations

What about the presidents and other officials at the international federations who had assisted in covering up the Russian doping scheme by ensuring that any positive results from the federations' own testing of Russian athletes were not effectively pursued?

The former IAAF President, Lamine Diack, was put under house arrest in Paris from November 2015 until September 2020, when he was convicted by a French court of accepting bribes to cover up doping by Russian athletes. He was sentenced to four years in prison (two suspended) and fined 500,000 euros, but due to his age (by now he was 87) he was allowed to go back to Senegal pending resolution of other bribery allegations, and he died in December 2021. The French courts also convicted his son, the IAAF's '*marketing consultant*', Papa Massata Diack, who was sentenced to five years in prison and fined one million euros for his corrupt handling of Russian doping cases, but also remained in Senegal, prompting Interpol to issue a Red Notice for his arrest at the request of the French authorities.[111] In September 2025, the media reported that following his appeal the criminal case against him would be re-tried in part,[112] and at the time of writing that appeal had not yet been resolved. But his lifetime ban from the sport of athletics issued by the IAAF Ethics Commission (see fn 38) remains in place.

Meanwhile, information provided by a whistle-blower in November 2016 prompted WADA to open an investigation into the handling of Russian doping cases by the International Biathlon Union and its autocratic Norwegian president, Anders Besseberg, who had been in that post since 1993. WADA passed on its findings to Interpol and the Norwegian and Austrian police (the IBU's headquarters are in Salzburg) in 2017, and the Austrian police then tapped the phones of Besseberg and the IBU Secretary-General, Nicole Resch, leading to police raids of the IBU headquarters and of the homes of Besseberg and Resch in April 2018, following which Mr Besseberg resigned as IBU President. The IBU Executive Committee then appointed an External Review Commission to ensure the criminal authorities were given full support in their investigations, to consider whether Mr Besseberg, Ms Resch and/or any other IBU officials had a case to answer for breach of the IBU's rules, and to advise on reforms of the IBU's constitution to strengthen its governance and integrity protections. I chaired that Commission, alongside former biathlete Vincent Defrasne, German lawyer Tanja Haug, and Austrian lawyer Christian Dorda. Bird & Bird's Lauren Pagé acted as counsel to the Commission, ensuring (among other things) that the Austrian and the Norwegian police had full access to documents and other information in the IBU's files. We also reviewed thousands of documents in the IBU's own files, and interviewed approximately sixty witnesses, including Grigory Rodchenkov, who by that stage was in witness protection in the US. We issued our report in September 2020,[113] and the findings it contained draw together many of the different threads of the Russian doping conspiracy discussed in this chapter:

> 1.1. This final report of the independent IBU External Review Commission exposes systematic corrupt and unethical conduct at the very top of the IBU for a decade (2008 to 2018) and more, by a president (Anders Besseberg, IBU President 1993 to 2018) who had no regard for ethical values and no real interest in protecting the sport from cheating. Enabled by a complete lack of basic governance safeguards that left integrity decisions in the sole hands of the President and his allies on the IBU Executive Board, with no checks and balances, no transparency, and no accountability whatsoever to keep them honest, Mr Besseberg's proclaimed commitment to clean sport was a charade. He and his allies

recounted by rote their supposed *'zero tolerance for doping'*, but did only the absolute minimum that was necessary to preserve a veneer of respectability for the sport.

1.2 In the Commission's view, the pattern of corrupt and unethical decision-making was apparent long before evidence of an institutionalised doping conspiracy in Russia started to emerge in 2014 and 2015, but it was clearly exposed by Mr Besseberg's woeful response to that evidence, even as [the flow of evidence] turned inexorably from a trickle to a stream to a torrent. He and his allies insisted that Dr Grigory Rodchenkov was a liar and a fantasist, that Professor Richard McLaren was a gullible fool, and that even if the Russian Ministry of Sport and the Moscow doping control laboratory had conspired to cheat the anti-doping system, there was no evidence that the Russian Biathlon Union (the RBU) or any of its athletes were knowingly involved. They did not trouble themselves with wondering why the RBU would be excluded from such a conspiracy, or how an athlete could be injected with rEPO or doped with steroids without knowing about it. Doping, they said, had to be proved by catching athletes with prohibited substances in their systems. Anything less than a positive drugs test was not good enough, whatever any commission or doping panel might say.

1.3 Eventually, thanks to the bravery of whistle-blowers, the stalwart efforts of investigative journalists and of the Intelligence & Investigations Department of the World Anti-Doping Agency (WADA), and the steadfastness of a few biathlon leaders who were determined to fight for clean sport notwithstanding the hostile and intimidating reaction from Mr Besseberg and his allies, the evidence of the nature and scope of the Russian doping conspiracy, and the scale of its impact on biathlon, have finally emerged. The long list of proven doping cases that is set out in this Final Report reveals not only that blood doping and steroid abuse were widespread within the Russian national biathlon team in the period 2008 to 2014, but also that conspirators intervened at every stage to cover up that doping and to enable the cheating to continue.

...

1.6.4 It was Mr Tikhonov and Mr Kravtsov that Dr Rodchenkov witnessed discussing in the summer of 2013 how much they had paid Mr Besseberg to do their bidding. The Austrian and Norwegian criminal authorities have identified financial evidence sufficient to warrant setting up a joint taskforce to investigate the bribery allegation against Mr Besseberg, while the Commission has identified extensive provision of favours by the Russians to Mr Besseberg, particularly in the form of free hunting trips and the services of prostitutes. That Mr Besseberg acted under improper Russian influence may (in the Commission's view) be inferred from his consistent and implacable favouring of Russian interests, even when doing so was against all reason, [and] even when doing so took him well over the line of propriety into clear breach of his duties as IBU President.

...

1.7.1 In reaction to the initial disclosures by the Pound Commission, and the suggestion that biathlon should consider whether it had been affected by the conspiracy, Mr Besseberg did not propose that the IBU set up its own commission to investigate. Instead, the IBU Executive Board that he presided over instructed the IBU Secretary General to write an indignant letter to WADA, demanding that evidence be produced to justify the suggestion that biathlon may have been affected.

1.7.2 Similarly, Mr Besseberg reacted to WADA's call for international federations to honour their commitment as Code signatories not to grant their World Championships to a country whose corrupt national anti-doping organisation had been declared non-compliant by complaining that Russian biathlon should not have to suffer from the wrongdoing of others, and by telling the IBU's member federations at the 2016 IBU Congress that they could grant the 2021 IBU World Championships to Tyumen, Russia, without breaching that commitment, when that was clearly not the case. When WADA and the Czech national biathlon federation called him out on these actions, he had no defence, but was forced to capitulate, pausing only to state falsely to his detractors that the IBU Legal Committee had confirmed that the IBU had complied with its Code obligations, when in truth that committee had done no such thing.

1.7.3 The evidence reflects that, even while acknowledging on the side that there had been a conspiracy between the Moscow laboratory and the Russian Sports Ministry, Mr Besseberg reacted to Professor McLaren's report detailing the conspiracy by insisting loudly that it was not worth the paper it was written on, because it relied solely on the evidence of a man, Dr Rodchenkov, who was not to be trusted. The fact that two separate IOC Disciplinary Commissions (the Oswald Commission and the Schmid Commission) agreed with Professor McLaren that Dr Rodchenkov's testimony was corroborated by the objective evidence and was credible did not give Mr Besseberg pause. And while he agreed with his fellow IBU Executive Board members that the IBU should support the IOC's decision (based on the Schmid Commission's findings) to ban the Russian team from the 2018 Olympic Games, and should not lobby the IOC to allow Russian athletes to compete in Pyeongchang, there is clear evidence that he then disregarded that decision and went behind the IBU Executive Board's back to argue to the IOC that the RBU and its athletes were blameless and should be allowed to participate in the 2018 Games.

1.7.4 In late 2017 and early 2018, leading biathletes and IBU member federations and even the IBU's broadcasters pleaded to the IBU to send a message in support of clean sport by moving the 2018 IBU World Cup final event out of Tyumen. However, Mr Besseberg insisted that it was for the IBU Executive Board alone to make that decision, and then ensuring it did so in favour of Russia, first by using his double (casting) vote to defeat a motion at the Executive Board to move the event ..., and then by telling the Executive Board members that they could be held personally

> liable for the losses of the Tyumen Organising Committee, and may lose their houses, if they took the event away from Russia after the hosting contract had been signed. …

We noted that Mr Besseberg had denied any wrongdoing, but said the evidence we had seen established a clear case for him to answer for breach of his duties under the IBU rules to act at all times with the utmost of integrity, to protect the rights of clean athletes, and not to take any actions that were contrary to the interests of the sport. At the 2019 IBU Congress, the IBU's member federations accepted our recommendation to adopt a new IBU constitution and new governance systems moving forward. In particular, the new constitution introduced (a) term limits for IBU Executive Board members; (b) more transparency and more accountability for IBU decision-making; (c) integrity-related eligibility requirements for anyone wishing to hold IBU office; and (d) the transfer of exclusive authority over the policing and enforcement of new IBU integrity rules to a properly-resourced and independent Biathlon Integrity Unit (the '*BIU*'). We noted it would be for the BIU to decide what cases, if any, should be brought against IBU officials and/or Russian biathletes based on the evidence we had found.[114]

In October 2022, the BIU brought disciplinary charges against Mr Besseberg for breach of the IBU Code of Ethics, on the basis that he had received bribes from Russian officials to influence IBU decisions impacting Russian biathlon. A CAS panel upheld the charges in March 2025, and banned Mr Besseberg from the sport for life.[115]

In March 2023, the Norwegian public prosecutors charged Mr Besseberg with criminal corruption on the same basis. He was convicted in April 2024, on 2 September 2025 a criminal appeal court affirmed his first instance conviction and sentenced him to three years in prison,[116] and on 23 December 2025 the Supreme Court of Norway declined to hear his appeal against that decision. In the accompanying press release, the prosecutor who had brought the case, Marianne Djupesland, said: '*We assume that the judgement will send a message beyond Norway's borders. The case will hopefully raise awareness of the risk of corruption in sport. International top-level sport generates substantial revenues, and decisions of great importance to athletes, host nations and businesses tend to be made by international federations with limited transparency and accountability. That may increase the risk of corruption*'.[117]

Finally, in January 2020 another Hajo Seppelt documentary asserted that Tamás Aján, President of the International Weightlifting Federation since 2000, had covered up positive doping tests of elite weightlifters, including World Championship medallists.[118] A subsequent investigation by Richard McLaren concluded that '*Dr. Aján's autocratic authoritarian leadership of the International Weightlifting Federation resulted in a dysfunctional, ineffective oversight of the organisation by the Executive Board*', that this had enabled Aján to interfere with the operations of the IWF Anti-Doping Commission, and that forty positive drugs tests had been buried.[119] Meanwhile a WADA I&I investigation looked into related claims, including that Tamás Aján was paid to promote Russian interests and to protect Russian athletes from detection.[120] Evidence was passed to the Hungarian National Bureau of Investigations Financial Crime and Anti-Corruption Department, and also to the International Testing Agency (the '*ITA*'), a new independent anti-doping agency that had been founded as part of the response to the Russian scandal. The ITA's investigation culminated in charges against Aján and IWF Vice-President Nicolae Vlad for covering up, obstructing and/or delaying results management against several athletes so that they could compete in the Olympic Games and other events.[121] Those athletes were not Russians, but the report also noted that cases had been brought against 20 Russian weightlifters based on the LIMS data recovered from the Moscow anti-doping laboratory, and that as of June 2021 12 of them had been sanctioned by the IWF Hearing Panel.[122] The remaining cases were resolved and sanctions imposed either by the IWF Hearing Panel or by the CAS Anti-Doping Division.[123] In June 2022, the CAS upheld the charges brought by the ITA on behalf of the IWF against Aján and Vlad, and banned them both for life.[124]

Postscript

While it became very clear in 2016 that WADA, the sports movement, and the system created under the 2009 World Anti-Doping Code were woefully ill-equipped to punish the state-sponsored doping that took place in Russia between 2011 and 2015, ultimately there was at least a reckoning of sorts. In particular, no Russian politicians, team, flag or anthems were permitted at three Olympic Games. Instead, only individual Russian athletes who could show they were not tainted by that doping scheme were permitted to compete, as '*Olympic Athletes from Russia*' in Pyeongchang 2018,[125] and under the name 'ROC' rather than 'Russia' in Tokyo 2020 and Beijing 2022 (see p. 112). There were similar exclusions from other events. In addition, those at the very top of the IAAF, IBU, and IWF who had been complicit in the Russian scheme were exposed and punished; a comprehensive new system was introduced for WADA to police Code compliance and punish non-compliance by Signatories moving forward, supported by a new WADA Intelligence & Investigations Department; international federations transferred the policing of their anti-doping rules to independent integrity units and/or to the ITA and the CAS Anti-Doping Division; and hundreds of Russian athletes who had doped as part of the conspiracy were banned and had their results disqualified and their medals forfeited, so that the record books could be re-written and the medals could be re-allocated to the rightful winners. While that is certainly not as much as many wanted, hopefully the history books will at least say that the crisis was not entirely wasted.

Notes

1 WADA Director-General Olivier Niggli, *WADA ExCo approves 2026 List, alleges Kenyan NADO non-compliance*, WADA press release, 11 September 2025.
2 Pound R. et al, *Independent Commission Report No. 1*, 9 December 2015, p.3.
3 Daily Mirror front page headline, 10 November 2015.
4 Rodchenkov G., *The Rodchenkov Affair: How I Brought Down Putin's Secret Doping Empire* (Penguin 2021), Introduction and p.249.
5 See Franke W. and Berendonk B., *Hormonal doping and androgenization of athletes: a secret program of the German Democratic Republic government* (1997) Clinical Chemistry, 43:1262–1279; Ungerleider, *Faust's Gold: Inside the East German Doping Machine* (St Martins Press, 2001).
6 See generally Sottas P. et al., *The Athlete Biological Passport* (2011) 57(7) Clinical Chemistry 969– 976.
7 Rodchenkov G., *The Rodchenkov Affair: How I Brought Down Putin's Secret Doping Empire* (Penguin 2021).
8 *Icarus*, directed by Bryan Fogel, released January 2017, available on Netflix (netflix.com/title/80168079).
9 Rodchenkov G., *The Rodchenkov Affair: How I Brought Down Putin's Secret Doping Empire* (Penguin 2021), p.267.

10 Associated Press, *WADA: Russia lab must improve*, 17 November 2013.
11 Pound R. et al, *Independent Commission Report No. 1*, 9 December 2015, pp.207-09.
12 Walsh D., *The Russian Affair: The True Story of the Couple who Uncovered the Greatest Sporting Scandal* (Simon & Schuster 2020).
13 See WADA, *Progress of the Anti-Doping System in light of the Russian Doping Crisis*, 2 July 2019.
14 Available at youtube.com/watch?v=iu9B-ty9JCY (accessed 30 August 2025).
15 WADA, *Independent Commission – Terms of Reference*, 2015 (wada-ama.org/en/resources/independent-commission-terms-of-reference, accessed 5 December 2025).
16 Walsh D., *From Lance to Landis: Inside the American Doping Controversy at the Tour de France* (Ballantine Books, 2007); Walsh D., *Seven Deadly Sins: My Pursuit of Lance Armstrong* (Simon & Schuster UK, 2013).
17 Available at youtube.com/watch?v=nlkiC3iT0GA, accessed 30 August 2025.
18 Calvert J. and Arbuthnott G., *Revealed: Sport's Dirtiest Secret*, The Sunday Times, 2 August 2015.
19 Associated Press, *Lord Coe: allegations against IAAF are a declaration of war on my sport*, The Guardian, 4 August 2015.
20 Independent Commission, *Statement regarding Extended Mandate of Independent Commission*, 14 August 2015, available on wada-ama.org (emphasis in original).
21 House of Commons Digital, Culture, Media and Sport Committee, *Combatting doping in sport*, 5 March 2018.
22 *Paula Radcliffe denies cheating*, RTE, 8 September 2015.
23 *'Bayes's theory shows that the probability that A will occur if B occurs will generally differ from the probability that B will occur if A occurs'*: Mlodinow L., *The Drunkard's Walk* (Penguin, 2008), p.117. The prosecutor's fallacy is to ignore this premise and to assume instead that a low probability of evidence occurring if a defendant is innocent means that if that evidence exists (eg a 1-in-a-million DNA match) there is a low probability that the defendant is innocent. See McLaren R., *Athlete Biological Passport: The Juridical Viewpoint* [2012] I.S.L.R., Issue 4, pp.83-84, 93 (*'Currently the recommended level of variation required to initiate a review based on the ABP is a blood marker outside the 99.9th percentile. This means that the probability that the same value would be observed in a similar healthy, non-doping athlete is approximately one in every thousand times tested. ... This part of the review should not be confused with the probability of doping. The profile only establishes the likelihood of observing certain values assuming that the athlete is healthy and not doping. ... The profile cannot establish the probability of doping. ... A blood marker outside the acceptable levels cannot establish that an athlete has engaged in blood doping. It is only after experts have reviewed the profile and discounted all other possible explanations ... that a likelihood of doping can be determined. ... Otherwise sanctions will be delivered based on the faulty reasoning earlier referred to as the prosecutor's fallacy'*).
24 IAAF press release, *IAAF's response to allegations of blood doping in athletics*, 27 November 2015, linking to *IAAF Blood-Testing 2001-2012: IAAF's Response to Allegations of Blood Doping in Athletics*, Monaco, November 2015.
25 Ingle S., *'Disgraced' IAAF has failed its athletes, say embattled anti-doping scientists*, The Guardian, 28 November 2015.
26 House of Commons Digital, Culture, Media and Sport Committee, *Combatting doping in sport*, 5 March 2018.
27 Pound Commission Report No.2, 14 January 2016, amended 27 January 2016, at para 73.
28 Pound Commission Report No.2, 14 January 2016, amended 27 January 2016, pp.51-52, 69, 74, 76-78.
29 The Commission noted that as of December 2015, the IAAF had brought the most ABP cases (70) of any anti-doping organisation, with 51 of them leading to athletes being sanctioned, eight under appeal at CAS, six awaiting decisions, and five with ABP documentation packs prepared.
30 *Anti-doping experts Michael Ashenden and Robin Parisotto issue statements in response to WADA IC Report – both men are willing to let Seb Coe lead the IAAF moving forward*, letsrun.com, 15 January 2016.
31 Broadbent R., *Radcliffe wants her name cleared in public*, The Times, 15 January 2016.
32 The Committee did not publish any report until 5 March 2018. In that report, it acknowledged that WADA's experts had criticised the conclusions of Ashenden and Parisotto, but insisted that there remained a good faith dispute between those two scientists and the IAAF as to *'whether the IAAF should have been more proactive in following up results'*. House of Commons Digital, Culture, Media and Sport Committee, *Combatting doping in sport*, 5 March 2018, p.20.
33 See the Athletics Integrity Unit's homepage, athleticsintegrity.org (accessed 22 September 2025).

34 Ingle S., *Lamine Diack, former IAAF head, under investigation in corruption and doping inquiry*, The Guardian, 4 November 2015.

35 Pound R. et al, *Independent Commission Report No. 1*, 9 December 2015, p.124, p.48 and *passim*.

36 IAAF press releases, *IAAF provisionally suspends Russian Member Federation ARAF*, 13 November 2015, and *ARAF accepts full suspension – IAAF Council meeting, Monaco*, 26 November 2015.

37 Ingle S., *Russian Anti-Doping Agency suspended by Wada for non-compliance*, The Guardian, 18 November 2015.

38 Shobukhova's agent referred the matter to the IAAF Ethics Commission, chaired by Michael Beloff QC, ruled on 7 January 2016 that Valentin Balakhnichev, Alexei Melnikov, Gabriel Dollé and Papa Massata Diack had breached the IAAF Code of Ethics by covering up anti-doping rule violations by Ms Shobukhova and by extorting money from her in return for that cover-up, and banned Dollé for five years and the others for life. See IAAF Ethics Commission decision 02/2016, 7 January 2016 (blackstonechambers.com/documents/IAAF_Ethics_Commission_-_Decision_02-2016.pdf, accessed 30 August 2025). Appeals by Balakhnichev, Melnikov and Diack against their life bans were rejected by CAS in August 2017. See CAS press release, *CAS upholds the life bans imposed by the IAAF on Valentin Balakhnichev, Alexei Melnikov and Papa Massata Diack*, tas-cas.org, 21 August 2017,

39 *The Independent Commission Report 2*, 14 January 2016, amended 27 January 2016, p.47 and *passim*.

40 Ruiz R. and Schwirtz M., *Russian Insider Says State-Run Doping Fueled Olympic Gold*, New York Times, 12 May 2016. See also Keteyian, *Russian doping at Sochi Winter Olympics exposed*, 8 May 2016.

41 WADA, *Independent Investigation into the Sochi Allegations made by Grigory Rodchenkov, Terms of Reference.*

42 IOC press release, *Olympic Summit on 21 June 2016- information for the media*, 16 June 2016.

43 IOC press release, *Declaration of the Olympic Summit*, 21 June 2016.

44 McLaren R., *The Independent Person Report*, 16 July 2016.

45 WADA press release, *WADA statement: Independent investigation confirms Russian State manipulation of the doping control process*, 18 July 2016.

46 For example, *'[f]ormer Olympic champion Yuriy Burzakovskiy is now the head coach of the Russian national team, and is said to lead "a new generation" of clean Russian athletes. However Mr Burzakovskiy, and fellow Olympic champion Yelena Isinbaeva have both publicly dismissed the contents of the WADA Independent Commission's report as "groundless", even though in interviews with the Taskforce it emerged that neither of them has ever actually read that report'*: Taskforce Report to IAAF Council, 17 June 2016.

47 Taskforce Report to IAAF Council, 17 June 2016, paras 6.5 and 6.6.

48 Walsh D., *Coe: How he played the long game and won*, Sunday Times, 19 June 2016.

49 On 9 July 2016, the Doping Review Board ruled that Russian long-jumper Darya Klishina had met the requirements of IAAF Rule 22.1A in that, being based in the US since October 2013, she had been subject to fully compliant drug testing equivalent to the testing conducted on the athletes she would be competing against in Rio. But on 10 August 2016 it reversed that ruling based on evidence provided by Professor McLaren that one urine sample provided by Klishina in February 2014 had had a T/E ratio of 8.5, but had been the subject of a '*save*' order from the Ministry of Sport, and a sample collected from her in October 2014 sample bore scratches and marks indicative of sample swapping. On 15 August 2016, a CAS Panel sitting in Rio upheld her appeal against that decision, on the basis that even if she was subject to non-compliant drug-testing in Russia during the relevant period, she was still subject to fully compliant drug-testing in the USA during the same period, and so could be taken not to have been affected or tainted by the corrupted Russian testing system: *Klishina v IAAF*, CAS ad hoc Division OG 16/024. Klishina therefore became the only Russian track & field athlete to compete in Rio. She finished ninth in the women's long jump competition.

50 *ROC & Lyukman Adams et al v IAAF*, CAS 2016/O/4684, paras 119, 121, 122-24, 126-27, 128, 129, 131, 133, 141, 147, 148-50, 165, 167-68, 171.

51 IOC press release, *Statement of the Executive Board of the International Olympic Committee on the WADA Independent Person Report*, 19 July 2016.

52 *Russian Weightlifting Federation v International Weightlifting Federation*, CAS OG 16/09.

53 *Rio 2016: IOC to have final say on Russia competitors*, Al Jazeera, 31 July 2016.

54 *Rio 2016 Olympics: Russians "have cleanest team" as 271 athletes cleared to compete*, BBC, 5 August 2016.

55 Herbert I., *Rio 2016: Russia given Paralympics ban as 'medals over morals attitude' leaves president Philip Craven disgusted*, The Independent, 7 August 2016.

56 In his second report, published in December 2016, Professor McLaren made clear which approach he had preferred: *'After its release, the IOC chose to take actions based upon the Report from the perspective of individual competitors, in contrast to the International Paralympic Committee ("IPC"), which chose to take actions based upon the Report for what it was – a description of a systemic system of cover up and manipulation of the doping control process'. Independent Person Second Report*, 9 December 2016, p.8.

57 *Russian Paralympic Committee v International Paralympic Committee*, CAS 2016/A/4745. See also *Russian Paralympic Committee v International Paralympic Committee*, Swiss Federal Tribunal decision number 4A_470/2016 dated 20 August 2016 (SFT rejected request for provisional measures staying CAS award and requiring IPC to allow Russian para athletes to participate in Rio Paralympics); *Safronov et al v IPC*, 20 O 323/16, Landgericht Bonn decision dated 5 September 2016; *Arestova et al v IPC, Safronov et al v IPC*, Oberlandesgericht Dusselforf decisions dated 13 September 2016; and Bundesverfassungsgericht decision 1 BvQ 38/16 dated 15 September 2016 (German courts requesting requests from the athletes themselves for the same relief).

58 *Report of the Independent Observers, Games of the XXXI Olympiad, Rio de Janeiro 2016.*

59 Pound R. et al, *Independent Commission Report No. 1*, 9 December 2015, p.274.

60 IOC press release, *Background Information to the decision of the IOC Executive Board concerning the participation of Russian athletes in the Olympic Games Rio 2016*, 24 July 2016.

61 McLaren R., *Independent Person Second Report*, 9 December 2016, pp. 5, 18, 22; Whitmore, *Russia: Powerful New Investigative Body Begins Work*, rferl.org, 10 September 2007.

62 WADA press release, *WADA publishes RUSADA Roadmap to Code Compliance*, 2 August 2017.

63 Minutes of WADA Foundation Board meeting, Glasgow, 20 November 2016 (available on wada-ama.org), p.13.

64 Minutes of WADA Foundation Board meeting, Seoul, 16 November 2017 (available on wada-ama.org).

65 Minutes of WADA Foundation Board meeting, Seoul, 16 November 2017 (available on wada-ama.org).

66 Minutes of WADA Foundation Board meeting, Seoul, 16 November 2017 (available on wada-ama.org).

67 IOC Disciplinary Commission's Report to the IOC Executive Board, Lausanne, 2 December 2017.

68 IOC press release, *IOC suspends Russian NOC and creates a path for clean individual athletes to compete in PyeongChang 2018 under the Olympic Flag*, olympics.com, 5 December 2017. In the press release, the IOC pointedly noted: *'Due process, to which every individual and every organisation is entitled, was followed. This opportunity was not available to the IOC prior to the Olympic Games Rio 2016'.*

69 Chappell B., *Panel Dismisses 47 Russians' Appeal To Be Allowed Into Winter Olympics*, National Public Radio, 8 February 2018.

70 *Ahn et al v IOC*, CAS OG 18/02; *Legkov et al v IOC*, CAS OG 18/03.

71 Minutes of WADA Foundation Board meeting, Montreal, 17 May 2018 (available on wada-ama.org).

72 Letter from Craig Reedie and Olivier Niggli to Minister Kolobkov dated 22 June 2018 (available on wada-ama.org).

73 See eg *Blatter v FIFA*, CAS 2016/A/4501, para 95 (*'The prohibition against retroactivity is a fundamental principle of Swiss law and forms part of international public policy'*); *Anderson et al v IOC*, CAS 2008/A/1545, para 10 (*'[...] any determination of [...] what sanctions can be imposed must be done in accordance with the law in effect at the time of the allegedly sanctionable conduct'*).

74 Letter from Minister Kolobkov to Craig Reedie dated 13 August 2018 (available on wada-ama.org).

75 Letter from Minister Kolobkov to Craig Reedie dated 13 September 2018 (available on wada-ama.org).

76 x.com/danroan/status/1040296736995110913, 13 September 2018 (accessed 1 October 2025).

77 Letter from Jonathan Taylor QC to WADA Director General Olivier Niggli dated 14 September 2018 (available on wada-ama.org).

78 Letter dated 14 September 2018 from Beckie Scott to Craig Reedie, Olivier Niggli and Jonathan Taylor, reproduced in Convington's Report to the World Anti-Doping Agency Concerning Allegations of Bullying and Harassment, 15 May 2019 (available on wada-ama.org), at pp.22-23.

79 AFP. *'A catastrophe for clean sport': Wada set to reinstate Russia after doping suspension*, 15 September 2018.

80 BBC, *Russian doping ban: Panel advises WADA to bring end to RUSADA ban*, 14 September 2018; Reuters, *WADA committee recommends reinstatement of Russia's anti-doping agency*, 14 September 2018.
81 *Edwin Moses: WADA's credibility rides on its Russia decision*, NY Times Op-Ed, 15 September 2018.
82 At sportsintegrityinitiative.com/wada-denies-moving-the-goalposts-on-access-to-moscow-lab-data/ (accessed 2 October 2025).
83 WADA press release, *WADA Executive Committee decides to reinstate RUSADA subject to strict conditions*, 20 September 2018.
84 Reuters, *Doping: WADA didn't put money above clean sport on Russia, says chief*, 24 September 2018.
85 Morgan L., *WADA criticise "one-sided" anti-doping summit at White House*, insidethegames.biz, 31 October 2018.
86 Minutes of WADA Foundation Board meeting, Baku, 15 November 2018 (available on wada-ama.org).
87 Samuelsson S., *Open Letter to the Chair of WADA Compliance Committee, Mr. Jonathan Taylor*, 3 January 2019 (sportsintegrityinitiative.com/open-letter-to-the-chair-of-wada-compliance-committee-mr-jonathan-taylor/, accessed 27 September 2025). The response I sent to Mr Samuelsson the next day can be found at sportsintegrityinitiative.com/response-to-open-letter-from-sebastian-samuelsson/, accessed 27 September 2025.
88 WADA Intelligence & Investigations Department, Case 2017-10, *Final Report to the CRC regarding the Moscow data*, wada-ama.org, 20 November 2019.
89 *CRC Recommendation in relation to RUSADA*, 21 November 2019 (available on wada-ama.org).
90 WADA press release, *WADA Executive Committee unanimously endorses four-year period of non-compliance for the Russian Anti-Doping Agency*, 9 December 2019.
91 *'Russia pariah of world sport', says sports writer David Walsh*, Channel 4 News, 9 December 2019 (channel4.com/news/russia-pariah-of-world-sport-says-sports-writer-david-walsh, accessed 11 January 2026).
92 See eg UKAD statement, *UKAD response to WADA Executive Committee decision to impose four-year Russia ban*, ukad.org.uk, 9 December 2019; Australian Government, *Statement on WADA Russia decision*, health.gov.au, 10 December 2019; Institute of National Anti-Doping Organisations statement, *iNADO comments on today's decision of WADA's Executive Committee*, inado.org, 9 December 2019.
93 See Rob Koehler's attack, *WADA's very future at stake over Russian doping sanctions*, The Sunday Times, 15 December 2019 (*'If this level of egregious offence and disdain doesn't warrant a complete ban, it's difficult to imagine what will. There is no deterrence factor'*), and my response: *WADA has not treated Russia softly*, The Sunday Times, 22 December 2019 (*'… we cannot use the new rules that came into force in 2018 to punish the original wrongdoing; that would not stand up at CAS. To punish a new generation of Russian athletes not implicated in the original wrongdoing or by the latest transgressions would cut across WADA's mission to protect clean athletes, whatever their nationality. … I respect the athletes demanding a blanket ban in Tokyo, including Victoria Aggar, who quit the WADA Athletes Committee in protest. Yet many others believe WADA has struck the right balance, including eight of the 17 members of the WADA Athletes Committee, as well as the British Athletes Commission that Victoria chairs. While US anti-doping chief Travis Tygart pursues his longstanding anti-Russia and anti-WADA line, many other anti-doping organisations (including from the UK, Germany, and Australia) support WADA's stance. So while I am happy for Koehler to disagree with WADA's position, I am not happy for him to suggest that anyone who disagrees with him must be in thrall to the IOC or Russia. He should respect the views of all athletes, not just those sharing his views'*).
94 *Jonathan Taylor QC explains WADA's decision to sanction Russia*, lawinsport.com, 20 December 2019.
95 *WADA v RUSADA*, CAS 2020/O/6689.
96 *WADA v RUSADA*, CAS 2020/O/6689, para 582.
97 *WADA v RUSADA*, CAS 2020/O/6689, paras 509 and 609.
98 *WADA v RUSADA*, CAS 2020/O/6689, paras 614-15, 660, 670, 674.
99 *WADA v RUSADA*, CAS 2020/O/6689, para 744.
100 David Walsh speculated that this was a compromise made by the CAS Panel chair, Mark Williams, to get Dr Hamid Gharavi (RUSADA's nominee to the Panel) onside, so that the decision would be unanimous: Walsh D., *Reduction in Russia's ban should not be seen as a failure*, Sunday Times, 19 December 2020.
101 Morgan L., *Former WADA compliance panel chairman rejects Russian criticism of sanction recommendation*, insidethegames.biz, 2 January 2021.

102 USADA press release, *Statement from USADA CEO Travis T. Tygart on Russia CAS Appeal and Ruling*, 17 December 2020.
103 WADA 2024 Annual Report, August 2025 (available on wada-ama.org). See also Savinova, *RUSADA has completed the processing of athletes' cases from the database of the Moscow laboratory*, Sport Express Russia, 28 September 2025.
104 Unpublished email correspondence with WADA, 24 November 2025.
105 en.wikipedia.org/wiki/List_of_stripped_Olympic_medals, accessed 12 Sept 2025.
106 All of the IAAF Russia Taskforce's reports to Council and related documents were posted contemporaneously on the IAAF's website, and as of the time of writing they remain available there, at worldathletics.org/about-iaaf/documents/member-federation-resource-centre, under the heading '*Russian Reinstatement Conditions*'.
107 *Yuliya Stepanova: what do Russians think of doping whistleblower?*, bbc.co.uk, 30 December 2016.
108 World Athletics press release, *World Athletics Council issues package of sanctions in relation to RusAF's breach of anti-doping rules*, Monaco, 12 March 2020.
109 Report of the Russia Taskforce, November 2022 (available on worldathletics.org).
110 World Athletics press release, *World Athletics Council decides on Russia, Belarus and female eligibility*, Monaco, 23 March 2023.
111 Interpol, *Interpol issues Red Notice against Papa Massata Diack at France's request*, 14 January 2016.
112 BBC, *Lamine Diack: Former IAAF head found guilty of corruption and jailed*, bbc.co.uk, 16 September 2020; Newswire, *Paris Court postpones corruption retrial of ex-IAAF chief's son*, 3 September 2025.
113 *Final Report of the IBU External Review Commission*, 28 January 2021 (assets.ctfassets.net/cz0vl36hcq0x/7qVMY41VSetZAfKFMDL3ix/9ee089840f6321162af1de3d3ccff2e8/ERC_Final_report._Redacted_publication_version_28.01.2021.pdf, accessed 22 September 2025) (internal cross-references omitted).
114 *Final Report of the IBU External Review Commission*, 28 January 2021 (assets.ctfassets.net/cz0vl36hcq0x/7qVMY41VSetZAfKFMDL3ix/9ee089840f6321162af1de3d3ccff2e8/ERC_Final_report._Redacted_publication_version_28.01.2021.pdf, accessed 22 September 2025) at para 1.14 (emphasis in original).
115 BIU press release, *Biathlon Integrity Unit acknowledges CAS decision in case of Anders Bessberg*, biathlonintegrity.com, 14 March 2025, with link to award in *IBU v Besseberg*, CAS 2023/O/9541.
116 Okokrim press release, *Former biathlon president sentenced to 3 years in prison for aggravated corruption*, okokrim.no, 4 September 2025.
117 Okokrim press release, *Refusal to hear appeal to the Supreme Court: judgment against former biathlon president now final and enforceable*, okokrim.no, 23 December 2025.
118 EyeOpening Media GmbH, *Doping Top Secret: the Lord of the Lifters – How an Olympic sport is being destroyed*, 5 January 2020 (youtube.com/watch?v=EokLZCKgcFg, accessed 12 September 2025).
119 McLaren Global Sport Solutions, *Independent Investigator Report to the Oversight and Integrity Commission of International Weightlifting Federation*, 4 June 2020 (available on iwf.sport).
120 WADA press release, *WADA develops new method of identifying sample tampering as part of weightlifting investigation*, 22 October 2020.
121 *International Weightlifting Federation v Tamás Aján*, CAS 2022/ADD/41; *International Weightlifting Federation v Nicu Vlad*, CAS 2021/ADD/42.
122 *ITA Report on IWF Anti-Doping Rule Violations and Related Allegations of Misconduct*, 24 June 2021.
123 Unpublished email correspondence with WADA, 24 November 2025.
124 *International Weightlifting Federation v. Tamás Aján*, CAS 2022/ADD/41; *International Weightlifting Federation v. Nicu Vlad*, CAS 2021/ADD/42; ITA press release, *Former IWF president and IWF vice-president sanctioned with a lifetime ban as a result of ITA's prosecution*, ita.sport, 16 June 2022.
125 *IOC suspends Russian NOC and creates a path for clean individual athletes to compete in PyeongChang 2018 under the Olympic Flag*, IOC press release, olympics.org, 5 December 2017.

Chapter 5

A Different Kind of Girl

I support the fight for societal, political, and economic equality between the sexes. I also believe that anyone who identifies as a woman is entitled to have that identity respected, without prejudice or discrimination. And the sports governing bodies that I have represented share those values. They want as many people as possible to participate in their sports, and they also want to be a force for tolerance, diversity, equality, and inclusion in society generally. They would agree that '*[s]port has the power to change perceptions, prejudices, and behaviours. It must not be used to reinforce them*'.[1]

Why, then, have I spent the past decade helping many of those SGBs to restrict or prevent transgender and *'intersex'* athletes with a female gender identity from competing in the female category? Are critics right that I am just *'offensive and stupid'*?[2] Or *'bigoted ... sexist, racist [and] queerphobic'*?[3] Is Caster Semenya right that I should cut my tongue out and throw it away for defending those restrictions?[4] Is Kristen Worley right that I am *'the darkest of dark lawyers in world sport, ... a MONSTER'*?[5]

I hope the answer is no, but read on and judge for yourself.

Why do most sports have separate competitions for men and women?

Sport is a powerful weapon in the fight for female emancipation, because it empowers girls and women to realise their potential. *'Girls who play sport stay in school longer, suffer fewer health problems, enter the labor force at higher rates, and are more likely to land better jobs. They are also more likely to lead. [Ernst & Young] research shows stunningly that 94% percent of women C-Suite executives today played sport, and over half played at a university level. Competition – celebrating wins, surviving losses, requiring teamwork, rewarding persistence, resilience and discipline, these are the experiences we need in leaders and these are the experiences they gain in sport'*.[6] A great example is Doriane Lambelet Coleman, whose prowess as an elite middle-distance runner in the 1980s earned her a scholarship that enabled her to go first to college and then to law school in the US. She is now an eminent law professor at Duke University, one of the USA's most prestigious law schools.[7] It is therefore unsurprising that she is also a forceful advocate for the power of sport to promote sex equality in society generally.[8]

The international governing body of athletics, World Athletics, doesn't just say it believes in sex equality. It puts its money where its mouth is, staging both male and female competitions in all of the events at its major championships and in all but one event at the Olympic Games, and offering equal prize money to men and women across those competitions, including paying equal prize money to male and female Olympic gold medallists from Paris 2024 onwards.[9]

Why is it necessary, though, to stage separate male and female competitions? Why not have female athletes compete with the male athletes? I gave up the study of biology at the age of 16, and am sure my biology teachers thought that was not a moment too soon. But still I will try to explain, based on the painstaking education I have subsequently received from Stéphane Bermon, David Handelsman, Angelica Hirschberg, and the other amazing experts that I have met in the course of representing World Athletics and other SGBs in this area:

- Before puberty, a boy's testes and a girl's ovaries produce the same amount of testosterone (approximately 0.25 mg a day), giving them both between 0.06 and 1.68 nanomoles of testosterone per litre (nmol/L) of blood.[10]
- From puberty onwards:[11]
    - The girl's ovaries will continue to produce the same low levels of testosterone as they did pre-puberty, or perhaps slightly more. But they will also produce much more estradiol, the most potent and biologically active form of estrogen, which triggers development of the adult female body, geared for reproduction (monthly menstruation, the hips shifting down and out to facilitate childbirth, the storage of fat to support the baby *in utero* and at the breast), leading to reduced explosivity and a lower ratio of muscle to fat, both of which tend to impair sports performance.[12]
    - In contrast, the boy's testes start producing about 7 mg of testosterone per day, a 28-fold increase that generates circulating testosterone in the range 7.7 to 29.4 nmol/L.[13] That surge in testosterone drives a series of physiological changes that females do not experience. On average, adult males have bigger hands and feet, broader shoulders, narrower hips, and longer limbs than adult females (on average, they are 7-8% taller); they have less fat and larger and stronger muscles (on average, men have 18% more muscle mass than adult females; and adult females have only 50-60% of adult males' upper limb strength, and 60-80% of their leg strength); they have bigger hearts and therefore greater cardiac output (pumping more blood to the muscles) than adult females, and they have 12% more haemoglobin in that blood, which means their maximal oxygen transfer from lungs to muscles is about 10% more efficient.[14]
- As a result of these physiological differences, a significant sex difference in sports performance emerges from puberty onwards,[15] at least in those sports where power, strength and/or endurance play a decisive role.[16] The very best adult male athletes better the performances of the very best adult female athletes by 10-12% in track events, by 15-19% in jumping events, by 6-13% in swimming events, by 12-17% in cycling events, by 7-10% in speed skating, by 23-32% in weightlifting, and by much larger percentages in explosive power sports disciplines such as pitching, wrestling, and boxing.[17] In fact, hundreds if not thousands of the next best adult male athletes *also* outperform the very best adult female athletes, albeit by a smaller margin. For example, in 2022 the women's 100m world record (10.49, by Florence Griffith-Joyner) was beaten or equalled by 1,138 male athletes, the women's 200m world record (21.34, also by Griffith-Joyner) was beaten or equalled by 1,458 male athletes, the

> women's 400m world record (47.60 – Marita Koch) was beaten or equalled by 1,258 male athletes, the women's 800m world record (1.53:28 – Jarmila Kratochvilova) was beaten or equalled by 3,023 male athletes, the women's high jump world record (2.09m – Stefka Kostadinova) was beaten or equalled by 556 male athletes, and the women's long jump world record (7.52m – Galina Chistyakova) was beaten or equalled by 526 male athletes.

Historically, the sex difference in sports performance was undoubtedly exacerbated by the relative lack of opportunities and resources afforded to female athletes compared to their male counterparts. But that performance gap has not narrowed since the 1980s, even in those countries that now strive to give the same support and opportunities to female as to male athletes.[18] And because of the innate physiological advantages that males enjoy over females, no amount of training or resources will ever close that gap completely,[19] as occasional '*battles of the sexes*' have tended to show.[20] So in most sports there will always be a need for separate competition categories to ensure equal opportunities. If male and female athletes competed together, the female athletes would have no chance to succeed, *not* because of a lack of talent or effort on their part, but instead because of the male athletes' insurmountable physiological advantages. The best male athletes would win all the prize money, all the scholarship funds, and any other prizes on offer. Female athletes would never make it near the finals, let alone get onto the podium, however hard they worked. They would be lost in the crowd of also-rans, because of an innate disadvantage that they can do nothing to overcome. That would surely discourage many females from participating in the sport at all, let alone making the extreme sacrifices required in order to excel. And so the clear societal benefits that female participation in sport can deliver would be lost.

But if separate male and female competition categories are necessary, there have to be rules determining who is eligible to compete in the male category and who is eligible to compete in the female category. And that puts sports governing bodies right in the middle of the culture war that is currently raging between those who say that all that should matter is your gender identity (*'If Caster [Semenya] identifies as a woman, she should be able to compete as one* [...]. *It's as simple as that'*[21]) and those who say that in certain contexts, including sport, biology has to trump gender identity (*'You cannot guarantee a level playing field for women by letting in athletes according to what they perceive themselves to be, only according to what they immutably are'*[22]).

Is sex really binary?

The division of sporting competition into male and female categories assumes that sex is binary. And that is indeed the orthodox understanding, which is grounded in reproductive capacity: there are only two viable gametes (reproductive cells) in humans – sperm and eggs – and therefore there are only two sexes. Males have testes that produce sperm; females have ovaries that produce eggs. From this perspective, individuals cannot be both male and female, or a mix of male and female, or something between the two. Nor can they be some *other* sex, because there isn't one.[23]

There is a counter-argument, championed by feminist academic Dr Anne Fausto-Sterling,[24] that this orthodox understanding of a strict male/female binary is an illusion, that in fact *'male and female stand on the extreme end of a biological continuum'*,[25] and between those *'extremes'* sit *'intersex'* people, whose bodies *'contain a mixture of male and female parts'*.[26] For example, they may have both testicular and ovarian tissue (ovo-testes),[27] or they may have testes and a vagina (eg Complete Androgen Insensitivity Syndrome, 5-alpha reductase deficiency) or ovaries and a penis (Congenital Adrenal Hyperplasia/'*CAH*'). Dr Fausto-Sterling accepts that such *'intersex'* individuals may be a very small minority. Her estimate in 2000 that 1.728% of all births are intersex[28] is still widely cited,[29] even though she cautioned that was just an *'order of magnitude'* estimate. In 2003, she accepted a revised estimate of 0.373%,[30] and subsequently she has noted that the estimate reduces to 0.028% if you exclude cases of 46XX CAH.[31] So male and female are the overwhelming norms, not the *'extremes'*. But she insists that the very low prevalence of *'intersex'* individuals does not make them abnormal or unnatural. She also insists they are definitely not *'really'* male or female. Instead *'they constitute a category other than male or female'*.[32]

Dr Fausto-Sterling has never hidden the fact that her scientific analysis is driven by her political views, and in particular by her desire for social, economic and political equality between the sexes. In fact, she maintains there is no such thing as objective science; she insists it is all driven by underlying but unstated value judgements. For her, in other words, *'the biological debate does not stand separately. It is part of the political struggle. And so are we all'*.[33] Her contribution to that struggle has included skilfully demonstrating that perceived sex differences in cognitive ability, which are used as a purported justification for workplace discrimination, and in competitiveness, which are used as a purported explanation for male over-representation in leadership positions, are not due to innate biological differences, which cannot be changed, but rather to social conditioning (expectations and opportunities), which can. And in her view the existence of *'intersex'* people helps the sex equality argument, because there cannot be innate differences between the sexes, potentially justifying different rights for men and women, if there are people who are a mixture of male and female.[34] *That* is why she does not agree that *'intersex'* people are *'really'* males or females with unusual physiology, that *'lurking inside the mixed-sex child is a real male or female body'*, or that doctors need to decide whether a *'mixed-sex'* baby was *'supposed'* to be a boy or a girl, and to subject the baby to surgery to *'correct nature's mistake'*.[35]

Yes, sex is binary

I share Dr Fausto-Sterling's desire for social, political, and economic equality between the sexes. But in the context of sport, as already explained there are innate biological differences between men and women that necessitate separate competition categories in order to deliver that equality. And the scientific experts that I have worked with on this issue are clear that the so-called *'intersex'* 46XY athletes who compete at the elite levels of female competition are not *'a mixture of male and female'* whose *'bodies contain a mixture of male and female parts'*.[36] Instead, they are unmistakably and undeniably biological males:[37]

- Every foetus has primitive, bipotential (ie sex indifferent) gonads, as well as Wolffian ducts and Mullerian ducts.

- If the foetus has 46XX chromosomes, the primitive gonads develop into ovaries, the Wolffian ducts degenerate, and the Mullerian ducts develop into oviducts, uterus, fallopian tubes, cervix, and vagina.
- If the foetus has 46XY chromosomes, however, the SRY gene on the Y chromosome* triggers the primitive gonads to develop into testes, the Mullerian ducts degenerate, and the Wolffian ducts develop into the vas deferens, epididymis, and ejaculatory ducts.
- The 46XX foetal tissues will then form female external genitalia (vagina, labia, clitoris), while the 46XY foetal tissues, upon interaction with dihydrotestosterone, a powerful androgen (*'DHT'*), will form male external genitalia (penis, testes, scrotum).
- In very rare cases, this process is disrupted; hence the term *'difference in sex development'*, or *'DSD'*. As already noted, most commonly this happens to 46XX babies with CAH. The best estimate is that only 1 in 20,000 of 46*XY* babies have a DSD,[38] ie about 0.007% of the estimated 140 million births a year, which is just under 10,000 births globally per year.[39]
- In two 46XY DSD conditions, 17β and 5-ARD, the individual has a deficiency of an enzyme that is responsible for converting androstenedione into testosterone in the foetus (17β-hydroxysteroid dehydrogenase type 3) or of an enzyme (5-alpha reductase) that converts that testosterone into DHT, which drives the final stages of foetal development of the male genitalia. In each case, the resulting DHT deficiency means that the testes may not descend from the abdomen, and penis growth and scrotum formation will not occur to the usual degree in the womb. As a result, at birth the external genitals will be potentially ambiguous/female in appearance – for example, the under-virilised penis may resemble a large clitoris, and the unfused scrotum may resemble labia[40] – and therefore such babies might, in Dr Fausto-Sterling's words, be *'mistaken for girls'*.[41]
- Crucially, however, the testes of 46XY individuals with 5-ARD or 17β still function normally, and the DHT deficiency only has localised effects, in the genitals, prostate, and hair tissues, not systemic effects, eg on bone, muscle, or cardiovascular function. As a result, from puberty onwards those testes will start producing levels of testosterone within the normal adult male range, which will trigger development of the bigger and stronger bones and muscles, bigger heart and lungs, and higher levels of haemoglobin that cause the sex difference in adult sports performance. The 5-ARD and 17β pubescents may also experience penis growth, because there is now enough circulating testosterone to activate the relevant androgen receptors directly, without having to be converted to DHT first, and their testes, which may or may not descend, will produce sperm, enabling them to father children, using *in vitro* fertilisation if necessary.[42]
- For these reasons, the standard medical practice is to recommend that the parents raise a 46XY 5-ARD or 17β baby as male.[43] Currently only about a third of 46XY 5-ARD or 17β babies are raised as female, and this is likely to decrease over time as medical understanding of these conditions proliferates. Furthermore, because of the penis growth and other virilisation that takes place from puberty onwards (a transition that is known colloquially as *'guevedoche'* – *'balls at twelve'*

* *'SRY'* stands for sex-determining region on the Y chromosome.

– in the Dominican Republic, and *'turniman'* in New Guinea), 56-63% of the 5-ARD individuals who are initially raised as female and 39-64% of the 17β individuals who are initially raised as female adopt a male gender identity after puberty. As a result, only a small minority (12.5% to 20%) of all 5-ARD and 17β individuals have a female gender identity after puberty.[44]

- Two other 46XY DSDs are Complete Androgen Insensitivity Syndrome (CAIS) and Partial Androgen Insensitivity Syndrome (PAIS). In these cases, again the testes develop normally, although they remain undescended, and produce levels of testosterone in the normal adult male range from puberty onwards. Due to a gene mutation, however, the androgen receptors in the affected individual's cells are completely or partially insensitive to that testosterone, so negating (CAIS) or reducing (PAIS) its virilising effect on the individual's body. In cases of complete insensitivity, the male external genitalia do not develop at all, and nor do the secondary male sex characteristics at puberty. Instead, because their receptors *are* sensitive to the estradiol that is produced by conversion of testosterone from the testes by aromatase activity,[45] CAIS individuals have external genitals that are female in appearance (albeit that the *'vagina'* is short and blind-ending, because there is no cervix or uterus or ovaries for it to connect to[46]), and as a result they are usually reared as female.[47] In PAIS cases, gender assignment at birth largely depends on the degree of (in)sensitivity and therefore the degree of virilisation (or lack thereof) of the external genitals. In most PAIS cases (c.60%), the advice given is to rear the child as male rather than female;[48] and where the individual is raised as female, again the virilisation that takes place at puberty may lead to gender re-assignment at that point from female to male.[49]

What does all of this tell us?

- First, it tells us that *'intersex'* – which is a sociological term, not a scientific one[50] – is a misnomer. People with a 46XY DSD are not *'a mixture of male and female'*, with *'a mixture of male and female parts'*. Instead they are males with an enzyme deficiency or an androgen insensitivity that means at birth their testes remain in the abdomen or the inguinal canal, and their penis and scrotum are under-developed and may in some cases look more like a clitoris and labia.

- Second, it tells us that, for the same reasons, these extremely rare conditions do not change the fundamental bipolarity of biological sex, just as the (also rare) incidence of people with only one kidney or with a heart with fewer than four chambers does not change the fact that the human body has two kidneys and a heart with four chambers.[51]

- Third, it explains why the majority of *'intersex'* individuals *'view themselves as ordinary men or women who happen to have been born with an unusual medical condition'*.[52]

- Fourth, it tells us why most 46XY individuals with 5-ARD or 17β identify as male rather than female, including many of the minority of those individuals who were reared as female until puberty.

- And fifth, it tells us that 5-ARD and 17β adults have normally functioning testes, have undergone normal male puberty, and therefore have all of the same physiological advantages over biological females as 46XY males without DSDs enjoy. Their only potential differences from other 46XY biological males, due to their DHT deficiency, are in the appearance of their external genitals, their hair pattern (they may have male pattern baldness), and the size of their prostate.

In sport, biological sex has to trump gender identity

The Encyclopaedia Britannica states: *'Sex is a biological classification that divides a species into two complementary categories based on physiological characteristics, including chromosomes and reproductive organs. ... . By contrast, gender is a social construct ... . Because one's sex and gender identity may not always correspond, it's important to distinguish between the two in order to create appropriate health care, programs, and policies for all people'.*[53] This seems indisputable. Even if an individual has a female gender identity, if they have testes rather than ovaries they need to be monitored for testicular cancer, not ovarian cancer. And if they want to understand their reproductive options, they need advice on the chances of paternity using their sperm and IVF; they have no maternity options, because they have no ovaries or womb. Even Dr Fausto-Sterling agrees: *'If we are talking about groupings needed for reproduction, then it makes sense to discuss people who produce eggs and sperm'.*[54]

Is sport another context where biology has to trump gender identity? More specifically, what if an athlete has the SRY gene, and so has testes rather than ovaries, and so has levels of circulating testosterone in the adult male range, and so (unless they are androgen-insensitive) has all of the physiological advantages that biological males have over biological females, *but* due to a DSD their external genitals were ambiguous or female in appearance at birth, and as a result they were raised with a female gender identity, which they have maintained even after undergoing male puberty? Should they be able to compete in the female category, or should they have to compete in the male category?[55]

One side of this debate notes: *'You cannot guarantee a level playing field for women by letting in athletes according to what they perceive themselves to be, only according to what they immutably are'.*[56] The other counters: *'We cannot have a woman legally recognised as a trans woman in society and not be recognised that way in sports. Focusing on performance advantage is largely irrelevant because this is a rights issue. We shouldn't be worried about trans people taking over the Olympics. We should be worried about their fairness and human rights instead'.*[57] Those seeking a compromise ask: *'How do we support and protect women's sport and, at the same time, honor the rights of a marginalized segment of humanity?'*[58] And commentators note: *'This is easily the most complex issue that sports has had to deal with, perhaps ever'.*[59]

To me, however, it is not complex. Instead, the only logical answer is that if you have received the physiological benefits of male puberty, sporting fairness requires that you compete in the male category, not in the female category. In other words, in the context of sport it is your biology that counts, not your gender identity.[60]

It is striking how seldom the gritty biological reality is acknowledged and addressed in this debate. Often it is buried in scientific jargon. For example, ethicists critiquing World Athletics' regulatory approach, rather than straightforwardly acknowledging that 46XY DSD athletes have testes, instead say their high testosterone levels are due to *'altered gonadal steroidogenesis'*.[61] Sometimes this obfuscation may simply be due to squeamishness. But more often protagonists in the debate deliberately ignore, disguise or distort the fundamental distinction between biological sex and gender identity because they know that it undermines their arguments. For example:

- Katrina Karkazis, a Professor of Sexuality, Women's and Gender Studies at Amherst College in the USA, asserts that *'[c]onsiderations of fairness support an approach that allows all legally recognized females to compete* [in sport] *with other females, regardless of their hormonal levels, providing their bodies naturally produce the hormones'*.[62] This is classic doublespeak. Not only does it conflate biological sex and gender identity. It also ignores the fact that individuals can only *'naturally produce'* the *'hormonal levels'* at issue here (testosterone in the adult male range: 7.7 to 29.4 nmol/L) if they have testes rather than ovaries, ie if they are biological males. Whether that should or should not resolve the issue is up for debate, but failing to acknowledge these facts, instead trying to bury and ignore them, is in my opinion simply misleading.

- In a 2016 opinion piece titled *'Naturally Occurring High Testosterone Shouldn't Keep Female Athletes out of Competition'*, the editors of Scientific American asserted: *'[The IOC] should allow women with naturally "high T" to compete in all international track competitions. ... Hormone levels akin to [Dutee] Chand's are natural, and there is no evidence that they enhance performance ...'*.[63] Once again, this conflates gender identity and biological sex, without ever acknowledging the difference between the two; and once again it ignores the fact that this *'naturally high'* testosterone is the result of the individual in question having testes rather than ovaries.

- The same is true of the South African journalist who wrote that *'in layman's terms, [Caster Semenya] is a woman but without the entire internal female reproductive organs. She, therefore, does not menstruate and her body produces an elevated amount of testosterone'*;[64] and of the advocates in the *Chand* case who argued that the testosterone levels of a 46XY DSD athlete are *'the product of a natural genetic gift, which should not be viewed differently from other natural advantages derived from exceptional biological variation'*.[65] Individuals with a 46XY DSD do not lack *'the entire internal female reproductive organs'*: they do not have *any* female reproductive organs, because they are biologically male. And their *'natural genetic gift'/'exceptional biological variation'* is simply having a Y chromosome (46XY) and so an SRY gene that triggers the primitive gonads in the foetus to turn into testes, rather than two X chromosomes (46XX) that cause them to become ovaries. Again, in my view, it is just misleading to try to bury this biological reality.

- Finally, in their critique of the CAS decision in *Semenya v IAAF*, Madeleine Pape and Roger Pielke assert: *'Whether 46XY DSD individuals are either female or male depends not on testosterone levels, or even on chromosomal make-up, but on the sex assigned to them at birth, based primarily on an examination of their genitalia and maintained from that moment forward (or not) depending on how their gendered lives unfolded'*.[66] Once again, this confuses sex and gender, and (in my view) serves only to obscure the issues, not to illuminate them.

Neither I nor any sports organisation I have represented has any desire to disrespect the dignity or gender identity of 46XY DSD athletes. But burying or obscuring the scientific facts prevents a proper and informed debate as to what is or is not necessary to protect fair competition in the female sports category. Therefore, when I refer to males and females in this chapter, unless I say otherwise I am not referring to their gender identity. Instead, because the context is sport, where biology is largely determinative of outcome, I am referring to biological males (46XY, with testes) and biological females (46XX, with ovaries). And for the reasons I have explained above, 46XY individuals with DSDs like 5-ARD and 17β are biological males, whether their gender identity is male or female.

Transgender male to female athletes

Transgender male to female ('*MTF*') athletes also have male chromosomes (46XY), and so (prior to any medical intervention) have testes rather than ovaries, and so have levels of circulating testosterone in the adult male range rather than in the adult female range, and so (if they transition after puberty) have all of the physiological advantages that male puberty confers. In other words, from a biological perspective, there is no material biological difference between 46XY transgender MTF individuals and individuals with 46XY DSDs like 5-ARD or 17β, other than (possibly) the appearance of their external genitals, which has no relevance to sports performance. This is a point the IAAF emphasised in the *Semenya* CAS proceedings (see *Figure 1*).

Figure 1: Adapted from exhibit used in *Semenya v IAAF*, CAS 2018/O/5794. First re-published in Coleman, Semenya and ASA v IAAF: Affirming the Lawfulness of a Sex-Based Eligibility Rule for the Women's Category in Elite Sport, (2019) 19 ISLR 83–90 (2019). The bold horizontal line divides factors that influence sports performance (above the line) from factors that do not (below the line).

	Typical Male	**Person with 5-ARD**	**Transgender MTF person**	**Typical Female**
Chromosomes	46XY	46XY	46XY	46XX
Gonads and Gametes	Testes & sperm	Testes & sperm	Testes & sperm	Ovaries & eggs
Endocrine system and sex hormones	Androgenic T levels in male range	Androgenic T levels in male range	Androgenic T levels in male range	Estrogenic T levels in female range

Primary sex characteristics (develop in utero)	Testes, epididymis & vas deferens, prostate	Testes, epididymis & vas deferens, prostate	Testes, epididymis & vas deferens, prostate	Ovaries, fallopian tubes, uterus, vagina
Virilisation on puberty	Yes	Yes	Yes	No
Secondary sex characteristics (develop at puberty)	Male	Male	Male	Female
External genitalia	Penis, scrotum	Varies	Penis, scrotum	Clitoris, labia
Legal sex	Male	Varies	Varies	Female
Gender identity	Male	Varies	Female	Female

It is striking, however, that those on the other side of this debate appear very anxious to distinguish 46XY DSD athletes with a female gender identity from 46XY MTF transgender athletes. For example, Caster Semenya has said of transgender athletes: *'I love them, I support them in everything that they do, but when it comes to my situation, it's way irrelevant to mix it'*.[67]

It is not difficult to see why they want to draw this distinction. First, the comparison drives home the point that 46XY DSD athletes, like transgender MTF athletes, are biologically male. Second, it means that if 46XY DSD athletes with a female gender identity are to be accommodated in the female competition category, then logically transgender MTF athletes have to be accommodated too, meaning that the displacement of biologically female athletes increases. Dr Eric Vilain described the CAS decision in the *Chand* case (see pp 141 et seq) as *'a victory of identity politics and activism. Now I'm really worried about the future of women in sports because if we push this argument, anyone declaring a female gender can compete as a woman. We're moving towards one big competition, and the very predictable result of that competition is that there will be no women winners'*.[68] And a report to the UN General Assembly in August 2024 stated: *'According to information received, by 30 March 2024, over 600 female athletes in more than 400 competitions have lost more than 890 medals in 29 different sports'* to biologically male competitors.[69]

The distinction usually made is that the 46XY DSD athletes in question were raised as female from birth, whereas 46XY transgender athletes were raised male and '*chose*' to transition to female at a later date:

- In the *Semenya* hearing at CAS, Dr Vilain and his fellow expert witness Roger Pielke argued that if an individual has been reared as female and consistently lived as a female, they should be permitted to compete in the female category, but if they were initially reared as male, and subsequently transitioned to female, they should not (see p 155).

- Roger Pielke and Madeleine Pape reiterated this proposed distinction after the case was over, arguing that 46XY DSD individuals with a female gender identity are different from transgender MTF individuals because they *'have experienced a continuity of gender assignment and identity since birth'.*[70] In other words, unlike transgender individuals, they have never *'changed lanes'.*[71]

But this appears to be a distinction without a difference, and therefore does not justify different treatment. There is evidence that transgender individuals can start to experience gender dysphoria as early as the age of three.[72] They may be reared male initially, and legal and other barriers, including minimum age requirements for gender-affirming surgery and/or hormonal treatment, may mean that they do not actually transition to the female gender until their teens at the earliest. But given that they will likely have considered themselves female from early childhood, it seems illogical and unfair to deny them, due to their unchosen, unwanted gender of rearing, the same rights of access to the female category as the 46XY DSD athletes who were by chance reared female from birth. And again that makes the argument for the inclusion of 46XY DSD athletes in the female competition category harder, because it means the risk of displacement of biological females is even greater.

What is 'an unfair and disproportionate advantage'?

Some accept that 46XY transgender MTF athletes and 46XY DSD athletes have a performance advantage over biological females, but insist that advantage is not unfair or disproportionate, and argue it is therefore an acceptable cost of respecting their gender identity.[73] Logically this means that the performance advantage conferred by male puberty should not be grounds for exclusion from the female category unless the 46XY transgender athlete or 46XY DSD athlete in question would beat the best time ever achieved by a 46XX female athlete in that discipline. If they cannot beat that record, the logic goes, their advantage is not unfair or disproportionate, and so they should be allowed to compete without condition.[74] I doubt that many of the biologically female athletes who are thereby displaced entirely from the podium, as happened in the women's 800m final at the Rio Olympics in 2016,[75] or from a place in the Olympic final, or from a place on their nation's Olympic team, or from a place in the national championships, would agree with this. Instead, as sports ethicist Jon Pike says, the notion that people with male advantage should be permitted in the female category as long as they do not outperform all cisgender females is *'a snare and a delusion'.*[76] Displacement is just as unfair, whatever level it occurs at. And in sport, fair competition is the overriding requirement; a desire for inclusion cannot be permitted to trump or limit it.[77]

In her 2023 autobiography, Caster Semenya points to the fact that *'my times are well within the women's category. ... I'm just better than a lot of the women I was running against'* as evidence: (1) that she does not have an unfair advantage;[78] and (2) that *'[w]omen like me are not men. The IAAF knew that not one woman with a confirmed DSD diagnosis had even approached the running times of male elite runners'.*[79] But the fact that the best times of Caster Semenya and her 46XY DSD colleagues are within the range of times recorded in the female category, albeit at the very highest end of that range, is not a surprise. It is only the top 10-12%

of male track athletes who can beat the very best female track athletes. Caster Semenya asks: *'if speed was all about testosterone, then why wasn't I as fast as my male colleagues?'*[80] The answer, bluntly, is that Caster Semenya is not an elite athlete by male standards. That does not make it fair for her to compete in the female category.

Meanwhile, the lawyers for Dutee Chand and Caster Semenya argued that *'[a]ny performance advantage that [46XY DSD] athletes enjoy is the product of a natural genetic gift, which should not be viewed differently from other natural advantages derived from exceptional biological variation. Athletes are not prohibited from competing in sport because they possess other natural genetic advantages – for example, height, lung capacity, foot size, or visual acuity above a certain limit. On the contrary, athletes who achieve sporting success are usually those who fall outside normal parameters. There is therefore no principled or permissible reason for prohibiting a female athlete from competing because of an unusual natural genetic trait, even if that trait confers an advantage over fellow female competitors who lack that trait'.*[81] This is another *'snare and delusion'*:

- As previously explained (see p vi), the purpose of competition categories is to ensure that it is natural talent and hard work that determine success, not factors outside the athlete's control, such as age, or weight, or degree of disability. We have male and female competition categories because no amount of natural talent or effort would enable biological females to bridge the physiological advantages enjoyed by biological males, any more than a flyweight could beat a heavyweight in a boxing match. Sports ethicists call the male physiological superiority a *'category advantage'* that is not worthy of celebration and therefore should be excluded by means of carefully defined competition categories. They contrast it with *'competition advantages'* that enable certain athletes within that category to excel, which *are* worthy of celebration.[82]
- The *'natural genetic gift'* that 46XY DSD athletes have been given is a pair of testes producing levels of testosterone that give them massive physiological advantages over 46XX athletes with ovaries. Unlike the fast twitch muscles of female Jamaican sprinters, testes are not an *'exceptional biological variation'* within the female (XX) athlete population. Instead they are the completely unexceptional consequence of having a Y chromosome. The only *'exceptional biological variation'* seen in 46XY DSD athletes is that because of an enzyme deficiency or partial androgen insensitivity their external genitals are under-virilised (the reason why some of them may be assigned a female legal sex at birth), which (again) does not affect sports performance in any way. So 46XY DSD athletes are not achieving sporting success because they *'fall outside normal parameters'*. Instead, they are achieving sporting success because they fall inside the normal parameters for biological males, but are competing against biological females.

That is why celebrating the diversity of female talent means allowing female Jamaican sprinters with their superior fast twitch muscles to sweep the podium, but preventing 46XY transgender or DSD athletes doing the same.[83] Anything else would be category-defeating.

'Sex testing' (also referred to, inaccurately, as 'gender verification')[84]

Why have sports governing bodies found it so difficult to address these issues? The answer is that they and the lawyers and scientists and medical professionals advising them have had to learn as they have gone along, and have made numerous mistakes along the way.

Until the 20th century, females were excluded entirely from most sports, based on concerns that they were physically too weak and might be injured, impairing their ability to bear children. They were barred completely from competing at the first modern Olympic Games, in 1896. Twenty-two females were permitted to compete in the 1900 Games, but only in sports that were considered not to involve strenuous (read: unfeminine) effort, namely tennis, lawn golf, sailing, croquet, and equestrian sports. The 1928 Olympics saw the first female gymnastics and athletics events (but no races longer than 800 metres), and female athletes were given more access to different events and sports from 1936 on, even if they remained very much in the minority at the Olympics until they finally reached parity with male athletes in 2024.[85]

The first concerns that biological males were seeking to compete in female competitions seem to have been prompted by newspaper reports in 1936 of two female athletes with a male gender identity seeking to compete in the *male* category – a Czechoslovakian runner, Zdena Koubková, who became Zdenek Koubek, and a British shot putter and javelin thrower, Mary Weston, who became Mark Weston.[86] Then US athlete Helen Stephens won the 100m gold at the 1936 Olympic Games in Berlin, beating Poland's Stanisława Walasiewicz (subsequently known as Stella Walsh), the defending champion. Decades later, a post-mortem autopsy determined that Walsh had XY and XO chromosomes and under-virilised male genitals. In 1936, however, the concern was about the *'maleness'* of Helen Stephens, prompting an inspection of her genitals to confirm her eligibility for female competition.[87] The scandal prompted a recommendation from Avery Brundage, then president of the US Olympic Committee, that every female Olympic athlete should be examined by doctors *'to certify her womanhood'*.[88] This approach was confirmed in 1939, after Dora Ratjen, a German athlete who had come fourth in the women's high jump at the Berlin Games[89] and set a new women's world record of 1.70m at the 1938 European Championships, was arrested on suspicion of impersonating a man. Subsequent investigation established that Dora had ambiguous genitalia and male secondary sex characteristics, leading to a change of legal sex and gender presentation from female to male, and to a change of name to Heinrich.[90]

In 1946 the IAAF started requiring female competitors to produce a medical certificate from a team or family doctor confirming their eligibility to compete in the female category, and in 1948 the IOC followed suit. But as Cold War tensions increased in the 1960s, sports administrators (read, the Western Bloc) were no longer so willing to trust national authorities (read, the Eastern Bloc) not to cheat.[91] Instead, starting at the 1966 Commonwealth Games, and continuing at the 1966 European Athletics Championships, the 1967 Pan-American Games, and the 1968 Olympic Games, female athletes were required to submit to a physical examination of their genitals at the event to prove they were competing in the right category. It has been suggested that *'[u]nexpectedly, five world record holders did not attend'* the physical examinations held at the 1966 European Athletics Championships.[92] Several accounts note in particular that Irina and Tamara Press, two Ukrainian sisters who had set 26 world records and won six Olympic gold medals in track and field during the 1950s and 1960s, did not turn up for examination and never competed again.[93] Meanwhile the physical examination at the 1967 European Cup of Ewa Klobukowska, who had won bronze in the women's 100m and gold in the women's 100m relay at the 1964 Tokyo Olympics, triggered an investigation that revealed she had unusual (XXY) chromosomes and had had testes surgically removed. She was promptly barred from competing in the female category.[94]

These '*nude parades*' were highly intrusive and demeaning, and (unsurprisingly) extremely unpopular with female athletes.[95] They were also not fit for purpose, because (as explained at pp 129–130 above) an athlete may be 46XY with fully functioning (internal) testes, and yet – because of an enzyme deficiency or an insensitivity to androgens – have more or less female-looking external genitals. Therefore the IOC switched to the sex chromatin test, aka the buccal smear test, involving examination of cells taken from inside the cheek for evidence of a nuclear marking, known as a Barr body, that is only found in cells with an inactive X chromosome. Since one X chromosome is always active, the cells of 46XX females have one Barr body, while the cells of 46XY males have none. Austrian downhill ski world champion Erika Schinegger failed the Barr body test in the lead-up to the 1968 Winter Olympics in Grenoble, and was found to have XY chromosomes and undescended testes. She subsequently re-named herself Erik, adopted a male gender identity, and later fathered a child.[96] Three more athletes reportedly failed the sex chromatin test at the 1972 Olympics in Munich, and six more at the 1984 Olympics in Los Angeles.[97] But the test had a high rate of false results, and was not foolproof even when accurate, because (as explained above) in rare cases a 46XY individual, who will '*fail*' the Barr body test, may be completely insensitive to androgens (CAIS), meaning that the testosterone produced by their testes has no virilising effect on their body. A famous example is María José Martínez-Patiño, a Spanish athlete I had the pleasure to meet in the course of the *Chand* proceedings described below. Maria has CAIS and was raised female. She passed the Barr body test in 1983 (a false negative) and was given a '*certificate of femininity*', but she forgot to bring that certificate to the 1985 World University Games in Japan, and so was required to provide a further buccal smear, which revealed that she was 46XY, not 46XX, something she and her family had not previously known. Her eligibility for the female category was revoked, her sports scholarship was withdrawn, and her running times were erased from the records, despite the fact that she had never gone through male puberty.[98]

Chastened by this case, for which it received heavy criticism, in 1992 the IAAF formally abandoned any general test to determine eligibility to compete in the female category, and instead simply reserved the right to undertake medical examinations on a case-by-case basis when the need arose. The IOC in contrast continued with general testing, although it replaced the Barr body test with DNA-based methods using a polymerase chain reaction to detect the presence of the SRY gene on the Y chromosome.[99] Five female athletes tested positive for the SRY gene at the 1992 Olympic Games in Barcelona, and were referred for further examination, but the results of those examinations have never been made public.[100] At the 1996 Olympic Games in Atlanta, eight female athletes tested positive for the SRY gene, and further examination established that seven of them had CAIS or PAIS, while one had 5-ARD but had had her testes removed several years previously.[101] In 1999 the IOC joined the IAAF in abandoning such general testing in favour of an *ad hoc*, case by case approach.

In 2004 the IOC adopted the '*Stockholm Consensus on Sex Reassignment in Sport*', permitting transgender MTF athletes to compete in the female competition category at the Olympics if they had acquired a female legal sex and if their testosterone levels had been suppressed (by gonadectomy or hormonal treatment) either prior to puberty or for sufficient time after puberty (at least two years) to minimise the physiological advantages conferred by puberty.[102] In 2006 the IAAF adopted a similar '*Policy on Gender Verification*', which stated that in '*sex reassignment*' cases a physical and endocrinological evaluation would be conducted two years after gonadectomy to determine whether the transgender MTF athlete was still *'enjoying the benefits of natural testosterone predominance normally seen in a male'*, while DSD cases would continue to be dealt with on an *ad hoc* basis – although the policy noted that cases of CAIS, gonadal dysgenesis, and Turner's syndrome conferred no advantage over *'other females'* and therefore should not render the athlete in question ineligible for the female category, while Congenital Adrenal Hyperplasia, androgen-producing tumours, and Polycystic Ovarian Syndrome *'may accord some advantages but [are] nevertheless acceptable'*.[103]

The problems with this *ad hoc* approach for DSD cases became all too apparent when Caster Semenya won gold in the 800m women's final at the IAAF World Championships in Berlin in August 2009.

'A different kind of girl'[104]

Caster Semenya was born in January 1991 in a rural village in South Africa. She grew up loving sports, and excelled at running. She began competing locally, then regionally, then nationally, and was soon selected by Athletics South Africa ('*ASA*') to represent her country in international competition. In October 2008, at the age of 17, she won 800m gold at the Commonwealth Youth Games in India in a time of 2:04.23. In March 2009, she competed in her first ever senior 800m race, winning in a time of 2:02. And in July 2009, after receiving professional coaching for the first time, she won 800m gold at the African Junior Championships in a time of 1:56.72, which was the fastest 800m run by *any* woman of *any* age in the world that year. Two weeks later, ASA sent her to compete in the IAAF World Championships in Berlin, and again she won 800m gold, in a time of 1:55.45, another personal best and the world best for that year, and almost two seconds ahead of the runner-up, Janeth Jepkosgei. These results were remarkable. Rarely if ever has any other athlete achieved such a rapid ascent to the very top of the sport.

In her 2023 autobiography, Caster Semenya says that when she was growing up, she was always conscious that she was different from the other girls. She preferred wearing shorts and trousers to skirts and dresses, she went hunting and played soccer with the boys whenever she could, and she was often mistaken for a boy. When she started running competitively, the other runners and their coaches would say she looked like a boy, and *'the girls didn't see me as one of them'*. On 7 August 2009, after a claim was made in a South African blog that she was *'a hermaphrodite'*, Athletics South Africa sent her to a Pretoria hospital for what she was told was *'a gender test'*. A doctor examined her genitals, did a sonogram of her abdomen, and took a blood sample for testing. He told her that her testosterone levels were high and that her chances of running in the World Championships were *'very low'*. She travelled to Berlin the next day. On 14 August 2009, the results of the tests conducted in Pretoria were communicated to Dr Harold Adams, the ASA team doctor, in Berlin. He told ASA president Leonard Chuene that the results were *'not good'* and recommended that Caster Semenya be withdrawn from the World Championships. Mr Chuene initially agreed. Caster confirms that she was told in Berlin by ASA Vice-President Attlee Maponyane that the results of the Pretoria tests *'will not be good'*, and that it would be best if she feigned injury and withdrew from the championships. But Caster refused, believing that the IAAF was trying *'to shame me out of the final'*, and the next day Mr Chuene, having consulted with unnamed politicians in South Africa, changed his stance and agreed with her, insisting that since no definitive test results were yet available she must be permitted to run. At a meeting on 15 August 2009 with IAAF officials, he asserted that no tests had yet been conducted on Caster and so she must be allowed to compete, or else Athletics South Africa would sue the IAAF. *'He warned them that the Oscar Pistorius case would be a Sunday school picnic compared with what would happen if Ms Semenya did not run'*.[105] In response, the IAAF officials said that if there were no test results then she was entitled to the benefit of the doubt, and therefore she could compete if that was what Athletics South Africa wanted, but she would then be subject to IAAF jurisdiction for gender verification purposes.[106] On 16 August 2009, Caster was sent for further examinations at a Berlin hospital, including an ultrasound of her internal organs.[107]

After the 800m semi-final heat on 17 August 2009, when a journalist asked Caster about rumours that she was *'born a man'*, she responded that she had no idea what he was talking about. In her autobiography, Caster describes her reaction to this sort of speculation: *'I was angry because there was no need for the world to know my business. That is what I found unfair. It wasn't the world's business what I was carrying around inside of me – they didn't have a right to that'*. But she continues: *'Looking at it the other way, whoever leaked the results did me a big favor. I now knew what was going on with my body. I had top-level medical information, free of charge. I thought of all the people in the world who were like me and would never have access to this kind of knowledge. At least I knew'*.[108]

Showing remarkable strength of character, Caster Semenya did not let any of this affect her performance in the 800m final on 19 August 2009. In fact, she says *'[t] he test made me all the more determined to win'*. Before the final, IAAF spokesman Nick Davies sought to quell the growing chatter, saying: *'It's a medical issue. It's not an issue of cheating. We're more concerned for the person not to make this something which is humiliating for her and something which is going to affect her in a negative way. This is why you will appreciate we have to be discreet. She is a human being who was born as a woman and who has grown up all her life as a woman but who is now in a position where this is being questioned'*.[109] By the time Caster Semenya returned to South Africa on 25 August 2009, however, the fact that she had elevated testosterone levels had become public knowledge, and in September 2009 an Australian paper reported that she had *'male sex organs and no womb or ovaries'*.[110] IAAF Secretary-General Pierre Weiss said: *'It is clear that she is a woman but maybe not 100 per cent. We have to see if she has an advantage from her possibly being between two sexes compared to the others'*.[111]

Meanwhile Caster Semenya was contacted by Greg Nott, a lawyer with Norton Rose in South Africa. He advised her that the IAAF's rules infringed her rights and would be overturned in court if she challenged them, but she decided not to take that route. Instead, she committed to taking oral contraceptive pills to reduce her serum testosterone levels to below 10 nmol/L, and so was permitted to compete in the female category again from July 2010 on.[112] Apart from second place finishes in the 800m at the IAAF World Championships in Daegu in 2011 and at the Olympic Games in London in 2012 (upgraded to gold when the winner was subsequently disqualified for doping), her 800m times over the next five years were relatively poor. She attributed that not to her lower testosterone levels but rather to the debilitating side effects (in particular, weight gain and nausea) of the contraceptive pills.[113]

In 2011, the IAAF adopted *'Regulations Governing Eligibility of Females with Hyperandrogenism to Compete in Women's Competition'*, which formalised the approach it had taken in Caster Semenya's case by stating that a hyperandrogenic athlete was only permitted to compete in the female category if: (1) she had androgen levels below *'the normal male* range', defined as 10 nmol/L or higher; or (2) she showed that she *'has an androgen resistance such that she derives no competitive advantage from having androgen levels in the normal male range'*, to be determined by a panel of independent medical experts, including by assessment of breast size and appearance of genitalia.[114] Similarly, the IOC adopted rules for the 2012 Olympic Games in London and for the 2014 Winter Olympics in Sochi that provided for any athlete with a DSD to be evaluated by a genetic expert, a gynaecologist, and an endocrinologist to determine: *'(i) whether the investigated athlete's androgen level, measured by reference to testosterone levels in serum, is within the male range, and if so, (ii) whether such hyperandrogenism is functional or not'*.[115]

While Caster Semenya initially chose the path of least resistance, in 2015 another athlete impacted by the IAAF's 2011 Hyperandrogenism Regulations decided not to comply with those regulations but instead to challenge them in court.

Chand v AFI & IAAF[116]

Eighteen-year-old Indian sprinter Dutee Chand won two gold medals at the Asian Junior Athletics Championships in June 2014, and was due to go to the World Junior Athletics Championships in Oregon in July 2014.[117] However, the Sports Authority of India required her to undertake a series of clinical tests, karyotyping, blood tests and MRI examinations, and subsequently told her she could not compete in Oregon. The Athletics Federation of India suspended her from competition and advised her to follow the IAAF's 2011 Hyperandrogenism Regulations in order to establish her eligibility to compete in the female category.[118]

Instead, however, supported by gender activist Payoshni Mitra, together with Bruce Kidd (former Olympic athlete, and Professor of Sport and Public Policy at the University of Toronto) and Katrina Karkazis, on 18 September 2014 Dutee responded to the Athletics Federation of India as follows:[119]

> The high androgen level produced by my body is natural. I have not doped or cheated. If I follow the IAAF guidelines you have attached, I will have to undergo medical intervention in order to reduce my naturally-produced

> androgen level. Experts tell me that the basis for this policy is unscientific and that these interventions are invasive, often irreversible, and will harm my health now and into my future. I feel perfectly healthy and I have no health complaints so I do not want to undergo these procedures because the experts also tell me they are likely to have serious side effects. I also understand that these interventions will most likely decrease my performance level because of the serious side effects and because they will interfere with the way my body has worked my whole life. Also, I am unable to understand why I am asked to fix my body in a certain way simply for participation as a woman. I was born a woman, reared up as a woman, I identify as a woman and I believe I should be allowed to compete with other women, many of whom are either taller than me or come from more privileged backgrounds, things that most certainly give them an edge over me.
>
> I request that you allow me to compete again in national events without having to undergo medical intervention. I also request you to allow me to be a part of the Indian team in international competition. The IAAF policy has a provision that says you can make me provisionally eligible while I contest my case.

On 26 September 2014, Dutee appealed the Athletics Federation of India's decision to suspend her from female competition to the Court of Arbitration for Sport, and named the IAAF as an additional respondent to the appeal, asserting that its 2011 Hyperandrogenism Regulations were unlawful and therefore unenforceable against her. The CAS Panel convened to hear the case was chaired by Annabelle Bennett, a former Australian federal court judge, sitting alongside Canadian lawyer Richard McLaren (Dutee's nominee) and Swiss lawyer Hans Nater (the IAAF's nominee). Canadian lawyers Jim Bunting and Carlos Sayao represented Dutee, while Liz Riley and I from Bird & Bird represented the IAAF. The AFI did not appear and was not represented.

The CAS Panel heard the case in Lausanne from 23 to 26 March 2015. Dutee's lawyers argued that:

- The Hyperandrogenism Regulations *'discriminate unlawfully against female athletes and against athletes who possess a particular natural physical characteristic'*, namely, elevated levels of endogenous testosterone. They argued (see p 135) that *'[a]ny performance advantage that those athletes enjoy is the product of a natural genetic gift, which should not be viewed differently from other natural advantages derived from exceptional biological variation'.*[120]
- They also disputed that Dutee's *'naturally high'* testosterone levels gave her any advantage over her competitors. They asserted that *'differences in athletic performance between males and females are not attributable to sex-based differences in testosterone levels, but are instead due to other factors'*, such as the sex differences in levels of lean body mass and human growth hormone.[121]
- In support of the proposition that testosterone is not the cause of the sex difference in sports performance: (a) they suggested that *'there is a complete overlap of endogenous testosterone levels between the sexes'*;[122] (b) they noted that many female athletes have very low levels of endogenous testosterone, and/or are completely or partially insensitive to testosterone (CAIS or PAIS), and yet still manage to compete at an elite level; and (c) they insisted that even

though *exogenous* testosterone (ie synthetic testosterone, used in breach of anti-doping rules) is clearly beneficial to performance, it does not follow that *endogenous* testosterone (ie testosterone produced by the body) is beneficial to performance, because *'the former involves the introduction of a new biochemical agent that upsets the body's equilibrium by dislodging its natural hormonal stasis, while the latter does not'.*[123]

- Finally, they argued that the 2011 Hyperandrogenism Regulations were disproportionate, ie their harmful side effects outweighed any benefits they might deliver, because they caused female athletes with hyperandrogenism: (a) to be publicly stigmatised; (b) to suffer serious damage to their self-esteem and gender identity, by pressuring them *'to conform to stereotypical expectations of "feminine" behaviour and appearance for fear of being investigated and prevented from competing'*; (c) to be subjected to medical tests without their fully informed consent; and (d) to be forced to undergo unnecessary medical treatment/procedures that could have serious long-term side effects.[124]

The following witnesses testified in support of Dutee Chand's case:

- Professor Richard Holt, an endocrinologist, argued that it had not been proven that there was a sex difference in testosterone levels, let alone that this was the reason for the sex difference in sports performance. He asserted that in fact there is *'a very wide range of testosterone levels in both elite male and female athletes'*, which results in *'a complete overlap of endogenous testosterone levels between the sexes'*.[125] He also noted that there is no correlation between testosterone levels and sports performance among female athletes. For example, female athletes with 3 nmol/L of circulating testosterone do not perform 30 times better than those with 0.1 nmol/L. He suggested that a better explanation for the sex difference in sports performance is the sex difference in lean body mass or in levels of human growth hormone.[126]
- Sari van Anders, an associate professor of psychology and women's studies at the University of Michigan specialising in the relationship between hormones and social behaviour, agreed with Professor Holt that it had not been proven that differences in testosterone levels are the cause of the sex difference in sports performance. Reflecting her research interests, and her debt to Dr Fausto-Sterling, she suggested a cause of that sex difference may be *'gender-socialisation during puberty'*, ie girls are culturally programmed not to be athletes. She also claimed that endogenous testosterone does not trigger the same muscle growth as exogenous testosterone, and that the scientific research showed that *'endogenous testosterone cannot be the basis for successful athletic performance'*.[127]
- Katrina Karkazis, who at the time was a senior research scholar in bioethics at Stanford University, and who is another Fausto-Sterling acolyte, suggested that there is *'a great deal of mythology'* about the physiological effects of testosterone, there is very little data on the effects of testosterone on female sports performance, and there is no evidence that successful athletes have higher testosterone levels than less successful athletes.[128]
- Madeleine Pape, a former elite athlete and a *'sociologist who studies policy enactments of sex in biomedicine and sport'*, who also shares the Fausto-Sterling disdain for *'oppressive ontologies of sex'*,[129] argued that the 2011 Hyperandrogenism Regulations *'target women whose self-presentation is inconsistent with dominant gender stereotypes'*.[130]

Of these witnesses, in my view, only endocrinologist Professor Holt was qualified to venture an opinion on the physiological reasons for the sex difference in sports performance, and his particular expertise was in diabetes and growth hormone rather than testosterone physiology. And only Madeline Pape had any experience of elite sport. In fact, Katrina Karkazis acknowledged to me during cross-examination that she had never been to a sporting event in her life. But even so she felt sufficiently qualified to tell the IAAF how it should be regulating its sport. I fully accept that sports governing bodies must understand the requirements of human rights law. But by the same token, surely those who want to offer opinions on whether a sport should sort competition based on sex or gender need to educate themselves about that sport first?

In any event, we responded with fact evidence from Paula Radcliffe and María José Martínez-Patiño, as well as a statement from Joanna Harper, a medical physicist and a transgender MTF athlete, who presented a study she had conducted that indicated the running times of transgender MTF athletes decreased after their testosterone levels were lowered from the male to the female range.[131] We also presented expert evidence from Professor Martin Ritzen, an endocrinologist who had published many papers about sex differentiation, from Professor Angelica Hirschberg, a specialist in obstetrics and gynaecology who treats many individuals with DSDs, and from Dr Stéphane Bermon, the IAAF's medical director, who was in charge of implementation of the IAAF's 2011 Hyperandrogenism Regulations and therefore also had significant practical experience with individuals with DSDs. They noted that:

- From puberty onwards, there is a significant sex difference in sports performance.[132]
- From puberty onwards, there is also a significant sex difference in testosterone levels, with the normal range for males beginning at around 10.5 nmol per litre of serum (even if some men may have levels slightly lower than that), and the normal range for females being 0.1 to 3.08 nmol/L. Female athletes with healthy ovaries and normal adrenal function would not have endogenous testosterone levels anywhere near 10.5 nmol/L, and therefore there is no overlap in the normal ranges of male and female testosterone levels. The contrary claim from the experts for Ms Chand depends on treating the elevated testosterone levels of 46XY DSD individuals with a female gender identity as part of the normal adult female range.[133]
- Notwithstanding the limited studies published on the point to that date, it is clear that endogenous testosterone, with all of its anabolic effects, is the most significant reason for the sex difference in sports performance. In particular, the sharp increase in levels of circulating testosterone from male puberty onward triggers fat breakdown, protein synthesis, and muscle fibre growth, and so is the reason why adult males have significantly more lean body mass than adult females, as well as bigger and stronger bones, and greater concentrations of haemoglobin in their blood.[134]
- There is clear evidence that exogenous testosterone enhances sports performance in female athletes. Since the body's androgen receptors cannot distinguish between exogenous and endogenous testosterone, it is fair to assume that elevated levels of endogenous testosterone will have the same physiological effects and therefore the same performance-enhancing effects as exogenous testosterone, which is why the World Anti-Doping Agency bans

the administration of substances that boost the production of endogenous testosterone.[135]

- In normal sex development, the primitive gonads will develop into ovaries (if the chromosomes of a foetus are 46XX) or testes (if they are 46XY).[136] In a 46XY DSD individual, however, an enzyme deficiency or an androgen insensitivity mean the testes remain internal and the external genitals may appear ambiguous at birth, which in some cases may lead to assignment of a female legal sex. But from puberty onwards their testes will produce normal adult male levels of testosterone, triggering all of the physiological advantages that drive the sex difference in sports performance, save only in cases of complete androgen insensitivity.[137]
- That is why 46XY DSD individuals are disproportionately represented in the elite female athlete population. In the general population, only 1 person in every 20,000 is 46XY DSD; but in the elite female athlete population that figure rises to 142 in every 20,000, ie a 142 times greater prevalence.[138] When these athletes have competed with their testosterone suppressed, they have not been able to match the results they previously achieved.[139]
- Clinical experience shows that oral contraceptives are a simple way to reduce endogenous testosterone levels in 46XY DSD individuals with a female gender identity to the normal female range, and are generally well-tolerated, with limited side effects.[140]

This was all very important evidence that became the foundation for the case we successfully advanced in the *Semenya* proceedings. But looking back now, it is remarkable how naïve and under-prepared we were when the *Chand* case was tried. In particular, we made several mistakes that cost us dearly in *Chand* and that we had to work hard to correct subsequently in *Semenya*:

- We did not challenge Dutee's proposition that *'sex in humans is not simply binary'*, but rather *'is a continuum with no clear or singular boundary between men and women'*, and that *'some people are intersex, meaning they do not neatly fall into one category or another'*.[141] I have explained above the fallacies in these statements.
- In addition, we were careful to respect the gender identity of 46XY DSD athletes competing in the female category by referring to them as women throughout, but we failed to explain how important it is in this context to distinguish between gender identity and biological sex. For example, we agreed that *'whether a person is female is a matter of law'*; we said that *'in rare cases, female athletes may have conditions which, through no fault or their own, cause their bodies to produce male rather than female levels of testosterone'*; and we said the purpose of the 2011 Hyperandrogenism Regulations was *'to protect women from having to compete against other women'* who were *'benefiting from the androgenising effect of male levels of testosterone'*.[142] This conflation of sex and gender explains why the CAS Panel decided that the 2011 Hyperandrogenism Regulations treated some *'females'* differently from other *'females'*, by restricting their eligibility to compete *'on the basis of a natural physical characteristic (namely the amount of testosterone that their bodies produce naturally)'*.[143] That meant the IAAF had to prove that such discrimination – ie between different *'females'* – was a necessary and proportionate means of achieving fair competition in the female category.[144]

- We also noted, and even acknowledged as *'problematic'*, *'the lack of definitive research linking female hyperandrogenism and sporting performance'*.[145] Once again, this failure to distinguish between biological females on the one hand and biological males with a female gender identity on the other cost us dear, because it meant that we, and therefore the CAS Panel, were focused on whether testosterone levels within the normal female range determine results in the female category (they do not, because that range is so small, 0.06-1.68 nmol/L), rather than on the mountains of evidence demonstrating that the much higher levels of testosterone seen in biological males (7.7 to 29.4 nmol/L) give them a massive performance advantage over biological females.

- The 2011 Hyperandrogenism Regulations adopted the standard medical definition of hyperandrogenism, ie any condition causing levels of testosterone above the normal female range, and therefore encompassed not only the DSDs that affect 46XY individuals (in particular, 5-ARD, 17β, and PAIS) but also conditions that affect 46XX individuals (ie biological females), namely Polycystic Ovary Syndrome (*'the most common cause'* of female hyperandrogenism[146]) and Congenital Adrenal Hyperplasia.[147] This made no sense, because 46XX individuals with PCOS or CAH have ovaries rather than testes, and so either: (a) they only have very slightly elevated testosterone levels (still nowhere near the normal male range) that do not come close to generating the performance-enhancing benefits of a male puberty (PCOS); or (b) they only have elevated testosterone levels if the condition is untreated (CAH), in which case they will generally have severe side-effects that would harm performance, not enhance it, which is why no case of CAH or its variants has ever been seen in elite athletics.[148] There was therefore no good reason for the 2011 Hyperandrogenism Regulations to place any restrictions on individuals with PCOS or CAH competing in the female category, which is why those conditions had been excluded from the IAAF's 2006 Policy on Gender Verification mentioned above.

- The 2011 Hyperandrogenism Regulations also stated that *all* cases of hyperandrogenism would be assessed by specialists to determine whether the athlete's elevated testosterone has had a material androgenising effect on their body. This counted against us, because that specialist assessment is physically intrusive. But making the requirement universal made little sense. An assessment of virilisation is important in cases of Partial Androgen Insensitivity Syndrome, for the reasons explained above (see p 130), but the other DSDs (5-ARD and 17β) will have the normal androgenising effect of male puberty on the affected individual's body, making such assessment entirely unnecessary in those cases.

- We did not dispute Dutee's assertion that a performance advantage of *'only'* 2-3% is acceptable. At the elite level of athletics, where the winning margin may be tenths or even thousandths of a second,[149] a performance advantage of 2-3% is huge.

- Finally, athletes covered by the 2011 Hyperandrogenism Regulations could not compete *either* in the female competition category (because of their elevated testosterone levels) *or* in the male competition category (because of their female legal sex). In other words, they were excluded from the sport altogether.[150]

We soon regretted those mistakes. In July 2015 the CAS Panel issued its award, finding that:

- Ensuring fair competition conditions for female athletes is a legitimate objective.[151]
- Therefore, it is necessary for the IAAF *'to formulate a basis for the division of athletes into the male and female categories for the benefit of the broad class of female athletes. The basis chosen should be necessary, reasonable and proportionate to the legitimate objective being pursued'*.[152]
- However, *'every athlete must in principle be afforded the opportunity to compete in one of the two categories and should not be prevented from competing in any category as a consequence of the natural and unaltered state of their body. ... Excluding athletes from competing at all on the basis of a natural genetic advantage, or conditioning their right to compete on undergoing medical intervention which reduces their athletic performance, imposes a significant detriment on the athletes concerned, and is therefore only valid if it is clearly established to be a necessary and proportionate means of achieving fair competition'*.[153]
- *'Once an athlete is legally recognised as female, the Panel considers that an athlete must be permitted to compete in the female category unless her naturally high androgen levels confer a significant performance advantage over other female competitors, comparable to the performance advantage that male athletes enjoy over female athletes. Has the IAAF established that women with levels of endogenous testosterone of at least 10 nmol/L and who are androgen-sensitive have a sufficiently clear and significant competitive advantage over other females such that there may be a fairness-based reason why they should be precluded from competing as females, or at all?'*[154]
- To determine the *'normal'* female range of circulating testosterone, it is appropriate to exclude the testosterone levels of individuals with 46XY DSDs. When that is done, there is no overlap in adult male and female testosterone levels.[155]
- Professor Holt's hypothesis that the sex difference in sport performance is due to the sex difference in levels of human growth hormone is not supported by any evidence.[156] His alternative suggestion that the sex difference in lean body mass is a contributing factor may be correct, but lean body mass is linked to testosterone. The IAAF's experts established that it is more likely than not that testosterone contributes to sport performance, albeit that their evidence was mainly about exogenous testosterone. While the Panel could not decide whether endogenous testosterone will have exactly the same effects on the body as exogenous testosterone, *'[t]he onus is on the Athlete to demonstrate that the Hyperandrogenism Regulations are unsupported by, or not based on, scientific data and that a difference does exist between the effects of endogenous and exogenous testosterone. She has failed to meet that onus'*.[157] As a result, the Panel accepted that *'testosterone is the best indicator of performance difference between male and female athletes'*.[158]
- On the other hand, *'[o]n the basis of the evidence currently before the Panel, the Panel is unable to conclude on the balance of probabilities that androgen-sensitive hyperandrogenic female athletes enjoy such a substantial performance advantage over non-hyperandrogenic female athletes that excluding them from competing in the female category, and thereby excluding them from competing at all unless they take medication or undergo treatment, is a necessary and proportionate means of preserving fairness in athletics competition and/or policing the binary male/female*

> *classification'*. This is where our failure to distinguish clearly between biological females on the one hand and biological males with a female gender identity on the other really cost us dear. The Panel continued: *'It is not self-evident that a female athlete with a level of testosterone above 10 nmol/L would enjoy the competitive advantage of a male athlete, which performance advantage would be, on the IAAF's evidence, in the order of 10 – 12% (the approximate difference, on the evidence of the IAAF, between men and women and, therefore, an unfair advantage), rather than, say, 1% (a relatively marginal advantage, having regard to the many other variables that contribute to athletic performance). ... Further evidence as to the quantitative relationship between androgen levels in hyperandrogenic females and increased athletic performance is therefore required before the IAAF can discharge its onus of establishing that the Hyperandrogenism Regulations are a necessary and proportionate means of achieving the IAAF's stated objective'.*[159]

The CAS Panel concluded: *'The Panel therefore suspends the Hyperandrogenism Regulations for a period of two years, subject to the following provisos. At any time during that two-year period, the IAAF may submit further written evidence to the CAS concerning the magnitude of the performance advantage that hyperandrogenic females enjoy over other females as a result of their abnormally high androgen levels. In the event that the IAAF submits such evidence, the Panel will issue further directions enabling the Athlete to respond to that evidence and listing the matter for a further hearing for the Panel to consider whether that evidence is sufficient to establish the validity of the Regulations. In the event that the IAAF does not file any evidence within that two-year window (or if it notifies the CAS in writing that it does not intend to file such evidence) then the Hyperandrogenism Regulations shall be declared void'.*[160]

Gathering the evidence

The IAAF was aided enormously in its efforts to gather the arguments and evidence by Stéphane Bermon and Angelica Hirschberg and also by three new experts: Doriane Lambelet Coleman (Professor of Law at Duke Law School), the elite athlete turned law professor whose ground-breaking article *Sex in Sport* had caught our attention;[161] David Handelsman (Professor of Reproductive Endocrinology and Andrology at the University of Sydney), who had read the *Chand* award and was very concerned at what he regarded as bad science being propagated by the athlete's expert witnesses in that case; and Richard Auchus (Professor of Translational Medicine at the University of Michigan), who (like Angelica Hirshberg) is a world-leading expert on the proper diagnosis and treatment of DSD individuals.

In July 2018, David, Angelica and Stéphane published a landmark scientific paper in Endocrine Reviews, the official journal of the Endocrine Society, and the most highly regarded endocrinology journal in the world,[162] that put beyond dispute two fundamental points that had been challenged by the athlete's experts in *Chand*:

- Based on all of the reported data that has been produced using reliable testing methods, the normal adult female range of serum testosterone is 0.06 to 1.68 nmol/L. If females with PCOS are included, the upper limit increases to 3.1 nmol/L. Meanwhile the normal adult male range of serum testosterone is 7.7 to 29.4 nmol/L. There is therefore no overlap between the normal female adult range and the normal male adult range. Instead, there is a marked sex difference in adult levels of circulating testosterone from puberty onwards.[163]

- It is that difference in levels of circulating testosterone that drives the marked sex difference in athletic performance that emerges at the same time. The rising levels of testosterone in pubertal males bind to the androgen receptors in target tissues (including muscle, bone, and bone marrow), stimulating protein synthesis in the muscle cells (leading to increased muscle mass and strength), bone growth (leading to longer, thicker and stronger bones), and erythropoiesis, ie erythrocyte production and haemoglobin synthesis (leading to a higher concentration of haemoglobin in the blood). Placebo-controlled, double-blind randomised experiments have established that the more testosterone there is circulating in the body, the greater the person's muscle mass and strength, and the more haemoglobin in their blood. This dose-response relationship exists from castrate levels through normal female levels to the normal adult male range and beyond. It corresponds to a classic sigmoid curve, with lower and upper plateaus where there is little response to dose (which is why women are not virilised by their low testosterone levels), connected by a logarithmic curve in the mid-section that reflects a rapidly increasing response to rising dose. That is why it is only upon puberty, when male testosterone production increases 28-fold, and testosterone levels therefore rise from the lower plateau (0.06 to 1.68 nmol/L) to the higher (7.7 to 29.4 nmol/L), that males grow taller, stronger, and more powerful than females. It is also why, within those two respective plateaus, there is little or no correlation between testosterone concentration and performance, which is why athletes with CAIS are able to compete at elite level in the female category, and also why there is no need to establish an upper testosterone limit for the male category.[164]

Meanwhile, thanks to Doriane's contacts and organisational efforts, 42 of the world's leading sports science and sports medicine scientists signed up to a statement agreeing that the sex difference in testosterone levels is the primary driver of the sex difference in athletic performance:

> Based on our collective expertise and experience, the undersigned specialists in the sports science and sports medicine communities consider the following to be indisputable scientific facts:
>
> 1. The main physical attributes that contribute to elite athletic performance are:
>   - power generation (speed and strength), which is based on muscle mass, muscle fiber type, and biomechanics;
>   - aerobic power (VO2 max), which is based on hemoglobin concentration, total blood volume, maximal stroke volume, cardiac size/mass/compliance, skeletal muscle blood flow, capillary density, and mitochondrial content;
>   - body composition, i.e., lean body mass and fat mass;
>   - fuel utilization, i.e., glycogen breakdown and anaerobic capacity; and
>   - economy of motion.
> 2. Biological males and biological females are materially different with respect to these attributes.

Compared to biological females, biological males have greater lean body mass (more skeletal muscle and less fat), larger hearts (both in absolute terms and scaled to lean body mass), higher cardiac outputs, larger hemoglobin mass, larger VO2 max (also both in absolute terms and scaled to lean body mass), greater glycogen utilization, higher anaerobic capacity, and different economy of motion.

3. The primary reason for these sex differences in the physical attributes that contribute to elite (> 99th percentile) athletic performance is exposure in gonadal males with functional androgen receptors to much higher levels of testosterone during growth and development (puberty), and throughout the athletic career.

   No other endogenous physical or physiological factors have been identified as contributing substantially and predominantly to these differences. As a policy matter, the exogenous factors that influence elite athletic performance – nutrition, training, sports psychology, environmental manipulation, sports medicine techniques, etc – should be equally accessible to biological male and biological female athletes.

4. Therefore, the primary driver of the sex difference in elite athletic performance is exposure in biological males to much higher levels of testosterone during growth, development, and throughout the athletic career.[165]

We also got a clear and detailed explanation from Angelica, Richard and David of how individuals with 46XY DSDs such as 5-ARD and 17β are biologically the *same* in every material respect as biological males without DSDs. As already explained (see p 129), they have the same male chromosomes (XY) and SRY gene, which produces the same male gonads (testes), which from puberty onwards produce the same adult male levels of serum testosterone, which have the same virilising effect on the body as those testosterone levels have in biological males without DSDs, building bone and muscle size and strength and increasing the level of serum haemoglobin in exactly the same way. Angelica, Richard and David explained very clearly that the *only* material physical differences between 46XY DSD individuals and biological males without DSDs are that the external genitals of 46XY DSD individuals may be under-virilised (the reason why some are assigned a female legal sex at birth) and they may have male pattern baldness and a reduced prostate, none of which impacts upon sports performance.

As evidence of the male performance advantage that 46XY DSD athletes enjoy over 46XX athletes, we needed to demonstrate how 46XY DSD athletes with a female gender identity were massively over-represented in the female category in athletics, not only in the upper levels of the sport – the '142 times more prevalent' figure we had presented to the *Chand* Panel – but also, and in particular, on the podium at elite athletics events. This information was not publicly known, because the IAAF had been able to keep the identities of affected athletes confidential. We negotiated strict confidentiality undertakings with the other parties that allowed us to use this evidence in the *Semenya* proceedings. It still cannot be made public, but it was compelling. And it was made all the more so by what happened after the *Chand* award in July 2015 enabled 46XY DSD athletes to compete again in the female category without suppressing their testosterone levels.

When three DSD athletes had dropped their testosterone levels (to comply with the 2011 Hyperandrogenism Regulations) from above 20 nmol/L to below 2 nmol/L, their 800m times had slowed by 5.7-7.8% (roughly 5-8 seconds).[166] But after the regulations were suspended in July 2015 and so DSD athletes no longer had to suppress their testosterone levels, the 800m times of Caster Semenya and two other affected athletes (Francine Niyonsaba and Margaret Wambui – who have publicly acknowledged that they are also 46XY DSD[167]) improved from above two minutes to the 1:54-1:57 range. From 14 September 2015 to 30 June 2019, Caster Semenya won 31 consecutive 800m races, including a series of World Championship and Olympic golds, and in June 2018 she ran the 800m in 1:54.25, which was then, and remains as of the time of writing, the fourth best female 800m time ever. She, Niyonsaba and Wambui came in first, second and fourth respectively in the 2017 IAAF World Championships, first and second in the 2016 IAAF World Indoor Championships and in the 2018 Commonwealth Games (when only two of them competed), and first in the 2018 IAAF World Indoor Championships (when only one competed). One of them also came first in every single 800m race that one or more of them entered in the 2016, 2017 and 2018 Diamond League series. Their 46XX female opponents, lacking the physiological advantages conferred by male puberty, were unable to compete with them.

All of this evidence was compelling, but what brought it vividly to life was the sight of the same three 46XY DSD athletes sweeping the female 800m podium at the 2016 Olympic Games in Rio. As one commentator put it: *'If that doesn't make you understand from a simple odds perspective that there needs to be a limit on testosterone in women's sports, then I don't know what will'.*[168] Because of my role as chair of the WADA Independent Observer Team at the Rio Olympics, I was able to be in the athletics stadium watching the female 800m final in Rio, and I knew there and then that the result was such a striking demonstration of the overwhelming advantage that 46XY DSD athletes have over 46XX athletes that it virtually guaranteed that we would win the case eventually, cold comfort though I know that will be to the other athletes who competed in the race that day.

Revising the regulations

Before we went back to court, however, we had to fix the flaws in the 2011 DSD Regulations that had been exposed by the *Chand* proceedings. The new 2018 DSD Regulations, which came into effect in April 2018,[169] changed the position dramatically:

- The title of the regulations was changed from *'Regulations Governing Eligibility of Females with Hyperandrogenism to Compete in Women's Competition'* to *'Eligibility Regulations for the Female Classification (Athletes with Differences of Sex Development)'*. It would have been wrong for the regulations to apply to all females with hyperandrogenism, because in normal medical parlance that would include biological females with PCOS or CAH or testosterone-secreting adrenal or ovarian tumours. Because an excess of androgens is only a threat to fair competition in the female category if it confers the physiological advantages of male puberty that drive the sex difference in sports performance, we reverted to the position taken in the IAAF's 2006 Policy on Gender Verification by excluding from the scope of the regulations 46XX females with PCOS or CAH. Instead, the 2018 DSD Regulations only applied to individuals who had male chromosomes (46XY) and therefore had the SRY gene and so testes rather than ovaries, and therefore had testosterone in the normal adult male range, with all of the consequent physiological and ergogenic benefits, but who also had an enzyme deficiency (5-ARD or 17β) or an androgen insensitivity (PAIS)[170] that caused their external genitals to be under-virilised and therefore ambiguous in appearance at birth, resulting in them being reared as female.

- The new regulations permitted such 46XY DSD athletes to compete in the female category if they had a female gender identity and if they first suppressed their testosterone levels for at least six months, on the basis that this would reduce the concentration of haemoglobin in their blood, even if the other legacy benefits of male puberty would remain.[171] And they now had to suppress their testosterone levels to below 5 nmol/L (rather than 10 nmol/L), based on the studies that established the normal adult male range of circulating testosterone goes down to 7.7 nmol/L, while the normal female range only goes up to 1.68 nmol/L (or 3.01 nmol/L for women with PCOS), and also based on the evidence that an increase in the level of circulating testosterone from the normal female range up to 9.9 nmol/L would confer a material ergogenic advantage.[172]
- Where a 46XY athlete has partial androgen insensitivity syndrome (PAIS), the degree of insensitivity will vary, and therefore so will the extent to which the adult male levels of testosterone that their testes produce will virilise their body. Therefore, the 2018 DSD Regulations only applied to athletes with androgen insensitivity if they were *'sufficiently androgen-sensitive for [their] elevated levels of testosterone* [5 nmol/L or above] *to have a material androgenising effect'*.[173] If the athlete chose to undergo further investigation, the extent of their virilisation would be assessed by an independent panel of medical experts who were experienced in assessing clinical signs of virilisation as part of their regular medical practices and could do so reliably based on physical examination and laboratory tests, with the regulations specifying that the benefit of any doubt should be resolved in favour of the athlete.
- The scope of the regulations was also narrowed in other ways:
- Whereas the 2011 Hyperandrogenism Regulations had applied not only to international competitions, but also to all national competitions held under the rules of a member federation, the 2018 DSD Regulations applied *only* to international competitions. In other words, 46XY DSD athletes competing below international level were not subject to the 2018 DSD Regulations.
- Even at international competitions, the 2018 DSD Regulations applied *only* to track events over distances from 400m to one mile (referred to in the regulations as '*Restricted Events*'). They permitted 46XY DSD athletes to compete without restriction in any other track event, and in any field event. The many criticisms that were levelled at this aspect of the regulations were misplaced. We were well aware that the sex difference in sports performance applies across all events, but the *Chand* Panel had warned us not to go further than we could prove at that stage was necessary to protect fair competition in the female category. And to that date, a large percentage of the known DSD athletes had competed over distances between 400m and one mile; very few DSD athletes had competed at the highest levels in other events. That is why we limited the 2018 DSD Regulations to track events between 400m and one mile,[174] where they would have the most immediate impact, and to avoid any argument that the regulations were disproportionate. But we expressly noted that if 46XY DSD athletes started to be over-represented in other events, the regulations would

have to be extended, and we knew that ultimately that was exactly what would happen. In effect, this was a beachhead strategy: we wanted to establish the principle first, and then build from there.

In September 2017 we advised the *Chand* Panel that the IAAF was withdrawing the 2011 Hyperandrogenism Regulations and replacing them with the new 2018 DSD Regulations. The new regulations would not impact Dutee, because she only ran the 100m and 200m sprints, rather than any Restricted Event, and so the *Chand* proceedings were terminated. But the 2018 DSD Regulations did impact Caster Semenya, because her favoured events were the 800m and 1500m. And whereas in 2010 she had felt too young and not ready to take on the world governing body,[175] in 2018 she was very ready to do so, not just for herself but also for future generations of athletes like her. She insisted: *'This fight is not just about me, it's about taking a stand and fighting for dignity, equality and the human rights of women in sport. All we ask is to be able to run free, as the strong and fearless women we are'.*[176] Whereas others noted: *'If Caster wins her case, the IAAF will have to let people compete in female categories based on their legal sex, which these days can be a matter of choice. That means that you will have people with testes and high male levels of testosterone competing in the female category, and that will mean women with ovaries and low levels of testosterone have no chance of winning. That will in the long run threaten to destroy women's sport'.*[177]

'The sporting trial of the century'[178]

In June 2018 Caster Semenya filed a complaint against the IAAF with the CAS, seeking a declaration that the 2018 DSD Regulations were unlawful. She was represented by Greg Nott and Patrick Bracher of Norton Rose Fulbright South Africa, as well as by the lawyers who had represented Dutee Chand, Jim Bunting and Carlos Sayao, then of Davis Ward Phillips & Vineberg in Toronto, Canada, now of Tyr LLP. Together they formed an excellent team who were highly professional but also courteous and collegial in their approach, and therefore a pleasure to work with. (In my experience it is better to have strong legal adversaries in a case rather than weak ones. It means no one gets distracted by unimportant side issues, and everyone can remain focused on the issues that are really in dispute). Liz Riley and I, together with our Bird & Bird colleague Chris Lavey, represented the IAAF. Athletics South Africa, represented by Dev Maharaj & Associates from Bryanston, South Africa, instructing Norman Arendse SC and Ncumisa Mayosi, filed separate proceedings that were consolidated with Caster Semenya's for trial. Annabelle Bennett was appointed by the CAS to chair the Panel hearing the case; the IAAF nominated Hans Nater again to sit alongside her; and Caster Semenya nominated Hugh Fraser, a Canadian lawyer and former elite athlete. In exchange for the claimants' agreement to an expedited schedule that would see the case heard in February 2019, we agreed that the 2018 DSD Regulations would not be implemented before an award had been issued.

In their pre-hearing submissions, Caster Semenya's legal team based their case, as Dutee's team had done before them, on a conflation of biological sex and gender. They said:

- The 2018 DSD Regulations discriminate against 46XY DSD athletes: (1) on the basis of *'a natural or genetic trait which they have possessed since birth and over which they have no* control', ie levels of endogenous testosterone above the normal female range; (2) on the basis of their female sex, because no male athletes are subject to the restrictions placed on 46XY DSD athletes; (3) on the basis of their gender, by refusing to recognise their female gender; and (4) on the basis of their physical appearance, by *'deliberately seek[ing] out women with a stereotypically male phenotype, while not targeting women who possess a stereotypically female appearance'*.[179]

- Such discrimination is not necessary to safeguard fair competition in the female category, because DSDs are simply *'a form of genetic difference that should be celebrated in the same way'* as other genetic differences seen within the diverse population of female athletes, such as the superior fast-twitch muscles of Jamaican sprinters.[180] In support of that argument, Caster Semenya's lawyers put forward as an expert witness Dr Alun Williams of Manchester Metropolitan University, who submitted that the genetic variations that cause DSDs and the consequent elevated testosterone levels are not qualitatively different from other performance-enhancing genetic variations, and therefore there is no reason to treat individuals with DSDs any differently from other athletes.[181]

- Dr Eric Vilain (then Professor and Chair of the Department of Genomics and Precision Medicine at George Washington University), who had switched from supporting (see p 134) to attacking World Athletics' position because he disagreed with our description of 46XY DSD individuals as *'biological males'*,[182] asserted that *'the current scientific mainstream … recognises that sex is not binary but rather a spectrum, where no single factor (e.g., presence or absence of testes) prevails above all others'*.[183]

- Several experts, led by Roger Pielke, Professor of Environmental Studies and Director of the Sports Governance Centre at the University of Colorado, focused on a paper published by Stéphane Bermon and Pierre-Yves Garnier in July 2017, in response to a suggestion made by CAS arbitrator Richard McLaren during the *Chand* proceedings, which reported a correlation between the testosterone levels and the performance levels of female athletes in the 400m, 400m hurdles, and 800m at the 2011 and 2013 IAAF World Championships.[184] Pielke et al insisted the paper was statistically flawed, and established only correlation, not any causative relationship, between testosterone levels and female athletic sports performance. They also noted that there were no other studies establishing any causative relationship between levels of endogenous testosterone and sports performance in female athletes.[185]

- Caster Semenya's experts did not dispute the aspects of the Handelsman/Hirschberg/Bermon review paper that established that the sex difference in adult testosterone levels is the main reason for the physiological sex differences that drives the difference in sports performance between adult males and adult females. But (still conflating sex and gender) they asserted that that paper does not establish what degree of performance advantage (if any) *'females with DSD have over females without DSD'*, especially given that (they said) *'there are differences in how testosterone acts in the bodies of females with DSD compared with males and women without DSD'*. They asserted that females with CAIS and PAIS, whose receptors are completely or largely insensitive to testosterone, have success at the highest level of elite international athletics, which they said was further proof that testosterone is not important to female sport performance. Therefore, they insisted, the proposition that testosterone levels determine female sports performance has still not been established.[186]

- Professor Richard Holt also repeated the arguments he had made in *Chand* that there is an overlap between male and female testosterone ranges (if you include within the female range the testosterone levels of 46XY DSD individuals with a female gender identity), and that there is no positive correlation between testosterone levels and female athletic performance. He proposed that the sex difference in sport performance was instead due to the sex difference in growth hormone levels (as he had argued in *Chand*), or else it was due to (unspecified) benefits conferred by the Y chromosome (an argument originally advanced by Dr Fausto-Sterling).[187]

- Caster Semenya's lawyers argued that the IAAF could not show that the restrictions in the 2018 DSD Regulations were rationally connected to the objective of protecting fair competition in the female category because: (1) if testosterone affects performance at all, it does so not just in Restricted Events but also in other events (in other words, they used our attempt to be proportionate as a stick to beat us with); (2) there is no empirical data suggesting that females with testosterone over 5 nmol/L have a performance advantage over females with testosterone under that threshold; (3) females with PCOS are not covered by the DSD Regulations even though they may have testosterone levels greater than 5 nmol/L; and (4) the process of determining whether 46XY DSD athletes are sufficiently androgen-sensitive to be virilised by their elevated testosterone levels is subjective, uncertain, and arbitrary.[188]

- Nor (they argued) could the IAAF show that the 2018 DSD Regulations are proportionate, because they will cause *'prolonged and severe harm'* to affected athletes, who will be subject to highly intrusive examinations that will undermine their dignity and self-esteem; their cases will inevitably become public and as a result they will be stigmatised; and the medical treatment they will be required to undergo if they wish to continue to compete in Restricted Events carries the risk of serious physical and mental side-effects, and will not be the product of informed and voluntary consent.[189]

- This left the question of how eligibility for the female category should be determined, if not as the IAAF had proposed. Roger Pielke and Eric Vilain suggested that this should depend: if an individual has been reared as female and consistently lived as a female, they should be permitted to compete in the female category, but if they have been reared as male, and subsequently transitioned to female, ie if they have *'changed lanes'*, they should not.[190] They did not explain why they drew this distinction, although, as noted above (see p 134), Eric Vilain had previously worried about *'the future of women in sports … if … anyone declaring a female gender can compete as a woman'*. In any event, as already explained (see pp 133–135), the attempted distinction does not stand up to scrutiny: there is no relevant biological difference between 46XY DSD athletes and transgender MTF athletes, and the latter will likely have experienced gender dysphoria from an early age, but been unable, for social and/or legal reasons, to *'change lanes'* until they were much older.

Many of these arguments were also made by ASA's expert witnesses.[191] On cross-examination I asked Ross Tucker why he was appearing for the other side when he had previously noted that *'the presence of the Y-chromosome …, and specifically the SRY gene on it, which directs the formation of testes and the production of testosterone, is a key criteria* [sic] *on which to separate people into categories'*.[192] The answer was that Ross was there only to speak to his criticisms of the Bermon/Garnier paper,[193] but because he is a scientist of integrity he had to acknowledge that otherwise he agreed with our case.

In response, bolstered by our own team of expert witnesses (Bermon, Handelsman, Hirschberg, Auchus, and Coleman, joined by Dr Ben Levine of the University of Texas and Dr Aaron Baggish of Harvard Medical School, as well as Joanna Harper), we were able to point out that most of the claimants' arguments simply missed the mark, because the 2018 DSD Regulations distinguished between 46XY individuals with testes (biological males) and 46XX individuals with ovaries (biological females):

- Contrary to what Caster Semenya says in her book, we did not claim that the IAAF was above the law and so *'could discriminate at will'*.[194] We noted that the IAAF is not a public authority, exercising state powers, and therefore it is not a party to the European Convention on Human Rights or other international human rights treaties, but we also acknowledged that the IAAF's own constitution expressly commits it not to discriminate improperly between different athletes. We pointed out, however, that it is not improper to differentiate between athletes if they are objectively different in relevant ways, if that differential treatment is necessary to achieve fair competition, and if it is rationally related and proportionate to the achievement of that objective.[195]

- We noted that the Handelsman/Hirschberg/Bermon review paper establishes definitively the clear sex difference in adult levels of serum testosterone. It also establishes that that difference is the cause of the physiological advantages conferred by male puberty that are the main reason for the clear sex difference in athletic performance that emerges from puberty onwards.[196]

- Because of that clear sex difference in sports performance, everyone accepts that the only way to give female athletes the same chance as male athletes to excel in and benefit from the sport is to create a female-only competition category. And that means you have to decide who is eligible to compete in that category. While legal sex works well as a proxy in most cases, it falls down in the case of biological males with a female gender identity, whether transgender MTF or 46XY DSD, because they have all of the physiological benefits conferred by male puberty. While the IAAF believes that individuals should be accepted in society based on their gender identity, in the context of sport, where physical prowess is crucial to outcome, *'biology has to trump identity'*.[197]

- Just as an SGB is entitled to create age categories and weight categories to ensure that victory is determined by what its stakeholders value (natural talents perfected by hard work) and not by factors they do not value (eg differences in age or weight), so too it is entitled to create a protected competition category that excludes biological males, because the testosterone produced by their testes gives them a massive physiological advantage that biological females cannot overcome by talent and hard work. And if the testes, and the physiological advantages they confer, require and justify the exclusion of biological males from the female category, then they also require and justify the exclusion of 46XY DSD athletes from the female category, because the 46XY DSD athletes covered by the regulations have testes and undergo normal male puberty, and therefore have all of the same consequential physiological advantages as other biological males, whether their gender identity is male or female.[198]

- There is a clear difference between physiological advantages caused by natural variations occurring within the 46XX female athlete population, such as the fast twitch muscles of Jamaican athletes, and physiological advantages caused by the testes of 46XY DSD athletes, because testes are not a *'natural genetic advantage'* within the 46XX female athlete population. Instead, they only occur within the 46XY athlete population, and are the very reason why the female-only competition category has been created.[199]

- Crucially, the question posed by the *Chand* Panel – whether endogenous testosterone levels determine performance within the female competition category – has no relevance for this case, because this case *'is not about biological females and how their bodies respond to testosterone; it is about biological males with 5-ARD (and other 46XY DSDs), how their bodies respond to testosterone, and the performance advantages of that response when they compete against biological females'*.[200] And that made the much-criticised Bermon-Garnier study of the testosterone levels of female athletes at the Daegu and Moscow World Championships (see p 154) irrelevant. Steph and Pierre-Yves also pointed out that their paper had not suggested any causative relationship between female testosterone levels and sports performance, because differences of testosterone levels within the narrow range of the adult female plateau – 0.06-1.68 nmol/L – will not make any ergogenic difference.[201]
- Athletes with one of the 46XY DSDs covered by the 2018 DSD Regulations are *'biologically ... the same in every material respect as male athletes without DSDs'*. For example, because they have testes that produce adult male levels of testosterone from puberty onwards, and they are androgen-sensitive, *'5-ARD individuals have all the ergogenic physiological advantages of high testosterone levels that adult males have, irrespective of their natal or legal sex, their gender identity, or the appearance of their genitals'*.[202] As a result, all of the scientific evidence that establishes the clear dose-response relationship between testosterone (whether endogenous or exogenous) and muscle mass, strength and serum haemoglobin concentration, and the consequent physiological advantages that biological males have over biological females, applies equally and fully to 46XY DSD athletes.[203]
- Testosterone causes the body to produce more erythrocytes and thereby to produce more haemoglobin. The data showed that the average haemoglobin levels of three DSD athletes were similar to the average haemoglobin levels of other biologically male athletes, giving them a performance advantage over biological females.[204]
- The data also showed that when four DSD athletes were required to drop their testosterone levels down from 21-25 nmol/L to below 2 nmol/L, their times slowed by between 5.7% and 7.8%.[205]
- The performance advantage that the 46XY DSD athletes have over biological females is demonstrated by their enormous over-representation in elite female competition.[206] While the claimants are right that no 46XY DSD athlete has yet won a women's event by a margin of 10-12%, this is not because 46XY DSD athletes lack the performance advantages that other biologically male athletes enjoy. Instead, it is just because *'the particular [46XY DSD] athletes we have seen thus far are not as good as the best males'*.[207]
- The 2018 DSD Regulations are much narrower and more focused in scope than the 2011 Hyperandrogenism Regulations. In particular, they are limited in scope to the Restricted Events, because a majority of the 46XY DSD athletes with a female gender identity have competed in the 400m and 800m, with

great success, which suggests that *'these are the events where 46XY DSD athletes derive the greatest performance-enhancing benefits from their elevated levels of endogenous testosterone'*, while they have also had success in longer events, up to a mile.[208]

- The evidence does not support the claimants' contention that the 2018 DSD Regulations have adverse effects that outweigh the benefits they confer. The suggestion that affected athletes would be publicly stigmatised is refuted by the fact that World Athletics has kept confidential the names of the many DSD athletes who have competed at the highest level, and there are new provisions in the regulations to prevent the sorts of leaks at a national level that were seen in the cases of Dutee Chand and Caster Semenya. In addition, potential DSD athletes will not be identified based on their physical appearance or behaviour, but rather by objective means such as their drug test results revealing levels of endogenous testosterone above the normal female range. As for the side effects of reducing those testosterone levels, gonadectomy or hormone treatment to reduce testosterone levels are the recognised gender-affirming standard of care for 46XY DSD individuals with a female gender identity, in order to avoid virilisation of their bodies.[209] And Professors Hirschberg and Auchus, medical doctors with extensive experience of dealing with DSD cases, are not aware of any evidence that lowering the serum testosterone levels of 46XY DSD athletes to the normal female range has any significant harmful consequences for those individuals' physical health, even if it does adversely affect their sports performance.[210]

- The oft-repeated claim that the IAAF has required 46XY DSD athletes to have their testes surgically removed in order to compete in the female category[211] is simply untrue. Gonadectomy is not a requirement under the regulations; hormone treatment to reduce testosterone levels is another valid option.[212]

Caster Semenya's lawyers and witnesses were not happy at our change of tack (moving from arguing about the impact of endogenous testosterone on female sports performance to noting that 46XY DSD individuals are biological males who enjoy the same performance advantages over biological females as all other biological males enjoy). In reply, they argued that:

- By describing athletes covered by the 2018 DSD Regulations as *'biological males'*, the IAAF is attempting *'to convert the DSD Regulations into a shadow transgender rule'*, and regressing to *'an egregious form of sex testing'*.[213]

- While it is true that the elevated testosterone levels of females with 5-ARD give them increased muscle mass and strength and higher levels of serum haemoglobin, which would likely be performance-enhancing in certain disciplines, their deficiency of DHT (a potent and performance-enhancing androgen that is banned by WADA) means that it is *'"certain" that the overall androgenic advantage that women with 5-ARD enjoy over other women is not the same as the advantage that men have over women. In this regard, the evidence shows that no woman with a DSD, including 5-ARD, has demonstrated athletic performances that come anywhere close to the performance of elite male athletes'*.[214] Note the implicit assumption that this failure to match the performances of elite male athletes was because of the deficit of DHT, rather than because the 5-ARD individuals were not elite athletes.

- The fall in performance levels of three DSD athletes after they started suppressing their testosterone levels by taking oral contraceptives was not because of their lower testosterone levels but rather because of the adverse side-effects of the medication.[215]

The Semenya hearing

The CAS Panel heard the case in Lausanne from 18 to 22 February 2019, amid significant media interest. Seb Coe opened our case by underlining the importance of protecting fair competition in the female category. Caster Semenya in turn testified that the IAAF's suggestion that she is a biological male *'re-opens my wounds from 2009'*.[216] She described the medical examinations that she was forced to undergo in Pretoria before the 2009 IAAF World Championships and then in Berlin itself at the World Championships. She said the leaking of the fact that she had been *'gender tested'* had led to *'relentless public scrutiny'* that has continued ever since. She said that in Berlin she was *'profoundly confused that her gender was being questioned for the first time in her life'*.[217] I did not challenge that statement on cross-examination because I was not aware until I read her 2023 memoir that in fact her gender had been frequently questioned by friends during her childhood, and by other athletes and coaches in South Africa, and that she had been advised by the doctor in Pretoria and by an ASA official in Berlin that the test results would not be good for her and it would be better if she feigned injury and withdrew from the event.[218]

Caster Semenya then explained that in 2010 she started taking oral contraceptives to reduce her testosterone levels below 10 nmol/L because that was the only way the IAAF would let her continue to race. She insisted that her subsequent slower race times were not due to her lower testosterone levels, but rather to the adverse side-effects of the contraceptive pill, which included hot sweats, fever, and weight gain. Her performances improved again when she stopped taking the pill after the *Chand* Panel suspended the 2011 Hyperandrogenism Regulations in July 2015, but again she insisted that this was not because her testosterone levels increased, but rather because she *'stopped feeling sick and was once again able to sharpen her mental focus'*. She disputed that her *'naturally high testosterone levels'* gave her an advantage over her female competitors, noting that she had been beaten several times by those competitors and at other times had only won narrowly, while she could not get close to the times posted by the best male athletes.[219]

Caster Semenya apparently was not impressed by my cross-examination of her.[220] This was not just because of my appearance: she describes me as *'an overweight, puffy-faced boy'* who *'I don't think had ever run across a street, much less gotten near a track'*. To be fair, she was right, I was overworked and unfit at the time. It was also because of my suggestion that it was slightly unusual that she ran negative splits, ie she ran the second half of the 800m faster than the first half, and that her testosterone levels seemed to spike immediately before major events, including the 2012 Olympics. She said that those spikes were not due to her skipping her medication – she insisted that she always took the contraceptive pills every day – but instead were natural increases due to the fact that in the lead-up to those events she reduced the intensity of her training and rested more.[221] She says in her autobiography that I also suggested (inaccurately) that she had hidden from a blood test at the 2012 Olympics, that she never ran on the inside lane, and that she had *'never lost a race'*, but I have checked the transcript of the cross-examination, and in fact I didn't suggest any of those things. Nevertheless, I regret that Caster felt that I was *'using nonsense to make [her] look bad as an athlete and as a person'*. That was not my intent. In fact, in my eyes her cross-examination was something of a side-show, because our case was simply that her testes and normal male levels of circulating testosterone give her all the normal male physiological advantages that make a separate female competition category necessary. This was all scientific fact; there was no need to put it to her in cross-examination.

The parties' respective expert witnesses gave evidence not sequentially but concurrently, in a series of '*hot tubs*' organised by subject matter.[222] This approach (which had also been adopted in *Chand*) is somewhat unusual and requires some explanation. The normal adversarial process of cross-examining expert witnesses individually and sequentially does not sit particularly well with the standard scientific method, which is to resolve differences by identifying competing hypotheses and allowing a consensus of opinion to emerge and coalesce behind the hypothesis that has the strongest supporting arguments and evidence. Therefore, a different method has been developed (originally in Australia), known as '*hot tubbing*', in which the experts testify concurrently in a structured discussion chaired by the judge that is designed to encourage the experts to put points and questions to each other and ideally to arrive at a consensus on particular points, while identifying the reasons for a divergence of opinion on any remaining points. Where the judge permits, the advocates may also ask questions to test particular propositions, but the judge remains in control and ensures that the experts are not confined to answering those questions but instead engage directly with their professional colleagues on the other side and so (ideally) feel constrained to acknowledge where the weight of the evidence and considered opinion lie.[223]

In my experience, hot-tubbing can be very effective, but only if the judge is skilled enough and informed enough to control and conduct the discussion. In both *Chand* and *Semenya*, the Panel chair was Annabelle Bennett, an eminent Australian judge with a strong scientific background, including a biochemistry doctorate. She was therefore both familiar with hot tubbing and able to shepherd the expert witnesses skilfully through the key scientific issues. In *Semenya* she heard concurrent evidence from three to nine scientific experts at a time in a series of six different hot tubs. She was able to take each group of experts through a list of pre-agreed issues, quickly identify areas of common ground, and focus on the reasons for the remaining differences. The experts were clearly more comfortable with this format than they would have been with individual cross-examination. Significant time was saved, and they were discouraged from making unsupported points, because they knew they would be immediately challenged by learned colleagues who were fully familiar with the evidence in the field. Instead, there was a largely respectful exchange that enabled the experts to debate, to make their own points, and to comment immediately on what others said. This allowed the key points and evidence to emerge naturally, so that the Panel could understand clearly what was agreed and what remained in dispute, and why.

The process undoubtedly tested the nerves of the parties' respective legal teams, since we were all far more used to cross-examination, and were nervous about giving up the opportunity to win concessions from the other side. However, Annabelle Bennett gave all counsel a fair opportunity to ask further questions, and in the event we seldom felt the need to do so, given her skill in covering the necessary ground fully and fairly to all parties. The account given in the award of the hot tub evidence illustrates how that process helped the Panel to cut through the morass of detail to the key issues it had to resolve and the key evidence it had to consider.

The CAS award

The CAS Panel reserved judgment at the end of the hearing, and on 1 May 2019 it released a long and detailed award that remains a landmark judgment on this topic and in CAS jurisprudence generally.[224]

- The Panel started by noting: *'This case … involves a collision of scientific, ethical and legal conundrums. It also involves incompatible, competing, rights. It is not possible to give effect to, or endorse, one set of rights without restricting the other set of rights. Put simply, on the one hand is the right of every athlete to compete in sport, to have their legal sex and gender identity respected, and to be free from any form of discrimination. On the other hand is the right of female athletes, who are relevantly biologically disadvantaged vis-à-vis male athletes, to be able to compete against other female athletes and not against male athletes and to achieve the benefits of athletic success, such as positions on the podium and consequential commercial advantages'*.[225]

- The Panel also noted that *'once it is recognised that it is legitimate to have separate categories of male and female competition, it inevitably follows that it is necessary to devise an objective, fair and effective means of determining which individuals may, and which may not, participate in those categories. … The Panel accepts the IAAF's submission that reference to a person's legal sex alone may not always constitute a fair and effective means of making that determination. This is because … the reason for the separation between male and female categories in competitive athletics is ultimately founded on biology rather than legal status. The purpose of having separate categories is to protect a class of individuals who lack certain insuperable performance advantages from having to compete against individuals who possess those insuperable advantages. In this regard, the fact that a person is recognised in law as a woman and identifies as a woman does not necessarily mean that they lack those insuperable performance advantages associated with certain biological traits that predominate in individuals who are generally (but not always) recognised in law as males and self-identify as males. It is human biology, not legal status or gender identity, that ultimately determines which individuals possess the physical traits which give rise to that insuperable advantage and which do not'*.[226]

- *'On true analysis, therefore, the purpose of the male-female divide in competitive athletics is not to protect athletes with a female legal sex from having to compete against athletes with a male legal sex. Nor is it to protect athletes with a female gender identity from having to compete against athletes with a male gender identity. Rather, it is to protect individuals whose bodies have developed in a certain way following puberty from having to compete against individuals who, by virtue of their bodies having developed in a different way following puberty, possess certain physical traits that create such a significant performance advantage that fair competition between the two groups is not possible'*.[227]

- *'Once it is recognised that the reason for organising competitive athletics into separate male and female categories rests on the need to protect one group of individuals against having to compete against individuals who possess certain insuperable performance advantages derived from biology rather than legal status, it follows that it may be legitimate to regulate the right to participate in the female category by reference to those biological factors rather than legal status alone. Since those biological factors do not correspond perfectly with legal sex in every case, the Panel accepts the IAAF's submission that it is sometimes necessary to devise eligibility conditions that are not exclusively based on [legal] sex. The Panel stresses, however, that the necessity criterion can only be established where the evidence establishes to the requisite degree of proof that the biological factor which is the subject of the regulation confers a sufficiently significant performance advantage in each athletic discipline which is covered by the regulation'.*[228]

- The Panel noted that it had heard a large amount of expert evidence that had not been available to the *Chand* Panel.[229] In particular, it noted there was now clear evidence, including from the Handelsman/Hirschberg/Bermon paper, and a fair degree of consensus among the experts, that the normal adult female male range of circulating testosterone is 0.06 to 1.6 nmol per litre of blood, while the normal adult male range is 7.7 to 29.4 nmol/L;[230] and it is this sex difference in testosterone levels that drives the sex differences in size and strength of bone and muscles and levels of serum haemoglobin, and as such is the primary reason for the sex difference in sports performance.[231]

- The Panel also noted, however, that the *Chand* Panel's ruling meant that it was up to the IAAF to demonstrate that 46XY DSD athletes enjoy a performance advantage over female athletes that is the same as or similar in magnitude to that enjoyed by male athletes over female athletes, and that the cause of that performance advantage is their higher testosterone levels.[232] In this regard, the Panel noted that:

  - The experts agreed that from puberty onwards, 46XY DSD athletes have greater lean body mass, larger hearts and higher cardiac output, larger haemoglobin mass and higher VO_2 max than 46XX athletes, because they have much higher levels of circulating testosterone.[233]

  - More specifically, the experts agreed that 46XY DSD athletes with 5-ARD have serum testosterone levels in the normal male range, and therefore have greater muscle mass and haemoglobin than 46XX female athletes. The Panel concluded by a majority, ie with one dissent, that this gives the 46XY female athletes a '*significant*' performance advantage over 46XX female athletes in the Restricted Events.[234]

  - The experts agreed that 5-ARD individuals have a DHT deficiency. They did not agree on whether DHT is expressed in skeletal muscle or on whether it affects sports performance, but they did agree that DHT acts locally rather than systemically, with tissue-specific effects in the urogenital sinus during foetal life, so that a deficiency stunts the development of male external genitalia. The Panel concluded that if DHT has any effect on sports performance, it is *'at most modest'*.[235]

  - Individuals with 5-ARD are fully androgen-sensitive, and therefore their testosterone levels have the same virilising effect on their bodies as those levels have on the bodies of males without 5-ARD.[236]

- ○ The fact that the haemoglobin levels of three DSD athletes fell when they were required to suppress their levels of endogenous testosterone is evidence that elevated testosterone levels would increase their haemoglobin levels and so give them a performance advantage.[237]

- ○ Furthermore, *'[t]he contrast between the rare incidence of 5-ARD in the general population and the overwhelming success that women with 5-ARD have achieved [in elite female athletics] provides powerful evidential support for the conclusion that female athletes with 5-ARD have a significant performance advantage'* over female athletes without a DSD *'which is of such a magnitude as to be capable of subverting fair competition within the female category'.*[238]

- *'On this basis, the majority of the Panel accepts that the IAAF has discharged its burden of establishing that regulations governing the ability of female athletes with 46XY DSD to participate in certain events are necessary to maintain fair competition in female athletics by ensuring that female athletes who do not enjoy the significant performance advantage caused by exposure to levels of circulating testosterone in the adult male range do not have to compete against female athletes who do enjoy that performance advantage'.*[239]

- The majority of the Panel also found that the 2018 DSD Regulations were rationally connected to their objective of ensuring fair competition in the female category in elite athletics, because they only restricted participation in the Restricted Events, where 46XY DSD athletes were particularly over-represented, reflecting their undoubted performance advantage in those events.[240] This vindicated our '*beachhead*' strategy (see p 152).

- The Panel found that the allegedly adverse effects of the regulations *'are, in the main, either hypothetical, or supported by challenged or inconclusive data, or are not relevant to the facts of the present case'.* It noted that if a female athlete has high testosterone levels, that has to be investigated to rule out doping in any event, and if those levels are due to a DSD the investigation will yield information that will help the athlete make an informed decision about possible medical treatments. The Panel accepted the evidence of Richard Auchus and Angelica Hirschberg that the process of assessing the degree of virilisation in PAIS cases is not arbitrary and inconsistent but rather is workable and reliable. It found that requiring 46XY DSD athletes to take oral contraceptives to lower their testosterone levels if they wish to compete in the female category is not disproportionate and does not outweigh the need to protect fair competition in the female category. It acknowledged the concerns expressed by the claimants' witnesses that there could be fluctuations in testosterone above 5 nmol/L even if the pills were taken every day, but decided these concerns *'were speculative … [and] do not provide an evidentiary basis for a conclusion that they* [ie the DSD Regulations] *are presently and on their face disproportionate'.* It therefore found that *'the IAAF has shown that the DSD Regulations are reasonable and proportionate on their face'.*[241]

On that basis, the Panel ruled that the 2018 DSD Regulations were valid and enforceable. But it noted: *'Nevertheless, the Panel has some grave concerns as to the future practical application of the DSD Regulations. While the evidence has not established that those concerns are justified, or that they negate the conclusion of ex facie proportionality, this may change in future unless constant attention is paid to the fairness of how they are implemented'.* In particular, it expressed concern *'as to an athlete's potential inability to remain in compliance with the DSD Regulations in periods of full compliance with treatment protocols, and, more specifically, the resulting consequences of unintentional and unavoidable non-compliance. In addition, the evidence of actual (in contrast to theoretical) significant athletic advantage by a sufficient number of 46XY DSD athletes in the 1500m and 1 mile events could be described as sparse. The IAAF may consider deferring the application of the DSD Regulations to these events until more evidence is available'.*[242]

Caster Semenya has since said that *'I'd hoped things would go our way, but I also knew we were dealing with a rigged system'.*[243] She doesn't explain how it was *'rigged'*, and I reject that suggestion. The CAS Panel was selected by the parties, and was absolutely rigorous throughout in testing the case that we put forward. It upheld that case not because the process was rigged but rather (in my view because it was clear that the facts and the science were on our side. The same lawyers who had represented Caster Semenya subsequently agreed to Annabelle Bennett also sitting on the CAS Panel convened to hear another challenge to World Athletics' DSD regulations, which hardly suggests that they thought she was biased. If Caster Semenya's argument is rather that the system was *'rigged'* because it did not consider fully her human rights arguments, that too is without merit: the award makes clear that her human rights were carefully considered, but were balanced against the rights of biologically female athletes to fair competition.

Similarly, I don't understand why critics of the *Semenya* award suggest that the CAS Panel *'said that it did not have to consider human rights, medical ethics, or the quality of the science'.*[244] In fact, the CAS Panel concluded, following careful and detailed analysis, that the DSD Regulations *'reflect a rational resolution of conflicting human rights'.*[245] As the Swiss Federal Tribunal subsequently noted (see below), the Panel also conducted a comprehensive review of the claimants' ethical and scientific arguments.

Post-Semenya CAS award

The IAAF quickly amended the 2018 DSD Regulations to provide that inadvertent and temporary non-compliance with the 5 nmol/L testosterone limit would not render the DSD athlete ineligible. On the other hand, it decided to maintain the application of the regulations to the 1500m and the mile events, because it remained satisfied that the performance advantage applies to those events as well. In fact, we were never in doubt that the performance advantage applies to *all* track and field events. And that was borne out by subsequent developments. After the *Semenya* award was issued, various 46XY DSD athletes who did not want to lower their testosterone levels instead switched from the Restricted Events to the shorter sprints (100m and 200m) or to races longer than a mile, and quickly excelled: Namibia's Christine Mboma and Beatrice Masilingi came second and sixth respectively in the 200m final at the 2021 Tokyo Olympics;[246] Niger's Aminatou Seyni came fourth in the 200m final at the 2022 World Championships in Oregon and second in the 100m final at the 2022 Championships;[247] and Burundi's Francine Niyonsaba came fifth in the 10,000m at the 2021 Tokyo Olympics, and subsequently recorded the fifth best time ever in the 3,000m and set a world record in the 2,000m.[248]

In June 2019, Caster Semenya's lawyers asked the Swiss Federal Tribunal to overturn the CAS award on the basis that it was contrary to Swiss public policy. In August 2020, the SFT rejected that request, ruling that *'the award under appeal is not incompatible with substantive public policy … no matter how you approach it'*. It said: *'the CAS has performed a comprehensive review of the grievances raised by the parties. Furthermore, the arbitrators accounted for all elements and did not neglect any significant detail. … It has in fact conducted a careful weighing of the different interests present. On the one hand, the CAS has taken into account the interest in ensuring fair competition within female athletics and to defend the "protected class" in order to allow female athletes not having DSD to excel at the highest level. On the other, it considered the effects of oral contraceptives on the health of the 46XY DSD athletes, the infringements associated with the intrusive physical examinations to assess androgen sensitivity, privacy issues, and the possibility for 46XY DSD athletes to successfully maintain their testosterone levels below the regulatory limit. … [T]he conclusion reached by the challenged award is not untenable or even unreasonable'*. In particular, the SFT agreed that the restrictions placed on 46XY DSD athletes' rights and freedoms were justified, because the DSD Regulations *'constitute a measure, that is suitable, necessary and proportionate to the legitimate aims of fairness in sports and maintaining the "protected class". Moreover, such interests cannot be qualified as "clearly less important" in relation to the rights of 46XY DSD athletes'*.[249]

The World Medical Association and the UN High Commissioner for Human Rights nevertheless urged physicians not to implement the 2018 DSD Regulations, arguing that the testosterone suppression required of 46XY DSD athletes if they want to participate in the female category is not in line with medical ethics and could be harmful to the athlete.[250] But the International Federation of Sports Medicine countered that *'[t]his argument is an outdated approach to protect the privacy of patients. If the athlete is fully informed of the consequences of treatment and not coerced into undergoing treatment, the athlete has free choice to do so, which is a fundamental human right'*.[251]

Caster Semenya and her legal team fought on, filing a case with the European Court of Human Rights in February 2021 against the state of Switzerland, arguing that the Swiss legal system had failed to ensure that the CAS and the SFT took proper account of ECtHR jurisprudence in making their respective assessments of the 2018 DSD Regulations, thereby infringing her rights under the European Convention of Human Rights to a fair trial, to equal treatment, to respect for her privacy, and not to be subjected to torture. On 11 July 2023, she successfully negotiated the first stage of that challenge when four of the seven judges of the ECtHR Chamber agreed with her submission that the CAS and the SFT had not adequately taken into account ECtHR jurisprudence in making their respective assessments. The three judges in the minority filed a vigorous dissent, on the ground that protecting fair competition in the female category is *'undeniably'* a legitimate aim, and sports governing bodies *'should have a wide margin of discretion in devising measures to achieve it'*. They noted that the majority, in asserting an infringement of Caster Semenya's right to be treated the same as *'other women'*, had ignored her genetic differences from those women. The minority considered that those differences make it *'necessary and reasonable'* to condition her participation in female competition on observing the restrictions set out in the 2018 DSD Regulations.[252] The case was duly referred on to the ECtHR Grand Chamber (the full court of 17 judges), where the argument was focused on the scope of review by the SFT of the CAS award, rather than on the merits of the DSD Regulations, which was something of a relief to us, given that World Athletics was not a party to the proceedings, and was denied permission to appear at the hearing. In its July 2025 judgment, the Grand Chamber held that because Caster Semenya was forced to submit her claim that

World Athletics' regulations infringed her human rights to private arbitration before the CAS, the SFT was required to carry out a particularly rigorous examination of the compatibility of the CAS award with substantive public policy, including ECHR principles. The Grand Chamber decided that the SFT had not examined sufficiently rigorously the proportionality of the DSD Regulations on issues flagged by Caster Semenya (in particular, her alleged difficulty in maintaining her testosterone levels below 5 nmol/L), and as a result she had not received the fair hearing guaranteed to her under ECHR Article 6(1).[253]

The case was therefore referred back to the SFT for reconsideration. On 30 July 2025, however, World Athletics announced that it was changing its rules to exclude anyone with the SRY gene from the female category (see p 167), and in October 2025 Caster Semenya announced that there was therefore no reason for her to continue to pursue her case against the old regulations before the SFT.[254]

Paris 2024 (Berlin 2009 redux)

The issue came sharply into focus at the 2024 Olympic Games in Paris when Italian boxer Angela Carini stopped fighting just 46 seconds into her bout with Imane Khelif of Algeria, protesting that she feared for her safety. Khelif and a second boxer, Lin Yu-ting of Taiwan, had both been disqualified from female competition in 2023 by the International Boxing Association (the '*IBA*') after failing to meet the eligibility criteria for the female category set out in the IBA's rules.[255] The IBA Technical Competition Rules 2024 state that only *'individuals with chromosome XX'* may compete in the female category, and that *'individuals with chromosome XY'* are excluded from that category,[256] and the IBA President, Umar Kremlev, said: *'According to the results of DNA tests, it was proved that they* [ie Khelif and Yu-ting] *have XY chromosomes'*.[257] As explained above, it is the SRY gene on the Y chromosome that triggers development of testes that produce the levels of testosterone that create the massive sex differences in size, strength and power. A study suggests that male boxers have on average 162% greater punching power than female boxers, which is by far the largest of all the many sex differences in sports performance.[258] Khelif and Yu-Ting both subsequently won gold in their respective weight categories.

Reem Alsalem, the UN's Special Rapporteur on Violence against Women and Girls, commented the next day: *'I think yesterday was the manifestation of how disregard for certain important criteria can actually cause a lot more harm than good. Women and girls in sports have been saying for decades that it is important to maintain... single-sex sport, particularly in elite sport. And, I think yesterday we saw this was not the case and that it created problems for safety, fairness, but also put the players in very difficult positions that neither of them controls and should have not been in. I have been consulting with a wide range of stakeholders, including women and girl athletes – and this issue is important to them. This issue has come up. They would like me to address this issue... it's a fundamental principle in sports to ensure fairness, to ensure safety'*. Ms Alsalem advocated going back to chromosome testing to ensure that any person with an SRY gene (and so having testes) does not compete in the female category: *'It's really important to make sure that the physical safety of any player is upheld. We know that there are simple, efficient, dignified ways of testing sex ... that are not invasive, that are cheap and that are reliable. So I think that will be one of the first things really to come back on is, why is that such a problem? If it can particularly resolve an issue and if it can allay fears, and concerns which are very valid. …'.*[259]

Back to the future

As the table below shows, over the past decade or so SGBs have gradually tightened the testosterone suppression requirements for transgender MTF athletes to compete at elite level in the female category, and many are now abandoning that approach altogether based on the emerging scientific consensus that: (1) testosterone suppression does not materially lessen the performance advantage conferred by a male puberty;[260] and (2) even if the transgender MTF athlete avoids male puberty entirely, which is increasingly unlikely, given the restrictions on access to hormonal puberty blockers,[261] they will still enjoy an advantage over biologically female athletes because (a) they get some exposure to high testosterone levels even before puberty (in the uterus and then during '*mini-puberty*' in the first three to six months after birth),[262] conferring physiological advantages (increased growth velocity, less fat, greater muscle mass and strength) that are likely the reason for the small sex differences in sports performance that emerge even prior to adolescent puberty;[263] and (b) they do not experience the increase in estradiol that comes with female puberty, which has material performance-impairing physiological effects.[264] Further impetus in this direction was supplied by Donald Trump's February 2025 Executive Order, declaring that the US federal government will '*use all appropriate and available measures to see that the International Olympic Committee amends the standards governing Olympic sporting events to promote fairness, safety, and the best interests of female athletes by ensuring that eligibility for participation in women's sporting events is determined according to sex and not gender identity or testosterone reduction*'.[265] In the UK, there was also the Supreme Court's decision in *For Women Scotland Ltd v The Scottish Ministers* that references to '*females*' in section 195 of the Equality Act 2010 are to biological females, and therefore the Act does not require sports bodies to permit biological males to compete in the female category based on their female legal sex and/or gender identity.[266]

In particular, World Boxing announced in May 2025, World Athletics announced in July 2025, and FIS (the International Ski Federation) announced in September 2025 that athletes wishing to participate in the female category at its events will have to prove, through PCR testing of a buccal swab, saliva, or a blood sample, that they do not have the SRY gene.[267] In March 2026 the IOC issued a new policy for all Olympic events that excludes biological males (46XY, with testes) from the female category, even if they have a female gender identity, the only exception being 46 XY DSD individuals with CAIS or other DSD conditions that mean they do not experience the normal physiological effects of male puberty.[268]

Figure 2: Rules on transgender MTF athletes competing in the female category, as of December 2025

1	Permitted without restriction if they declare their gender identity is female, irrespective of male biology.	International Chess Federation (2023-) (as long as they maintain same gender in '*non-chess life*' and that gender identity is recognised under national law).
2	Permitted if testosterone levels are reduced to below 10 nmol/L for at least 12 months.	IOC 2015 consensus.
3	Permitted if testosterone levels are reduced to below 5 nmol/L for at least 12 months.	UCI 2020-22.
4	Permitted if testosterone levels are reduced to below 5 nmol/L for at least 24 months.	UCI 2022-23.
5	Permitted if testosterone levels are reduced to below 2.5 nmol/L for at least 24 months.	World Athletics (2023-2025); WTA (2024-2026); International Tennis Federation (2024-).
6	Permitted if they have not gone through male adolescent puberty, and so they have never experienced the biological effects of adult male levels of testosterone.	World Rugby (2021-); World Aquatics (2023-); UCI (2023-); ICC (2023-); USA Powerlifting (2023-); US Golf Association (2024-); LPGA (2015).
7	Not permitted if 46XY, because they have not gone through female puberty.	World Athletics (2025-); World Boxing (2025-); FIS (2025-); WTA (2026-).

It appears, therefore, that a political, scientific and legal consensus has emerged that eligibility for the female category should be determined by biological sex, not by gender identity, at least at the elite level. However, SGBs will continue to look for ways to accommodate all those who wish to compete in their sports. For example, at grass roots level, where the emphasis is on participation rather than performance, some SGBs may choose to strike a different balance between fairness and inclusion.

Notes

1 *UN experts urge States to uphold the ideal of sport that is inclusive of LGBT and intersex persons*, ohchr.org, 31 October 2023.

2 Anonymous email from *'Citizen Advocate'*, received 3 August 2024.

3 Andrew, *New IAAF Testosterone Regulations are Bigoted and Targeted*, victorypress.com, 2 May 2018.

4 Reuters, *Semenya offered to show her body to officials to prove she was female*, reuters.com, 24 May 2022 (*'World Athletics lawyer Jonathan Taylor, speaking during the HBO Real Sports interview, disagreed with medical panels, including the World Medical Association, that condemned the sport's governing body for requiring women with differences in sex development (DSDs) to take drugs to compete. "You say 'medically it's not healthy for me', then my question back to you is: 'Why do the world's leading experts say that that is what we would prescribe?'" said Taylor. Semenya fired back: "Jonathan must cut his tongue and throw it away. If he wants to understand how that thing has tortured me, he must go and take those medications. He will understand"'*).

5 Kristen Worley, x.com/kristenworley, 3 September 2024.

6 World Economic Forum, *Amazing things happen when you give equal funding to women in sport*, 25 August 2016. See also *Girls who play after-school sport in UK 50% more likely to later get top jobs, study finds*, The Guardian, 11 September 2025.

7 Duke Law Directory, *Professor Doriane Lambelet Coleman*, law.duke.edu, accessed 24 May 2024.

8 Lambelet Coleman D., *On Sex and Gender, A Commonsense Approach* (Simon & Schuster 2024).

9 World Athletics press release, *World Athletics introduces prize money for Olympic gold medallists*, worldathletics.org, 10 April 2024.

10 Some male physiological advantages become evident even before puberty, probably as a result of transiently higher levels of testosterone produced by the testes in the uterus and then at around three to six months, a *'mini-puberty'*. See Becker M and Hesse V, *Minipuberty: Why Does It Happen?*, Hormone Research in Paediatrics, 93:76-84 (2020); Lanciotti L et al, *Up-To-Date Review About Minipuberty and Overview on Hypothalamic-Pituitary-Gonadal Axis Activation in Fetal and Neonatal Life*, 2018(9) Frontiers in Endocrinology, 23 July 2018; Joyner M, Hunter S, and Senefeld JW, *Evidence on sex differences in sports performance*, J Appl Physiol 138:274-281 (2025).

11 Senefeld JW, Lambelet Coleman D, Johnson PW, Carter RE, Clayburn AJ, Joyner MJ, *Divergence in Timing and Magnitude of Testosterone Levels Between Male and Female Youths*, JAMA, 2020 Jul 7;324(1):99-101.

12 See papers cited at footnote 260.

13 Hooven C., *Testosterone: The Story of the Hormone that Dominates and Divides Us* (Cassell 2021), Chapter 5 (*'Getting an Edge'*), and see papers cited at footnote 161. See also *Carol Hooven on Testosterone*, The Dishcast Podcast with Andrew Sullivan, 18 June 2021.

14 Handelsman DJ, Hirschberg A. and Bermon S., *Circulating Testosterone as the Hormonal Basis of Sex Differences in Athletic Performance*, (2018) Endocrine Reviews 39: 803 – 829; Hunter S. et al, *The Biological Basis of Sex Differences in Athletic Performance: Consensus Statement for the American College of Sports Medicine*, Translational Journal of the ACSM 8(4): 1-33, Fall 2023; Hilton E. & Lundberg T., *Transgender women in the female category of sport: perspectives on testosterone suppression and performance advantage*,, Sports Med. 2021, 51(2):199-214; Heather AK, *Transwoman Elite Athletes: Their Extra Percentage Relative to Female Physiology*, Int J Environ Res Public Health, 2022 Jul 26;19(15):9103.

15 Handelsman DJ, *Sex differences in athletic performance emerge coinciding with the onset of male puberty*,, Clin Endocrinol (Oxf), 2017 Jul;87(1):68-72.

16 But not in sports where they do not play a decisive role, such as certain shooting events, where the average sex difference in sports performance is less than 1%. See Hamilton BR et al, *Integrating transwomen athletes into elite competition: The case of elite archery and shooting*, Eur J Sport Sci. 2021 Nov;21(11):1500-1509); Goldschmied N et al, *Do women and men compete equally on a level playing field? An empirical investigation into the 2021 Olympic shooting competitions*, PLoS One. 2023 Sep 27;18(9):e0291017. For example, from 1968 to 1992 the skeet shooting event at the Olympic Games was open to both males and females. At the 1992 Barcelona Games, the gold medal was won by a Chinese female, Zhang Shan, one of seven females in a field of 60: *ZHANG Shan: The only female shooter to win gold in a mixed competition*, olympics.com, 5 July 2020. See also Leong N., *Against Women's Sports*, 95 Wash. U. L. Rev. 1251 (2018) at p. 1266 et seq (citing examples of superior female performance in sports such as long distance swimming, rock climbing, ultramarathon, and dog-sledding, but acknowledging that there is a sex difference in

performance in sports that primarily test speed and strength, due to the sex difference in testosterone levels).

17 Hunter S. et al, *The Biological Basis of Sex Differences in Athletic Performance: Consensus Statement for the American College of Sports Medicine*, Translational Journal of the ACSM 8(4):p 1-33, Fall 2023, Table 2.

18 Dr Fausto-Sterling suggested in 1992 that those physiological differences may be due less to sex differences in circulating testosterone and more to the fact that females are expected not to exercise and compete in sport in the same way or to the same degree as males, and that if females are given more opportunities and resources to participate in sport those differences will narrow and potentially disappear entirely. Fausto-Sterling A., *Myths of Gender: Biological theories about women and men* (Basic Books 2nd Edn 1992), pp. 214-220. For a similar view expressed ten years later, see Wackwitz LA, *Verifying the Myth: Olympic Sex Testing and the Category "Woman"*, (2003) Women's Studies International Forum, Vol. 26, No. 6, pp. 553 – 560 (*'Preservation of the category "woman" for athletic competition is considered necessary because it is commonly assumed that women are simply not capable of achieving the same sort of physical prowess as men. Women, or so the story goes, are weaker than men; they do not jump as high or throw as far; they do not travel as quickly on foot, skis, or skates, across land or through water; they do not throw, hit, punch, or kick as well or as hard; they do not set the same sorts of records or win the same types of competitions as do their male counterparts. These myths about the clear demarcations between the characteristics of men and the characteristics of women support the sexual division of sport by facilitating the assumption that such divisions are natural, when in fact, they are socially constructed. Because of the extent to which these assumptions are ingrained in human cultures—including those surrounding the Olympic Games—women have had less opportunity to compete and to realize their full potentials as athletic beings. Women have been frequently excluded from participation in sport based upon the assumption that they need a special level of protection in and from athletic arenas (Blue, 1987). During the 1928 Olympics, for instance, women were grudgingly allowed to run the 800-m track event for the first time. After several runners "collapsed" near the finish line, Olympic officials declared the race a danger to women and eliminated it from the schedule of events. Women were not allowed to run the 800 m in the Olympics again until 1960 (Blue, 1987). However, despite active measures taken to prevent women from participating in and excelling at athletic competition, at this point in history, the gap between elite male and elite female athletes is remarkably slight. In 1988, for example, the fastest woman in the 100-m race at the Olympic Games ran less than 1 s behind the fastest man in the 100 m, and the gap is closing in other events as well. It may be, then, that cultural restrictions, not genetic differences, have prevented women from exceeding the athletic achievements of men (Hubbard, 1990). The myth of male athletic superiority within a binary sex – gender system, however, is so strong that even some feminists may find it difficult to accept the possibility of other alternatives'*).

To date, however, the performance gap has remained steady: see Seiler S. et al, *The Fall and Rise of the Gender Difference in Elite Anaerobic Performance 1952-1966*, Medicine & Science in Sports & Exercise 39(3):p 534-540, March 2007; Thibault V. et al, *Women and Men in Sport Performance: The Gender Gap has not Evolved since 1983*, J Sports Sci Med. 2010 Jun 1;9(2):214-23; Hallam LC, Amorim FT, *Expanding the Gap: An Updated Look Into Sex Differences in Running Performance*, Front Physiol. 2022 Jan 4;12:804149.

19 See study cited at footnote 160, and Harper J., *Transgender Athletes and International Sports Policy*, (2022) 85 Law and Contemporary Problems 151-165; Tucker R. et al, *Fair and Safe Eligibility Criteria for Women's Sport*, Scand J Med Sci Sports, 34: e14715 (*'[E]ndogenous testosterone production during male development leads to performance advantages arising from well-established sex-based differences in body size, muscle mass, endurance, speed, strength, and power. These physical advantages are so large that they necessitate a separate and protected female category that excludes male advantage to ensure fair and safe competition for female athletes'*).

20 For example, German tennis player Karsten Brassch, who was ranked 203 in men's singles at the time, beat Serena Williams 6-1 and Venus Williams 6-2 in exhibition matches at the 1998 Australian Open; and in December 2025 women's no 1 Aryna Sabalenka lost an exhibition match in Dubai 6-3 6-3 to Nick Kyrgios, who had been a top ten men's singles player but in December 2025 was ranked 670th after a string of injuries.

In 1945 Babe Didrikson Zaharais became the first and only woman in history to make the cut on the PGA Tour, a feat she achieved three times, at the Los Angeles Open, the Phoenix Open, and the Tucson Open. In 2003, Swedish golfer Annika Sörenstam was the first woman since Zaharias to compete in a PGA Tour event, in Fort Worth, Texas. She was the no. 1 ranked woman golfer in the world at the time, but missed the cut by four strokes.

21 Graffam C., *I know how Caster Semenya feels – as an intersex person, I've been harassed my entire life*, independent.co.uk, 21 August 2016.
22 Brown O., *World Athletics is right: Caster Semenya has an unfair advantage*, telegraph.co.uk, 12 July 2023.
23 Wright, C.M., *Sex is Not a Spectrum*, realityslaststand.com, 1 February 2021 (*'the nature of biological sex … is connected to the distinct type of gametes (sex cells) that an organism produces. As a broad concept, males are the sex that produce small gametes (sperm) and females produce large gametes (ova). There are no intermediate gametes, which is why there is no spectrum of sex. Biological sex in humans is a binary system'*); Wright, C.M., *Why There Are Exactly Two Sexes*, Arch Sex Behav (2025) (*'in anisogamous organisms there are only two gamete types, sperm and ova, and thus only two sexes. Sexual ambiguity is not a third or intermediate sex because developmental variation does not correspond to producing new gamete types'*); Goymann W., Brumm H., Kappeler P. , *Biological sex is binary, even though there is a rainbow of sex roles*, BioEssays, 2023;45:2200173, December 2022 (*'While we fully endorse efforts to create a more inclusive environment for gender-diverse people, this does not require denying biological sex. … Denying the concept of biological sex, for whatever cause, ultimately erodes scientific progress and may open the floodgates to "alternative truths"'*); Marinov, *In Humans, Sex is Binary and Immutable*, Acad. Quest (2020) 33:29-288; Pike J. and Hilton, E., *Sex, fairness and the World Athletics regulations: a reply to Bowman-Smart et al*, (2025) Journal of the Philosophy of Sport, 1-18.
24 Fausto-Sterling A., *Why Sex Is Not Binary*, newyorktimes.com, 25 October 2018; Fausto-Sterling A., *Myths of Gender: Biological theories about women and men* (Basic Books 2nd Edn 1992); Fausto-Sterling A., *Sexing the Body (Gender Politics and the Construction of Sexuality)* (Basic Books, updated edition 2020). See also Wackwitz LA, *Verifying the Myth: Olympic Sex Testing and the Category "Woman"*, (2003) Women's Studies International Forum, Vol. 26, No. 6, pp. 553–560.
25 Fausto-Sterling A., *Sexing the Body (Gender Politics and the Construction of Sexuality)* (Basic Books, updated edition 2020), p. 33. See also the remarkable claim in Jordan-Young, R. and Karkazis, K., *Some of Their Parts: "Gender Verification" and Elite Sports*, Anthropology News, 1 May 2012, that individuals who are neither male nor female are *'the rule rather than exceptions in the lived mode'*.
26 Fausto-Sterling A., *Sexing the Body (Gender Politics and the Construction of Sexuality)* (Basic Books, updated edition 2020), pp. 44 ,68.
27 In extremely rare cases, an individual may have both testes and ovaries, or a combination of the two (ovo-testes). Successful pregnancies have been reported in such individuals, as well as one case of successful paternity. See eg Acién P, Acién M., *Disorders of Sex Development: Classification, Review, and Impact on Fertility*, J Clin Med. 2020 Nov 4;9(11):3555, section 4.2.2.
28 Fausto-Sterling A., *Sexing the Body (Gender Politics and the Construction of Sexuality)* (Basic Books, updated edition 2020), pp. 56, 324.
29 See eg Samuels M., *Dehumanised, dispossessed – who considered Imane Khelif's life beyond boxing?*, thetimes.com, 14 August 2024.
30 Hull C., letter to the editor, and response of Fausto-Sterling A., (2003) 15(1) Am J Hum Biol. pp. 112-116.
31 Fausto-Sterling A., *Sexing the Body (Gender Politics and the Construction of Sexuality)* (Basic Books, updated edition 2020), pp. 56, 324; Lambelet Coleman D., *On Sex and Gender, A Commonsense Approach* (Simon & Schuster 2024), pp. 23 24.
32 Fausto-Sterling A., *Sexing the Body (Gender Politics and the Construction of Sexuality)* (Basic Books, updated edition 2020), p. 54. See also Viloria H. and Nieto M., *The Spectrum of Sex* (Jessica Kingsley Publishers, 2020), *passim*.
33 Fausto-Sterling A., *Myths of Gender: Biological theories about women and men* (Basic Books 2nd Edn 1992), p. 270. See also Jordan-Young R. and Karkazis K., *You Say You're a Woman? That Should Be Enough*, New York Times, 17 June 2012 (*'If we want a clear answer to who is eligible for women's competitions, it is time to stop pawning this fundamentally social question off onto scientists'*); Wackwitz LA, *Verifying the Myth: Olympic Sex Testing and the Category "Woman"*, (2003) Women's Studies International Forum, Vol. 26, No. 6, pp. 553–560 at p. 558 (*'By requiring conformity to social norms and situating people into seemingly distinct, but nevertheless constructed categories, governing bodies of sport wield oppressive power that serves to create and reinforce a system of difference based upon hierarchy and grounded in oppression. Imposition of dichotomous categories is an enactment of cultural power relations, in which one group dominates another through categorization and enforced difference. … What, after all, would patriarchy be without the discrete categories of men and women?'*).
34 Fausto-Sterling A., *Sexing the Body (Gender Politics and the Construction of Sexuality)* (Basic Books, updated edition 2020), pp. 4-5, p. 9 (*'Since intersexuals quite literally embody both*

sexes, they weaken claims about sexual difference') and pp. 33, 42 (*'the science of physical difference was often invoked to invalidate claims for social and political emancipation'*).

35 Fausto-Sterling A., *Sexing the Body (Gender Politics and the Construction of Sexuality)* (Basic Books, updated edition 2020), pp. 34, 51, 53, 54, 59, 81. See also Reis E., *Bodies in Doubt: An American History of Intersex* (John Hopkins University Press, 2d Edn, 2021), p. xxi (*'Not everything should be "fixed", especially when the fix is motivated by social concerns rather than medical necessity'*) and p. 70.

36 Dr Fausto-Sterling's contrary claim apparently arises because of her focus on so-called *'true hermaphrodites'*, ie those with chromosomal mosaicism and/or ovo-testes. Such cases are extremely rare in the general population (see paper cited at footnote 27), let alone in elite athletics, and so I do not address them further in the text, but simply note that it is testosterone that produces the secondary sex characteristics that influence sports performance, and therefore the key question in such cases is whether or not the individual has functioning testicular tissue producing levels of circulating testosterone in the normal male range.

37 Hooven C., *Testosterone: The Story of the Hormone that Dominates and Divides Us* (Cassell 2021), pp. 54-64; Martínez-Patiño M. et al, *An approach to the biological, historical and psychological repercussions of gender verification in top level competitions*, October 2010 Journal of Human Sport and Exercise 5(3).

38 Morel Y., Rey R., Teinturier C., et al, *Aetiological diagnosis of male sex ambiguity: a collaborative study*, Eur J Pediatr. 2002;161:49–59; Wisniewski AB, Batista RL, Costa EMF, Finlayson C., Sircili MHP, Dénes FT, Domenice S., Mendonca BB, *Management of 46,XY Differences/ Disorders of Sex Development (DSD) Throughout Life*, Endocr Rev. 2019 Dec 1;40(6):1547-1572, at 1548.

39 Looking back at Dr Fausto-Sterling's original prevalence estimate of 1.728% (*Sexing the Body (Gender Politics and the Construction of Sexuality)* (Basic Books, updated edition 2020), p. 324), there was no express mention of cases of 5-ARD or 17β in the table she provided (p. 56), but it appears that she treated them as a form of partial androgen insensitivity (see fn 82 to chapter 4 of *Sexing the Body*, where she refers to 5-ARD/DHT deficiency as *'a form of androgen insensitivity'*). If so, they will have been included in the figure she gives in that table for cases of partial androgen insensitivity, namely 0.0076%, which is consistent with the 1:20,000 estimate I have quoted in the text (taken from the works cited at footnotes 28-31, above). See further Sax L., *How common is intersex? A response to Anne Fausto-Sterling*, (2002) Journal of Sex Research, 39:3, 174-78 (including only conditions in which chromosomal sex is inconsistent with phenotypic sex, or in which the phenotype is not classifiable as either male or female, and so excluding non-intersex conditions, such as Klinefelter syndrome, Turner syndrome, and late-onset CAH, the true prevalence of intersex is about 0.018%) and (*'The available data support the conclusion that human sexuality is a dichotomy, not a continuum. More than 99.98% of humans are either male or female'*).

40 Hooven C., *Testosterone: The Story of the Hormone that Dominates and Divides Us* (Cassell 2021), pp. 75-81; Kang HJ, Imperato-McGinley J., Zhu YS, Rosenwaks Z., *The effect of 5-alpha-reductase-2 deficiency on human fertility*, (2014) Fertil. Steril. 101:310-316 (*'The affected subjects are 46XY males with testes and male accessory ducts but predominantly female external genitalia. Because the Wolffian ducts develop normally owing to normal fetal testosterone levels, the ejaculatory ducts, epididymides, vasa deferentia, and seminal vesicles are formed. However, since external genitalia development is dependent on intracellular conversion of testosterone to DHT, the urogenital sinus and genital tubercle fail to differentiate normally into the external genitalia, urethra and prostate. At birth, males homozygous for 5α-reductase-2 mutation typically have a clitoral-like phallus, bifid scrotum, hypospadias, blind shallow vaginal pouch from incomplete closure of the urogenital sinus and a rudimentary prostate. Because of this genital ambiguity, most males are assigned a female gender at birth and reared as such'*).

41 Fausto-Sterling A., *Sexing the Body (Gender Politics and the Construction of Sexuality)* (Basic Books, updated edition 2020), p. 111.

42 Ozbey H. and Etker S., *Disorders of sexual development in a cultural context*, Arab J Urol. 2013 Mar; 11(1): 33–39; Kang HJ, Imperato-McGinley J., Zhu YS, Rosenwaks Z., *The effect of 5-alpha-reductase-2 deficiency on human fertility*. (2014) Fertil. Steril. 101:310-316 (*'At puberty, the surge in mainly testosterone production causes individuals to virilize, with a noticeable increase in muscle mass, deepening of the voice, and an increase in libido, prompting most to transition to the male gender. This pubertal rise in androgens increases penile length, results in scrotal rugation and pigmentation, and is involved in testicular descent'*); Bramble MS et al, *Effects of Chromosomal Sex and Hormonal Influences on shaping Sex Differences in Brain and Behavior: Lessons from Cases of Disorders of Sex Development*, J Neurosci Res. 2017 Jan 2;95(1-2):65-74 (*'During teenage years, the undescended testes begin to secrete high levels of testosterone and trigger male puberty, characterized by the deepening of the voice, increased*

muscle mass, and increased height. In addition, there can be a dramatic increase in the growth of the phallus and occasional descent of the testes into the scrotal region').

43 See eg Lee PA et al, *Global Disorders of Sex Development Update Since 2006: Perceptions, Approach and Care*, Horm Res Paediatr. 2016;85(3):158-80 (*'Male assignment is recommended for those with 5α-reductase deficiency, since 60% later identify themselves as male, and for 17β-HSD3 deficiency, since >50% later switch to male'*); Wisniewski AB, Batista RL, Costa EMF, Finlayson C, Sircili MHP, Dénes FT, Domenice S, Mendonca BB, *Management of 46,XY Differences/Disorders of Sex Development (DSD) Throughout Life*, Endocr Rev. 2019 Dec 1;40(6):1547-1572 at 1556 (male rearing recommended for individuals with 5ARD or 17β); Ozbey H. and Etker S., *Disorders of sexual development in a cultural context*, Arab J Urol. 2013 Mar; 11(1): 33-39.

44 Cohen-Kettenis PT, *Gender change in 46,XY persons with 5alpha-reductase-2 deficiency and 17beta-hydroxysteroid dehydrogenase-3 deficiency*, Arch Sex Behav. 2005 Aug;34(4):399-410; Mendonca BB et al, *Male pseudohermaphroditism due to steroid 5alpha-reductase 2 deficiency. Diagnosis, psychological evaluation, and management*, Medicine (Baltimore), 1996 Mar;75(2);64-76; Mendonca BB et al, *Steroid 5α-reductase 2 deficiency*, J Steroid Biochem Mol Biol. 2016 Oct;163:206-11 (*'Most affected males are raised as females, but virilization occurs at puberty, and male social sex develops thereafter with high frequency'*); Imperato-McGinley J, Peterson RE, Gautier T, Sturla E, *Androgens and the evolution of male gender identity among male pseudohemaphrodites with 5-a reductase deficiency*, (1979) N. Engl. J. Med. 300:1233-1237. In cases of 5-ARD and 17β, *'female rearing is associated with a high likelihood of patient-initiated male reassignment later in life'*: Wisniewski AB, Batista RL, Costa EMF, Finlayson C, Sircili MHP, Dénes FT, Domenice S, Mendonca BB, *Management of 46,XY Differences/Disorders of Sex Development (DSD) Throughout Life*, Endocr Rev. 2019 Dec 1;40(6):1547-1572 at 1555; Bramble MS et al, *Effects of Chromosomal Sex and Hormonal Influences on shaping Sex Differences in Brain and Behaviour: Lessons from Cases of Disorders of Sex Development*, J Neurosci Res. 2017 Jan 2;95(1-2):65-74 (*'the vast majority'* of 5-ARD individuals who are reared as girls change gender to male during the pubertal years). See also Babu R, Shah UJ, *Gender identity disorder (GID) in adolescents and adults with differences of sex development (DSD): A systematic review and meta-analysis*, Pediatr Urol. 2021 Feb;17(1):39-47 (noting high incidence of gender identity disorder in 5-ARD individuals (53%) and 17β individuals (53%) who are reared as females, with half of them changing gender to male following virilisation at puberty); Lee PA, Fuqua JS, Houk CP, Kogan BA, Mazur T, Caldamone A., *Individualized care for patients with intersex (disorders/differences of sex development): part 1*, J Pediatr Urol. 2020 Apr;16(2):230-237 (*'The risk of an incongruence between initial gender assignment and adult gender identity is highest for 46, XY DSD and tends to occur most often when 46, XY DSD patients are initially assigned female'*). But cf Maimoun et al, *F1000 Commentary: Phenotypical, biological, and molecular heterogeneity of 5alpha-reductase deficiency: an extensive international experience of 55 patients*, J Clin Endocrinol Metab. 2011 Feb; 96:296-307 (of 40 5ARD individuals initially assigned a female gender, only five (12.5%) assumed a male gender identity in peripuberty).

45 See Hess RA, *Estrogen in the adult male reproductivec tract: a review*, Reprod Biol Endocrinol. 2003 Jul 9;1:52 (explaining role played by estrogen in regulating fluid dynamics in the male reproductive tract); Angier, *Woman: An Intimate Geography* (Virago Press 2014), pp. 59-61, Bramble MS et al, *Effects of Chromosomal Sex and Hormonal Influences on shaping Sex Differences in Brain and Behaviour: Lessons from Cases of Disorders of Sex Development*, J Neurosci Res. 2017 Jan 2;95(1-2):65-74 (*'If inguinal testes are not removed before puberty, there is often normal breast development resulting from the high levels of circulating testosterone which is locally aromatized into active estrogens, stimulating breast growth'*).

46 Rogol AD, Pieper LP, *Genes, Gender, Hormones and Doping in Sport: A Convoluted Tale*, Frontiers in Endocrinology, Perspective, 12 October 2017, 2017 Oct 12;8:251 (*'Those with [CAIS] appear at birth as normal females, but only have the outer one-third of a "vagina" given that it is derived from non-Mullerian structures … .The rest of the female reproductive tract is missing, since the 46XY females have testes that had produced anti-Mullerian hormone responsible for the disappearance of the uterus, Fallopian tubes, and the inner two-thirds of the vagina'*).

47 Bramble MS et al, *Effects of Chromosomal Sex and Hormonal Influences on shaping Sex Differences in Brain and Behaviour: Lessons from Cases of Disorders of Sex Development*, J Neurosci Res. 2017 Jan 2;95(1-2):65-74 (*'46XY patients born with CAIS are universally assigned as females at birth, as a result of the outward female phenotypic appearance of the genitalia'*).

48 National Health Service, *Androgen Insensitivity Syndrome*, nhs.co.uk (accessed July 2024); Khorashad, B.S., Gardner, M., Lee, P. A. *et al.*, *Recommendations for 46,XY Disorders/*

Differences of Sex Development Across Two Decades: Insights from North American Pediatric Endocrinologists and Urologists, Arch Sex Behav (2024) (in 2020, 61% of survey participants recommended rearing a neonate with PAIS as male, and 11% recommended rearing as female); Gürbüz F. et al, *Gender Identity and Assignment Recommendations in Disorders of Sex Development Patients: 20 Years' Experience and Challenges*, J Clin Res Pediatr Endocrinol. 2020 Nov 25;12(4):347-357 (four of six babies with PAIS reared as male, two as female).

49 Babu, R., & Shah, U., *Gender identity disorder (GID) in adolescents and adults with differences of sex development (DSD): A systematic review and meta-analysis*, (2021) Journal of Pediatric Urology, 17(1), 39–47 (review reporting that 12% [14 out of 113 cases] of PAIS individuals reared as girls developed gender dysphoria later in life, although so did 25% [7 out of 28 cases] of those reared as boys).

50 The authors of the 2006 Consensus Statement on Management of Intersex Disorders recommended that *'intersex'* be dropped and *'disorders in sex development'* used instead, as an umbrella term for specific diagnoses such as 5-ARD and AIS. See Hughes IA, Houk C, Ahmed SF, Lee PA; LWPES Consensus Group; ESPE Consensus Group, *Consensus statement on management of intersex disorders*, Arch Dis Child. 2006 Jul;91(7):554-63. However, some patients and advocates dislike *'disorders'*, preferring *'differences'* or *'variations'* instead. See Wisniewski AB, Batista RL, Costa EMF, Finlayson C, Sircili MHP, Dénes FT, Domenice S, Mendonca BB, *Management of 46,XY Differences/Disorders of Sex Development (DSD) Throughout Life*, Endocr Rev. 2019 Dec 1;40(6):1547-1572; Lee PA et al, *Global Disorders of Sex Development Update Since 2006: Perceptions, Approach and Care*, Horm Res Paediatr. 2016;85(3):158-80.

51 Wright CM, *Why There Are Exactly Two Sexes*, Arch Sex Behav (2025) (*'in anisogamous organisms there are only two gamete types, sperm and ova, and thus only two sexes. Sexual ambiguity is not a third or intermediate sex because developmental variation does not correspond to producing new gamete types'*); Handelsman, D. and Bermon, S. (2025), *Biology and Management of Male-Bodied Athletes in Elite Female Sports*, Drug Test and Analysis 17, no. 9 (2025): 1703–1714, at 1704 (*'It is sometimes considered that sex "is not quite binary"; however, this confuses inevitable, rare deviation in natural biological process with the binary process itself. For example, people are born with a heart with less than four chambers, no spleen, no gallbladder, or a single kidney—genetic disorders occurring at up to 100 times the frequency of DSDs—but these findings do not change our understanding of the characteristic features of the human body as having a four-chambered heart, a spleen, a gallbladder, and two kidneys. Similarly, the fact that DSDs occur does not detract from the underlying biology that in humans, there are two distinct sexes'*); Soh D., *Science Shows Sex is Binary, Not a Spectrum*, realclearpolitics.com, 31 October 2018 (*'most of us have 10 fingers. There exist individuals who possess fewer or more than 10 digits on their hands, but this hasn't called for a re-conceptualization of how many fingers a human being has'*).

52 Emi Koyama, Director, Intersex Initiative, *Frequently Asked Questions About the 'DSD' Controversy*, 29 June 2008. See also Reis E., *Bodies in Doubt: An American History of Intersex* (John Hopkins University Press, 2d Edn, 2021), p. 177 (*'Though some people may come to adopt a gender identity a "intersex", nonbinary, or genderqueer, many simply identify as women or men who have an intersex trait'*).

53 Encyclopaedia Britannica, *The difference between sex and gender explained*, Britannica.com, accessed 15 May 2024.

54 Fausto-Sterling A., *Sexing the Body (Gender Politics and the Construction of Sexuality)* (Basic Books, updated edition 2020), p. 325.

55 For the opposing arguments on this issue, see Shin PS, *Sex and Gender Segregation in Competition Sport: Internal and External Normative Perspectives*, 80 *Law and Contemporary Problems* 47-61 (2017).

56 Brown O., *World Athletics is right: Caster Semenya has an unfair advantage*, telegraph.co.uk, 12 July 2023.

57 Transgender cyclist Rachel McKinnon (now known as Veronica Ivy), quoted in *Transgender athletes have an unfair advantage*, heraldsun.com.au, 4 November 2018.

58 Dr Joanna Harper, quoted in *Hyperandrogenism and women vs women vs men in sport: A Q&A with Joanna Harper*, sportscientist.com, accessed 4 August 2024.

59 Ross Tucker, *Hyperandrogenism and women vs women vs men in sport: A Q&A with Joanna Harper*, sportscientist.com, accessed 4 August 2024.

60 See Handelsman DJ, *Toward a Robust Definition of Sport Sex*, Endocr Rev. 2024 Sep 12;45(5):709-736.

61 Bowman-Smart, H., Savulescu, J., O'Connell, M., & Sinclair, A., *World Athletics regulations unfairly affect female athletes with differences in sex development*, (2024) Journal of the Philosophy of Sport, 51(1), 29–53.

62 *Chand v Athletics Federation of India & the IAAF*, CAS 2014/A/3759, para 263.

63 Editors, *Naturally Occurring High Testosterone Shouldn't Keep Female Athletes out of Competition*, scientificamerican.com, 1 August 2016.

64 Anthony J., *Stripped of dignity: Semenya's ordeal in race for gender identity*, Nation, 24 February 2024 (*'[Caster Semenya] was unbeaten for almost four years and as her talent showed no sign of fading, international attention was maliciously turned to her physique. Instead of focusing on her historic achievements on the track, false publications dominated by racist undertones were persistently implanted by unscrupulous athletics organisations. These institutions considered anything that did not conform to their lily-white Eurocentric version of femininity as ineligible. Caster has definite muscles and her voice is deep. She was born with what is medically referred to as a difference in sex development, a term of varying genetic conditions, where an embryo responds in a different way to the hormones that spark the development of internal and external sexual organs. In layman's terms, she is a woman but without the entire internal female reproductive organs. She, therefore, does not menstruate and her body produces an elevated amount of testosterone'*).

65 *Chand v Athletics Federation of India & the IAAF*, CAS 2014/A/3759, para 113.

66 Pape M. and Pielke R., *Science, Sport, Sex, and the Case of Caster Semenya*, Issues in Science and Technology, Vol 36(1) (Fall 2019), pp. 56-63, critiqued in *Forum, A discussion of Science, Sport, Sex, and the Case of Caster Semenya*, Issues in Science & Technology, Vol 26(2) (Winter 2020).

67 Quoted in Wilson J., *Caster Semenya: I sympathise with trans athletes but their issues are irrelevant to mine*, telegraph.co.uk, 15 December 2023.

68 Quoted in Macur J., *The Line Between Male and Female Athletes Remains Blurred*, nytimes.com, 28 July 2015.

69 Reem Alsalem, UN Special Rapporteur on Violence against Women and Girls, *Report of the Special Rapporteur on violence against women and girls, its causes and consequences*, A/79/325, 27 August 2024, p. 5. However, the only supporting reference for this assertion is to '*Submissions from WOLF, ICSF and Dianne Post on behalf of Lavendar Patch*'. No further information is provided about those sources, and I was not able to track down these submissions (or any other supporting documentation) online.

70 Pape M. and Pielke R., *Science, Sport, Sex, and the Case of Caster Semenya*, Issues in Science and Technology, Vol 36(1) (Fall 2019), pp. 56-63, critiqued in *Forum, A discussion of Science, Sport, Sex, and the Case of Caster Semenya*, Issues in Science & Technology, Vol 26(2) (Winter 2020).

71 Roger Pielke, in Lance Armstrong's podcast, *The Forward*, 20 May 2019 (*'Caster Semenya, born a girl, raised as a girl, into school as a girl, all her life, never has changed lanes'*).

72 Zaliznyak M, Yuan N, Bresee C, Freedman A, Garcia MM., *How Early in Life do Transgender Adults Begin to Experience Gender Dysphoria? Why This Matters for Patients, Providers, and for Our Healthcare System*, Sex Med. 2021 Dec;9(6). See also Encyclopaedia Britannica, *The difference between sex and gender explained*, Britannica.com, accessed 15 May 2024 (*'An individual's internal sense of their gender … is generally established in children by the age of three'*).

73 See eg Gleaves, J., & Lehrbach, T., *Beyond fairness: the ethics of inclusion for transgender and intersex athletes*, (2016) Journal of the Philosophy of Sport, 43(2), 311–326.

74 See eg Jordan-Young, R. and Karkazis, K., *Some of Their Parts: "Gender Verification" and Elite Sports*, Anthropology News, 1 May 2012 (*'None of the women who have been suspended because of questions about their sex (and who likely have hyperandrogenism) have been world record holders; they aren't "outliers" among their elite female peers'*).

75 See footnote 167.

76 Pike J., *Why "Meaningful Competition" is not fair competition*, (2023) Journal of the Philosophy of Sport, 50:1, 1-17.

77 Pike J., *Safety, fairness and inclusion: transgender athletes and the essence of Rugby* (2023) Journal of the Philosophy of Sport, 48:2, 155-168. See also Binney N, *Fairness in handicap and championship sport* (2025) Journal of the Philosophy of Sport, 52:1, 60-79.

78 Caster Semenya, *The Race To Be Myself* (Merky Books, 2023), p. 283.

79 Caster Semenya, *The Race To Be Myself* (Merky Books, 2023), pp. 268-69.

80 Caster Semenya, *The Race To Be Myself* (Merky Books, 2023), p. 283.

81 *Chand v Athletics Federation of India & the IAAF*, CAS 2014/A/3759, paras 4 and 113. See also Schultz J., *Caster Semenya and the "Question of Too": Sex Testing in Elite Women's Sport and the Issue of Advantage*, Quest, 2011, 63, 228-243 (*'Suppose, hypothetically, that Caster Semenya does have a genetic condition that gives her a competitive edge. Is this any different from a volleyball or basketball player with Marfan syndrome, which can make one unusually tall? Why does Michael Phelps possess "genetic gifts" that make him "built to swim" while Semenya gets labelled an "anomaly" with an "unfair advantage"? In other words, why are genetic variations that affect autosomal chromosomes an advantageous endowment while*

those that affect sex chromosomes amount to a curse that can effectively drum one out of competitive sport?'); Rogol AD, Pieper LP, *Genes, Gender, Hormones, and Doping in Sport: A Convoluted Tale*, Frontiers in Endocrinology, Perspective, 12 October 2017, 2017 Oct 12;8:251 (same).

82 Pike J., *Why "Meaningful Competition" is not fair competition*, (2023) Journal of the Philosophy of Sport, 50:1, 1-17, at 10 et seq; Pike J. and Hilton, E., *Sex, fairness and the World Athletics regulations: a reply to Bowman-Smart et al*, (2025) Journal of the Philosophy of Sport, 1-18.

83 See eg Hamilton BR et al, *Response to the United Nations Human Rights Council's Report on Race and Gender Discrimination in Sport: An Expression of Concern and a Call to Prioritise Research*, Sports Med. 2021 Apr;51(4):839-842 (*'As competitors, athletes accept that a degree of unfairness is inherent to sport since the best performing athletes usually possess genetically mediated advantages like the greater height of an athlete in basketball, or architecture of skeletal muscle that determines whether an individual has the potential to become a champion sprinter or marathon runner, but not both. However, not all natural advantages are left unregulated or uncategorised. Rules have been created for weight and age categories to maintain fairness and for safety reasons. In the absence of such categories, sporting competitions may lose their meaning, rewarding factors such as maturity/age or size/mass, rather than the attributes that sport is intended to reward. The same is true of biological sex, necessitating the separation of those who lack the performance-enhancing effects of testosterone from those who benefit from it'*); Tucker R., *Hyperandrogenism and women vs women vs men in sport: A Q&A with Joanna Harper*, sportscientist.com, accessed 4 August 2024 (*'this is not the same as tall people dominating in basketball, or people with fast-twitch fibres dominating sprints. We do not compete in categories of height, because we have decided that there is no need to "protect" short people. We certainly do not compete in categories of muscle biochemistry or neurology. … [T]hink about weight classes in boxing, contact sports, rowing. Would it be fair if someone said "I can't help my physiology, and I'm 2kg over the limit for "lightweight", so let me in?" Or, if you did create a division for height in basketball, should we allow people who can't help that they're tall because of genes to come down and play with those under 6 foot? Of course not. Point is, if you create a division to ensure performance equality based on a known performance advantage, then you absolutely must defend that division, however "arbitrary" the line appears to be. The division between men and women is clear. It is obviously significantly influenced by testosterone, and few physiological variables are as clearly (if imperfectly) separate like testosterone is. If that division is to be respected, as it should, then hyperandrogenic women should have some regulation in place'*).

84 See generally Ritchie R, Reynard J, Lewis T., *Intersex and the Olympic Games*, J R Soc Med. 2008 Aug;101(8):395-9; Ferguson-Smith MA and Ferris EA, *Gender verification in sport: the need for change?*, Br J Sp Med 1991; 25(1); Heggie V., *Testing sex and gender in sports: reinventing, reimagining and reconstructing histories*, Endeavour, 2010 Dec;34(4):157-63; Rupert JL, *Genitals to Genes: The History and Biology of Gender Verification in the Olympics*, Canadian Bulletin of Medical History, 2011 28:2, 339-365; Dickinson B. et al, *Gender verification of female Olympic athletes*, Med Sci Sports Exerc. 2002 Oct;34(10):1539-43; Harper J., *Sporting Gender: The History, Science and Stories of Transgender and Intersex Athletes* (Rowman & Littlefield, 2020), Chapter Three (Intersex Athletes in the 1930s) and Chapter Four (Postwar Sex Testing); Waters M., *The Other Olympians: A True Story of Gender, Fascism and the Making of Modern Sport* (Ebury Press 2024).

85 Ripa Y., *Women and the Olympic Games*, Encyclopédie d'histoire numérique de l'Europe, ehne.fr, 22 June 2020; *#GenderEqualOlympics: Paris 2024 making history on the field of play*, olympics.org, 28 July 2024; Harper J., *Sporting Gender: The History, Science and Stories of Transgender and Intersex Athletes* (Rowman & Littlefield, 2020), Chapter One ("Pre-Historic" Women's Sport).

86 Waters M., *At the Paris Olympics, Sex Testing Will Be in Full Force. How Did We Get Here?*, nytimes.com, 21 June 2024. Joanna Harper suggests that they were both likely 46XY DSD but were initially reared as female rather than male because they had ambiguous genitals as newborns: Harper, *Sporting Gender: The History, Science and Stories of Transgender and Intersex Athletes* (Rowman & Littlefield, 2020), pp. 46-47. That impression is reinforced by the detailed account of their stories in Waters M., *The Other Olympians: A True Story of Gender, Fascism and the Making of Modern Sport* (Ebury Press 2024).

87 Time Magazine, *Sport: Olympic Games*, 17 August 1936 (*''Last week in Berlin, muscular Helen Stephens reached the climax of a career that began three years ago when her Fulton, Mo. high-school track coach chanced to glance at his stop watch as she was finishing a practice sprint. When Coach Bert Moore had assured himself that his watch was not wrong he began to train Sprinter Stephens seriously without telling her how good she was. In her first meet, at St. Louis last year, she surprised herself by breaking a U. S. record and beating Polish Stella Walsh, most famed woman sprinter in the world. Said Stella Walsh: "I can beat her any time I try."*

Last week in Berlin Sprinter Stephens proved Sprinter Walsh, running for Poland under her real name of Stella Walasiewicz, wrong, by two full yards. Her time in the 100-metre final was 11.5 sec., a new record for women. When a Warsaw newspaper, with what is now a routine lack of chivalry toward female Olympic competitors, suggested that Sprinter Stephens was a man, the possibility that Sprinter Stephens' ignorance of her own abilities might include her sex was promptly destroyed by German Olympic officials. They announced that they had foreseen the dispute, investigated Sprinter Stephens before the race, found her a thoroughgoing female').

88 Tannenbaum R., *The Life and Murder of Stella Walsh, Intersex Olympic Champion*, longreads.com, 18 August 2016; *Stanislawa Walasiewicz: The Curious Story of Stella Walsh*, Encyclopaedia Britannica, 19 January 2006; Dohle M., *'They say I'm not a girl': Case Studies of Gender Verification in Elite Sports* (McFarland & Co., 2020), pp. 90-102.

89 *Dora Ratjen – 1.55m: 1936, High Jump, Women, XI Olympic Games, Berlin*, youtube.com (accessed 18 September 2024).

90 Berg S., *How Dora the man competed in the high jump*, spiegel.de, 15 September 2009; Beamish R. & Ritchie I., *'Totalitarian Regimes and Cold War Sport'*, pp. 16-17, in *East Plays West: Sport and the Cold War* (Routledge 2007); Dohle M., *'They say I'm not a girl': Case Studies of Gender Verification in Elite Sports* (McFarland & Co., 2020), pp. 43-53; Waters M., *The Other Olympians: A True Story of Gender, Fascism and the Making of Modern Sport* (Ebury Press 2024), pp. 248-50 and 267-68.

91 Heggie V., *Testing sex and gender in sports: reinventing, reimagining and reconstructing histories*, Endeavour, 2010 Dec;34(4):157-63. However, accusations could go both ways. On 22 August 1960, page 4 of 10, under the headline *Olympic women "have medical certificates": official's answer to criticism*, The Times reported as follows: *'Mr Jack Crump, secretary of the British Amateur Athletic Board, commenting on press reports that two countries had challenged the sex of one of the British women competitors in the Olympic Games, said yesterday: "We require of every woman before an international competition that she supplies us with a certificate signed by her own medical practitioner. This has been done for all Britain's athletes and the 16 entered have all produced on the proper from as provided by the International Olympic Committee a certificate duly signed by a medical practitioner. These forms are signed by myself, and every woman entrant sent to Rome was accompanied by a form duly signed by her registered medical practitioner. It would be unthinkable for us and for anybody else to challenge the integrity and capability of a registered practitioner. In that respect we have completely complied with the rule"'*.

92 Ferguson-Smith MA and Ferris E, *Gender verification in sport: the need for change?*, Br J Sp Med 1991; 25(1).

93 Ritchie R, Reynard J, Lewis T., *Intersex and the Olympic Games*, J R Soc Med. 2008 Aug;101(8):395-9.

94 Ferguson-Smith MA and Ferris EA, *Gender verification in sport: the need for change?*, Br J Sp Med 1991; 25(1); Heggie V., *Testing sex and gender in sports: reinventing, reimagining and reconstructing histories*, Endeavour, 2010 Dec;34(4):157-63; Dohle M., *'They say I'm not a girl': Case Studies of Gender Verification in Elite Sports* (McFarland & Co., 2020), pp. 70-78.

95 Ferguson-Smith MA and Ferris E, *Gender verification in sport: the need for change?*, Br J Sp Med 1991; 25(1).

96 Harper J., *Sporting Gender: The History, Science and Stories of Transgender and Intersex Athletes* (Rowman & Littlefield, 2020), pp. 60-63; Dohle M., *'They say I'm not a girl': Case Studies of Gender Verification in Elite Sports* (McFarland & Co., 2020), pp. 79-89.

97 Ferguson-Smith MA and Ferris E, *Gender verification in sport: the need for change?*, Br J Sp Med 1991; 25(1).

98 María José Martínez-Patiño, *Personal Account, A Woman Tried and Tested*, Lancet 2005; 366: S38.

99 Dingeon, B., Hamon, P. , Robert, M. *et al*, *Sex testing at the Olympics*, Nature 358, 447 (1992).

100 Serrat A, García de Herreros A., *Gender verification in sports by PCR amplification of SRY and DYZ1 Y chromosome specific sequences: presence of DYZ1 repeat in female athletes*, Br J Sports Med. 1996 Dec;30(4):310-2. Three historians of sex testing in sport have asserted that *'[u]pon further analysis, experts determined that one sample was a false positive, six samples identified the wrong gene, and five samples were from athletes with DSDs'* (Pieper L., Schultz J. and Krieger J., *Regression, Not Progress: A Response to World Athletics' Return to Sex Testing*, idrottsforum,org, 3 April 2025), but they cite only the Serrat paper as support for that statement, and the Serrat paper says only that the five athletes whose samples were positive for the SRY gene were referred for physical examination, and does not say anything about the results of that examination,

101 Elsas LJ, Ljungqvist A, Ferguson-Smith MA, Simpson JL, Genel M, Carlson AS, Ferris E, de la Chapelle A, Ehrhardt AA, *Gender verification of female athletes*, Genet Med. 2000 Jul-Aug;2(4):249-54.
102 *Statement of the Stockholm Consensus on Sex Reassignment in Sports*, 12 November 2003, stillmed.olympic.org (accessed 11 August 2024).
103 IAAF Policy on Gender Verification (2006), unique-sportstime.de (accessed 2 November 2025).
104 Caster Semenya, *The Race To Be Myself* (Merky Books, 2023), title of Chapter Two. See also BBC documentary *Too Fast to be a Woman: The Story of Caster Semenya* (2011), available on youtube.com.
105 *Athletics South Africa v Chuene, Maponyane, and Dlamini*, decision of disciplinary inquiry (Norman Arendse SC, chair) dated 7 February 2011, p. 40 (static.pmg.org.za/docs/110816hearing_2.pdf, accessed 26 November 2025).
106 *SA chief issues Caster Apology*, bbc.co.uk, 19 September 2009; *Athletics South Africa v Chuene, Maponyane, and Dlamini*, decision of disciplinary inquiry (Norman Arendse SC, chair) dated 7 February 2011, para 41 (static.pmg.org.za/docs/110816hearing_2.pdf, accessed 26 November 2025).
107 Caster Semenya, *The Race To Be Myself* (Merky Books, 2023), pp. 124-30, 142-46; *Athletics South Africa v Chuene, Maponyane, and Dlamini*, decision of disciplinary inquiry (Norman Arendse SC, chair) dated 7 February 2011, para 41 (https://static.pmg.org.za/docs/110816hearing_2.pdf, accessed 26 November 2025); Sindane L., *Semenya saga: Chuene's trail of lies*, Mail & Guardian, 18 September 2009 (mg.co.za/article/2009-09-18-semenya-saga-chuenes-trail-of-lies/, accessed 26 November 2025); Sindane L., *Secret report reveals Chuene plotting*, Mail & Guardian, 23 October 2009 (mg.co.za/article/2009-10-23-secret-report-reveals-chuenes-plotting/, accessed 26 November 2025).
108 Caster Semenya, *The Race To Be Myself* (Merky Books, 2023), pp. 157-60, 165, 174-75.
109 *Gold medal athlete Caster Semenya told to prove she is a woman*, theguardian.com, 19 August 2009.
110 Hurst M., *Caster Semenya has male sex organs and no womb or ovaries*, dailytelegraph.com.au, 11 September 2009; Caster Semenya, *The Race To Be Myself* (Merky Books, 2023), pp. 20-25, 80-93, Chapter 11 (The Troubles Begin), pp. 135-36, 139, 156, 159, 173.
111 *Semenya 'maybe not 100pc' a woman*, abc.net.au, 10 September 2009. In her memoir, Caster Semenya says that Mr Weiss said this at the press conference held in Berlin immediately after her victory in the 800m final, but in fact he said it the following month.
112 Caster Semenya, *The Race To Be Myself* (Merky Books, 2023), pp. 182-83, 187-88.
113 *Semenya v IAAF*, CAS 2018/O/5794, para 79.
114 *IAAF Regulations Governing Eligibility of Females with Hyperandrogenism to Compete in Women's Competition*, summarised in *Chand v IAAF*, CAS 2014/A/3759, paras 41-68.
115 Clause 8F, *IOC Regulations on Female Hyperandrogenism, Games of the XXX Olympiad in London, 2012*, IOC Medical and Scientific Department, 22 June 2012, stillmed.olympic.org (accessed 11 August 2024).
116 *Dutee Chand v Athletics Federation of India & the IAAF*, CAS 2014/A/3759 ('*Chand v IAAF*'). For an insider's account of the *Chand* case, see Harper J., *Sporting Gender: The History, Science and Stories of Transgender and Intersex Athletes* (Rowman & Littlefield, 2020), Chapters 13 and 14.
117 However, the Sports Authority of India required her to undertake a series of clinical tests, karyotyping, blood tests, and MRI examinations, and subsequently told her she could not compete in Oregon'.
118 *Chand v IAAF*, CAS 2014/A/3759, paras 8-27, 371 et seq.
119 *Chand v IAAF*, CAS 2014/A/3759, para 29.
120 *Chand v IAAF*, CAS 2014/A/3759, paras 4, 113.
121 *Chand v IAAF*, CAS 2014/A/3759, paras 119-123, 137, 143, 155-58, 461.
122 *Chand v IAAF*, CAS 2014/A/3759, paras 141.
123 *Chand v IAAF*, CAS 2014/A/3759, para 124.
124 *Chand v IAAF*, CAS 2014/A/3759, paras 231, 234-37.
125 *Chand v IAAF*, CAS 2014/A/3759, para 145.
126 *Chand v IAAF*, CAS 2014/A/3759, paras 136-158.
127 *Chand v IAAF*, CAS 2014/A/3759, paras 123, 159, 162-63, 169, 170.
128 *Chand v IAAF*, CAS 2014/A/3759, para 173.
129 Pape, M., Latham, J., Karkazis, K.A., & Ritz, S.A., *Resisting and Remaking Sex in the Petri Dish, the Clinic, and on the Track*, Catalyst: Feminism, Theory, Technoscience, Vol.6 No. 2 (2020) (accessed 28 July 2024).

130 *Chand v IAAF*, CAS 2014/A/3759, para 354.
131 Harper, J., *Race Times for Transgender Athletes*, Journal of Sporting Cultures and Identities, 2015; 6:1-9.
132 *Chand v IAAF*, CAS 2014/A/3759, para 205.
133 *Chand v IAAF*, CAS 2014/A/3759, paras 130-31, 184, 188-89, 194-95, 212, 215 (Dr Bermon noting that the threshold of 10 nmol/L had been selected on the basis that it was five standard deviations away from the typical testosterone levels of females with PCOS).
134 *Chand v IAAF*, CAS 2014/A/3759, paras 126, 128, 183-5, 198, 205, 461.
135 *Chand v IAAF*, CAS 2014/A/3759, paras 186-87, 206, 214, 218, 461.
136 *Chand v IAAF*, CAS 2014/A/3759, paras 180-81.
137 *Chand v IAAF*, CAS 2014/A/3759, paras 184-85.
138 Bermon S. et al, *Women with Hyperandrogenism in Elite Sports: Scientific and Ethical Rationales for Regulating*, J Clin Endocrinol Metab, doi: 10.1210/jc/2014-3603; Bermon S. et al, *Serum Androgen Levels in Elite Female Athletes*, J Clin Endocrin Metab, doi: 10.1210/jc/2014-1391. In fact, even that is considered to be an understatement, although confidentiality issues prevent me from explaining why here.
139 *Chand v IAAF*, CAS 2014/A/3759, paras 206, 210.
140 *Chand v IAAF*, CAS 2014/A/3759, para 193. Now see Elliott-Sale KJ et al, *The Effects of Oral Contraceptives on Exercise Performance in Women: A Systematic Review and Meta-analysis*, Sports Med. 2020 Oct;50(10):1785-1812.
141 *Chand v IAAF*, CAS 2014/A/3759, paras 35(e), 504 and 293.
142 *Chand v IAAF*, CAS 2014/A/3759, paras 127, 285, 288, 510.
143 *Chand v IAAF*, CAS 2014/A/3759, paras 448, 508.
144 *Chand v IAAF*, CAS 2014/A/3759, paras 448-450, 508.
145 *Chand v IAAF*, CAS 2014/A/3759, para 530.
146 Cleveland Clinic, *Hyperandrogenism*, myclevelandclinic.com (accessed 22 May 2024).
147 A biological male (46XY) could also have CAH, but in such cases the only effect would be early (male) puberty, resulting in testosterone levels in the normal male range: *Chand v IAAF*, CAS 2014/A/3759, para 484.
148 Auchus R., *Endocrinology and Women's Sports: The Diagnosis Matters*, (2017) 80(4) Law & Contemporary Problems 127, at p. 136.
149 *Chand v IAAF*, CAS 2014/A/3759, para 274 (noting evidence of Ross Tucker that the results of 100m to 1500m races taken from sixteen world championships, seven Olympic Games and 18 world best lists revealed an average margin between first and second place of 0.57-0.6%).
150 *Chand v IAAF*, CAS 2014/A/3759, paras 221, 239.
151 *Chand v IAAF*, CAS 2014/A/3759, para 230.
152 *Chand v IAAF*, CAS 2014/A/3759, para 35(f).
153 *Chand v IAAF*, CAS 2014/A/3759, para 513.
154 *Chand v IAAF*, CAS 2014/A/3759, para 519.
155 *Chand v IAAF*, CAS 2014/A/3759, para 494.
156 In fact, the evidence is clearly against. See Handelsman DJ, *Toward a Robust Definition of Sport Sex*, Endocr. Rev. 2024 Sep 12;45(5):709-736 (*'endogenous GH secretion in young women is consistently higher (typically twice) that in young men of similar age. Women are about 30% less sensitive than men to exogenous GH, based on the final, optimized GH replacement dose for GH-deficient adults. Yet, even discounting the doubled GH secretion in females by 30% indicates that young women still have greater exposure to endogenous GH than young men. Consequently, differences in endogenous GH secretion and/or action cannot account for the differences in male and female athletic performance that originate at the onset of male puberty'*).
157 *Chand v IAAF*, CAS 2014/A/3759, paras 454-472, 488, 490, 491, 497-99.
158 *Chand v IAAF*, CAS 2014/A/3759, para 534.
159 *Chand v IAAF*, CAS 2014/A/3759, paras 522, 528, 532.
160 *Chand v IAAF*, CAS 2014/A/3759, para 548.
161 Doriane Lambelet Coleman, *Sex in Sport*, 80 Law and Contemporary Problems 63-126 (2017).
162 Handelsman DJ, Hirschberg A. and Bermon S., *Circulating Testosterone as the Hormonal Basis of Sex Differences in Athletic Performance*, (2018) Endocrine Reviews 39: 803 – 829.
163 Handelsman DJ, Hirschberg A. and Bermon S., *Circulating Testosterone as the Hormonal Basis of Sex Differences in Athletic Performance*, (2018) Endocrine Reviews 39: 803 – 829, at note 4. See also RV Clark et al, *Large divergence in testosterone concentrations between men and women: Frame of reference for elite athletes in sex-specific competition in sports, a narrative review*, Clinical Endocrinology 90(1):15-22, 2019; Erratum, Clinical Endocrinology 91(3):471-473, which came up with slightly different ranges (males: 8.8 to 30.9 nmol/L;

females: 0.4-2.0 nmol/L), but only because it included a sub-set rather than the entirety of the data pooled by Handelsman et al.

164 Handelsman DJ, Hirschberg A. and Bermon S., *Circulating Testosterone as the Hormonal Basis of Sex Differences in Athletic Performance*, (2018) Endocrine Reviews 39: 803 – 829 (*'Similar to all hormones and drugs, over their effective range of biological activity the dose-response relationship for testosterone is usually a sigmoidal curve with lower and upper plateaus joined by a monotonically rising middle region, which may be linear in the natural scale but more often log-linear (linear on the log or similar transformed scale). In the middle portion of the typical sigmoidal dose-response curve for the same increase in testosterone dose (or concentration), the response would be increased in simple proportional (i.e., linear) but more often on a logarithmic scale. In contrast, at the lower and upper plateaus of dose or concentrations, changes in testosterone exposure may evoke minimal or no response on the endpoint'*); Hooven C., *Testosterone: The Story of the Hormone that Dominatesand Divides Us* (Cassell 2021), p. 109 (*'T[estosterone] is not the master key to performance differences within each sex. Many studies show that among elite athletes, T level (when it is within normal range) is not related to performance, within sex. That is, if we measure the T levels of healthy, typical male (or female) athletes, we will not find that the men with the highest T levels relative to the other healthy men are always the best at their particular sport. … But the conclusion that T levels don't explain differences between the sexes is the result of a subtle bait and switch. The scientifically backed claim, that T doesn't always predict sporting success within males, or within females, has been replaced by a similar-sounding but unsupported claim that T doesn't explain sporting differences between males and females'*) (emphasis in original).

165 *The Role of Testosterone in Athletic Performance* (January 2019), available at web.law.duke.edu.

166 Bermon S., *Androgens and athletic performance of elite female athletes*, Curr Opin Endocrinol Diabetes Obes, 2017;24:246-51.

167 See e.g. Phyllis Ellis's documentary, *Category: Women* (Orama Filmworks, 2022); Canadian Running, *New Canadian documentary explores Caster Semenya story in human-rights terms*, 29 April 2022.

168 Johnson R., *What No One Is Telling You About Caster Semenya: She Has XY Chromosomes*, letsrun.com, 2 May 2019; *Semenya, Francine and Margaret miss Stockholm Diamond League after gender ruling*, Region Week 18 May 2019.

169 IAAF Eligibility Regulations for Female Classification (Athletes with Differences of Sex Development), April 2018, critiqued in Karkazis K, Carpenter M., *Impossible "Choices": The Inherent Harms of Regulating Women's Testosterone in Sport*, J Bioeth Inq. 2018 Dec;15(4):579-587.

170 Or a genetic disorder involving disordered gonadal steroidogenesis, which can be found in individuals whose chromosomes are 46XY, 46XX, or mosaic (XX and XY). See Ballantyne K, Kayser M. and Grootegoed JA, *Sex and gender issues in competitive sports: investigation of a historical case leads to a new viewpoint*, Br J Sports Med 2012;46:614-617 (proposing that Dutch sprinter Foekje Dillema had a 46XX/46XY mosaic condition, leading to development of ovaries with some testicular tissue present); Dohle M., *'They say I'm not a girl': Case Studies of Gender Verification in Elite Sports* (McFarland & Co., 2020), pp. 54-69.

171 *Semenya v IAAF*, CAS 2018/O/5794, para 333.

172 *Semenya v IAAF*, CAS 2018/O/5794, para 332.

173 IAAF Eligibility Regulations for Female Classification (Athletes with Differences of Sex Development), April 2018,, clause 2.2(a)(iii) and footnote 6.

174 IAAF press release, *IAAF introduces new eligibility requirements for female classification*, 26 April 2018 (*'We have seen in a decade and more of research that 7.1 in every 1000 elite female athletes in our sport have elevated testosterone levels, the majority are in the restricted events covered by these regulations. This is around 140 times what you will find in the general female population which demonstrates to us in statistical terms a recruitment bias'*).

175 Podcast, *Changes with Annie McManus: Caster Semenya*, 27 November 2023.

176 Caster Semenya post on twitter.com, 25 February 2021.

177 Kelner M., *A bitter battle is raging in athletics – and it could get very ugly*, news.sky.com, 18 February 2019.

178 *Semenya v IAAF*, CAS 2018/O/5794, *Athletics South Africa v IAAF*, CAS 2018/O/5798 (together, '*Semenya v IAAF*'). See Ingle S., *Caster Semenya v IAAF: the inside story of sporting trial of the century*, theguardian.com, 1 May 2019; Harper J., *Sporting Gender: The History, Science and Stories of Transgender and Intersex Athletes* (Rowman & Littlefield, 2020), Chapter 20.

179 *Semenya v IAAF*, CAS 2018/O/5794, para 51.

180 *Semenya v IAAF*, CAS 2018/O/5794, paras 52-53, 348.

181 *Semenya v IAAF*, CAS 2018/O/5794, paras 142-151.

182 *Semenya v IAAF*, CAS 2018/O/5794, para 158.

183 *Semenya v IAAF*, CAS 2018/O/5794, paras 152-162.

184 Bermon S. and Garnier P. , *Serum androgen levels and their relation to performance in track and field: mass spectrometry results from 2127 observations in male and female elite athletes*, British Journal of Sports Medicine 2017;51:1309-1314, 3 July 2017; and see *Correction: Serum androgen levels and their relation to performance in track and field: mass spectrometry results from 2127 observations in male and female elite athletes*, British Journal of Sports Medicine 2021;55:e7, 1 September 2017.

185 *Semenya v IAAF*, CAS 2018/O/5794, paras 131-138. See also Sonksen PH, Bavington LD, Boehning T, Cowan D, Guha N, Holt R, Karkazis K, Ferguson-Smith MA, Mircetic J, Bohning D., *Hyperandrogenism controversy in elite women's sport: an examination and critique of recent evidence*, Br J Sports Med. 2018 Dec;52(23):1481-1482; Pielke R, Tucker R, Boye E., *Scientific integrity and the IAAF testosterone regulations*, Int Sports Law J. 2019;19(1–2):18–26.

186 *Semenya v IAAF*, CAS 2018/O/5794, para 55.

187 *Semenya v IAAF*, CAS 2018/O/5794, paras 116-128. This argument is refuted in Handelsman DJ, *Towards a Robust Definition of Sport Sex*, Endocr Rev. 2024 Sep 12;45(5):709-736.

188 *Semenya v IAAF*, CAS 2018/O/5794, paras 58-61.

189 *Semenya v IAAF*, CAS 2018/O/5794, para 64.

190 *Semenya v IAAF*, CAS 2018/O/5794, paras 139-141, 159.

191 *Semenya v IAAF*, CAS 2018/O/5794, paras 241-282.

192 Tucker, R., *The Caster Semenya debate*, sportscientist.com, 16 July 2016.

193 Pielke R., Tucker R., Boye E., *Scientific integrity and the IAAF testosterone regulations*, Int Sports Law J. 2019;19(1–2):18–26.

194 Caster Semenya, *The Race To Be Myself* (Merky Books, 2023), p. 278.

195 *Semenya v IAAF*, CAS 2018/O/5794, para 293.

196 *Semenya v IAAF*, CAS 2018/O/5794, paras 315-17, 353, 356.

197 *Semenya v IAAF*, CAS 2018/O/5794, paras 289, 295-96. See also Pike J. and Hilton, E., *Sex, fairness and the World Athletics regulations: a reply to Bowman-Smart et al*, (2025) Journal of the Philosophy of Sport, 1-18.

198 *Semenya v IAAF*, CAS 2018/O/5794, para 298.

199 *Semenya v IAAF*, CAS 2018/O/5794, para 298.

200 *Semenya v IAAF*, CAS 2018/O/5794, para 292.

201 Bermon S, Hirschberg AL, Kowalski J, Eklund E., *Serum androgen levels are positively correlated with athletic performance and competition results in elite female athletes*, Br J Sports Med. 2018 Dec;52(23):1531-1532.

202 *Semenya v IAAF*, CAS 2018/O/5794, paras 289, 296-97, 318, 386.

203 *Semenya v IAAF*, CAS 2018/O/5794, para 359.

204 *Semenya v IAAF*, CAS 2018/O/5794, para 323.

205 *Semenya v IAAF*, CAS 2018/O/5794, para 325. See Bermon S., *Androgens and athletic performance of elite female athletes*, Curr Opin Endocrinol Diabetes Obes, 2017;24:246-51.

206 *Semenya v IAAF*, CAS 2018/O/5794, para 289.

207 *Semenya v IAAF*, CAS 2018/O/5794, para 289.

208 *Semenya v IAAF*, CAS 2018/O/5794, para 321.

209 See eg Wisniewski AB, Batista RL, Costa EMF, Finlayson C, Sircili MHP, Dénes FT, Domenice S, Mendonca BB, *Management of 46,XY Differences/Disorders of Sex Development (DSD) Throughout Life*, Endocr Rev. 2019 Dec 1;40(6):1547-1572; Cools M, Nordenström A, Robeva R, Hall J, Westerveld P, Flück C, Köhler B, Berra M, Springer A, Schweizer K, Pasterski V; COST Action BM1303 working group 1, *Caring for individuals with a difference of sex development (DSD)*, Nat Rev Endocrinol. 2018 Jul;14(7):415-429. See also Neena A. Xavier, Janet B. McGill, *Hyperandrogenism and Intersex Controversies in Women's Olympics*, The Journal of Clinical Endocrinology & Metabolism, Volume 97, Issue 11, 1 November 2012, pp. 3902–3907 (*'In patients with some DSD, gonadectomy of undescended testes is recommended to reduce testosterone levels and to prevent malignant transformation. When should this occur? This procedure may reduce athleticism and cause side effects such as hot flashes that may further impede training of an individual with no functioning ovaries. Indeed, physicians and patients will have to weigh the short-term and long-term health consequences of androgen reduction therapy or procedures, or the converse, the addition of feminizing treatment. Although reducing excessive androgen levels in women with hyperandrogenism is considered the standard of care, treating an elite athlete who may have additional motives for needing treatment or limiting treatment will add a new dimension to decision making. Selected cases may present an ethical quagmire for physicians. Should treatment of a young woman with the potential to become an elite athlete be aimed at long-term health or short-term performance? Will physician recommendations and patient desires be aligned? When does patient autonomy trump physician recommendations?'*); Harper J., *Transgender Athletes and International Sports*

Policy, 85 Law and Contemporary Problems 151-165 (2022). On the risk of malignancy, see Kathrins & Kolon, *Malignancy in disorders of sex development*, Translational Andrology and Urology, 2016;5(5):794-798 (*'Post-pubertal complete AIS patients remain prone to tumor development if the testes remain in the abdomen—historical estimates place the risk of malignancy at 3.6% at 25 years and 33% at 50 years (13). In cohorts based on prophylactic gonadectomy, the incidence of GCT* [giant cell tumor] *in partial AIS (usually AIS patients raised female) is significantly higher—15% … . The standard of care remains orchiectomy, the timing of which (pre- or post-pubertal) remains controversial. The finding of the majority of tumors in the post-pubertal age group argues for later surgery while the treatment of associated inguinal hernia and psychological issues related to the gonad may warrant pre-pubertal surgery'*). Cf Wünsch L, Holterhus PM, Wessel L, Hiort O., *Patients with disorders of sex development (DSD) at risk of gonadal tumour development: management based on laparoscopic biopsy and molecular diagnosis*, BJU Int. 2012 Dec;110(11 Pt C):E958-65 (*'In patients with DSD, gonadectomy is frequently recommended and depending on the age and the molecular diagnosis, an increased gonadal tumour risk exists and undesired hormone effects may arise. However, gonadectomy is irreversible and impacts considerably on body image. It represents an overtreatment for some patients and should be considered after a comprehensive diagnostic evaluation'*). See also Wylie C Hembree, Peggy T Cohen-Kettenis, Louis Gooren, Sabine E Hannema, Walter J Meyer, M Hassan Murad, Stephen M Rosenthal, Joshua D Safer, Vin Tangpricha, Guy G T'Sjoen, *Endocrine Treatment of Gender-Dysphoric/Gender-Incongruent Persons: An Endocrine Society Clinical Practice Guideline*, The Journal of Clinical Endocrinology & Metabolism, Volume 102, Issue 11, 1 November 2017, pp. 3869–3903; Dubon, Mary E. MD; Abbott, Kristin MD; Carl, Rebecca L. MD, MS., *Care of the Transgender Athlete*, Current Sports Medicine Reports 17(12), pp. 410-418, December 2018.

210 *Semenya v IAAF*, CAS 2018/O/5794, paras 310, 334, 408.

211 See eg Brown, A., *Challenging harm caused by sport's gender rules*, sportsintegrityinitiative.com, 1 August 2025.

212 See IAAF press release, *IAAF response to false claims by athlete regarding DSD treatment*, worldathletics.org, 11 October 2019: *'The IAAF does not advise, nor has it ever advised, an athlete on a preferred treatment route. The IAAF encourages relevant athletes to seek independent, medical advice and will, if requested, provide athletes with information on independent experts and reference centre specialists. The IAAF has never forced any athlete affected by its regulations to undergo surgery, nor paid for any of their treatment. It has in some cases paid for the medical investigation and diagnosis of the athlete by an independent medical centre so the athlete is fully aware of her condition. Regarding the Ugandan athlete, Annet Negesa, interviewed in the ARD documentary, the IAAF strongly denies any suggestion that the IAAF or Dr. Stephane Bermon was involved in her treatment or recommended any course of treatment to her. Furthermore, contrary to the athlete's interview in the ARD documentary, Dr. Bermon has never met the athlete in question and was not at either the consultation in Nice nor the surgery she speaks of in Uganda'*. In October 2020, Ms Negesa said that she could not remember which doctor recommended a gonadectomy, that previously she thought it must have been Dr Bermon, but she no longer maintains that allegation: Winterfeldt and Mebus, *'Gender Battle' – now the doctor has his say*, WDR, sportschau.de, 6 October 2020.

213 *Semenya v IAAF*, CAS 2018/O/5794, paras 67, 69.

214 *Semenya v IAAF*, CAS 2018/O/5794, paras 68, 116-128.

215 *Semenya v IAAF*, CAS 2018/O/5794, para 56.

216 *Semenya v IAAF*, CAS 2018/5794, para 86.

217 *Semenya v IAAF*, CAS 2018/O/5794, para 76.

218 Caster Semenya, *The Race To Be Myself* (Merky Books, 2023), pp. 126-30, 131.

219 *Semenya v IAAF*, CAS 2018/O/5794, paras 73-87, 189.

220 Caster Semenya, *The Race To Be Myself* (Merky Books, 2023), pp. 279-82.

221 *Semenya v IAAF*, CAS 2018/O/5794, para 87.

222 Much of this discussion of hot tub evidence comes from an article that Doriane Coleman and I wrote for Judicature: *Experts in the Hot Tub at the Court of Arbitration for Sport*, judicature.duke.edu, Vol 104, No.2, summer 2020.

223 See generally Justice Peter Garling RFD, *Concurrent Expert Evidence – The New South Wales Experience*, University of Oxford Faculty of Law, 1 December 2015 (supremecourt.nsw.gov.au/documents/Publications/Speeches/2015-Speeches/Garling_20151201.pdf, accessed 11 January 2026); Civil Justice Council, *Concurrent Expert Evidence and 'Hot-Tubbing' in English Litigation Since the 'Jackson Reforms'*, 25 July 2016 (judiciary.uk/wp-content/uploads/2011/03/cjc-civil-litigation-review-hot-tubbing-report-20160801.pdf, accessed 11 January 2026).

224 Such was the public interest in the case that CAS Secretary-General Matthieu Reeb read out a summary of the award to the press outside the CAS building. See video posted at *IAAF*

rules necessary to preserve integrity of female competition says CAS on Caster Semenya, 1 May 2019, available on theguardian.com (accessed 29 July 2024).
For discussion of the case from the respective perspectives of two of the protagonists, see Krech M., *The Misplaced Burdens of "Gender Equality" in Caster Semenya v IAAF: The Court of Arbitration for Sport Attempts Human Rights Adjudication* [2019] I.S.L.R. Issue 3, p. 66, and Lambelet Coleman D., *Semenya and ASA v IAAF: Affirming the Lawfulness of a Sex-Based Eligibility Rule for the Women's Category in Elite Sport* [2019] I.S.L.R. Issue 4, p. 83.
225 *Semenya v IAAF*, CAS 2018/O/5794, para 460.
226 *Semenya v IAAF*, CAS 2018/O/5794, paras 557-58.
227 *Semenya v IAAF*, CAS 2018/O/5794, para 559.
228 *Semenya v IAAF*, CAS 2018/O/5794, para 560.
229 *Semenya v IAAF*, CAS 2018/O/5794, para 470.
230 *Semenya v IAAF*, CAS 2018/O/5794, paras 481, 490.
231 *Semenya v IAAF*, CAS 2018/O/5794, paras 488-493, 528-30, 571.
232 *Semenya v IAAF*, CAS 2018/O/5794, para 472.
233 *Semenya v IAAF*, CAS 2018/O/5794, para 479.
234 *Semenya v IAAF*, CAS 2018/O/5794, para 484, 535, 571.
235 *Semenya v IAAF*, CAS 2018/O/5794, paras 482, 494.
236 *Semenya v IAAF*, CAS 2018/O/5794, paras 498-99.
237 *Semenya v IAAF*, CAS 2018/O/5794, paras 531-32.
238 *Semenya v IAAF*, CAS 2018/O/5794, para 537.
239 *Semenya v IAAF*, CAS 2018/O/5794, para 580.
240 *Semenya v IAAF*, CAS 2018/O/5794, para 583.
241 *Semenya v IAAF*, CAS 2018/O/5794, paras 487, 585, 599, 601, 603, 609, 618-20, 622.
242 *Semenya v IAAF*, CAS 2018/O/5794, paras 623-24.
243 Caster Semenya, *The Race To Be Myself* (Merky Books, 2023), p. 278.
244 Bruce Kidd, in *Forum, A discussion of Science, Sport, Sex, and the Case of Caster Semenya*, Issues in Science & Technology Vol 26(2) (Winter 2020).
245 *Semenya v IAAF*, CAS 2018/O/5794, para 589.
246 Granville S., *Namibian teens vow to fight Olympics testosterone ban*, bbc.co.uk, 7 July 2021. Mboma's story is covered in detail in the *Tested* podcast series, CBC Stories, July 2024.
247 *Aminatou Seyni profile*, worldathletics.org (accessed 4 August 2024).
248 *Francine Niyonsaba: Burundi runner sets new 2,000m world record in Zagreb*, bbc.co.uk, 14 September 2021.
249 *Semenya & ASA v IAAF*, SFT 4A_248/2019, paras 9.5, 9.8.3.1, 9.8.3.2, 10.5, 12. The text quoted from the SFT judgment is an informal translation from the original French.
250 World Medical Association, *World Medical Association urges physicians not to implement IAAF rules on classifying women athletes*, 2020; Report of the United Nations High Commissioner for Human Rights, *Intersection of race and gender discrimination in sport*, A/HRC/44/26, 15 June 2020, para 34(c).
251 Hamilton BR et al, *Integrating Transwomen and Female Athletes with Differences of Sex Development (DSD) into Elite Competition: The FIMS 2021 Consensus Statement*, Sports Med. 2021 Jul;51(7):1401-1415. See also Hamilton BR et al, *Response to the United Nations Human Rights Council's Report on Race and Gender Discrimination in Sport: An Expression of Concern and a Call to Prioritise Research*, Sports Medicine (2021) 51:839-842.
252 *Semenya v Switzerland*, application no. 10934/21, ECtHR, Third Section (11 July 2023), joint dissenting opinion of Judges Grozev, Roosma, and Ktistakis.
253 *Semenya v Switzerland*, no 10934/21, 10 July 2025, paras 211-239. See Kennedy R. and Lavey C., *The ECHR Grand Chamber judgment in Semenya v Switzerland and its wider impact on international sport*, lawinsport.com, 3 October 2025.
254 Associated Press, *Caster Semenya ends legal battle over track's sex eligibility rules*, espn.co.uk, 2 October 2025.
255 *Statement made by the International Boxing Association regarding Athletes Disqualification in World Boxing Championships 2023*, 31 July 2024, iba.sport (accessed on 2 August 2024).
256 See clause 4.2 of the IBA Technical & Competition Rules 2024, iba.sport (accessed on 2 August 2024).
257 Lawton M., *Women's bout involving failed gender test fighter ends in 46 seconds*, thetimes.com, 1 August 2024.
258 Morris JS, Link J., Martin JC, Carrier DR, *Sexual dimorphism in human arm power and force: implications for sexual selection on fighting ability*, J Exp Biol 15 January 2020; 223 (2); Kathryn Knight, *Evolution built men to pack a punch*, J Exp Biol 1 February 2020; 223 (3).
259 Harris R., *Imane Khelif: Olympics should reintroduce sex testing in wakeof Imane Khelif boxing row, UN adviser says*, news.sky.com, 3 August 2024.

260 Handelsman, DJ. and Bermon, S., *Biology and Management of Male-Bodied Athletes in Elite Female Sports*, (2025) Drug Test and Analysis 17, no. 9 (2025): 1703–1714 (even sustained complete testosterone suppression leaves an unfair legacy of physical advantages).
261 Movement Advancement Project, 2025, *Equality Maps: Bans on Best Practice Medical Care for Transgender Youth*, data as of 24 June 2025 (puberty-blocking treatment banned in 25 US states, although challenges are pending in certain of those states); SEGM, *Italy Joins the List of Countries Recommending Restrictions on Puberty Blockers for Gender Dysphoria*, December 2024; Euronews, *The UK is the latest country to ban puberty blockers for trans kids. Why is Europe Restricting Them?* (December 2024).
262 Becker M and Hesse V, *Minipuberty: Why Does It Happen?*, Hormone Research in Paediatrics, 93:76-84 (2020); Lanciotti L et al, *Up-To-Date Review About Minipuberty and Overview on Hypothalamic-Pituitary-Gonadal Axis Activation in Fetal and Neonatal Life*, 2018(9) Frontiers in Endocrinology, 23 July 2018; M. Joyner, S. Hunter, and J. Senefeld, *Evidence on sex differences in sports performance*, J Appl Physiol 138:274-281 (2025)).
263 See e.g. Davis SM et al, *Sex differences in infant body composition emerge in the first 5 months of life*, J Pediatr Endocrinol Metab. 2019 Nov 26;32(11):1235-1239; Atkinson M et al, *Sex Differences in Track and Field Elite Youth*, Medicine & Science in Sports & Exercise 56(8):1390-1397, August 2024 (sex differences up to 12yo: 100-800m 4%; long jump 6.8%; high jump 5.3%); Brown, G.A., Shaw, B.S. and Shaw, I., *Sex-based differences in shot put, javelin throw, and long jump in 8-and-under and 9-10-year-old athletes* (2025) Eur J Sport Sci. 25 (long jump 3.7-4.9%; shot put 6.5-19.3%; javelin 23.5-32.6%).
264 See e.g. M. Joyner, S. Hunter, and J. Senefeld, *Evidence on sex differences in sports performance*, J Appl Physiol 138:274-281 (2025); John Hopkins Medicine, *Estrogen's effects on the female body*, hopkinsmedicine.org (accessed 2 December 2025); Tønnessen E et al, *Performance Development in Adolescent Track and Field Athletes According to Age, Sex and Sport Discipline*, (2015) PLOS ONE 10(6) (*'during puberty girls begin to produce higher levels of circulating estrogen and other female sex hormones. Compared to their male counterparts, they experience a less pronounced growth spurt and a smaller increase in muscle mass, but a continuous increase in fat mass, thereby lowering the critical ratio between muscular power and total body mass. Fat free mass (FFM) in males and females is nearly identical up to 12–13 years of age. Subsequently, FFM plateaus in females at 15–16 years of age, but continues to increase in males up to 19–20 years of age'*); *Female Athletes Need to Train Differently: It's Biological*, relentlessathleticsllc.com (accessed 24 June 2025) (*'when a female athlete goes through puberty her tendons and ligaments become loose. This helps accommodate their growing bones without an equal muscle growth. BUT when it comes to explosiveness, loose tendons and ligaments lead to force dissipation, meaning an even slower, less explosive athlete on the field'*). See also World Athletics' Working Group on Gender Diverse Athletes, Final Report, 11 November 2024, p. 33 (*'Less is known about the nature and extent of the male advantage retained by XY athletes who do not experience endogenous puberty. However, we do know that it exists: [i] Puberty blockers and T suppression cannot mitigate the organizational effects of chromosomes and hormones acting on sex chromosomes receptors, proteins, and physiological systems. [ii] These organizational effects include important drivers of both pre- and post-pubertal athletic performance. [iii] XY athletes will not experience the competitive disadvantages associated with sports relevant aspects of female sexual development, the menstrual cycle and post-partum issues that can adversely affect females after childbirth'*).
265 Executive Order, *Keeping Men Out of Women's Sports*, White House, 5 February 2025 (whitehouse.gov/presidential-actions/2025/02/keeping-men-out-of-womens-sports/, accessed 21 October 2025).
266 *For Women Scotland Ltd v. The Scottish Ministers*, [2025] UKSC 16, especially paras 234-36.
267 *World Boxing to introduce mandatory sex testing for all boxers that want to participate in its competitions*, World Boxing press release dated 30 May 2025, updated 6 June 2025; *World Athletics introduces SRY gene test for athletes wishing to compete in the female category*, World Athletics press release, 30 July 2025; *FIS Council reinforces commitment to athlete safety*, FIS press release, 24 September 2025.
268 IOC Policy on the Protection of the Female (Women's) Category in Olympic Sport and Guiding Considerations for International Federations and Sports Governing Bodies, 26 March 2026.

Chapter 6

The Fastest Man on No Legs

Blake Leeper was born with no feet, shin bones, or calf muscles. His parents were told he would never walk, but they refused to accept that, and so did he. Not only did he walk, using prosthetic legs; he insisted on joining in with the sports that the other kids were playing. Initially he mainly played baseball and basketball, but after watching Oscar Pistorius – described as *'the fastest man on no legs'*[1] – compete in front of 90,000 people at the 2008 Beijing Olympics, he was inspired to turn to athletics. In a December 2019 podcast, he explained the feeling he got when he put on his first pair of bespoke running-specific prosthetics (*'RSPs'*, or *'blades'*), stepped onto the track, and sprinted properly for the first time: *'That was the fastest I had ever run in my life, and I was 18 years old. And the way the wind was hitting my face, nothing mattered in that moment. I didn't care that I was disabled, I didn't care that I was missing my legs. ... In that moment, I was free. And I fell in love with that feeling, I really did'*.[2]

Concentrating on the short sprints (100m to 400m), Blake soon started performing to an outstanding level, so much so that he competed on the US team at the 2012 London Paralympics, winning a silver medal in the 400m (behind Oscar Pistorius) and bronze in the 200m (behind Pistorius and Alan Oliveira). Many further medals followed in subsequent years, and in 2019 he ran the 400m in 44:38 seconds, which was only 1.35 seconds slower than the *able-bodied* world record of 43:03 seconds set by Wayde van Niekerk in 2016. However, despite 44:38 seconds being well within the qualifying standard for the 2020 Olympics, the IAAF refused to let Mr Leeper run either at the Olympics or in any of its other events, because – it insisted – his blades gave him an unfair advantage.

Mr Leeper was incredulous: *'They tell me, me, that I have an unfair advantage! I couldn't believe it'*.[3] He immediately appealed the IAAF's decision to the Court of Arbitration for Sport. It was *'heart-breaking'*, he told the CAS Panel, *'that instead of seeking to be inclusive, the IAAF had used his disability to diminish his achievements and aspirations'*.[4] He *'explained that his lifetime goal has been to compete in the Olympic Games. Achieving that goal would, he believes, both help to change perceptions of individuals with disabilities and help to inspire disabled persons not to accept lower expectations from others. Mr. Leeper therefore urged the Panel to overturn the IAAF's decision, in order to give him the opportunity to realise his dream and to serve as an inspiration for other disabled athletes to do likewise'*.[5]

What was the IAAF thinking? How could it possibly believe that a double amputee had an unfair advantage over able-bodied sprinters? Was this just a fig leaf concealing the IAAF's prejudice against disabled people, against athletes who don't conform to traditional notions of athletic aesthetic and excellence?

The IAAF was accused of that and more. It instructed Bird & Bird to defend its decision at the CAS. Chris Lavey and I met with world-leading experts in biomechanics and human performance from the USA and Australia, who confirmed that Mr Leeper's RSPs were set at a height that gave him longer legs than he would have had if he had not been an amputee, which artificially increased his sprinting speed by a significant margin. Our job was to present that evidence to the CAS in defence of the IAAF's decision to exclude Mr Leeper from its events unless he shortened his RSPs to run at his '*natural*' height.

Before I explain how the case turned out, I want to discuss briefly the different reasons why SGBs regulate the use of equipment and technology in their sports, and how they have sometimes struggled to address the issues presented by the enormous technological advances made in recent decades.

When should a sports governing body be concerned about advances in sports equipment and technology?

At the pinnacle of any sport, truly tiny margins determine success or failure. In the short sprints in athletics, for example, the winning margins are often milliseconds.[6] And therefore there is a huge demand for anything that will deliver even tiny performance gains, and sports equipment manufacturers and technology companies spend enormous amounts developing new products to meet that demand. A famous example is the '*Vaporfly 4%*' running shoe that Nike brought out in 2018, with a carbon plate in the sole that had a spring-like effect. Independent testing suggested that the shoes increased the user's running economy by 4 per cent and running speed by 3.4 per cent.[7] A series of world records fell to athletes wearing them, including the men's marathon world record (broken by 78 seconds by Eliud Kipchoge in September 2018), the women's marathon world record (broken by 81 seconds by Brigid Kosgei in October 2019), and the 10 km road world record (broken by six seconds by Joshua Cheptegei in December 2019).[8]

The governing body of a sport will want to be open to technological progress and innovation, in order: (1) to improve the safety of the sport, eg by mandating the use of cricket helmets to limit the risk of serious head injuries[9] or of rugby mouthguards with inbuilt sensors generating real-time data about concussion injuries;[10] (2) to improve the accuracy and efficiency of on-field officiating, such as the use of Video-Assisted Refereeing technology in tennis, cricket, football, and other sports, albeit with varying levels of customer satisfaction;[11] and in particular (3) to keep the sport relevant and exciting enough to attract a constant stream of new participants and fans. As World Athletics President Seb Coe said in early 2024, when announcing changes to the long-jump take-off rules: '*Our sport is 150 years old. There are elements of it that you absolutely want to protect – they are sacrosanct – but there is stuff there that just leaves people a little cold. It is going to change; it has to. We can't just sit there. The holy grail of every sport is to remain salient, interesting and exciting to young people*'.[12]

But the SGB also needs to guard against the potentially negative effects of new equipment and technology. In particular:

- It has to ensure the new equipment or technology presents no safety risks for participants. For example, Major League Baseball banned the use of aluminium bats because they enable batters to hit pitches much harder and faster, potentially endangering fielders, umpires, and spectators.[13] Similarly, in 2000 the UCI banned competition bicycles that weigh less than 6.8 kilograms,[14] because the cyclist racing up a mountain may want the bike to weigh as little as possible but '[i]f the brakes, or wheels, or the frame disintegrate when the cyclist is descending at 50 or 60 miles per hour after a steep climb, death is a possibility – not only for that cyclist but for all those who follow him to the paving'.[15]

- It will want to maintain enough consistency with the past for historical comparisons, and record-setting performances, to remain meaningful.[16] For example, the UCI decreed in 2000 that the record for the longest distance travelled in one hour could only be broken by a rider using a '*tradition bike*', ie a bike similar to the one used by Eddy Merckx when he set the record in 1972, so without disc wheels or aero bars or any of the other technological improvements that had since been made to endurance race bikes.[17]

- It will want the new equipment or technology to be available to all, so that no one has an unfair advantage.[18] For example, in 2020 World Athletics decreed that a new type of running shoe may not be used in competition until it has been freely available for purchase for at least four months.[19]

- It will want to ensure that the sport continues to showcase and test a range of different skills. For example, another Major League Baseball concern about the aluminium baseball bat was that it would upset the balance between pitcher and batter, turning each match into a '*home run derby*'.[20] Similarly, a Times journalist suggested in April 2024 that the introduction of the Kookaburra cricket ball into English county cricket, with its less pronounced seam and therefore reduced movement through the air compared to the traditional Dukes ball, had tipped the balance against the bowler and in favour of the batter, '*mak[ing] some average batters look very good*'.[21] And when a golf club was developed in the 1980s that had U-shaped grooves on the club face instead of the traditional V-shaped grooves, enabling the user to generate more back spin even when hitting from the rough,[22] that made it less important to hit the fairway from the tee. The R&A and the US Golf Association therefore banned clubs that generated more back spin than the traditional V-shaped grooves, to ensure that driving accuracy remained a fundamental part of the sport.[23] More recently, golfers have developed faster swing speeds that enable longer drives, leading the R&A and USGA to stipulate that golf balls have to be calibrated so that they do not travel further than 320 yards when hit at a speed of 127 mph.[24]

- Most of all, the governing body needs to ensure that victory always belongs to the athlete with the best natural talent and work ethic (see pp v–vi), not the one with access to the best R&D department.[25] Sports ethicist Tom Murray argues this provides the key to distinguishing between performance-enhancing products that are acceptable, such as more supple baseball gloves, because they help to highlight the speed and skill involved in fielding a ground ball or a line drive,[26] and performance-enhancing products that are not acceptable, such as anabolic steroids, because they do not highlight but rather negate natural skill and effort.[27]

Striking the right balance between natural talent and effort on the one hand and innovative equipment/technology on the other is an issue for all sports,[28] but it is particular challenge in sports such as motor racing, where technical and engineering prowess are not just an accepted but a highly celebrated part of the sport. The rules governing the technical specifications of the power units, bodywork, electrical systems, and other components of Formula One racing cars run to hundreds of pages,[29] and are rigorously policed and enforced by the sport's governing body, the Fédération Internationale de l'Automobile (FIA). In those rules, the FIA decides what elements of the race should be a challenge for the engineers to tackle, and what should be left to the skill of the driver. As just one example, it has outlawed the use of traction control in Formula One cars,[30] leaving it to the driver's skill to navigate corners at speed without losing grip, in order to deliver *'much more unpredictable racing and a better spectacle for the fans'*.[31]

But while motor racing may be an extreme case, no sport is immune from the challenges that new equipment and technology can present. For example, the only equipment a swimmer needs is a swimsuit, a pair of goggles, and (in some cases) a swim cap. But swimmers who wore high tech full-body swimsuits made of polyurethane panels and ultrasonically-welded seams that dramatically reduce surface friction drag won more than 90 per cent of the races at the 2008 Beijing Olympics, setting 66 new Olympic records and 25 new world records in the process.[32] Commentators noted that '*the suit was regarded as a form of "technological doping"*' that '*only served to diminish natural ability, therefore threatening the integrity of the sport*'.[33] In July 2009, the international governing body of swimming, the Fédération Internationale de Natation, now known as World Aquatics, banned the full-body suits in an effort to ensure that it remains natural talent, not technology, that determines success in the sport.[34] Several of the records that were set by body suit users before that ban came into effect have not been beaten to this day.[35]

Tennis provides another example. Conventional tennis rackets have interwoven or bonded vertical and horizontal strings, but in the 1970s a '*spaghetti*' racket was produced with two additional layers of vertical strings that slid freely across the horizontal strings on impact with the ball, creating exaggerated top spin that forced the serve returner well back behind the baseline, thereby decreasing the number of successful serve returns and increasing the number of top spin shots played in any rally that did ensue. At the 1977 US Open, several players using these rackets beat higher-ranked opponents using conventional rackets, prompting threats by the latter to boycott tournaments that did not ban the use of the new rackets. In 1978 the International Tennis Federation announced that henceforth all racket strings had to be interlaced, in order '*to prevent undue spin on the ball that would result in a change in the character of the game*'. It explained: '*We encourage progress but want it to be in the best interests of the game as a whole*'.[36] By 2001, however, players were developing faster and flatter serves using the lighter carbon fibre rackets and polyester strings, particularly on Wimbledon's grass courts, and therefore the All England Lawn Tennis & Croquet Club switched to a '*stickier*' grass (100 per cent ryegrass, rather than a blend of ryegrass and '*creeping red fescue*') to produce higher bounces and therefore increase the chance of longer rallies.[37]

Going back to the '*Vaporfly 4%*' running shoe that Nike brought out in 2018, introducing new technology that allowed users to smash existing world records (see p 186), their rivals complained: '*It's the same as doping. It's simply cheating*';[38] while commentators questioned whether the new shoes, coupled with new pacing technology, '*make[] it impossible to compare race performances between records set before and after the introduction of these new technologies*', and suggested that records set using such technology '*should be differentiated from those records performed without the assistance of such technology with an "asterisk"*', *in order to 'allow for a fairer comparison between athletes'*.[39] World Athletics finally intervened in January 2020. It accepted that it was too late to ban the Vaporfly and similar running shoes that had already come to market, but it imposed an immediate moratorium on the use in competition of any new running shoe with a sole that was thicker than 40mm and had more than one rigid embedded plate, because *'there is sufficient evidence to raise concerns that the integrity of the sport might be threatened'*. Seb Coe explained: *'It is not our job to regulate the entire sports shoe market, but it is our duty to preserve the integrity of elite competition by ensuring that the shoes worn by elite athletes in competition do not offer any unfair assistance or advantage. As we enter the Olympic year, we don't believe we can rule out shoes that have been generally available for a considerable period of time, but we can draw a line by prohibiting the use of shoes that go further than what is currently on the market while we investigate further. I believe these new rules strike the right balance by offering certainty to athletes and manufacturers as they prepare for the Tokyo 2020 Olympic Games, while addressing the concerns that have been raised about shoe technology. If further evidence becomes available that indicates we need to tighten up these rules, we reserve the right to do that to protect our sport'*.[40] After this intervention, the rate at which new world records were set in running races slowed down from a high of eleven in 2021 back to the more normal rate of five per year in 2022 and 2023.[41]

What are the legal constraints on an SGB's ability to regulate the use of equipment and technology in its sport?

When the ITF banned the use of *'spaghetti'* tennis rackets in elite competitions in 1978, the racket manufacturer filed a lawsuit against the ITF and the US Tennis Association in the US, arguing that the ban amounted to an unlawful boycott of its product. However, the court decided that the purpose of the ban was not to injure the manufacturer but rather *'to accomplish the legitimate goals of preserving the essential character and integrity of the game of tennis as it had always been played, and preserving competition by attempting to conduct the game in an orderly fashion'*. Expert evidence presented by the ITF and USTA persuaded the court that *'rackets or stringing that impart excessive topspin to the ball alter the character of the game'*, and that *'the ITF and the USTA could rationally consider a racket's artificial enhancement of fundamental skills of the game [to be] a threat to the integrity and character of the game as it has been historically played'*. The court also noted that the ITF had drafted the rule narrowly *'so that it would be the least restrictive of technological improvements and developments, but still address the legitimate concern that such development not adversely alter the character of the game of tennis as it had been played historically or artificially enhance the skill and ability of players, thereby harming the integrity of competitive tennis'*. On that basis, the court rejected the manufacturer's claim that the ITF and USTA had acted unlawfully in banning its product.[42]

As already mentioned (see pp 11–12), that legal test – does the regulation pursue a legitimate objective, are the restrictions that it imposes rationally connected to the achievement of that objective, and are they proportionate, ie do they go any further than is necessary to achieve that objective, and do their benefits outweigh their detrimental effects? – has become ubiquitous in sports law, a test that every regulation must be able to pass, whatever its subject-matter. I stress that the test is *'is the rule rational?'*, ie could a reasonable person support it?, not *'is the rule reasonable?'*, ie do I agree with it? That is important. It is a fundamental principle of the jurisprudence of the CAS,[43] as indeed it is of English law,[44] that an SGB is better equipped than the court to decide what rules are best for its sport, and the court should only step in if it finds the rule to be irrational, ie one that no reasonable person could think was appropriate.

In the specific context of regulating the use of equipment and technology, the CAS has ruled that *'an international sports governing body … is legitimately entitled to take the view that fairness requires that the outcome of competitive athletics should be determined by natural physical talent, training and effort, and that athletes should not be able to use artificial technology during competitions in a way that provides them with an overall advantage over athletes who are not using such technology'*.[45] The CAS has also confirmed that SGBs, *'by virtue of their status, expertise and responsibility for protecting and reconciling the interests of all stakeholders in a particular sport, … enjoy a margin of appreciation in determining what factors are relevant to ensuring the fairness and integrity of the sport in question and what regulatory measures are necessary in order to achieve this'*.[46] However, SGBs do not have free rein. Instead, they must be ready to show that any restrictive regulations they issue are a necessary and proportionate means of preserving the fairness and integrity of the sport. And the CAS will scrutinise those regulations particularly rigorously when their effect is to exclude would-be participants from competing in the sport.

Maintaining the right balance between talent and technology in Paralympic sport

The International Paralympic Committee operates a complex classification system that separates para athletes into different competition categories depending on their degree of disability. The purpose is to ensure that the contest is determined not by their disability but rather by their natural talents and the hard work and training they put into perfecting those talents,[47] ie to ensure that success goes to *'the best athlete, rather than the athlete with the least impairment'*.[48] The rules have to protect and advance that imperative.

Where para sport differs from able-bodied sport, however, is that a para athlete may have to use special equipment or technology in order to be able to compete in the sport at all. This is surely to be encouraged: the para athlete's triumph over adversity is an inspiration for all.[49] However, there can't be carte blanche for a para athlete to use any equipment they want. To take an absurd example, an amputee couldn't be permitted to ride a motorcycle around the track, as that would destroy the level playing field, pose safety risks to other contestants, and obviate rather than celebrate the natural talents and effort of the competitors in the race.

On the other hand, why shouldn't an amputee athlete be permitted to use running-specific prostheses (RSPs) to compete, and (if good enough) to win the medals and prize money that their performances warrant? It may seem difficult to believe that this could be unfair to non-amputee athletes, but as better and better RSPs have been developed, the very best amputee athletes have started to match the performances of the very best non-amputee athletes. In such circumstances, how can we be sure that it is the amputee athlete's natural talent and effort that are driving their performance, and not the sophisticated RSPs that they are using? It is vital, including for the RSP users themselves,[50] that the RSPs simply enable the user to exploit the natural talents they have honed on the training field, and do not give them an artificial performance advantage. Otherwise, the achievements of these '*blade runners*' will always have a question mark against them, and their competitors will always be concerned that the playing field is not level.

This can be an issue for single amputees in field events such as long jump or high jump, particularly if they jump off their prosthetic leg.[51] However, the concern is particularly acute when the athlete is a double amputee, because that athlete can do something that no able-bodied athlete can do: by adjusting the height of both prosthetic blades, they can increase the length of their legs. As explained below, leg length determines stride length, which is a key component of top running speed, and therefore a double amputee can improve their sprint performance simply by increasing the length of their RSPs.

This issue has caused enormous controversy in both paralympic and non-paralympic athletics, prompting regulation, challenge, and consequent litigation, starting with the Pistorius case.

Pistorius v IAAF[52]

In March 2007, the IAAF Council adopted a rule banning the use in elite athletics of '*any technical device that incorporates springs, wheels or any other element that provides the user with an advantage over another athlete not using such a device*'.[53] Oscar Pistorius, a double amputee athlete from South Africa, sought permission to compete in IAAF competitions using '*Cheetah Flex-Foot' RSPs manufactured by Össur, on the basis that they did not give him an advantage over an athlete not using such RSPs. The IAAF denied that request after scientists at the Cologne Sport University examined Mr Pistorius's performance in race conditions and concluded that '[s]printing with the artificial limbs is – from a biomechanical perspective – a "bouncing" locomotion and is significantly different to sprinting of able-bodied athletes on hard surface. It is a different kind of locomotion at lower metabolic cost*'.[54]

Mr Pistorius appealed the IAAF's decision to the CAS, arguing that by excluding him without considering any alternative solution that might permit him to participate in its events on an equal basis with able-bodied athletes, the IAAF had breached its legal obligation not to discriminate against disabled athletes.[55] He was represented by Jeffrey Kessler, a prominent sports lawyer at Winston & Strawn in New York, who based the claim on the leading US case on the issue, PGA Tour v Martin. Briefly, in 2000 Casey Martin, an elite golfer with an atrophied right leg, argued that the PGA Tour's refusal to waive its rule that the golf course must be walked, so that he could use a golf cart to get from hole to hole, effectively denied him the reasonable accommodation he needed to enter its events, and therefore constituted discrimination in breach of the Americans with Disabilities Act of 1990. That legislation did not require an event organiser to make modifications if they would fundamentally alter the nature of the events they were staging – eg by changing an essential aspect of the sport, or by giving the disabled person an advantage over other competitors – and the PGA Tour contended that allowing Mr Martin to ride around the course on a cart would fundamentally alter the nature of the competition by removing fatigue as a factor, as well as putting those who were required to walk the course at a competitive disadvantage. The US Supreme Court rejected this argument on the basis that walking the course was not essential to the fundamental nature of the sport of golf (golfers were allowed to use carts in many events, including some PGA events), and that the evidence showed that Mr Martin did not get a competitive advantage from using a golf cart to get around the course at PGA Tour events. The Supreme Court therefore ruled that it was unlawful discrimination to refuse to allow him to use a cart.[56]

At the CAS seven years later, the IAAF did not argue that allowing Mr Pistorius to run on blades would fundamentally alter the nature of the races it was staging. Instead, it argued, and the CAS accepted, that '*disability laws only require that an athlete such as Mr Pistorius be permitted to compete on the same footing as others. This is precisely the issue to be decided by this Panel: that is, whether or not Mr Pistorius is competing on an equal basis with other athletes not using Cheetah Flex-Foot prostheses. As counsel for the IAAF rightly mentioned, if this Panel finds that Mr Pistorius' Cheetah Flex-Foot prostheses provide no advantage to Mr Pistorius, he will be able to compete on an equal basis with other athletes. If the Panel concludes that Mr Pistorius does gain an advantage, [disability laws] would not assist his case*'.[57]

The IAAF relied on the report from the scientists at Cologne Sport University to show that Mr Pistorius's blades would give him an artificial advantage over his competitors. The Cologne scientists, who were experts on the metabolic aspects of running, suggested that his blades had a spring-like effect, ie they returned more energy than the human ankle joint returns, which meant he did not need to expend the same amount of energy as able-bodied runners.[58] However, tests conducted by Mr Pistorius's experts showed there was no demonstrable additional energy return from the blades compared to ordinary tendons: Mr Pistorius consumed oxygen at the same rate as able-bodied athletes, and he experienced similar fatigue.[59] In addition, his lawyers noted that the IAAF had not asked the Cologne experts to consider other aspects of the blades that might be disadvantageous, eg when coming out of the blocks at the start, or when running around the curves in the track, and therefore there was no proper basis to conclude that the blades gave Mr Pistorius an overall net performance advantage. The CAS Panel agreed and so ruled his exclusion from IAAF competitions unlawful.[60]

One of Mr Pistorius's experts, Professor Peter Weyand, was careful afterwards to say that although the evidence relied on by the IAAF at the CAS had not proved that Mr Pistorius's blades gave him a performance advantage, it remained '*an open question*' whether those blades were in fact performance-enhancing.[61] Professor Weyand has since explained that the IAAF and its experts focused the CAS Panel on the wrong issues. Their claim that the blades generated a higher energy return than a normal ankle joint was not supported by the evidence, but in any event short sprints are the equivalent of a drag race, ie they are all about power (which is a function of sprint mechanics), not energy. Mr Pistorius's sprint mechanics had not been analysed in the CAS proceedings, and therefore the question of whether his blades gave him an advantage was not properly considered.[62]

I will pick this point up again below. At the time, however, the CAS ruling meant that Mr Pistorius was able to compete for South Africa at the 2012 London Olympics using his Cheetah Flex-Foot RSPs. Perhaps because he did not get near the podium (he finished eighth in the 400m semi-final, and was part of the relay team that finished eighth in the 4x400m competition), his participation in the London Olympics passed off without significant controversy. But Mr Pistorius also competed immediately afterwards in the 2012 Paralympics, and when he lost there in the 200m final to Alan Oliveira, another double amputee, who had reportedly increased the length of his blades by 5 cm shortly before the Games, Mr Pistorius complained bitterly that '*these guys are a lot taller and you can't compete with the stride length. You saw how far he came back. We aren't racing a fair race. I gave it my best. The IPC have their regulations. The regulations allow that athletes can make themselves unbelievably high*'.[63]

'Running tall': the IPC's MASH rule

Mr Pistorius was referring to the IPC's rule on Maximum Allowable Standing Height ('*MASH*'), which is intended to address the fact that the user of prosthetic blades can vary the height of the blades, and so the length of their legs, in a way that optimises their running performance. Taking the '*Ottobock 1E90 Sprinter*' model as an example, the user's residual limb goes into a socket that is connected to the prosthetic blade, and a '*clamping mechanism allows the adapter to be secured and released in order to determine the optimum position and height of the prosthetic*'.[64] To prevent abuse, the MASH rule predicts how long the athlete's legs would have been, and therefore how tall the athlete would have been if their legs had been intact, by reference to the dimensions of the rest of their body. It then permits them to run at that height but no taller.[65] That way, they cannot be said to have an unfair advantage over non-amputee or single amputee athletes, who are not able to alter their legs to run taller than their natural height.

One major premise of the MASH rule, then, is that leg length is a significant determinant of top running speed. That was a hotly contested issue in the Leeper case, and is discussed in detail below.

Another premise of the MASH rule, however, is that there is a correlation between the length of an individual's lower limbs and the dimensions of other parts of their body, so that the leg length of the individual, and therefore their '*natural*' height, ie the height they would have been if their legs had been intact, can be predicted based on those other dimensions.

At the time of the 2012 Paralympic Games, the IPC's MASH rule predicted a double amputee's natural height based on the length of their ulna (forearm bone) and demi-span (the distance between the mid-point of the sternum to the tip of the middle finger, with the arm outstretched laterally). However, as the controversy between Oliveira and Pistorius at those Games revealed, that method systematically over-estimated the natural height of double amputees, and so allowed them to '*run tall*'. Other athletes were also concerned. Para 400m runner David Prince said: '*The best way you can get a quick little boost is by taking some form of anabolic whatever-the-heck, but what we're seeing in the amputee classification predominantly is what we're referring to as technology doping. Guys that were previously not competitive are now competitive only because they gave themselves extra blade height*'.[66] And para sprinter and long jumper Lacey Hendersen agreed: '*It's getting a little crazy. These girls are tall. You're looking at them eye level when you're walking, and when they put on their racing legs, they're almost a foot taller than you*'.[67] The IPC therefore looked for a better method to replace it.

In 2009, Dr Alicia Canda had published a study that used measurements of the body segments of 1047 intact Spanish athletes (545 males and 502 females) to devise a series of regression equations that predicted standing height based on the lengths of other body segments.[68] One of those equations – the '*Canda-1 equation*' – predicted standing height based on thigh length, upper arm length, forearm, and sitting height. It did not require the length of the lower leg to be known, and so it could be used to estimate the natural height of transtibial (ie below the knee) double amputees.[69]

The IPC announced that from 1 January 2018 onwards it would use the Canda-1 equation to predict the natural height of its double amputee athletes, with a '*pure error*' factor of 1.91 cm added to the result of the equation to create a margin for error.* Because the IPC anticipated that this would lead to a marked decrease in leg length, and so a marked decrease in sprinting performance, it also said that world records set by amputees complying with the previous MASH rule would be archived, and the record book would start again.[70]

The introduction of this new, more accurate methodology did indeed mean that many double amputee runners had to decrease the lengths of their prosthetic blades by several inches. And sure enough their best performances thereafter were significantly slower than their best performances had been when running at the taller heights permitted under the former MASH rule.[71]

Blake Leeper

That brings us back to Blake Leeper, the US double transtibial amputee 400m runner. Complying with the IPC MASH rule in place when he started competing in 2009, which prescribed maximum leg length based on thigh length, Mr Leeper fixed his Ottobock 1E90 Sprinter prosthetic blades so that he ran at a height of 185.4 cm (6′ 1″). From September 2011, however, the IPC adopted the revised MASH rule described above, which predicted standing height based on the length of the ulna and demi-span. Mr Leeper's maximum permitted height under the new rule was 189.2 cm (6′ 2½″), and he immediately increased the length of his RSPs to run at that height. He insisted that he did so not because he thought that running taller would enable him to run faster, but rather '*as a result of his evolving understanding of running biomechanics, and in order to enable him to run at the height that was most comfortable*' for him.[72]

After his successes at the 2012 Paralympic Games in London (see p 185), Mr Leeper won silver medals in the 100m, 200m and 400m events at the 2013 IPC World Championships, and gold as a member of the US 4x100m relay team. A week later, he was interviewed at an annual design conference, and the interviewer reported: '*He has a question for materials experts, engineers and designers: Is it possible they can help create even more improvements to those blades? If diving across the line was the difference between a medal and no medal, imagine what could happen with improved aerodynamics or lighter and thinner composites or a refined curve. "We can*

* The pure error factor is a concept used in statistical modelling, particularly in design of experiments and regression analysis, to assess the variability in data that is not explained by the model and is due solely to random error.

take this to a whole new level," he said. … "Think back to that three-hundredths of a second, and if we can get into the labs and think about shaving just tenths of a second off, we're breaking world records," he said. "One day I believe the fastest man in the world will be wearing blades, and I'm hoping that person will be me"'.[73] He subsequently won the men's 400m gold at the 2015 U.S. Paralympics Track and Field National Championships in a new personal best time of 47:90 seconds, which was within five seconds of the able-bodied men's 400m world record.[74] However, a urine sample collected from him at that event tested positive for a metabolite of cocaine, and as a result he was banned from competition from June 2015 until June 2017 (see pp 58–59).

It was during this ban that the IPC adopted the more accurate MASH rule using the Canda-1 equation, which required many double amputee athletes to reduce the length of their blades. In Mr Leeper's case, for example, using the Canda-1 equation his relevant body measurements – seated height 91.4 cm; thigh length 44.5 cm; upper arm 29.0 cm; forearm 28.0 cm[75] – generated a predicted height of 172.53 cm. Adding the 1.91 cm pure error factor provided for in the new MASH rule, that meant Mr Leeper's maximum permitted racing height was 174.44 cm (just under 5′ 9″), ie nearly 15 cm (six inches) shorter than the height he had been running at before his drugs ban (189.2 cm, or 6′ 2½″). And all of that extra height came from the longer legs created by his RSPs. As the CAS panel subsequently noted: '*His bodily dimensions above the knee are those of a 1.74m (5′ 9″) tall male. On that basis, his legs should be 92 cm long. However, his RSPs are fixed at a length which makes his legs 107 cm long. As a result, Mr. Leeper runs on legs equal in length to the legs of 2.02m (6′ 8″) tall male*'.[76]

When he returned to competition in 2017, however, rather than shorten his RSPs by nearly six inches to comply with the IPC's new MASH rule, Mr Leeper instead started competing in able-bodied events organised by the IAAF's member federations, using the Ottobock RSPs that made him 189.2 cm tall (6′ 2½″), with legs equal in length to the legs of a 6′ 8″ man. He explained: '*I've been running at this height for the past 10 years, when I first got into the Paralympic Games, and this is the same height regulation that Pistorius abided by to run in the 2012 Paralympic Games and Olympic Games. So for me to compete, I've developed years and years and years of testing, and R&D, and muscle strength, and muscle memory to run fast at this height*'.[77]

At the 2017 US Track & Field National Championships, Mr Leeper recorded new personal bests for the 400m in both the semi-final (45:52 seconds) and final (45:25 seconds). And at a track event in Prague on 4 June 2018, he won the 400m in another new personal best of 44.42 seconds. This was the fastest 400m time ever recorded by a double transtibial amputee, and within the qualifying standard of 44.90 seconds that the IAAF had set for the men's 400m competition at the 2020 Olympic Games. At the US National Championships in July 2019, Mr Leeper won his 400m semi-final heat with a time of 44:38 seconds, which was another new personal best. The next day he ran 44:48 seconds in the 400m final, finishing fifth. He decided that moving forward he wanted to compete in international events sanctioned by the IAAF.

Mr Leeper seeks permission to race on his Ottobock blades in IAAF events, including at the Olympics

In 2014, Markus Rehm, a unilateral amputee, had won the long jump competition at the German national athletics championships, jumping off his prosthetic leg. The following year he won gold at the 2015 IPC World Athletics Championships with a jump of 8.40 metres, a distance that would have won him the gold medal at both of the two previous Olympic Games (London 2012 and Beijing 2008). And in 2016 he won gold at the 2016 Indoor Grand Prix in Glasgow, an able-bodied competition. Was Mr Rehm the best long jumper in the world, despite his disability, or were his performances artificially enhanced by his prosthetic blade? The German athletics federation asked the IAAF Council to adopt a new rule that took away any assessment of impact on performance, and simply scored amputee athletes separately from other athletes, because they were not competing under the same conditions. Instead, however, the IAAF Council adopted the more permissive Technical Rule 6.3.4, which prohibited '[t]he use of any mechanical aid, unless the athlete can establish on the balance of probabilities that the use of an aid would not provide them with an overall competitive advantage over an athlete not using such aid'. Athletes who could meet that requirement would have their results recognised in full. Those who could not meet it could still compete in international competitions, but their results would be listed separately, to reflect the different competition conditions.[78]

In July 2019, Mr Leeper applied to the IAAF pursuant to Technical Rule 6.3.4 for permission to race in its competitions on his Ottobock 1E90 Sprinter RSPs, at a height of 189.2 cm (6′ 2½″). He enclosed with his application a report prepared by Dr Elena Grabowski of the University of Colorado, who had been one of the team of experts that had supported Mr Pistorius's case back in 2008. Dr Grabowski and her colleagues Dr Paolo Taboga of California State University and Dr Owen Beck of the University of Texas reported that a series of treadmill and track tests that they had conducted with Blake Leeper in Boulder in August 2018 demonstrated that: (1) his RSPs prevented him from exerting maximal force from the starting blocks, compromising his acceleration and speed over the first 100m and costing him an estimated 1.41 seconds; (2) his RSPs were designed for straight movement, not curved movement, costing him an estimated 0.4 seconds when running around the curves of a 400m track; and (3) while he performed at an *'exceptional'* level in terms of maximum velocity, reaching 11.4 m/s on the treadmill, and in terms of running economy/aerobic capacity and sprint endurance (rate of fatigue), he did not perform those tasks any better than the very best non-amputee sprinters, and therefore there was no advantage that needed to be investigated to see if it was conferred by his RSPs.[79*] Dr Grabowski and her colleagues concluded that *'the differences between Blake Leeper and non-amputee athletes during the acceleration out of the starting blocks and curve-running indicate that if Leeper had biological legs and there were no interactions with other tasks that influence 400 m performance, he could theoretically run a 400m race 1.81 seconds faster compared to having artificial legs (running-specific prostheses). Thus, we have established on the balance of probabilities that the use of RSPs would not provide Leeper with an overall competitive advantage over non-amputee athletes not using such an aid'*.[80]

In February 2020, the IAAF denied Mr Leeper's application based on an expert group's advice that the Grabowski report did not establish that Mr Leeper got no overall competitive advantage from his RSPs.[81] Mr Leeper immediately appealed to the CAS for an order overturning that decision and allowing him to run in IAAF competitions, including at the 2020 Olympics. That appeal was heard in July 2020 by a CAS Panel made up of James Drake QC (now KC, chair), Klaus Reichart SC, and Murray Rosen QC (the '*Leeper 1* Panel'). Mr Leeper was represented in the CAS proceedings by Jeffrey Kessler of Winston & Strawn, the lawyer who had represented Oscar Pistorius in his CAS appeal back in 2008, while Chris Lavey and I represented the IAAF, with the invaluable assistance of our former Bird & Bird colleague Liz Riley, who by this point had joined the IPC as its General Counsel.

Mr Leeper's appeal raised the following issues for decision by the CAS:

- What did the IAAF's Technical Rule 6.3.4, properly interpreted, require to be shown? In particular, was the question whether the blades enabled Mr Leeper to run faster than the best non-amputee sprinters, as Mr Leeper contended, or whether they enabled him to run faster than he would have run if he had not been an amputee, as the IAAF contended?
- If Technical Rule 6.3.4 was interpreted as the IAAF contended, did it discriminate unlawfully against disabled people (in which case it would be void and unenforceable)?
- If Technical Rule 6.3.4 was valid and enforceable, could the IAAF rely on the IPC's MASH rule to show that Mr Leeper was running taller than his natural height, or (as Mr Leeper contended) was the MASH rule inapplicable outside of Paralympic sport, and unfair to apply in able-bodied sport, because Mr Leeper's able-bodied opponents were not subject to any height limit, and many of them had longer legs than him?
- If the IAAF could rely on the MASH rule to show that Mr Leeper was running taller than his natural height, did that extra height give him a performance advantage that was greater than the 1.81 second cumulative disadvantage (over 400m) that the Grabowski report had shown he suffered out of the blocks and around the curves?

What did Technical Rule 6.3.4, properly interpreted, require to be shown?

The IAAF's Technical Rule 6.3.4 prohibited *'the use of any mechanical aid, unless the athlete can establish on the balance of probabilities that the use of an aid would not provide them with an overall competitive advantage over an athlete not using such aid'*. Mr Leeper argued that what the rule therefore required was a comparison between: (1) the athlete who wishes to use a mechanical aid; and (2) the athletes that the athlete using the aid would be competing against, which in Mr Leeper's case would be the very best able-bodied sprinters in the world. He argued[82] that as long as his RSPs did not enable him to outperform those athletes, Technical Rule 6.3.4, properly interpreted, allowed him to use them.[83]

To be fair to Mr Leeper and his lawyers, Technical Rule 6.3.4, taken literally and considered in isolation, could possibly have been read that way. It was a good example of why, in my view, the wording of any proposed rules should be drafted, or at least reviewed, by the lawyers who are going to have to defend them in case of challenge and who will be familiar with the rules of interpretation that a tribunal will apply to determine their proper meaning. But if the rule was interpreted as

Mr Leeper's lawyers proposed, an athlete would be permitted to use a mechanical aid as long as it only made them as good as, not better than, the best athletes in the world.[84] Or, more precisely, *'their standard of not "better than ... the best non-amputee athlete" would warrant a "no advantage" conclusion for any amputee athlete who fails to set the World Record'.*[85] We noted that would be absurd, and completely contrary to the purpose of the rule, which was to ensure that the aid only *enabled* the user's performance, and did not artificially *enhance* it. Instead, we said, in order to give effect to the purpose of the rule, and to deliver the intended result, the required comparison was between the performance of the athlete using the mechanical aid, and the performance that athlete would be capable of achieving if they were not disabled and so did not have to use that aid.[86]

The *Leeper 1* Panel agreed with us. Noting that '*the interpretation of the Rule must be informed by the overarching object and purpose of the Rule, and by the need to ensure that the Rule is not interpreted in a way that gives rise to consequences which are absurd or unworkable*', the Panel decided that '*a rule which permits any athlete of any level of natural ability to use any performance-enhancing mechanical aid provided that their performance while using that aid does not exceed the performance of the very best athlete in the world ... would be illogical, arbitrary and absurd*'. Instead, the Panel ruled, '*the only logical, principled and workable construction of the Rule is one that ... requires a comparison to be undertaken between the athlete's likely athletic performance when using the mechanical aid and their likely athletic performance had they not had the disability which necessitates the use of that aid*'. Therefore Technical Rule 6.3.4, properly interpreted, required a comparison of '(a) Mr. Leeper's performance in the 400m event while using his RSPs to overcome his lack of fully intact biological legs; and (b) Mr. Leeper's likely performance in the 400m event had he been born with fully intact biological legs'.[87]

Did Technical Rule 6.3.4 discriminate unlawfully against disabled athletes?

Next, Mr Leeper argued that Technical Rule 6.3.4 discriminated unlawfully against disabled athletes, because it required them to establish that they did not derive an overall competitive advantage from their mechanical aids, whereas able-bodied athletes were not required to prove that they did not have any overall competitive advantage over their rivals, whether because of the length of their legs or otherwise, before they were allowed to compete.[88] He did not confine himself to arguing this was *indirect* discrimination, ie that the rule was intended to treat everyone equally, but had an unintended disproportionate effect on disabled people. Instead, he contended that it was *direct* discrimination, ie that the IAAF had adopted Technical Rule 6.3.4 specifically in order to keep disabled people out of its events.[89] It was not clear to us why Mr Leeper's lawyers took on this additional, unnecessary burden, as it would have been enough to prove unintentional discrimination. Perhaps it was just typical aggressive New York litigation tactics: when I worked there, I saw many breach of contract cases that were presented in the pleadings as fraud cases or even RICO (racketeering) violations.[90] Or perhaps the hope was that it would set the arbitrators against the IAAF and cause them to sympathise with and so find in favour of Mr Leeper.

In any event, the IAAF strongly rejected the suggestion that it was prejudiced against disabled athletes. It noted that its constitution sets out its commitment '*to preserve the right of every individual to participate in Athletics as a sport, without unlawful discrimination of any kind, undertaken in the spirit of friendship, solidarity and fair play*';[91] and that its Competition Rule 18.8 gives the event referee discretion to vary the rules as necessary to enable the participation of an athlete with a disability, where that can be done without giving the athlete an advantage over their competitors.[92] It also noted its proud history of including athletes with disabilities in its sport, going back to Harold Connolly, who won gold in the hammer throw for the USA at the 1956 Melbourne Olympics with an atrophied left arm and hand, and Sir Murray Halberg, who won a 5,000 m gold medal for New Zealand at the 1960 Rome Olympics with an atrophied left arm/shoulder girdle and an asymmetrical gait.[93] In 2020, when Mr Leeper's case came before the CAS, there were at least eighteen para athletes competing in events sanctioned by the IAAF or its members, including four double leg amputees, six single leg amputees, three single arm amputees, and three blind athletes.[94] We explained that the IAAF's only concern in such cases is to ensure, for the sake of all competitors, including the disabled athlete, '*that the outcome of IAAF-sanctioned competitions is determined by competitors' natural talent, training and effort, and not by the use of mechanical aids which confer an artificial competitive advantage over athletes who are not using such aids*'.[95] We argued that requiring the person seeking to use a mechanical aid to establish that the aid simply *enables* their performance, and does not artificially *enhance* it, is a necessary, rational, and proportionate way of achieving that objective.[96]

The *Leeper 1* Panel rejected Mr Leeper's suggestion that the IAAF was prejudiced against disabled athletes and had adopted Technical Rule 6.3.4 specifically in order to exclude them from the sport.[97] Instead, the Panel agreed with us that '*the aim of the Rule – and in particular the aspect of the Rule that places the burden on the athlete who wishes to use a mechanical aid to demonstrate the absence of a competitive advantage – is to ensure that where a disabled athlete requires a prosthetic aid in order to participate against able-bodied athletes in a particular event, the use of that aid does not enable the disabled athlete to achieve performances that are better than they would be able to achieve if they did not have the disability at all. […] The Panel considers this to be a legitimate objective for the IAAF to pursue*'.[98] However, the Panel noted that even though an SGB is afforded a margin of appreciation in deciding what regulations are required to protect the integrity of the sport, '*careful scrutiny is called for where … measures taken by a governing body are directed towards, and have a disparate impact on, individuals with disabilities or other particular protected characteristics*'.[99] It found that in practice Technical Rule 6.3.4 *did* have more of an impact on disabled athletes than on able-bodied athletes, because disabled athletes are more likely to have to use mechanical aids to compete. Therefore, the IAAF had to show that it was necessary, reasonable, and proportionate to the achievement of the underlying objective to put the burden on the disabled athlete to prove that they did not derive an artificial performance advantage from the mechanical aid.[100]

We felt we had strong observational evidence to justify requiring blade users to show their blades did not give them an artificial advantage. The CAS Panel in *Semenya* had held (see p 163) that the remarkable over-representation of 46 XY DSD athletes among elite female 800m runners strongly suggests that 46 XY DSD athletes have a performance advantage over biological females in that discipline.[101] The *Leeper 1* Panel agreed with us that that principle is not confined to 46 XY DSD cases, but rather applies generally, stating: '*the significant over-representation of athletes with a particular rare feature or characteristic among the cohort of top elite athletes is a compelling indication that such rare feature or characteristic potentially enhances athletic performance*'.[102] But by the same token, if a cohort with a particular characteristic is *not* over-represented in the elite athlete population, that is a good indication that that characteristic is *not* performance-enhancing.

- In its *Pistorius* decision, the CAS Panel specifically noted that its conclusion that Mr Pistorius's blades had not been shown to give him an overall competitive advantage was '*reinforced ... by the fact that the Cheetah Flex-Foot prosthesis has been in use for a decade, and yet no other runner using them – either a single amputee or a double amputee – has run times fast enough to compete effectively against able-bodied runners until Mr Pistorius has done so. In effect, these prior performances by other runners using the prosthesis act as a control for study of the benefits of the prosthesis and demonstrate that even if the prosthesis provided an advantage, and as noted none has been proven, it may be quite limited*'.[103]

- At the time (2008), that was fair comment. For example, Oscar Pistorius was the only double amputee who qualified for the men's 400m final at the 2008 Paralympic Games. All of the other finalists were single amputees, and the general perception was that double amputees were at a competitive disadvantage compared to single amputees. Mr Pistorius looked very much like an outlier, powered by truly exceptional natural talent and effort, not by his blades. In other words, it appeared that his blades merely enabled him to achieve his athletic potential, not to exceed it. After 2008, however, the landscape changed dramatically, possibly fuelled by the loosening of the MASH rule described at p 193. The total population of double amputee athletes is extremely small,[104] and only some of that very small pool will choose to compete in the sport of athletics, and in the 400 metres in particular, rather than in other sports or in other athletic disciplines. However, in the period from 2011 up to 2019 (when the competition schedule was disrupted by the Covid pandemic), 29 double amputees had appeared in the IPC/World Para-Athletics 400m rankings, and nine of them had run the 400m in under 50 seconds, the IAAF's benchmark for a world class athlete.[105] Seven of them had run under 47.4 seconds, a time that only 10 per cent of elite able-bodied athletes achieved; six of them had run times that would have placed them in the top 2 per cent or so of able-bodied 400m runners in the world; and two of them – Mr Pistorius and Mr Leeper – had run times that put them in the top 0.37 per cent of able-bodied 400m runners in the world. Mr Pistorius had a 400m personal best of 45.07 seconds; while Mr Leeper's 400m personal best (44.38 seconds) was only 1.35 seconds slower than the fastest time *ever* run by a non-amputee over 400 metres (Wayde van Niekerk's world record of 43.03 seconds). As the IAAF's expert witnesses noted, these results indicate that if a double amputee is sufficiently young, healthy, and motivated, and if they are able to afford state-of-the-art RSPs, they have '*a better than even chance of achieving times that will best nearly 98% of serious competitive 400m runners who do not have a disability*'.[106]

- We pointed out that there were two possible explanations for this significant over-representation of double amputees in the elite 400m rankings: either (1) world class 400m runners are disproportionately affected by double amputations; or (2) the amputees' blades are performance-enhancing.

The *Leeper 1* Panel was clear which of those explanations it preferred: '*The evidence presented by the IAAF does establish that there is a likelihood that RSPs enable some amputee athletes to run faster times in the 400m event than they would be able to achieve if they had intact biological legs. ... Since bilateral transtibial amputees make up a very small fraction of the overall population, the number of transtibial amputees who have run elite times (and top-level elite times) in the 400m event during this period is much higher than would be expected if those athletes' use of RSPs had no effect on their competitive performance. … Accordingly, the Panel considers that, as in Semenya, the significant over-representation of athletes with a particular rare feature or characteristic among the cohort of top elite athletes is compelling indication that such rare feature or characteristic potentially enhances athletic performance'.*[107]

However, the *Leeper 1* Panel was not persuaded that this justified putting the burden on amputee athletes to prove that their RSPs only enabled them to compete and did not enhance their performance. It noted that such proof would be burdensome and expensive to gather, and so was likely to be a significant barrier to entry.[108] It therefore ruled that the provision in Technical Rule 6.3.4 that put the burden on the amputee athlete should be deemed deleted, and instead '*the IAAF has the burden under the Rule of establishing that Mr Leeper (or any other disabled athlete who wishes to use prosthetic aids in order to run against able-bodied athletes) derives an overall competitive advantage from the use of the particular prosthetic aid*'.[109]

Discharging the burden of proof

As a result, the IAAF had to prove it was more likely than not (ie the odds were 51 per cent or greater) that Mr Leeper's RSPs enabled him to run faster than he would have run if he had not been an amputee. We sought to do so by proving two things: (1) that the height of Mr Leeper's RSPs meant that he was running on longer legs than he would have had if he had not been an amputee; and (2) that having those longer legs enabled him to run faster than he would have run if he had not been an amputee.

We were extremely fortunate to have some truly excellent expert witnesses to help us meet our burden on these two issues:

- Liz Riley introduced us to Sean Tweedy, Mark Connick, and Emma Beckman from the School of Human Movement and Nutrition Sciences at the University of Queensland, who had been involved in the development of the IPC's MASH rule that we were relying on to show that at 189.2 cm (6′ 2½″) Mr Leeper was running nearly six inches (15 cm) taller than his natural height. They agreed to explain the basis for the MASH rule to the CAS Panel, and to provide context and statistical analysis to explain the over-representation of double leg amputees at the top of para sport.
- When we went back to look at the *Pistorius* case, we discovered that the scientists who had testified on Mr Pistorius's behalf had published the data from the study they had conducted of Mr Pistorius,[110] but had disagreed among themselves on what that data showed, and had published their opposing views in a '*Point/ Counterpoint*' discussion in the Journal of Applied Physiology.[111] Peter Weyand and Matt Bundle noted that Mr Pistorius's swing time, ie the time it took him to reposition his limbs between strides, was nearly 10 per cent faster than the swing times of two of the fastest able-bodied sprinters in recorded history, most likely because his RSPs were lighter than biological legs. This meant that he could be in contact with the ground for longer than able-bodied sprinters, and therefore could achieve elite speeds even though he exerted less force while on the ground, only 1.2 times his body weight, compared to the 2.1 times body weight applied by the most elite sprinters. They calculated that if Mr Pistorius had had a normal swing time and therefore a normal ground contact time, the

lesser force he applied while on the ground meant that his top speed would reduce from 10.8 m/s to 8.3 m/s, and therefore his 400m time would increase by 12 seconds. They concluded that *'the moment in athletic history when engineered limbs outperform biological limbs has already passed'*. The other scientists from Mr Pistorius's team, including Roger Kram, Hugh Herr, and Elena Grabowski, strongly disagreed, arguing that the data did not permit any firm conclusions, and that the comments of Weyand and Bundle were *'absurd and insulting to Paralympic athletes'*.[112] In a further study published in 2010, Peter Weyand and Matt Bundle hypothesised that increasing the length of the RSPs, and so increasing contact length – the distance that the body travels forward while the foot is on the ground – *'could substantially increase the top running speed attained at the minimum period of foot-ground force application. For example, a relatively small increase in leg length of 10 cm would increase contact lengths by 9 cm and the top speeds of the subjects tested here from 9.1 to 9.8m/s'*.[113] This was obviously directly relevant to the second issue we had to address – did Mr Leeper's longer legs artificially increase his sprint speed? – and so we contacted Peter and Matt, who also agreed to provide their expertise to the CAS Panel.

Was Mr Leeper running tall?

To show that Mr Leeper was *'running tall'*, ie on longer legs than he would have had if he had not been an amputee, the IAAF relied on the IPC's MASH rule, which uses the Canda-1 equation described above to predict a transtibial double amputee's natural standing height based on the length of their thigh, upper arm, and forearm, and their sitting height. As already noted, based on Mr Leeper's measurements, his Maximum Allowable Standing Height was 174.4 cm (5' 9''), ie nearly 15 cm (6 inches) shorter than the height he wanted to run at (189.2 cm, or 6' 2½'').[114]

In response, Mr Leeper argued first that the IAAF could not rely on the MASH rule, because it was solely an IPC rule that *'has no application outside the context of regulating para-athletics'*.[115] The *Leeper 1* Panel disagreed, finding that the IAAF was entitled to take the MASH rule into account in applying Technical Rule 6.3.4, because it *'is grounded on similar considerations of fairness as underpin* [Technical Rule 6.3.4] *(viz. the need to ensure that disabled athletes do not use prosthetic aids that over-compensate for the absence of a missing limb)'*.[116] If the MASH rule provided *'an objective and reliable indication of Mr Leeper's likely maximum height if he had intact biological legs'*, that would help the Panel to determine whether Mr Leeper derived an overall competitive advantage from the use of his RSPs.[117]

Mr Leeper then argued that it was unfair to make him comply with the MASH rule when his able-bodied competitors were not subject to any height limit, and many of them had longer legs and/or were taller than him.[118] That argument was also rejected by the CAS Panel, which noted that *'this simply reflects the fact that the MASH rule assumes (on the basis of scientific evidence) that all able-bodied athletes have lower limbs that are proportionate to the length of the rest of their body, within a generous allowance. In other words, if the torsos and upper limbs of all able-bodied athletes were measured and those measurements were used to calculate those athletes' notional "MASH" heights using the established MASH formula, none of those able-bodied athletes would be taller, or significantly taller, than their notional "MASH" heights'*.[119]

The *Leeper 1* Panel concluded that: (1) '*the MASH rule provides an objective and reliable indication of Mr. Leeper's likely maximum height if he had intact biological legs. The MASH rule reflects the fact that among able-bodied individuals there is a general correlation between the length of an individual's lower limbs and the length of other parts of their body. That correlation is not exact, since there is a spectrum of bodily proportions across the general able-bodied population. Nevertheless, the correlation is sufficiently strong and established to enable scientists to calculate the maximum possible height a person could be based on the size/dimensions of certain parts of their body*';[120] and (2) by including an error factor in its calculation, the MASH rule ensures '*a generous margin of appreciation for the diverse shapes and sizes of the human body*'.[121] The Panel therefore accepted as reliable the MASH rule prediction that if Mr Leeper were not an amputee his height (including the error factor) would be 174.44 cm (5′ 9″), ie nearly 15 cm (6 inches) shorter than the height at which he was proposing to run.[122]

Did running nearly 15 cm (6 inches) taller artificially increase Mr Leeper's running speed?

On this final issue, the *Leeper 1* Panel noted that the respective experts agreed on the following points:

- The same basic physics apply to both able-bodied runners and amputee runners. Their physical performance and metabolism are governed by the same basic principles.
- In both cases, running speed is determined by a combination of contact length, contact time, step frequency, and ground reaction forces.
- Mr Leeper's RSPs do not give him any advantage in terms of running economy or aerobic capacity.
- Mr Leeper's RSPs compromise his ability to accelerate out of the blocks and therefore cause him to start the race slower than he would start if he had intact biological legs.[123]

Mr Leeper relied again on the report that Dr Grabowski and her colleagues had submitted to World Athletics in 2019, asserting – based on the results of their tests of Mr Leeper in Boulder in August 2018 – that his blades cost him 1.41 seconds out of the blocks and a further 0.4 seconds around the curves in the track, without identifying any offsetting performance advantages conferred by the blades.[124] He also submitted a supporting statement from Professor Hugh Herr of the Massachusetts Institute of Technology,[125] who endorsed their analysis and conclusions.[126]

In response, the IAAF noted that if Dr Grabowski and her colleagues were right that Mr Leeper's RSPs only *impaired* his performance, and did not confer any offsetting advantages, logically it followed that if Mr Leeper was not an amputee and so did not have to use RSPs, he would run the 100m race 1.41 seconds faster than his personal best of 10.91 seconds, ie in 9.5 seconds, breaking Usain Bolt's then world record by 0.08 seconds. And he would run the 400m 1.81 seconds faster than his personal best of 44.38 seconds, ie in 42.57 seconds, breaking Wayde van Niekerk's world record by 0.46 seconds. On that basis, Mr Leeper would be simultaneously both the fastest 100m runner *and* the fastest 400m runner who has ever lived, a feat that no one else in history, able-bodied or amputee, has ever achieved. Trusting to the power of understatement, we suggested that this seemed less plausible than the alternative explanation, which was that Mr Leeper's blades did not impair but in fact artificially enhanced his performance beyond what he would have been able to achieve had he not been an amputee.[127]

The *Leeper 1* Panel agreed with us. It accepted the contention of Dr Grabowski and her colleagues that Mr Leeper's blades conferred a disadvantage of up to 1.81 seconds in getting out of the blocks and in running around curves. But it noted that '*Dr. Grabowski's analysis fails to engage meaningfully with the question of how, notwithstanding the serious disadvantage that she concludes that Mr. Leeper experiences in respect of acceleration and curve running, he is nonetheless able to achieve overall 400m times that are quicker than 99.88% of all elite athletes. One theoretical possibility is that Mr. Leeper would be the fastest sprinter in the history of athletics if he had intact biological legs. Another possibility is that there are other features or consequences of Mr. Leeper's RSPs which enable him, partly or completely, to offset that disadvantage. Generally speaking, the more unusual a posited state of affairs or conclusion is, the less inherently likely it is to be the case. Without diminishing Mr. Leeper's significant natural talent and commitment to training, the Panel does not consider it to be more likely than not that Mr Leeper would be the fastest sprinter in history but for his disability. This conclusion makes Dr. Grabowski's analysis (which rests upon the proposition that Mr. Leeper would be the fastest sprinter in history if he had biological legs) difficult to accept*'. Instead, the Panel agreed with the IAAF that it was more likely that '*there are other features or consequences of Mr Leeper's RSPs which enable him, partly or completely, to offset that disadvantage*'.[128]

That was all well and good, but it was up to the IAAF to identify what that off-setting factor was. Fortunately, Professors Weyand and Bundle were crystal clear: it was the fact that Mr Leeper's blades made his legs nearly six inches longer than they would have been if he had not been an amputee.[129] They explained that because speed is equal to the distance travelled per unit of time, a runner's speed can be expressed as the distance their body travels forward while their foot is in contact with the ground ('*ground contact length*') divided by the duration of that contact. The ground contact length of an athlete is in turn determined mainly by leg length: the longer the athlete's legs, the further forward they move each time they make contact with the ground. Therefore, if a double-amputee runner's blades increase their leg length, that will increase their ground contact length, and so their sprinting speed.[130] The *Leeper 1* Panel accepted this explanation in full.[131]

Professors Weyand and Bundle presented observational evidence of this direct relationship between leg length and maximum running speed, noting that the best individual performers in Olympic sprint events '*exceed the sex-specific height norms of the larger population*', suggesting that '*being taller and having longer legs clearly is advantageous for sprint running*'. They noted that the magnitude of that advantage '*becomes larger as the duration of the sprint race increases*'.[132] They also noted that during the tests conducted by Dr Grabowski and her colleagues in Colorado in 2018, when Mr Leeper was running on RSPs that gave him a total height of 189.2 cm (6′ 2½″) and a leg length of 107 cm, his maximum speed was 11.4 m/s. They predicted that a 15 cm decrease in the length of Mr Leeper's RSPs, so that he ran at his MASH height of 5′ 9″, would reduce the distance by which his body moved forward on each contact with the ground by 15 cm and would reduce his maximum speed from 11.4 m/s to 9.8 m/s. In other words, a 14 per cent reduction in Mr. Leeper's leg length would result in a 14 per cent reduction in Mr. Leeper's top sprinting speed, meaning his 400 metres time would increase by eight seconds.[133]

Meanwhile the University of Queensland experts drew the Panel's attention to the performance data of the three double transtibial amputees who had reached the T44 400m final at the Rio 2016 Paralympic Games. They noted that the 400m times of those runners dropped by up to six seconds after they were forced to shorten their running blades by several inches to comply with the new (Canda-1) MASH rule.[134]

In response, Mr Leeper's experts – Dr Taboga, Dr Grabowski, and Dr Beck, ie the same three scientists who had conducted the tests on Mr Leeper in Colorado in 2018 – insisted that it was too simplistic to say that increased leg length equals increased ground contact length equals increased speed, because there are numerous other factors that also affect speed. They noted that no experiment had ever been reported that proves that an increase in leg length increases maximum speed. Instead, they asserted, the *only* published study on that issue, which they had authored and which had been reported in a peer-reviewed scientific journal (PLOS One), showed that in fact an increase in leg length does *not* increase maximum speed.[135]

That study,[136] referred to below as the '*Taboga 2020 study*', therefore assumed great importance at the hearing. It measured the top sprinting speeds achieved on a treadmill by five double transtibial amputee athletes when running on three different pairs of RSPs in turn, ie different models, different stiffness, and different heights. It reported that one participant had run 1.1 m/s slower on RSPs that were 10 cm longer, 1.8 m/s slower on RSPs that were 12 cm longer, and 2.8 m/s slower on RSPs that were 14 cm longer; while another participant had run 1.4 m/s slower using RSPs that were 2 cm longer and 1.25 m/s faster using RSPs that were 3 cm shorter. They suggested these results showed that there was no significant association between prosthetic height and maximum speed in double transtibial amputees, and therefore there was no need to limit the competition height of bilateral transtibial amputee athletes.

The IAAF's experts pointed out that:

- The Taboga 2020 study included only five subjects, which is too few to draw any statistically meaningful conclusions.
- Even ignoring that problem, the results of testing those five subjects did *not* support the hypothesis that prosthetic height has no effect on maximum speed. In brief, the study's statistical analysis showed a p-value of 0.76. A p-value tells you how surprising the results would be if prosthetic height had no real effect on speed. If the p-value is below 0.05, the results are considered unlikely to occur by chance alone. In the Taboga 2020 study, the p-value was 0.76, meaning the results were entirely consistent with random variation. Consequently, the results did not prove that prosthetic height has no impact on maximum speed, and did not provide any basis to reject the hypothesis that taller prosthetics allow athletes to achieve greater running speeds.[137]
- To provide reliable conclusions about the effect of RSP height on running speed, the study would have had to be designed to exclude the impact of potential confounding factors. For example, it takes a while for amputee

athletes to familiarise themselves with RSPs of a different height, model, and/or configuration. Indeed, that had been Mr Leeper's own justification for not shortening his RSPs when the IPC changed the MASH rule in January 2018. But in 14 out of the 15 configurations tested in the Taboga 2020 study, the subjects ran on RSPs with a different length and/or stiffness than they were used to, without being given adequate time to familiarise themselves with those differences. In addition, when testing maximum speeds of elite athletes, it is standard practice to allow at least two days of rest between each trial, to ensure proper recovery and avoid the result being affected by fatigue, but that had not been done in the Taboga 2020 study.

- These confounding factors undermined the reliability of the data generated and of the conclusions drawn by the study authors from that data. For example, if the confounding factor of unfamiliarity was removed (by looking only at the maximum speed achieved by each subject when using their usual RSPs at the usual stiffness), then of the three heights investigated (0, +2 cm and +4 cm), four out of five athletes achieved their maximum speeds when running at +2 cm or +4 cm. Therefore, to the extent that such limited data could show anything, it tended to support the hypothesis that increased RSP length permits higher maximum speed.[138]

The *Leeper 1* Panel agreed with each of these criticisms, and concluded that '*the Taboga 2020 Paper does not provide any reliable support for the proposition that increases in RSP height have no effect on running speed*'.[139]

This brought the Panel to its final decision: '*The Panel therefore concludes that, by virtue of the fact that he uses RSPs that enable him to run at a height that is several inches taller than his maximum possible height if he had intact biological legs, Mr. Leeper is able to run the 400m event in a time that is several seconds faster than the fastest time he would have been able to achieve with intact biological legs (even allowing for the disadvantage he experiences in the acceleration phase of the event and any potential disadvantage in respect of curve running)*'. As a result, the Panel ruled, the IAAF had established on the balance of probabilities that Mr Leeper's RSPs gave him a competitive advantage in the 400m event over an athlete not using RSPs. It therefore denied Mr Leeper's appeal against the IAAF's refusal to let him run in its competitions on those RSPs.[140]

In a press release reacting to the decision, Mr Leeper's lawyers said: '*The CAS panel's two rulings are incongruous with each other. On the one hand, the panel strikes down a World Athletics Rule which it finds to be discriminatory against the rights of disabled athletes to compete against the non-disabled. This was a just decision which we salute. On the other hand, the same panel issued a decision authorizing an even more insidious form of racial discrimination—against Black disabled athletes—by finding that their prosthetic limbs are subject to artificial height limitations based solely on the body proportions of Caucasian and Asian athletes. Data from Black athletes were not even considered in these studies, as if these athletes did not exist. It is ironic that Blake Leeper, who has been fighting for the rights of disabled athletes of every race, now finds himself the victim of discrimination against Black disabled athletes. We do not believe the courts will tolerate such discriminatory treatment and we will support Blake as he continues his fight to compete in the Olympics*'.[141]

This argument – that the MASH rule discriminates against black athletes because it is based on data from white and Asian athletes alone – had not been made in the *Leeper 1* proceedings. The IAAF, by now re-named World Athletics, responded robustly: *'World Athletics strongly rejects the (new) allegation from Mr Leeper's legal team that the finding that he "runs tall" is based on a "racist" Paralympic rule. The IPC rule on "Maximum Allowable Standing Height" (MASH) is based on the best available evidence of body dimensions and has been applied for several years to all Paralympic athletes (including African-American athletes) without issue. World Athletics is aware of no proof that African-American athletes have significantly different bodily dimensions (proportionality), and certainly not to the extent identified in this case. The 15 cm disparity found in Mr Leeper's case between his prosthetic leg length and his natural leg length is not due to racial differences in body dimensions'.*[142]

Leeper 2[143]

In December 2020 Mr Leeper applied again to the IAAF (by now re-named World Athletics), this time seeking permission to race in World Athletics competitions – including the Tokyo Olympics, which had been delayed to 2021 due to the Covid pandemic – on RSPs that were nearly 5 cm (2″) shorter than before, giving him a running height of 185.43 cm (6′ 1″). He said this was the lowest height he could run at without compromising his physical structure and so risking injury.[144]

Based on their prediction that a 1 cm change in leg length would cause a 0.1 m/s change in top speed, Professors Weyand and Bundle suggested that reducing the height of his RSPs by 5 cm would reduce Mr Leeper's maximum running speed by 0.5 m/s, ie from the 11.4 m/s top speed measured by Dr Grabowski et al in Colorado in 2018 down to 10.9 m/s, which would add 2.3 seconds to his 400 metres time. When Professor Weyand and his team tested Mr Leeper on his new RSPs at the Southern Methodist University's sprint lab in February/March 2021, the maximum speed he achieved was exactly what they had predicted (10.9 m/s). And when he ran in six para races in April and May 2021 at a height of 185.43 cm (6′ 1″), Mr Leeper's average time was 47.12, which was 2.3 seconds slower than his 2018/19 average, and his best time was 46.79, which was 2.41 seconds slower than his 2018/19 best.[145]

This indicated, Professors Weyand and Bundle said, that if Mr Leeper ran at his MASH height, ie 10 cm shorter still, his maximum running speed would reduce by a further 1 m/s, to 9.9 m/s, which would add 4.7 seconds to his 400m time. In other words, when running at 185 cm (6′ 1″), Mr Leeper was still getting an artificial performance advantage of 4.7 seconds over 400m, which was a lot more than the 1.81 seconds that his RSPs cost him out of the blocks and around the curves.

In April 2021 an expert panel convened by World Athletics turned down Mr Leeper's new application.[146] His lawyer, Jeffrey Kessler, issued the following statement: *'Unfortunately, this is what we have come to expect from World Athletics — a result-oriented and racist decision designed to prevent Mr. Leeper, as a disabled black athlete, from realizing his dream to compete in the Olympics based on his athletic merit. Blake will seek an expedited appeal before the Court of Arbitration for Sport, which will hopefully right this wrong in time for the U.S. Olympic Team trials'*; while Mr Leeper himself said: *'It's not right that World Athletics continues to discriminate against disabled Black athletes, and that the Panel they appointed has again sanctioned this discriminatory treatment. Basing this decision on standards and studies that completely excluded Black athletes goes against common sense and has no scientific basis, as my experts' submissions to World Athletics made clear. But despite this setback, I will appeal so I can continue to fight for athletes around the world who are discriminated against—whether on the basis of race, disability, or both—and look forward to making my case before the Court of Arbitration for Sport as I pursue my longtime dream of competing at the 2021 Tokyo Olympic Games'.*[147]

A new CAS Panel made up of three different arbitrators, Dr Georgios Petrochilos QC, Dr Ucheora Onwuamaegbu, and Dr Annabelle Bennett (the '*Leeper 2* Panel'), was convened to hear the appeal. Mr Leeper asked for the case to be expedited so that the decision would be handed down in time for him to be considered for selection for the US team at the Tokyo Olympics (assuming he won the appeal). That request was granted and the case was heard by video conference on 3, 4 and 8 June 2021. At the hearing, Mr Leeper's legal team argued that: (1) Technical Rule 6.3.4, properly interpreted, requires a comparison between Mr Leeper using the RSPs and other elite athletes not using such an aid, not between him with RSPs and him if he had intact biological legs, because no one can know how fast he would run if his legs were intact; (2) the MASH rule does not reliably estimate the height of black athletes; (3) his blades cost him 1.41 seconds out of the blocks and 0.4 seconds more when running around the curves; (4) he gains no off-setting performance advantage from his RSPs, and in particular no increase in top running speed, because there is no relationship between leg length and maximum running speed (citing the Taboga 2020 paper as the evidence for that); and (5) the results of the testing of Mr Leeper at the SMU sprint lab in February and March 2021 should be disregarded because *'the Dallas tests were conducted by self-interested experts and were ridden* [sic] *with "serious accuracy issues"'.*[148]

Arguments (1), (3) and (4) had been advanced in *Leeper 1*, and therefore we relied on the same evidence and arguments that had won the day there to refute those arguments again in these new proceedings. However, the argument that the MASH rule could not reliably predict Mr Leeper's natural height was new, and relied on the fact that the Canda-1 equation on which it is based was derived solely from the body proportions of Caucasians and Asians, and had not been validated for use on athletes of African descent. Mr Leeper's lawyers noted that a 1964 study by Dr James Tanner had established that people of African descent have shorter torsos and longer legs than Caucasians and Asians,[149] and asserted that this was confirmed by the case of another black athlete, Marko Cheseto, whose legs had been amputated after a frost-bite accident. They said Mr Cheseto's height pre-amputation had been 185.42 cm (6′ 1″), but his MASH-predicted height was only 175.26 cm (5′ 9″), ie the same as Mr Leeper. They argued this showed the MASH rule did not reliably predict the height of black athletes, and that Mr Leeper should be permitted to run on blades that gave him a height of 6′ 1″.

To rebut these arguments, we called the same experts as we had called in *Leeper 1*, who explained as follows:[150]

- It was true that the Canda equations used in the MASH rule were originally derived exclusively from measurements of Caucasian men and women in Spain. But the UQ experts and some colleagues had conducted a study in 2016 to determine whether those equations also accurately predicted standing height in other populations.[151]

- The American Association for Physical Anthropologists[152] accepts that natural biological variations between individual human beings, including differences in body dimensions, are caused by genetic variations, which in turn are driven *not* by race[153] but by geographical distance. In short, the greater the geographical distance between two populations, the less the gene flow between them, and therefore the greater the genetic variation between them.[154] The 2016 study had therefore sought to validate the Canda regression equations by measuring the body dimensions of populations in two locations that were geographically distant from Spain, namely Japan and Australia. The data collected showed that the Canda-1 equation provided accurate estimations of standing height across both Japanese and Australian subjects, even though Japanese males on average have significantly shorter thighs (average 41.5 cm) than Australian males (average 45.5 cm), and are also significantly shorter than Australian males (average 168.1 cm, compared to average 179.5 cm). The study concluded that the Canda-1 equation could be used to predict height accurately across different populations with different average body proportions.[155]

- The fact that the Canda-1 equation had been shown to work in two further distinct populations with a wide range of body proportions was strong evidence that it would also work for other populations with different body proportions, including people of African descent. The UQ experts noted that the Tanner study cited by Mr Leeper showed that the amount of variation in body dimensions between different human populations is very small. Dr Tanner had recorded an average difference between the white and black athletes he studied of 1 cm in sitting height and 3.2 cm in leg length, with a leg length to sitting height ratio of 0.90 in white athletes and 0.94 in black athletes. By contrast, the leg length to sitting height ratio for Asian subjects was much smaller, and yet the MASH rule also accurately predicted the stature of Asian subjects.[156] The UQ experts explained that the MASH rule is able to cope with these small variations because the Canda-1 equation predicts the height of a double transtibial amputee based on sitting height (where measurements of Caucasian subjects are longer on average), femur length, forearm length, and upper arm length (where measurements of black subjects are longer on average). Any differences in these measurements between different races offset one another, and the 1.91 cm pure error factor incorporated into the MASH rule addresses any remaining differences. As a result, the UQ experts explained, the MASH rule over-estimates height in the vast majority of cases (82 per cent), and under-estimates height in only a small minority of cases (18 per cent), and then only to a very small degree (on average, 1.2 cm).[157]

- The UQ experts noted that the IPC had applied the Canda-1 equation to black double amputees since January 2018 without any indication of systemic bias. They noted that Mr Chesoto's reported height pre-amputation was actually 6'0" (182.88 cm) and that based on his body dimensions, the Canda-1 equation predicted Mr Chesoto's natural height at 182.14 cm (5' 11.75"), ie it under-estimated Mr Chesoto's height by only 0.74 cm.[158]

- Meanwhile Professors Weyand and Bundle took the body measurements of the twelve elite black athletes photographed in the Tanner study, put those measurements into the Canda-1 equation, and found that it predicted the height of those athletes with the same accuracy as it predicted the height of the Caucasian and Asian athletes. Specifically, the Canda-1 equation over-estimated the height of ten out of the twelve black athletes, and under-estimated the height of the other two, but only by 0.2 cm and 1 cm respectively.[159]

The experts therefore maintained that it was appropriate for World Athletics to follow the IPC and World Para-Athletics in using the MASH formula to predict the natural height of double amputee athletes who are black, and to conclude, based on Mr Leeper's measurements, that Mr Leeper's natural height, ie the height he would be if he were not an amputee, is 174 cm (5′ 9″).[160]

As to issue (5), Professor Weyand reported on the results of the testing he had conducted with Mr Leeper at the SMU sprint lab in February/March 2021. He explained in detail why he emphatically rejected the opposing experts' challenge to the reliability of those results.[161]

In July 2021, the CAS announced that the *Leeper 2* Panel had rejected Mr Leeper's appeal, with the reasoned award to follow.[162] Winston & Strawn immediately issued a press release criticising that decision on the ground that *'[t]he MASH formula is based upon studies that did not include a single person of African heritage, like Mr. Leeper. In response to that absence of data, World Athletics relied in the proceeding on photos taken more than sixty years ago of athletes from the 1960 Rome Olympics, in which two of the twelve Black able-bodied athletes whose photos were taken would have required amputations to run at a shorter height to compete if MASH had applied to them'*. The release quoted both Mr Leeper (*'It is tragic and wrong that World Athletics will be permitted to continue its discrimination against me and other Black disabled athletes. I will continue my dedication to being the best athlete I can and will also continue to do all I can to fight for the rights of disabled and Black persons, regardless of this decision'*) and Mr Kessler (*'We are all so terribly disappointed by these rulings, which perpetuate the injustice against Mr. Leeper. Science and history will eventually prove that Mr. Leeper should be permitted an equal chance to compete against all. The fight for equality will continue. For now, the world will be deprived of seeing Mr. Leeper compete against the best able- bodied athletes and the glory of sports will be dimmed as a result'*).[163]

The *Leeper 2* Panel's reasoning was set out in its full award dated 4 November 2021:

- Like the *Leeper 1* Panel, the *Leeper 2 Panel* was clear that Technical Rule 6.3.4, properly interpreted, requires a comparison of the athlete's performance when using blades against the athlete's performance if their legs had been intact, not against the performances of other elite athletes. It explained: *'One must be careful not to construe Rule 6.3.4 as permitting aids which compensate for an athlete's anatomic features to the point of equiparating an athlete's competitive potential with the top athlete in the relevant discipline. Rule 6.3.4 cannot have the effect of allowing for an "arms race" to alter natural limitations in athletics. … If the Panel were to accept Mr Leeper's view, then Rule 6.3.4 would allow athletes, both disabled and able-bodied, to use mechanical aids that alter their anatomy to emulate their competitors' innate anatomical features and thus compensate for limitations resulting from their own anatomical features. The Panel is unable to accept a reading of Rule 6.3.4 that would lead to such an outcome'*.[164]
- The *Leeper 2* Panel noted that Mr Leeper's experts had identified only the performance disadvantages conferred by his blades out of the starting blocks and around the curves, and had not identified any advantages, but instead had effectively assumed that he would be the fastest sprinter in history but for his disability. The Panel agreed with the *Leeper 1* Panel that this seemed less likely than the alternative possibility, which was that his blades gave him a net performance advantage: *'According to Prof Grabowski, Prof Taboga, and Dr Beck,*

Mr Leeper obtains no advantage on his RSPs; he only suffers disadvantages. The Panel finds it difficult to reconcile this view with Mr Leeper's overall performance. The evidence before the Panel shows that Mr Leeper is able to achieve times quicker than 99.88% of the elite non-amputee 400m runners. The Panel agrees with the Leeper 1 panel that a range of factors may explain how Mr Leeper was able to achieve such times. It is possible that they are the result of natural talent, training, and sheer determination, meaning that Mr Leeper would be the fastest 400m sprinter if he had biologically intact legs. However, it is more likely that Mr Leeper was able to achieve these times because his RSPs confer on him a net performance advantage, which more than counterbalances any disadvantage in respect of initial acceleration and curve running'.[165]

- The *Leeper 2* Panel then addressed World Athletics' submission that there is a direct relationship between leg length and maximum speed. It declined to compare the results of the Dallas testing of Mr Leeper in 2021 to the results of the Colorado testing of Mr Leeper in 2018. It emphasised that it did *'not intend to cast any doubt on the validity of the Boulder and Dallas tests taken individually. Scientists design their tests differently, based on their own training and experience. But, given the differences between the two tests, the Panel is unable to draw safe conclusions by comparing those two tests'.*[166] However, it agreed with World Athletics that the Taboga 2020 paper did *not* show that increased RSP height had no effect on maximum speed, for the reasons given by the *Leeper 1* Panel.[167] Having weighed all of the other evidence, the *Leeper 2 Panel* joined the *Leeper 1* Panel in accepting *'the scientific evidence offered by WA's experts to the effect that a direct relationship exists between leg length and running speed. It accepts that a significant component of a runner's potential top speed is their contact length, which is determined by their leg length. The Panel also acknowledges that this direct relationship is reflected in the observational evidence put forward by WA's experts'.*[168]

- Finally, the *Leeper 2* Panel rejected Mr Leeper's argument that the MASH rule did not reliably predict what his height would have been if he had not been an amputee. It acknowledged that the Canda-1 equation had been validated against Australian and Japanese subjects rather than black subjects, and agreed that ideally it should be specifically validated against black subjects as well. But it noted that Mr Leeper did not dispute that geographic distance, not race, is the main driver of genetic variability in the body proportions of different populations. It also noted that the evidence in the record (the Tanner data, and the case of Mr Chesoto) tended to confirm the accuracy of the Canda-1 equation's predictions of the lower-leg length of black athletes. And it therefore accepted that the MASH prediction of Mr Leeper's natural height (175.26 cm/5′ 9″) was reliable, and so the height at which Mr Leeper's RSPs were set (185.43 cm/6′ 1″) meant that he was running 10 cm taller than his natural height, giving him a material performance advantage that clearly outweighed any disadvantage he might have out of the blocks and around the curves.[169]

Postscript (1): Blake Leeper's results when running at 5′ 9″

As noted above, Professors Weyand and Bundle predicted that if Mr Leeper ran at his MASH height of 174 cm (5′ 9″), his 400m time would be 6.8 seconds slower than the best time he had achieved when running 15 cm higher (44.38 seconds).

Mr Leeper did reduce the height of his prostheses down to 174 cm (5′ 9″) prior to the 2022 racing season, and in two races that season his best 400m time was 50.56 seconds, ie nearly 6.2 seconds slower than the personal best he had achieved on RSPs that were 15 centimetres longer (44.38 seconds).[170] Mr Leeper did get faster – he finished fourth in the 400m T62 final at the 2024 Paralympics, in a time of 47.32 seconds – but he never approached the times he had achieved when running on RSPs that were 15 centimetres longer.

Postscript (2): Retraction of the Taboga 2020 Paper

I am told that the retraction of a published scientific paper is very rare. However, in December 2022 the PLOS One editors announced that, following the receipt of objections to the Taboga 2020 Paper, they had had the paper re-evaluated by an academic editor and an expert in statistical analysis, who had decided that the conclusion that prosthetic height has no effect on maximum speed was not supported by the data reported and that the authors had misinterpreted statistical non-significance.[171] In fact, the reviewers said, the results reported in the paper *'provide evidence that prosthesis stiffness and height both impact running speed substantially, contrary to the claims in the article's title and conclusions'*. The PLOS One editors noted that the authors' response to these criticisms *'did not resolve the concerns about the data analyses or the validity of the article's results statements and conclusions. Therefore, the PLOS ONE Editors retract this article'*.[172]

Post-script (3): Validation of the MASH rule for application to black athletes

Perhaps most importantly, World Athletics did as the *Leeper 2* Panel had suggested and commissioned an independent study to determine whether the MASH rule reliably predicts the standing height of people of African descent. Scientists from the MIT Lincoln Laboratory fed the relevant dimensions – sitting height, thigh length, upper arm length, forearm length, and arm span – of 302 black American males and 1597 white American males into the equations used in the MASH rule, including the Canda-1 equation that had been used to estimate Mr Leeper's standing height, and then compared the height predicted by those equations to the intact subjects' actual height. The Canda-1 equation was found to under-estimate the height of both black and white subjects, but the mean under-estimate was only 0.54 cm. In addition, those results did not take into account the *'pure error'* factor that the MASH rule adds to the height predicted by the Canda-1 equation. The study was published in 2024. Its authors noted: *'Adding these values to our stature estimates yields overestimated mean statures in most cases …'*.[173] In other words, the predicted MASH height for Mr Leeper of 5′ 9″ (the measurement derived from the Canda-1 equation *plus* the 1.91 cm error factor) is most likely an *over*-estimate of Mr Leeper's *'natural'* height.

Notes

1 Rowbottom M., *Oscar Pistorius: The Fastest Man on No Legs*, Brand South Africa, 19 April 2007.

2 Chitra Ragavan podcast, *'When it mattered'*, Episode 25, 23 December 2019. See also *Abled: The Blake Leeper Story* (July 2023), abledfilm.com.

3 *New film tells the inspiring life story of double-amputee runner*, abcnews.go.com, 29 June 2023.

4 *Leeper v IAAF*, CAS 2020/A/6807 (the '*Leeper 1 award*'), para 131.

5 *Leeper v IAAF*, CAS 2020/A/6807, para 135.

6 The winning margin (the difference in performance by which a competitor misses a gold medal, any medal, or making the final) in elite athletic or swimming events at the 2008, 2012 and 2016 Olympics was less than 1 per cent. Handelsman DJ, Hirschberg AL, Bermon S., *Circulating Testosterone as the Hormonal Basis of Sex Differences in Athletic Performance*, Endocr Rev. 2018 Oct 1;39(5):803-829.

7 Burns GT & Tam N., *Is it the shoes? A proposal to regulate footwear in road running*, British Journal of Sports Medicine 2020;54:439-440.

8 *Factbox: Nike's Vaporfly running shoes and tumbling records*, reuters.com, 24 January 2020. See also Bermon S. et al, *Effect of Advanced Shoe Technology on the Evolution of Road Race Times in Male and Female Elite Runners*, Front Sports Act Living, 2021 Apr 22;3:653173.

9 The cricket authorities acted after the tragic death of Philip Hughes in 2014 from a brain haemorrhage, two days after he was struck on the neck by a bouncer in a domestic match in Australia. For example, the England & Wales Cricket Board has promulgated Head Protector Regulations that require all batters, wicket-keepers and close fielders to wear head protectors/helmets that *'have been certified as compliant with the most recent BSI Standard specification for the size of ball that is being used in that Match'* (clauses 1.2 and 3).

10 *World Rugby integrates smart mouthguard technology to the Head Injury Assessment as part of new phase of global player welfare measures*, worldrugby.org, 9 October 2023 (*'World Rugby will advance the Head Injury Assessment (HIA) by introducing in-game alerts from smart mouthguard technology to show if a player has experienced a high level of acceleration which could lead to an injury. … The smart mouthguards will work in real time to send alerts of high forces to the independent matchday doctor. This will, for the first time, enable players who have experienced a high acceleration event, but not shown symptoms or been seen by broadcast cameras, to be taken off and assessed. Elite rugby players will be required to wear smart mouthguards to be able to use the in game HIA1 test. The mouthguards will be required in training as well as matches, enabling coaches to better tailor drills, tackle skills and training load for each individual player, and best support their performance and welfare. The innovation is part of a wider package of changes recommended to World Rugby by its independent Concussion Working Group …'*). See Hayden, *Smart mouthguard data to be used to prevent players from getting high number of head impacts*, The Observer, 7 September 2025; Alderman, *Mouthguards that flash red after heavy impacts to be used at World Cup*, 11 August 2025.

11 *Sports Evolving Through the Hawk-Eye Technology*, opspl.com, 24 June 2020.

12 Broadbent R., *Lord Coe: Enhanced Games is bollocks – we'll ban morons taking part*, The Times, 29 February 2024. See Muniz-Pardos B. et al, *Technological advances in elite sport: Where does one draw the line?*, J Appl Physiol 2024 137:3, 646-648 (worrying that the change made *'would mean that every jump would count, which would discard the traditional skill of performing an optimal run phase prior to the jump'*). However in December 2025 World Athletics' CEO Jon Ridgeon announced that it was dropping the idea in the face of resistance from athletes, stating: *'You ultimately do not want to go to war with your most important group of people'*: Carro J., *World Athletics rules out takeoff zone*, insidethegames.biz, 7 December 2025.

13 *Why are Metal Bats Banned in MLB?*, EssentiallySports.com, 31 January 2022.

14 UCI Technical Regulations (26.01.23 version), uci.org, Article 1.3.019.

15 Murray T., *Ethics and Endurance-Enhancing Technologies in Sport*, in *Performance-Enhancing Technologies in Sport* (Murray, Maschke, Wasunna, eds, John Hopkins University Press 2009), p.151.

16 Fouché R., *Game Changer: The Technoscientific Revolution in Sports* (John Hopkins University Press, 2017), pp.16-17 (*'Comparing track and field athletes such as Jesse Owens, Carl Lewis, and Usain Bolt necessitates a belief that each athlete ran under roughly the same conditions. … [But] Owens did not have access to the Puma evoSpeed Electric Bolt Tricks track spikes that Bolt wore at the 2016 Olympics or the benefit of competing on the speedy Mondotrack WS synthetic track on which Bolt won his third consecutive round of gold medals in the 100 m, 200 m, and 4 × 100 m races'*).

17 *New UCI rules bring life back to cycling's hour record*, cyclingnews.com, 16 May 2014. In fact, if the changes are particularly revolutionary, *'[e]ventually it might be doubtful whether competitors were even playing the same sport'*. Simon RL, *The Ethics of Sport: What Everyone Needs to Know* (OUP 2016), p.114; Murray T., *Ethics and Endurance-Enhancing Technologies in Sport*, in *Performance-Enhancing Technologies in Sport* (Murray, Maschke, Wasunna, eds, John Hopkins University Press, 1990), p.144 (*'Yes, there could be a marathon on rollerblades and a high jump on trampolines. But they would be different events – not the marathon as foot race; not the high jump as unaided leap and acrobatic transit over the bar'*).

18 Loland S., *Fairness in Sport*, Chapter 8 in *Performance-Enhancing Technologies in Sport: Ethical, Conceptual and Scientific Issues* (Murray, Maschke, and Wasunna, eds., John Hopkins University Press 2009), p.168 (*'[E]quipment and technology should be identical for all competitors, or at least standardized as far as possible, and all competitors should be given equal access. Standardization procedures are found in sailing and in the throwing events in athletics, but they are more or less absent in other sports, such as skiing. There seems to be no acceptable justification for these inconsistencies. In tight skiing competitions, the quality and preparation of skis has a significant effect on the outcome. These inequalities are the responsibilities of ski manufacturers and support systems, not of athletes, and they should be eliminated or at least compensated for by standardization routine'*).

19 *World Athletics modifies rules governing competition shoes for elite athletes*, worldathletics.org, 31 January 2020.

20 *Why are Metal Bats Banned in MLB?*, EssentiallySports.com, 31 January 2022 (*'The introduction of aluminum bats to NCAA teams in the 1970s drastically affected batting averages and home runs. With batting averages rising about 20 points and home runs doubling almost overnight, it was evident that such technology enhanced performances. In light of this, many believed that if aluminum or other metals were allowed in the game, it would lead to records being shattered and the game losing its integrity as a stern test of player talent. There are advantages to using metal bats; however, stringent regulations have been implemented to ensure a fair experience for both teams involved'*).

21 *More spin but 'dreadfully dull' – backlash against Kookaburra experiment*, The Times, 23 April 2024.

22 Burnham P., Wilkinson M. and Goodall S., *The 2010 regulations on golf groove design: impact on ball flight characteristics during a controlled shot*, (2013) International Journal of Golf Science, 2(1), pp. 54-64; Boyd, *The Engines of Our Ingenuity* podcast, Episode 2596, Houston Public Media. The increased back spin was because the sharper angles created by the V-shaped rather than U-shaped grooves meant that on contact the ball did not slide but rather *rolled* up the club face.

23 USGA, *Notice to Manufacturers – New Groove Regulations*, 27 February 2007; and *USGA and R&A Rules Ltd Groove Measurement Procedure Outline*, August 2008.

24 R&A and USGA, *Notice of Decision Update to the Conformance Testing of Golf Balls to the Overall Distance Standard*, 6 December 2023. As justification for their decision, they explained: *'Protecting the integrity of golf courses, including their overall length, and ensuring that a variety of skills are needed to play them, preserves the fundamental elements of the sport. Both of these aspects have been impacted by increases in hitting distance and will continue to be impacted if nothing is done to address these trends now. In addition, our sport must be cognisant of the environmental impacts and what this means for golf courses, their operators and ultimately golfers and the communities around them. Longer golf courses require additional resources, including water and nutrients, all of which come with an environmental and economic cost'* (see R&A and USGA Update Note, 6 December 2023).

25 See eg the IPC's Policy on Sports Equipment, paralympic.org, 2 April 2011, at section 3.1.4 (*'human performance is the critical endeavour, not the impact of technology and equipment'*) and section 3.2 (*'Equipment that results in sport performance not primarily being generated by the athlete's own physical prowess but being generated by automated, computer aided, or robotic devices is prohibited*), critiqued in Zwierzchowski J., *People with disabilities in sport – legal aspect of unethical performance enhancement in Paralympics*, Baltic Journal of Health and Physical Activity, Vol 13 Issue 7 2021 Supplement 2 Article 13 2021. See also UCI General Regulations (01.10.23 version), uci.org, Chapter III (Equipment), Section 2 (*'Bicycles shall comply with the spirit and principle of cycling as a sport. The spirit presupposes that cyclists will compete in competitions on an equal footing. The principle asserts the primacy of man over machine'*); Clarification Guide of the UCI Technical Regulations (26.01.23 version), uci.org, p.1 (*'The UCI Regulations assert the primacy of man over machine. Observance of the regulations by all parties involved facilitates sporting fairness and safety during competition'*).

26 See Murray T., *Sports Enhancement*, in *The Ethics of Sport* (Caplan & Parent, eds., OUP 2017), at p.464 (*'Modern baseball gloves – supple, long-fingered, webbed – allow fielders to snatch line drives and scoop up hard grounders with relative ease. They improve performance, no*

doubt. But infielders still have to get to the ball, catch it, and throw accurately to base. They need quickness, agility, strength, and extraordinarily swift reaction times, qualities that great infielders have always possessed. This is one technology that has enriched rather than detracted from sport').

27 See Murray T., *Ethics and Endurance-Enhancing Technologies in Sport*, in *Performance-Enhancing Technologies in Sport* (Murray, Maschke, Wasunna, eds, John Hopkins University Press, 1990), p.157 (*'We understand sport, we grasp its meaning, when we see that sport aims to highlight the relationship between talents, what athletes do to perfect those talents, and athletic success. From this understanding comes a standard for judging the ethical acceptability of any particular form of endurance enhancement. Do the endurance-enhancing technology undermine the meaning of the sport? Does it do so by corrupting what we regard as natural talents …? Does it overwhelm the impact of virtuous activities …? … Endurance-enhancing technologies, like other performance-enhancing technologies, should be prohibited when they undermine the meaning of sport by interfering significantly with the relationship between natural talents, their virtuous perfection, and athletic success'*). See also Simon RL, *The Ethics of Sport: What Everyone Needs to Know* (OUP 2016), p.116 (*'there is a principled framework for discussing whether technological innovations, or adjustments for disabilities, are permissible at various levels of competition. That is, those charged with making the decision … need at least a rough theory of the sport at issue and the skills fundamental to it. A major consideration in their decision about the technology, then, will be the extent to which it undermines or reduces the fundamental skills of the game, … and whether, if it does, it reduces them to an unacceptable extent'*).

28 Fouché R., *Game Changer: The Technoscientific Revolution in Sports* (John Hopkins University Press, 2017), p.5 (*'From elite-level soccer blocking out any form of goal-line technology until the 2014 World Cup … to automobile racing's endless tweaking of regulatory formulas to blur engineering potency as a means to reclaim driver skill and ability, sports fans, competitors, governing bodies, and equipment manufacturers are now living in an era where tough decisions will have to be made in order to determine if sport, in the future, will be more about the [human] motor, the machine, or some transient equilibrium between these two poles'*).

29 For example, the 2025 F1 Technical Regulations are 178 pages long, and they are supplemented by the 2026 F1 Power Unit Technical Regulations, which are another 88 pages long.

30 Article 9.2.2 of the 2025 F1 Technical Regulations states: *'No car may be equipped with a system or device which is capable of preventing the driven wheels from spinning under power or of compensating for excessive torque demand by the driver. Any device or system which notifies the driver of the onset of wheel spin is not permitted'*.

31 *The Slippery History of Traction Control in F1*, racingnews365.com, 17 February 2021 (*'While traction control provided some immense stability benefits to drivers, it also took some of the natural hazard away from the sport. Without the looming threat of wheel spin, and the associated loss of time, drivers were free to hammer down 900hp+ with little fear of sending themselves for a trip to the gravel. Without it, we have much more unpredictable racing and a better spectacle for fans'*).

32 *Swimsuit controversy*, sportsscientists.com, 25 November 2008.

33 *The Technology Behind Speedo's High-Tech Swimsuits That Challenged the Olympics*, engineering.com, 2 December 2020. See also Fouché R., *Game Changer: The Technoscientific Revolution in Sports* (John Hopkins University Press, 2017), p.32 (*'the black techno-scientifically engineered materials became de rigeur for any swimmer wanting to compete for victory … The power of fast suit technoscience completely subsumed narratives of athletic ability'*).

34 *Swimming bans high-tech suits, ending an era*, nytimes.com, 24 July 2009 (quoting US coach Dave Salo: *'the whole suit situation has devalued athleticism. A lot of kids who aren't in very good shape can put on one of these suits and be streamlined like seals'*).

35 Gao, Z., Li, Y. and Wang, Z., *Restoring the real world records in Men's swimming without high-tech swimsuits*, Journal of Quantitative Analysis in Sports, Vol. 16, No. 4, 2020, pp. 291-300; Men's Freestyle World Records, worldaquatics.com (visited 10 May 2024).

36 Quoted in *Gunter Harz Sports Inc v United States Tennis Association*, 511 F. Supp. 1103 (D. Neb. 1981).

37 Miller S., *The Changing Grass at Wimbledon*, New York Times, 25 June 2022.

38 Athletics coach Matt Yates, quoted in *World Athletics gives seal of approval for controversial Nike Vaporfly shoes*, theguardian.com, 31 January 2020.

39 Muniz-Pardos B. et al, *Technological advances in elite sport: Where does one draw the line?*, J Appl Physiol 2024 137:3, 646-648.

40 *World Athletics modifies rules governing competition shoes for elite athletes*, worldathletics.org, 31 January 2020.

41 *Super shoe world records*, engineeringsport.co.uk, 1 December 2023.

42 *Gunter Harz Sports Inc v United States Tennis Association*, 511 F. Supp. 1103 (D. Neb. 1981) at pages 1115, 1117, 1120, and 1121, affirmed in *Gunter Harz Sports Inc v United States Tennis Association*, 665 F.2d 222 (8th Cir. 1981).

43 See eg *Sheikh Hazza Bin Sultan Bin Zayed Al Nahyan v FEI*, CAS 2014/A/3591, para 149 (*'[...] the FEI as a sporting association is afforded a wide margin of appreciation in making rules to regulate the conduct of its members. While this principle does not prevent a judicial or arbitral tribunal charged with examining the rules to determine whether they constitute an infringement of fundamental rights, it serves to emphasise that a sporting association will generally be in the best position to assess the rules which are required to address issues arising in the sport which it runs'*); *Dominguez v FIA*, CAS 2016/A/4772, para 101 (*'It is allowed to provide a discretion to the association and courts should not lightly exercise their power of review over the association's decisions made in the exercise of such discretion, especially in cases in which sports governing bodies have special expertise and experience in relation to their sport'*).

44 The *'margin of appreciation'* discussed in the CAS jurisprudence (see footnote 43) is the equivalent of the English law principle that the courts will not conduct a merits review of the decisions of a public body (determining whether the decision is reasonable) but only a rationality review (determining whether the decision is one that a rational person could make). Even if that principle has now been refined in cases of judicial review of government action (see eg speech of Lord Carnwath, *From Rationality to Proportionality in the Modern Law*, supremecourt.uk, 14 April 2014), it is still a central part of the grounds that the English courts have identified for challenging the decisions of sports governing bodies. See eg *Bradley v Jockey Club* [2004] EWHC 216, Richards J., para 43 (*'The test of proportionality requires the striking of a balance between competing considerations. The application of the test in the context of penalty will not necessarily produce just one right answer: there is no single "correct" decision. Different decision-makers may come up with different answers, all of them reached in an entirely proper application of the test. In the context of the European Convention on Human Rights it is recognised that, in determining whether an interference with fundamental rights is justified and, in particular, whether it is proportionate, the decision-maker has a discretionary area of judgment or margin of discretion. The decision is unlawful only if it falls outside the limits of that discretionary area of judgment. Another way of expressing it is that the decision is unlawful only if it falls outside the range of reasonable responses to the question of where a fair balance lies between the conflicting interests. The same essential approach must apply in a non-ECHR context such as the present. It is for the primary decision-maker to strike the balance in determining whether the penalty is proportionate. The court's role, in the exercise of its supervisory jurisdiction, is to determine whether the decision reached falls within the limits of the decision-maker's discretionary area of judgment. If it does, the penalty is lawful; if it does not, the penalty is unlawful. It is not the role of the court to stand in the shoes of the primary decision-maker, strike the balance for itself and determine on that basis what it considers the right penalty to be'*), affirmed on appeal, [2005] EWCA Civ 1056; *Chambers v British Olympic Association* [2008] EWHC 2028 (QB) (*'[...] though the court must not shrink from exercising a supervisory power which it has if it affects the claimant's right to work [...], the BOA, if acting honestly and not capriciously and within its powers, is and must be a body better fitted to judge what was needed than me, or any court'*).

45 *Leeper v IAAF*, CAS 2020/A/6807, para 325.

46 *Leeper v IAAF*, CAS 2020/A/6807, para 324.

47 See the opening lines of the Introduction to the 2015 IPC Athlete Classification Code: *'The vision of the Paralympic Movement is "to enable Para-Athletes to achieve sporting excellence and inspire and excite the world." The unique systems of Classification used in Para-sports perform two critical functions to support the realisation of this vision: (1) define who is eligible to compete in Para-sport and consequently has the opportunity to reach the goal of becoming a Paralympic Athlete; and (2) group Athletes into Sport Classes which aim to ensure that the impact of Impairment is minimised and sporting excellence determines which Athlete or team is ultimately victorious'*.

48 Mann DL and Ravensbergen HJC, *International Paralympic Committee (IPC) and International Blind Sports Federation (IBSA) Joint Position Stand on the Sport-Specific Classification of Athletes with Vision Impairment*, Sports Med. 2018; 48(9): 2011–2023. See also Tweedy SM, Vanlandewijck YC, *International Paralympic Committee position stand--background and scientific principles of classification in Paralympic sport*, Br J Sports Med. 2011 Apr;45(4):259-69.

49 Not least in the case of John McFall, a single amputee who won a bronze medal for Great Britain in the 100 metres at the 2008 Paralympic Games, then became a trauma and orthopaedic surgeon, and in 2024 applied to the European Space Agency to be the world's first amputee astronaut: *John McFall blazes trail to be world's first disabled astronaut*, The Times, 9 October 2023. Clearly Mr McFall is not a man for underachievement.

50 See Zettler P., *Is it cheating to use Cheetahs? The implications of technologically innovative prostheses for sports values and rules*, Boston Univ International Law Journal, Vo. 27:367, 394 fn 209: *'[A]t least some amputee athletes may not want to win "tainted" victories (or to be perceived as having won tainted victories)'.*

51 As in the case of German long jumper Markus Rehm, which is discussed at p 196. The issue would also arise with single arm amputees in throwing events (javelin and shot put) if the amputee throws with their prosthetic arm rather than their biological one.

52 *Pistorius v IAAF*, CAS 2008/A/1480. Instead, it was Mark Gay who acted for the IAAF in this case, instructing Michael Beloff QC.

53 *IAAF Council introduces rule regarding "technical aids"*, worldathletics.org, 26 March 2007 (Rule 144.2).

54 Brüggemann GP et al, *Biomechanics of double transtibial amputee sprinting using dedicated sprinting prostheses*, Sports Technol. 2008, 1, No.4-5, 220-227.

55 *Pistorius v IAAF*, CAS 2008/A/1480, para 24.

56 *PGA Tour Inc v Martin*, 532 U.S. 661 (2001). The evidence indicated that Mr Martin still had to walk more than a mile during a normal round, and thereby suffered more fatigue (due to his disability) than his able-bodied competitors suffered from walking the entire course. The trial court therefore found that the golf cart enabled Martin's performance but did not enhance it, and as such did not fundamentally alter the nature of the competition. On appeal, the Ninth Circuit affirmed the district court's judgment, and so did the US Supreme Court. The Supreme Court rejected the PGA's argument that battling fatigue was an essential and *'outcome-affecting'* feature of its events, first on the (surprising) basis that factors such as changes in the weather mean that it is *'impossible to guarantee that all competitors will play under exactly the same conditions or that an individual's ability will be the sole determinant of the outcome'* (532 U.S. 661 at 686-87), and secondly on the basis that the district court had already found as a matter of fact that fatigue was not really a debilitating factor for the able-bodied golfers, whose walking required them to expend only about 500 calories (*'nutritionally ... less than a Big Mac'*) (ibid), meaning that (in the Supreme Court's view) *'the walking rule is at best peripheral to the nature of petitioner's athletics events, and thus it might be waived in individual cases without working a fundamental alteration'* (ibid, p.689).

In a typically robust dissent, Justice Antonin Scalia pointed out that the playing rules of a sport are ultimately arbitrary (*'Eighteen-hole golf courses, 10-foot-high basketball hoops, 90-foot baselines, 100-yard football fields – all are arbitrary and none is essential. The only support for any of them is tradition and (in more modern times) insistence by what has come to be regarded as the ruling body of the sport ...'*), and therefore not even the United States Supreme Court can second-guess a sport's regulator's judgment that a particular element (eg walking the course) is fundamental to the nature of the sport. He used sarcasm to make his point: *'I am sure that the Framers of the Constitution ... fully expected that ... the judges of this august Court would some day have to wrestle with that age-old jurisprudential question, for which their years of study in the law have so well prepared them: Is someone riding around a golf course from shot to shot really a golfer? The answer, we learn, is yes. The Court ultimately concludes, and it will henceforth be the Law of the Lawn, that walking is not a "fundamental" aspect of golf'*.

Nor did Justice Scalia think much of the majority's view that allowing one golfer to ride while the others had to walk was unobjectionable because other factors (such as weather, or a *'lucky bounce'*) mean that in any event a player's talent is not outcome-determinative. He commented acerbically: *'I guess that is why those who follow professional golfing consider Jack Nicklaus the luckiest golfer of all time, only to be challenged of late by the phenomenal luck of Tiger Woods'*. He concluded: *'The statute seeks to assure that a disabled person's disability will not deny him equal access to (among other things) competitive sporting events – not that his disability will not deny him an equal chance to win competitive sporting events. The latter is quite impossible, since the very nature of competitive sport is the measurement, by uniform rules, of unevenly distributed excellence. This unequal distribution is precisely what determines the winners and losers – and artificially to "even out" that distribution, by giving one or another player exemption from a rule that emphasizes his particular weakness, is to destroy the game. ... Agility, strength, speed, balance, quickness of mind, steadiness of nerves, intensity of concentration – these talents are not evenly distributed. No wild-eyed dreamer has ever suggested that the managing bodies of the competitive sports that test precisely these qualities should try to take account of the uneven distribution of God-given gifts when writing and enforcing the rules of competition. And I have no doubt Congress did not authorize misty-eyed judicial supervision of such a revolution'. PGA Tour Inc v Martin*, 532 U.S. at 700-04, discussed by Syed M., *Sport is not fair and that's what makes it great*, Times, 17 February 2016.

57 *Pistorius v IAAF*, CAS 2008/A/1480, para 29.

58 As explained by Peter Weyand in *When Science Collides: The Blake Leeper Controversy Unpacked*, The Real Science of Sport Podcast, Season 4, Ep. 22, 19 October 2022.
59 *Study Revives Olympic Prospects for Amputee Sprinters*, Science Daily, 16 May 2008; *Pistorius v IAAF*, CAS 2008/A/1480, para 43.
60 *Pistorius v IAAF*, CAS 2008/A/1480, para 50.
61 Quoted in *'Blade Runner' back on track*, Science, 20 May 2008.
62 *When Science Collides: The Blake Leeper Controversy Unpacked*, The Real Science of Sport Podcast, Season 4, Ep. 22, 19 October 2022.
63 *Pistorius 'Sorry' Over Paralympic Blade Row*, sky.com, 3 September 2012.
64 Chapman M., *London 2012 Paralympics: Otto Bock Launches Prosthesis for Everyday Sports Use*, IB Times, 24 August 2012.
65 World Para Athletics Rules and Regulations (March 2024), Appendix Three.
66 Miner J., *The Battle of the Blades: The Oscar Pistorius Story and Tech Doping in Paralympic Games*, medium.com, 16 December 2019.
67 Taylor T., *Paralympics: a source of inspiration, advanced technology and (yes) doping*, si.com, 7 September 2016.
68 Canda A., *Stature Estimation from Body Segment Lengths in Youth Adults – Application to People with Physical Disabilities*, Journal of Physiological Anthropology, 2009 Volume 28 Issue 2 pages 71-82.
69 For those interested in the detail, the Canda-1 equation is -5.272 + (0.998 × sitting height) + (0.855 × thigh) + (0.882 × upper arm) + (0.820 × forearm).
70 Etchells D., *World records of double-leg amputees to be wiped following blade rule changes*, insidethegames.biz, 18 July 2017.
71 *Leeper v IAAF*, CAS 2020/A/6807, para 236.
72 *Leeper v IAAF*, CAS 2020/A/6807, para 133.
73 Miel R., *Carbon fibre prosthetics good as gold for Leeper*, Plastics News, 24 September 2013.
74 See *Records fall on final day of US Track and Field National Championships*, paralympic.org, 22 June 2015.
75 *Leeper v IAAF*, CAS 2020/A/6807, para 75.
76 *Leeper v IAAF*, CAS 2020/A/6807, para 195.
77 *'When it mattered'* podcast interview, Episode 25, 23 December 2019.
78 In 2021, Mr Rehm jumped 8.47m at an able-bodied event sanctioned by the German Athletic Federation, jumping off his prosthetic blade. And at the World Para Athletics European Championships in June 2021 he set a new world record (in the T64 class) of 8.62m. These distances were well within the qualifying standard set by World Athletics for the men's long jump event at the Tokyo Olympics, and later that month the German Athletic Federation nominated him for the German team for Tokyo. However, World Athletics said he could not compete using his prosthetic blade because he had not sought permission pursuant to Technical Rule 6.3.4 and so the blade had not been assessed. Mr Rehm appealed that decision to the CAS on 15 July 2021. A remote hearing was held on 21 July 2021 before James Drake QC, sitting alone. Chris Lavey and I appeared for World Athletics, alongside Vijay Parbat, in-house counsel at World Athletics. It was common ground between the parties that long jump performance depends principally on running velocity at take-off and velocity while airborne. We submitted an expert report from Peter Weyand, who explained that (1) running with one blade does not impair maximum sprinting speed or running velocity at take-off (Mr Rehm's blade would generate slightly less ground force that his intact limb, but such asymmetry is common for elite sprinters – Usain Bolt being the most famous example – and there is no evidence that it impairs their speed); and (2) jumping off the blade gives Mr Rehm an advantage (translating to a distance of 40 centimetres) that he would not have if he had been jumping off his intact leg, because the lower mass of the blade compared to an intact leg, as well as the smooth curvature at the bottom of the blade, means that Mr Rehm loses much less vertical velocity than able-bodied jumpers. Mr Drake QC accepted that Professor Weyand's expert opinion satisfied World Athletics' burden of showing that Mr Rehm's prosthetic leg gave him an overall competitive advantage over an athlete not using such an aid, and therefore dismissed Mr Rehm's appeal: *Rehm v IOC and World Athletics*, CAS 2021/A/8167.
79 The reader will note the unstated assumption that it was Mr Leeper's natural ability, not his RSPs, that enabled him to perform at the same level as those elite non-amputee athletes.
80 *Leeper v IAAF*, CAS 2020/A/6807, paras 24-32.
81 *Leeper v IAAF*, CAS 2020/A/6807, paras 35-46.
82 *Leeper v IAAF*, CAS 2020/A/6807, paras 294-95.
83 Mr Leeper's argument in 2020 that he should be permitted to use his blades as long as they did not enable him to outperform the very best athletes in the event is echoed by those who argue (see p 135) that trans MTF athletes should be permitted to compete in the

female category as long as they were not able to beat the world record set by a cisgender female athlete in their chosen discipline.

84 *Leeper v IAAF*, CAS 2020/A/6807, para 296.

85 Weyand PG et al, *Artificially long legs directly enhance long sprint running performance*, (2022) R. Soc. Open Sci. 9220397.

86 *Leeper v IAAF*, CAS 2020/A/6807, para 296.

87 *Leeper v IAAF*, CAS 2020/A/6807, paras 306-07, 310-13.

88 *Leeper v IAAF*, CAS 2020/A/6807, para 108.

89 *Leeper v IAAF*, CAS 2020/A/6807, para 114 (*'Mr Leeper submits that the history of the IAAF's treatment of him demonstrates that discriminatory intent. Although the Rule was enacted in 2015, the IAAF permitted Mr Leeper to compete with his RSPs until late 2017. It was only after he ran an Olympic qualifying time of 44.42 seconds that the IAAF decided to apply the rule in order to bar him from competing at the highest level of elite competitive athletics. This reveals the true object and purpose of the rule'*); and para 327 (*'Mr Leeper submitted that the imposition of a burden of proof on disabled athletes under the Rule was intended to advance the IAAF's discriminatory agenda by rendering it practically impossible for a disabled athlete such as him to gain authorisation to compete against able-bodied athletes in IAAF-sanctioned events, while at the same time concealing the IAAF's discriminatory motive under the guise of a facially neutral burden of proof'*).

90 The '*RICO*' Act is the federal Racketeer Influenced & Corrupt Organizations Act of 1970 (18 U.S.C. ss. 1961-1968).

91 World Athletics Constitution, worldathletics.org, Article 4.1(j).

92 See the commentary to Article 18.8 of World Athletics' 2019 Competition Rules, worldathletics.org: *'This Rule facilitates the participation of ambulant athletes with a disability to compete in athletic competitions with able-bodied athletes. For example, an arm amputee is not able to strictly comply with Rule 16.3 of the Technical Rules during a crouch start by putting both hands on the ground. This Rule enables a Start Referee to interpret the Rules in such a way to allow the athlete to place their stump on the ground, or to place wooden blocks or the like on the ground behind the start line on which an arm stump is placed, or in the case of a high upper arm amputee who is not able to make contact with the ground in any way, to adopt a start position without any contact with the ground'*.

93 See footage of Murray Halberg's performance at youtube.com/watch?v=9aW8B6BOLjs. Other examples of individuals with disabilities who have competed in World Athletics competitions include Marla Runyan (USA), a legally blind athlete who competed in long-distance disciplines including at the Sydney 2000 and Athens 2004 Olympic Games, Melinda Vernon (Australia), a deaf athlete who competed between 2003 and 2013 in (among other events) the IAAF World Cross Country Championships and IAAF World Half Marathon Championships, Jason Smyth (Ireland), a blind athlete who competed in the 100m at the 2011 Daegu IAAF World Championships, and Jaryd Clifford (Australia), a blind athlete who competed in the 1500m at the Tampere 2018 IAAF World U20 Championships.

94 Those athletes included Nick Rogers, Johannes Floors, Blake Leeper and Ntando Mahlangu (double leg amputees); Ivan Katanusic, Michail Seitis, Scout Bassett, Ronald Hertog and Markus Rehm (single leg amputees); Baktiar Eryanto, Carlee Beattie, and Holly Robinson (single arm amputees); and Elexis Gillette, Ilse Hayes, and Athanasios Gavelas (blind athletes).

95 *Leeper v IAAF*, CAS 2020/A/6807, para 332.

96 *Leeper v IAAF*, CAS 2020/A/6807, paras 328, 175-76.

97 *Leeper v IAAF*, CAS 2020/A/6807, para 329 (*'The Panel has carefully considered the evidence relied on by each of the parties on this issue. On the basis of that review, it is apparent that the materials relied on by Mr. Leeper are, when viewed in their fuller context, more nuanced than he submits. It is clear that the question of how the use of prosthetic running aids by amputee athletes should be regulated was a matter of significant concern, discussion and debate within the IAAF. The views of some contributors to that debate were expressed with force and vigour. This is perhaps unsurprising given the importance of the issue and the strong feelings which had been expressed by various stakeholders in the sport (including athletes). Having read the relevant internal IAAF documents, however, the Panel does not consider that the contemporaneous evidence establishes that the Rule was enacted for an improper discriminatory purpose'*).

98 *Leeper v IAAF*, CAS 2020/A/6807, para 333.

99 *Leeper v IAAF*, CAS 2020/A/6807, para 324.

100 *Leeper v IAAF*, CAS 2020/A/6807, paras 317-21, 334.

101 *Semenya & Athletics South Africa v IAAF*, CAS 2018/O/5794 & 5798, para 537.

102 *Leeper v IAAF*, CAS 2020/A/6807, para 337.

103 *Pistorius v IAAF*, CAS 2008/A/1480, para 51.

104 The prevalence of double amputees in the general population is estimated to be 1.5 in every 1,000. Of these, about one third are arm amputees and therefore about 1 in 1,000 are leg amputees. Furthermore, many of those amputations are due to old age and/or vascular disease (in particular, poorly controlled diabetes), which means the amputee is not healthy enough to be an athlete. Of the rest, many are unilateral amputees, and many of the bilateral amputees are transfemoral rather than transtibial, ie above rather than below the knee. So the pool of bilateral transtibial amputees who are of the right age and fit and healthy enough to be athletes is tiny. And even then, they can only compete if they can afford to spend substantial sums on a pair of specially-designed prosthetic sprinter blades.

105 In addition to Mr Leeper (personal best: 44.48 seconds in 2019) and Mr Pistorius (45.07 seconds in 2011), those athletes were Johannes Floors (45.78s in 2019), Liam Malone (46.2 seconds in 2016), David Behre (46.23 seconds in 2016), Hunter Woodhall (46.24 seconds in 2016), AJ Digby (47.23 seconds in 2017), Nick Rogers (47.5 seconds in 2017), and Alan Oliveira (48.58 seconds in 2013).

106 *Leeper v IAAF*, CAS 2020/A/6807, para 237.

107 *Leeper v IAAF*, CAS 2020/A/6807, para 337.

108 *Leeper v IAAF*, CAS 2020/A/6807, paras 339-59.

109 *Leeper v IAAF*, CAS 2020/A/6807, paras 360-62. In 2022, World Athletic codified this ruling at clause 3.3.3 of its new Mechanical Aid Regulations, which states: *'In any case where World Athletics does not authorise use by an athlete of a Mechanical Aid, it is World Athletics' burden to prove that use of that Mechanical Aid will provide that athlete with an overall competitive advantage. The applicable standard of proof is the balance of probabilities'.*

110 Weyand PG, Bundle MW, McGowan CP, Grabowski A, Brown MB, Kram R, Herr H, *The fastest runner on artificial legs: different limbs, similar function?*, J Appl Physiol 2009 Sep; 107(3):903-11.

111 Epstein D., *Fair or Foul? Experts split over whether Pistorius has advantage*, si.com, 3 August 2012.

112 Weyand PG, Bundle MW, *Point: Artificial limbs do make artificially fast running speeds possible*, J Appl Physiol (November 2009); 108(4):1011–2; Kram R. et al, *Counterpoint: Artificial legs do not make artificially fast running speeds possible*, J Appl Physiol (November 2009); 108(4):1012-14, discussion 1014, author reply 1020.

113 Weyand, PG, Sandell RF, Prime DNL, and Bundle MW, *The biological limits to running speed are imposed from the ground up*, Journal of Applied Physiology, 2010, 108(4): p. 950-961.

114 *Leeper v IAAF*, CAS 2020/A/6807, paras 75 and 378.

115 *Leeper v IAAF*, CAS 2020/A/6807, para 380.

116 *Leeper v IAAF*, CAS 2020/A/6807, para 383.

117 *Leeper v IAAF*, CAS 2020/A/6807, paras 381-84.

118 *Leeper v IAAF*, CAS 2020/A/6807, para 380.

119 *Leeper v IAAF*, CAS 2020/A/6807, para 384.

120 *Leeper v IAAF*, CAS 2020/A/6807, paras 381-82.

121 *Leeper v IAAF*, CAS 2020/A/6807, para 379.

122 *Leeper v IAAF*, CAS 2020/A/6807, paras 378, 385.

123 *Leeper v IAAF*, CAS 2020/A/6807, paras 366-69.

124 See p 196, and *Leeper v IAAF*, CAS 2020/A/6807, paras 23-32. They have since published a different report of the same data, suggesting that it shows that *'no athlete with bilateral leg amputations using running-prostheses, including the fastest such athlete, exhibits a single 400 m running performance metric that is better than those achieved by NA [non-amputee] athletes'.* Beck O., Taboga P. and Grabowski A., *Sprinting with prosthetic versus biological legs: insight from experimental data*, 2022 R. Soc. Open Sci. 9211799. In other words, Mr Leeper's experts are still contending that his blades give him no advantage because they do not help him run faster than the fastest ever elite athletes in his discipline. For swift rebuttals, see Weyand PG et al, *Artificially long legs directly enhance long sprint running performance*, 2022 R. Soc. Open Sci. 9220397, which notes (among other things) that *'their standard of not "better than that observed by the best non-amputee athlete" would warrant a "no advantage" conclusion for any amputee athlete who fails to set the World Record'*; and Connick MJ, Beckman EM, Tweedy SM, *Sprinting with bilateral transtibial running-specific prostheses versus biological limbs – are they comparable? Comments on Beck et al (2022)*, R Soc Open Sci. 2023 Sep 6;10(9):230086.

125 Professor Herr's commitment to Mr Leeper's cause, and to the cause of Mr Pistorius before him, is understandable when you know his backstory. According to a Sports Illustrated report in 2012, *'Herr was a mountain-climbing prodigy, known as the "Boy Wonder," until he suffered frostbite on a climbing trip as a 17-year-old in 1982 and lost both lower legs. Rather than accept the end of his climbing career, Herr immediately began designing climbing-specific prostheses that could change length mid-ascent and find purchase on nooks too small for*

human feet. And, almost as quickly, some of Herr's competitors who saw a potentially unfair advantage called for him to be disqualified from competitive climbing'. Epstein D., *Fair or Foul? Experts split over whether Pistorius has advantage*, si.com, 3 August 2012.

126 *Leeper v IAAF*, CAS 2020/A/6807, paras 156-168.

127 *Leeper v IAAF*, CAS 2020/A/6807, paras 372-73.

128 *Leeper v IAAF*, CAS 2020/A/6807, paras 372-74.

129 *Leeper v IAAF*, CAS 2020/A/6807, para 375 et seq.

130 *Leeper v IAAF*, CAS 2020/A/6807, paras 214-15.

131 *Leeper v IAAF*, CAS 2020/A/6807, para 388 (there is *'cogent evidence … that increases in RSP height do cause increases in running speed … . In particular, Dr Weyand and Dr Bundle provided a detailed explanation of the scientific evidence which establishes that, all other things being equal, increased leg length causes increased running speed. This is because there is a close correlation between an athlete's leg length and their ground contact length (ie, the distance that a runner's body travels while their foot is in contact with the ground). Increasing the size of a prosthetic limb beyond normal anatomical proportions therefore increases ground contact length. Since contact length is a direct determinant of running speed, an increase in limb length entails an increase in running speed'*).

132 *Leeper v IAAF*, CAS 2020/A/6807, para 224.

133 *Leeper v IAAF*, CAS 2020/A/6807, para 213.

134 *Leeper v IAAF*, CAS 2020/A/6807, para 236.

135 *Leeper v IAAF*, CAS 2020/A/6807, para 387.

136 Taboga P., Beck O., and Grabowski A., *Prosthetic shape, but not stiffness or height, affects the maximum speed of sprinters with bilateral transtibial amputations*, PLOS One, 2020; 15(2):e0229035.

137 Wasserstein RL, Lazar NA, *The ASA's Statement on p-Values: Context, Process, and Purpose*, The American Statistician, 2016, 70(2): 129-133. See Altman DG and Bland JM, *Absence of evidence is not evidence of absence*, BMJ 1995 Aug 19;311, 485: *'The non-equivalence of statistical significance and clinical importance has long been recognised, but this error of interpretation remains common. Although a significant result in a large study may sometimes not be clinically important, a far greater problem arises from misinterpretation of non-significant findings. By convention a P value greater than 5% (P>0·05) is called "not significant." Randomised controlled clinical trials that do not show a significant difference between the treatments being compared are often called "negative." This term wrongly implies that the study has shown that there is no difference, whereas usually all that has been shown is an absence of evidence of a difference. These are quite different statements'.* See also Dahiru T, *P-Value, A True Test of Statistical Significance? A Cautionary Note*, Ann Ib Postgrad Med. 2008 Jun;6(1):21-6.

138 *Leeper v IAAF*, CAS 2020/A/6807, paras 225, 234, 252-253.

139 *Leeper v IAAF*, CAS 2020/A/6807, paras 387-88.

140 *Leeper v IAAF*, CAS 2020/A/6807, paras 389-90.

141 *CAS Invalidates Burden of Proof on Disabled Athletes as Discriminatory, But Bars Double-Amputee Blake Leeper from Competing on His Blades on Racially Discriminatory Grounds*, winston.com, 28 October 2020.

142 *World Athletics' response to CAS announcement of decision in Leeper case*, worldathletics.org, 26 October 2020. Mr Leeper duly appealed the *Leeper 1* award to the Swiss Federal Tribunal on the ground that the IAAF's approach was racially discriminatory, because the MASH rule is based solely on data from Caucasians and Asians, it ignores the fact that black athletes have longer legs than Caucasian and Asian athletes, and so (he alleged) it requires double amputee black athletes to run at heights that are lower than their natural heights. In making these (new) arguments, he cited various materials that he had not cited to the *Leeper 1 Panel*. In response, the IAAF insisted that there was no unlawful discrimination under Swiss law, properly applied. The Swiss Federal Tribunal issued its ruling on 2 June 2021, rejecting Mr Leeper's appeal and leaving the *Leeper 1* award untouched: *Leeper v World Athletics*, 4A 618/2020, SFT judgment dated 2 June 2021.

143 *Leeper v World Athletics*, CAS 2021/A/7930.

144 *Leeper v World Athletics*, CAS 2021/A/7930, para 48.

145 Weyand PG et al, *Artificially long legs directly enhance long sprint running performance*, (2022) R. Soc. Open Sci. 9220397.

146 *World Athletics panel decision on application from Blake Leeper*, worldathletics.org, 26 April 2021 (linking to decision). The release summarised the decision as follows:

1 Does the MASH (Maximum Allowable Standing Height) rule have an application outside the context of regulating para-athletics? The Panel concluded that the MASH rule was established to maintain fairness in competition by preventing disabled athletes from over-compensating for the absence of a missing limb and that it therefore did have application outside the context of regulating para-athletics.
2 Does the MASH rule have any application to Black athletes? The Panel concluded that the weight of rational scientific opinion is to the effect that the MASH rule does have application to black athletes of African descent. The Panel carefully considered all the competing arguments and is confident that there is a scientifically proved basis upon which the MASH rule has the asserted application.
3 Does Mr Leeper run unnaturally tall in using his new RSPs which give him a standing height of 184 centimetres? At the CAS hearing last year, in relation to a previous application from Mr Leeper, it was not in dispute that, were Mr Leeper required to comply with the MASH rule, he would not be permitted to run at a height greater than 174.4 centimetres. At the tests conducted at the Southern Methodist University in February and March 2021 Mr Leeper's standing height with his new RSPs was measured at 184 centimetres with a leg length of 104 centimetres. The difference between the MASH and his standing height is thus 9.6 centimetres. The only conclusion that is open is that Mr Leeper is running unnaturally tall in using his new RSPs.
4 Does the height of Mr Leeper's RSPs result in Mr Leeper running faster in the 400 metre event than would otherwise be the case? The reports submitted satisfied the Panel that there is a direct relationship between leg length and running speed and that therefore the height of Mr Leeper's RSPs result in him running faster in the 400m event than would otherwise be the case.

147 *Double-Amputee Sprinter Blake Leeper to Appeal World Athletics' Use of Racially Discriminatory 'MASH' Rule To Ban Him From Competition Against Able-Bodied Athletes*, winston.com, 26 April 2021.

148 *Leeper v World Athletics*, CAS 2021/A/7930, paras 39-41.

149 Tanner JM, *The Physique of the Olympic Athlete* (George Allen & Unwin Ltd. 1964). In that study, Dr Tanner collected two sets of data. First, he recorded the race and sitting height for each athlete from a total of 200 male athletes who competed either at the 1958 Commonwealth Games in Cardiff or the 1960 Olympic Games in Rome. Second, he included a sequence of three photographic plates for a subset of 104 of those athletes.

150 *Leeper v World Athletics*, CAS 2021/A/7930, para 138.

151 Connick MJ et al, *Evaluation of methods for calculating maximum allowable standing height in amputees competing in Paralympic athletics*, Scand J Med Sci Sports, 2016 Nov 26(11): 1353-1359.

152 Now known as the American Association of Biological Anthropologists.

153 The 2019 American Association for Physical Anthropology Statement on Race and Racism (Fuentes A. et al, (2019) Am J Phys Anthropol. 169, pp. 400-402) states: *'Race does not provide an accurate representation of human biological variation. It never was accurate in the past and it remains inaccurate when referencing contemporary human populations. […] Variation exists within and among populations across the planet, and groups of individuals can be differentiated by patterns of similarity and difference, but these patterns do not align with socially-defined racial groups (such as whites and blacks)'*.

154 The citations our experts provided for this were Novembre J. et al, *Genes mirror geography within Europe*, Nature, 2008;456(7218):98-101; and Molnar S., *Human Variation: races, types and ethnic groups*, 2006 (6th ed), Upper Saddle River, N.J, Pearson Prentice Hall, pp.142-43 (*'Overall, the picture of genetic relationships … shows a strong relationship to the geographic distances between populations. … The expected relationship between geographic distance and genetic distance is explained by the isolation of distance model. Genetic similarity is a function of gene flow; the more gene flow between two populations, the more similar they are genetically. … in most organisms, including humans, geographic distance limits the amount of gene flow. We expect that the closer two populations are geographically, the more gene flow between them, and the smaller the genetic distance. The further apart two populations are geographically, the less gene flow between them, and therefore the greater the genetic distance'*).

155 Connick MJ et al, *Evaluation of methods for calculating maximum allowable standing height in amputees competing in Paralympic athletics*, Scand J Med Sci Sports, 2016 Nov 26(11): 1353-1359.

156 *Leeper v World Athletics*, CAS 2021/A/7930, para 141.

157 *Leeper v World Athletics*, CAS 2021/A/7930, para 52.

158 *Leeper v World Athletics*, CAS 2021/A/7930, para 142.

159 Professors Weyand and Bundle extracted the measurements of thigh, upper arm, and forearm lengths from the photographs of 100 of the 104 athletes appended to the Tanner study. For the fourth measurement required for the Canda-1 equation, the sitting height, they relied on the measurements that Dr Tanner recorded in an appendix for those 100 athletes. These included 76 white athletes, twelve black athletes, and nine Asian athletes. The experts then inputted these measurements for these 100 athletes into the Canda-1 equation. They found that it predicted the height of all 100 athletes accurately, within an average of 2.8 cm (*Leeper v World Athletics*, CAS 2021/A/7930, para 140).

160 *Leeper v World Athletics*, CAS 2021/A/7930, para 139. Before the pure error factor is applied, his predicted natural height is 172.53 cm (5′ 8″).

161 *Leeper v World Athletics*, CAS 2021/A/7930, para 59.

162 *The CAS dismisses the second appeal of Blaker Leeper*, CAS press release, tas-cas.org, 11 July 2021.

163 *Blake Leeper response to Court of Arbitration for Sport decision*, winston.com, 11 July 2021.

164 *Leeper v World Athletics*, CAS 2021/A/7930, paras 97-99.

165 *Leeper v World Athletics*, CAS 2021/A/7930, para 128.

166 *Leeper v World Athletics*, CAS 2021/A/7930 para 116.

167 *Leeper v World Athletics*, CAS 2021/A/7930, paras 113-14.

168 *Leeper v World Athletics*, CAS 2021/A/7930, para 112.

169 *Leeper v World Athletics*, CAS 2021/A/7930, paras 131-152.

170 Weyand PG et al, *Artificially long legs directly enhance long sprint running performance* (2022) R. Soc. Open Sci. 9220397.

171 Specifically, they said: '*When a sample size is small, statistical non-significance does not provide sufficient evidence for a trivial effect or "no effect". In fact, a non-significant observed substantial effect provides more evidence that the true effect is substantial rather than trivial. "Substantial" in this case is a change in running speed of at least 0.3%, since this change would give a top runner at least one extra medal in every 10 races*'.

172 *The PLOS ONE Editors (2022) Retraction: Prosthetic shape, but not stiffness or height, affects the maximum speed of sprinters with bilateral transtibial amputations*, PLoS ONE 17(12): e0280174, 30 December 2022.

173 Baum BS, Man C., *Race and geography impact validity of maximum allowable standing height equations for para-athletes*, Sci Rep. 2024 Mar 19;14(1):6551.

Chapter 7

Extra Time

Breakaway leagues

When I was growing up in the 1970s and 1980s, the television signal was terrestrial only, delivered via a large transmitter at Crystal Palace to an aerial on the roof of the house. There were three channels, BBC1, BBC2, and ITV, and sports coverage was largely limited to Grandstand on the BBC on Saturdays presented by Frank Bough, football highlights on Match of the Day on Saturday nights presented by Des Lynam, and one live match a week, on the Big Match on ITV on a Sunday afternoon, presented by Brian Moore. It was only in the late 1980s that the television market began to expand, first with the introduction of two further terrestrial channels, Channel 4 and Channel 5, and then with the advent of the Sky service, delivered by two new methods, cable and satellite. And these new broadcasters were well aware that high quality sports coverage was a driver of audiences and therefore of revenues from subscribers and advertisers. For example, Channel 5 launched in March 1997, but many households, ours included, did not bother to tune their television sets to pick it up until it secured the exclusive right to broadcast England's World Cup qualifier away to Poland in May 1997. And of course BSkyB acquired the exclusive rights to Premier League football from 1992 on, and invested millions of pounds in innovative production techniques that quickly made its Premier League coverage a '*must watch*' offering. Rugby union, cricket, and other sports also started attracting competition among broadcasters for the rights to their events, and therefore started attracting much higher rights fees than they had previously received from the BBC or ITV.

This was obviously good news for the sports governing bodies (SGBs) involved. As the custodians of their sports, entrusted with growing participation and maximising the health, social, cultural and other benefits of those sports, in the public interest and for the public good, they could invest this commercial income in new facilities, coaches and training programmes, to grow the playing base and to identify and develop the best emerging talent into the next generation of elite stars. This would then improve the offering and so increase the bids for the broadcast rights, creating a virtuous circle of investment, development, and commercial return that would allow the sport to continue to grow and flourish. But as the content became more and more attractive to consumers and so increasingly valuable to broadcasters, the elite players started to demand a greater share of the revenues that their talent was generating, and entrepreneurs began to look for ways to tap into those rising values, either by investing in the best of the existing teams – witness the acquisition of many leading English football clubs by US sports franchise owners and more recently by Middle East sovereign states – or by enticing the best teams or players to sign up for their own new rival competitions.

New entrants galvanising the market with fresh ideas and energy to stimulate greater consumer demand are what the free market does best. And their profit-maximising imperative has helped to drive the development of innovative new products and formats like football's Premier League, cricket's Twenty20, and basketball's 3x3 Champions Cup. But disrupting the status quo carries its own risks and threats, particularly when it comes to the public interest side of sport, as those at the top may be tempted to cash in on their success, regardless of the consequences for the rest of the sport. Witness the biggest Premier League clubs enthusiastically joining the European Superleague in 2021 before they were forced to retreat by the furious backlash from their fans. And witness also the grotesque spectacle of athletes chasing inflated prize money by taking the testosterone and enclomiphene (both banned substances under the World Anti-Doping Code) sold by the entrepreneurs organising the first '*Enhanced Games*', scheduled for May 2026.

In short, while innovation and risk-taking must always be encouraged and rewarded, the resulting revenues cannot go only to the entrepreneurs and the sport's elite professional athletes. Instead a sizeable portion has to be reinvested in the grass roots of the sport, to grow the playing base and to identify and nurture new elite talent that will improve the spectacle and so generate further revenues to underwrite the success of the sport into the long term. For a new entrant, it is much easier to pay elite athletes enormous amounts if you can free-ride on that investment instead of having to do the hard work yourself, no matter if that damages the sport in the long run. But after years of banging this drum, I feel a bit like King Canute commanding the waves to recede. Protectionist measures taken by the SGB, such as bans on taking part in '*unsanctioned*' events, are very susceptible to legal challenge, with competition law usually the weapon of choice, on the basis that the SGB is a monopolist that is seeking to '*abuse its dominant position*' and/or to conspire with its members to '*prevent, restrict or distort competition*' from new entrants for the services of players, to the detriment not only of those players but also of the consumer. We have seen such challenges in football,[1] rugby union (see p 10), rugby league,[2] cricket,[3] snooker,[4] darts (see p 227), basketball,[5] swimming,[6] golf,[7] and even ice-skating.[8] I have spent many hours developing arguments that the law has to recognise that the uncertainty of outcome that is key to the sporting spectacle can only be delivered if the teams are evenly matched, and that is only possible if their owners agree to accept broad restrictions on their commercial freedoms, including as to the competitions they play in and the rights they exploit. An SGB cannot stop stakeholders from pursuing new commercial initiatives if they see fit – unless it has legislative backing, such as the Football Governance Act 2025, which bars clubs from joining competitions that are black-listed by the new Independent Football Regulator – but in my view an SGB that organises commercially valuable competitions for its members must at least be able to require those who benefit from that effort not to do anything to harm those competitions. No one has a God-given right to run a sport; market entry by new event organisers is obviously entirely lawful; and clubs and players cannot be stopped (once they have honoured any contractual commitments to '*official*' events) from going off to play in new rival events. But they cannot insist on being allowed to play in both official events and in rival events. Instead, they should have to choose one or the other.[9]

Darts

In 1998/99, I was working on the response of the International Rugby Board (now World Rugby) to competition law complaints that had been filed by certain English and Welsh clubs, accusing the IRB of misusing its regulatory powers to protect its commercial interests and to stifle their own (see p 63). I happened to turn on a BBC documentary in the *Blood on the Carpet* series, featuring Ollie Croft, the then-chairman of the British Darts Organisation (the '*BDO*').[10] Ollie was being interviewed about a restraint of trade complaint that had been filed by several leading darts players against the BDO after it responded to their 1993 breakaway to form the Professional Darts Corporation (the '*PDC*') by banning them from competing in BDO events. The lawsuit was settled on the courthouse steps in June 1997, with the BDO lifting its ban on the claimants, and also acknowledging their right to organise their own world championship in competition with the BDO World Championship, but with the two sides agreeing that players could only enter and play in one world championship each season, and that the top 16 finishers in each championship could not enter the rival championship the following year. We contacted Ollie to ask for more details of the lawsuit, and he invited us to come and see him at the BDO's offices above his tile shop in Muswell Hill. Ollie's wife Lorna gave us cups of tea and slices of pork pie, and Ollie gave us the information we wanted about the lawsuit. But he also asked if we could help the BDO, and over the next few years we provided that assistance *pro bono*, given its lack of funds.

The BDO and its members organised many darts events for players from around the UK and overseas, and each year the best players qualified through those events for the annual BDO World Championship, which was staged at the Lakeside Hotel in Frimley Green, Surrey, in front of a large and raucous crowd clad mainly in fancy dress. The BBC broadcast extensive live coverage of the event, and the ticket revenues and broadcasting rights fees funded not only the event prize money but also the BDO's entire operating budget for the rest of the year, including all of the development work it did for the sport. But some of the best players, including Phil Taylor, Dennis Priestley and Eric Bristow, thought that the BDO was not doing enough to market the sport and increase its commercial revenues, which is why they eventually broke away and formed the PDC. Teaming up with Barry Hearn, the British sports promoter and entrepreneur, who secured a broadcast deal with BSkyB, the PDC soon offered significant prize money for its own version of the world championship. In the beginning, however, the PDC did not have any development tournaments of its own to supply enough players for that event, so instead it tried to recruit the BDO's best players. One of its most significant coups was to persuade Raymond van Barneveld, the winner of the 2005 BDO World Championship, to join the PDC in 2006. Other top player such as Jelle Klaasen (the winner of the 2006 BDO World Championship), Michael van Gerwen, and others followed him. Ollie wanted this free-riding by the PDC stopped, because it was diminishing the value of the BDO World Championship, which underwrote the BDO's development work, but he did not want the BDO to be taken to court again. We therefore put a clause in the BDO World Championship participation agreement that committed any player who reached the semi-finals of the BDO World Championship to return to play in the following year's event. Because the PDC had scheduled its own world championship to clash with the BDO World Championship, that effectively meant the four BDO semi-finalists could not switch to the PDC event the following year. We considered that to be a legitimate and proportionate restriction that we would be able to defend in court.

Ollie also asked for our help with Sport England, a government agency that distributes public funding to sports in England. The BDO's member clubs were unable to obtain an exemption from charging VAT to their individual members, because Sport England had refused to recognise darts as a sport. We looked into this and discovered there were several hurdles to that recognition:

- First, there was apparently some concern that archery might object to darts being recognised as a sport. This made no sense to me. While travelling the world promoting WADA's new whereabouts rules to its stakeholders (see p 63), I bumped into Tom Dielen, the World Archery general secretary, and it made no sense to him either, so he confirmed that World Archery had no objection to darts being recognised as a sport, and that solved that problem.
- We managed to persuade UK Sport's Anti-Doping Directorate to send a team to the BDO World Championship to deliver some anti-doping education to the players and then conduct the sport's first ever drug-testing. All was going smoothly on the night in question until I got a message that I was needed urgently in the doping control station. When I got there, the DCO explained that a player had been there for more than two hours but the only urine he had been able to produce was very dilute and so did not meet the minimum specific gravity requirements for testing. I spoke to the player, and he was very apologetic. He said he had drunk four pints of lager, but was willing to switch to Guinness if we thought that that might help. I thought that was a show of good faith from the player, and so I suggested to the DCO that they give him another half an hour. They did that, and ultimately he was able to produce a sample that met the WADA requirements.
- Lastly, Sport England suggested that darts did not involve sufficient physical skill or effort to qualify as a sport. The BDO was quite rightly outraged at this suggestion. Ollie offered to settle the issue with a game of darts, on the basis that if Sport England was right that there was no physical skill or effort involved, then its team would be able to beat the professionals fielded by the BDO, and in that case the BDO would immediately withdraw its request for recognition; but if it was wrong, the Sport England team would be soundly thrashed and it would have to immediately recognise darts as a sport. Surprisingly, Sport England declined that novel means of alternative dispute resolution. We then wrote it a very cross letter, threatening legal action on the basis that it was treating darts unfairly, since it had recognised archery, shooting, and even baton twirling as sports, none of which involved any more physical skill or effort than darts. We emphasised the substantial skill involved in throwing a dart accurately under pressure. We also highlighted, with the support of expert testimony from the team doctor for the England cricket team, the stamina required for long darts matches and the risk of repetitive strain injury in the throwing elbow. And we also gave the leading players pedometers to wear at the Lakeside during the week of the BDO World Championship, to demonstrate the amount of ground they covered going back and forth on the oche. In the video montage that we put together to support the BDO's case, former world champion Andy ('*The Viking*') Fordham compared himself to Geoff Capes, the elite shot-putter, on the basis that their respective sports both involved throwing a bit of metal, and said: *'these trainers I'm wearing aren't just for show'*. Faced with this overwhelming evidence, Sport England granted recognition by return.[11] Bruce Philipps, who was Sport England's Head of Communications at the time, told me a few years later that Sport England had found the whole thing hilarious, and had been happy to

grant the application, but I am sure it was really the force of our advocacy that won the day. When I called Ollie to give him the good news, the first thing he said was: *'That's great. Now can you get darts into the Olympics for London 2012?'* My reply was a short and unequivocal '*no*'. But Ollie still thanked me and Iain for our efforts by giving us our very own darts shirts emblazoned with our own darts names: Jon ('*The Truth*') Taylor, and Iain ('*The Professor*') Higgins.

Ollie also continued to give us tickets to the Lakeside each year for the BDO World Championship, and we used the opportunity to entertain some of our other clients. The evening was always memorable, with two thousand fans in fancy dress, beer flowing throughout, players entering to their favourite walk-on music, and dramatic on-stage shoot-outs compered by the redoubtable Martin (*'Let's play darts!'*) Fitzmaurice.[12] Kate Mittelstadt and Jenn Schrier from the US Anti-Doping Agency came along one year; I can still remember the look on Jenn's face when she walked into the venue and saw the raucous crowd, all in fancy dress and drowning in beer. Not what she was used to, I think, back in Colorado where USADA is based. We also got to go to the players' bar behind the stage, where the keen darters in our party would throw some arrows alongside players who were warming up for their matches. One year a rank outsider was about to clinch a famous semi-final victory, so we went back-stage to beat the post-game rush. As I stood at the bar waiting to be served, I heard a roar greet the outsider's victory, and then a commotion as he and his friends and family were welcomed back-stage. A minute or two later I looked behind me and there was the victor himself, standing with a tenner in his hand, waiting patiently to be served. I congratulated him and asked if I could buy him a pint, but he politely declined. Then I invited him to go in front of me in the queue, but he said he was happy to wait his turn. I doubt there are many other sports where someone who has just won a World Championship semi-final would need to queue for a drink afterwards, and even fewer who would be humble enough not to expect to be ushered to the front of the queue. Another reason to love darts!

For my 40th birthday party, in 2007, we held our own darts competition in a bar in the Riverside Stand at Craven Cottage, with mandatory fancy dress and walk-on music for all contestants. The BDO's then-reigning men's and women's world champions, Martin ('*Wolfie*') Adams and Trina ('*Golden Girl*') Gulliver, came along to captain a team each, and Martin Fitzmaurice also came along to act as compere for the competition. I arrived well before the party started, and asked Wolfie if he could give me a few tips, since I had hardly ever thrown a dart in my life, and didn't want to be embarrassed at my own event. Wolfie told me to imagine the darts board was a clock face, and to aim between 8 o'clock and 11 o'clock, where there is a cluster of high-scoring beds. So I stepped up to the oche, took careful aim between 8 and 11 o'clock, let fly, and hit a treble 20. Perhaps unsurprisingly, that trick did not work again when I tried to repeat it later under competition conditions. Despite wearing my full sleeve fake tattoos and my darts shirt emblazoned with my *nom de guerre* ('*The Truth*'), and despite my excellent walk-on music (The Clash's *'I fought the law and the law won'*), I crashed out ignominiously in the first round, soundly beaten by Andy ('*The Cardinal*') Parkinson (*'The Hallelujah Chorus'* from Handel's Messiah). Other contestants that night included Adam ('*Silver Surfer*') Lewis QC (*'O Fortuna'* from Carmina Burana) and his wife Beate ('*The Valkyrie*') Mjaaland (*'Ride of the Valkyries'* from Apocalypse Now), who was the eventual winner of the tournament.

Sports governance

Sports federations seeking to generate commercial revenues know that it is hard to sell the public a shiny spectacle, however appetising it may look on the surface, if people suspect it might be rancid inside (see p 18). For that reason, some sports leaders have been anxious to avoid headlines about drugs cheats in their sports. For example, Arne Llungqvist, a true leader in the fight against doping in sport, says that Primo Nebiolo, the IAAF President from 1981 to 1999, *'was never much fun when it came to [my] work in anti-doping. He didn't like the negative publicity the IAAF got because we continually caught athletes taking performance-enhancing substances'.*[13] The accomplished investigative journalist Andrew Jennings explained: *'The federations grew in prestige and wealth* [as broadcasters and sponsors began paying for sports rights]. *It could all be lost if the public discovered that many of their heroes were pumped up with illicit drugs. These fears created a culture of blindness. Sports officials who should have been rooting out doping looked the other way. Worse still, they then began to protect their stars from exposure'.*[14]

I have been lucky to work with some truly outstanding sports federation officials who have been ready to put their head above the parapet and fight to defend the integrity of their sports, without fear or favour, understanding the costs and risks but also understanding that the costs of compromising would be much greater. Many of the cases I have described in this memoir attest to those officials' courage and personal integrity. However, some of the other cases I have described (see pp 114–119) demonstrate, in my view, that the governance mechanisms of the sports movement have not always been strong enough to vet properly all candidates for high office, or to prevent serious corruption from those elected or appointed to such positions.For example, so complacent were Anders Besseberg (IBU president) and Tamás Aján (IWF president), so confident were they that the system of sports governance would never be rigorous enough to hold them to account, that they were happy to take up seats as sports movement representatives on WADA's Foundation Board, even while they were busy presiding over wholesale violations of the World Anti-Doping Code in their own sports (see pp 114–119).

I certainly do not want to tar everyone with the same brush. Many sports movement representatives are very fine people and excellent servants of their sports, and the miscreants are the exceptions rather than the rule. My point is only that historically the governance mechanisms in some sports have not always been strong enough to block the rise of corrupt individuals to the top or to prevent their abuses once they got there. However, things are beginning to change, and so there is hope for the future. After all, it was the WADA Investigations & Intelligence Department that eventually exposed both Besseberg and Aján. And more and more international federations are coming to understand that to maintain public confidence in their sports, they need to transfer responsibility for integrity decisions to operationally independent bodies such as the Athletics Integrity Unit (see p 86) and the Biathlon Integrity Unit (see p 118). Similarly, more and more countries are beginning to realise that the integrity responsibilities of their national federations should be transferred to competent and properly resourced independent bodies, including not only the anti-doping responsibilities (as happens, for example, in the case of UK Anti-Doping: p 57) but also the anti-corruption work and the crucial work of safeguarding athletes from sexual and other abuse (see eg Sport Integrity Australia).

In 2021, during the Covid lockdown, I recorded an interview with Seb Coe. He agreed that when you are elected president of a sports federation, the temptation is to hold all of the powers of your new office jealously to your chest. But he understood that the federation will always appear conflicted when it comes to enforcing its integrity rules against its biggest stars. After all, it is the federation's responsibility to generate as much revenue from its biggest competitions as it can, but if the sport's biggest stars are exposed as cheats, the broadcasters, sponsors and fans will walk away and the revenues will dry up. As a result, international federation presidents cannot win. If the sport's biggest star tests positive for a banned substance, but the federation decides not to charge them with a doping offence, the public will assume the federation simply wanted to avoid a scandal, even if in fact its lawyers have advised that there is a very good reason (eg a mistake in the way the sample was collected or analysed) why a charge could not be brought. That inescapable appearance of conflict is why there has been a clear trend in recent years towards transferring disciplinary decisions to independent integrity bodies, and in my view that trend needs to continue.

Still want to be a sports lawyer?

When I am asked for advice on how to become a sports lawyer, I always say you will obviously need a deep understanding of the sector, so pore over the sports pages and read the best sports books, for sure. And you will also need the judgement and sensibility to understand how to support and guide your clients with discretion and empathy through the difficult and often high-profile issues that confront them from day to day. But first and foremost, I say, become an excellent lawyer, because that is what clients in the sports sector need above all. As a sports lawyer, particularly a sports disputes lawyer, you will need to master many different areas of law, including commercial and intellectual property law, competition law, and public law and human rights law, and you will need to be ready to apply them to solve complex legal, commercial and/or political problems, sometimes with few if any precedents to guide you, and often in very high-profile circumstances and under a very public glare. So in the end, while it is always helpful if a candidate has sports-specific experience and understanding, what I really care about is that they are extremely well-trained lawyers with the hard core legal and practical problem-solving skills that our sports movement clients need.

Beyond that, all I can say is that the market for sports lawyers is not a big one, and the supply of ambitious young prospects always outstrips demand. So if you really want to break into this sector, you have to be committed, you have to be patient, and you have to be opportunistic, which means staying abreast of developments, finding interesting issues to blog or write articles about in order to show your worth (there are still several areas of sports law that remain relatively unmapped), and looking for opportunities to volunteer (eg as an independent non-executive director of a sports body, or as an ethics panel or disciplinary tribunal member, or as an athlete coordinator or educator) that will give you useful experience as well as exposure to people who might subsequently be able to give you a leg up in the field. You will need all of that, and some luck too, and I wish you a lot of it, because it is a very stimulating and exciting sector, and one where the application of legal skills can help to make a real difference. And what could be more satisfying than that?

Notes

1 *European Superleague Company SL v FIFA and UEFA*, Case C-333/21, European Court of Justice, 21 December 2023.

2 *News Ltd v Australian Rugby League Ltd (No 2) (Superleague)* (1996) 64 FCR 410 (Federal Court of Australia).

3 *Greig v Insole* [1978] 1 WLR 302 (Ch D 1977). See generally Haigh G., The Cricket War: The Story of Kerry Packer's World Series Cricket (John Wisden & Co., 2017).

4 Hendry v WPBSA [2001] EWCA Civ 1127.

5 Palmer D., FIBA throws eight countries out of EuroBasket with Olympic places at risk, insidethegames.biz, 16 April 2016 (sanctions imposed for backing the Euroleague).

6 Shields et al & International Swimming League v World Aquatics, No. 23-15092, 9th Cir. 17 September 2024; Enhanced US LLC v World Aquatics et al, 25-CV-7096 (JMF), S.D.N.Y. opinion and order dated 17 November 2025.

7 Poulter et al v PGA European Tour, Appeal Panel decision dated 3 April 2023 (sportresolutions.com/decisions/golfers-v-pga-european-tour, accessed 12 December 2023).

8 International Skating Union v European Commission, Case C-124/21, European Court of Justice, 21 December 2023.

9 See Gottrup-Klim e.a. Grovvuareforeninger v Kansk Landburgs Grovvareselskab AmbA, Case C-250/92, European Court of Justice, 15 December 1994, [1994] ECR I-5641, relied on in Poulter et al v PGA European Tour, Appeal Panel decision dated 3 April 2023 (sportresolutions.com/decisions/golfers-v-pga-european-tour, accessed 12 December 2023).

10 Olly Croft, darts supremo who popularised the sport but presided over a period of turmoil and acrimony – obituary, Daily Telegraph, 29 November 2019.

11 Kelso P., *Bull's eye! Darts achieves sporting* recognition, The Guardian, 25 March 2005.

12 Obituaries: World Darts Federation, *Martin Fitzmaurice has passed away*, dartswdf.com, 14 April 2016; Steve Russell, *In memory of Martin Fitzmaurice: 3rd June 1940-14th April 2016*, indyrs.co.uk, 27 April 2016.

13 Ljungqvist A. & Lager G., *Doping's Nemesis* (SportsBooks Limited, 2008), Chapter 8 (*'The Anti-Doping Police and the East German Underworld'*).

14 Simson V. & Jennings A., *The Lords of the Rings: Power, Money & Drugs in the Modern Olympics* (Simon & Schuster, 1992), p.188.

Index

[*all references are to page number*]

A Practitioner's Guide to Correcting Mistakes in Pension Schemes

For Emily